GW00632192

# Hayes

## A History of a Kentish Village

### Volume 2: 1914 to modern times

by

Jean Wilson and Trevor Woodman

Published by J Wilson
8 Redgate Drive, Hayes, Bromley, Kent, BR2 7BT

First published 2012

ISBN 978-0-9515178-3-3

Printed and bound by CPI Group (UK) Ltd, Croydon, CR0 4YY
www.hayeskenthistory.co.uk

# Foreword

When Jean asked if I would write the foreword to the second volume I was delighted as it gave me the opportunity to thank her for the unstinted dedication she has given to the finalisation of the project, which she and Trevor started after the Millennium Exhibition. These volumes bring together the thirty years of research they have both undertaken.

As I grew up in The Avenue, West Wickham, as a family we were always involved in Hayes. My father was a Sidesman and a member of the PCC over many years at St Mary's in Hayes and I went to Church and Sunday School there from a very young age. I remember playing on fields at the top of Pickhurst Lane and Mead Way before the latter was opened up to Pickhurst Lane. There was a pond where I caught my first newt behind Barnhill and I recall climbing the willow trees that overhung the little stream that ran, from the pond, down to Hayes Bottom, through what is now Hayesford Park Estate, and where Pickhurst Schools now are, picking wild roses to take home for my mother in summer time. I went to school in Beckenham when I was seven and used to walk down to Westmoreland Road to catch the 126 to St George's Church, long before there were any houses or shops built there. Well, that was a long while ago but these books have brought back many memories for me and I trust will do the same for many others who enjoy reading them.

Trevor had always been interested in local studies and worked with the Kent Archaeological Group, CIB but after his stroke he needed other interests and after reading *A History of Hayes* by Canon Thompson he was hooked and the rest is history! Though their researches for books and exhibitions both Jean and Trevor had accumulated an immense amount of information, which was used for the 2000 Millennium exhibition and many people said then – You should write a book. Well, friends, this is it.

Life in Hayes has changed out of all proportion in the last 50+ years. We are now in the digital age with things out of date as soon as they are bought but let us all remember, that those who have gone before worked very hard to pass on to us a lovely place to live, with access to country in which we can walk and relax while at the same time we are able to access the culture and life in the city of London. As I was told 'Hayes is the nearest Village to London', 'People move here but don't want to move out'. Long may that last, but that means we must all take an interest in the things around us and a watchful eye on the greenbelt and planning issues, to ensure we keep these benefits to pass on to future generations.

Elizabeth Woodman
October 2011

# Contents

# List of Maps

# Acknowledgements

My friend and co-author, Trevor Woodman, died suddenly in September 2007 and I am very grateful for the support and encouragement of so many local people to continue with *Hayes, A History of a Kentish Village*. At the time of his death Trevor had almost finished the first drafts of the chapters covering the years from 1880 to 1945. His wife, Elizabeth, has been a tower of strength in overseeing the completion of these chapters and in reading and commenting on the text. At her suggestion the book has been divided into two volumes, Volume 1 to the outbreak of World War I and Volume 2 from 1914 to the present day.

Mrs Patricia Knowlden, former Vice-President of the Bromley Borough Local History Society, who died in 2011, was particularly helpful in reading and commenting on the early chapters in Volume 2. Mr Roger and Mrs Anne Manning have assisted with proof reading both volumes and, together with Mr Laurie Mack, have made useful suggestions and contributions to the final chapters. Mr Laurie Mack has generously agreed that much of his unpublished work may be used in this history.

Over the years the staff of Hayes Public Library and the Local Studies Department of Bromley Central Library have given valuable advice. Miss E Plincke's early encouragement was followed by that of Mr Alex Freeman in the 1980s and later Mr Simon Finch. They have always been very willing to look for source information. Grateful thanks are given to all who have helped and especially to the archivists, Miss Elizabeth Silverthorne, Ms Sally Eaton (Deves), Ms Catrin Holland and archives assistant, Ms Lorraine Budge.

Many Hayes records are held in other archives and again we have received a great deal of help. Thanks go to the officers and staff of the following organisations: Australia War Memorial; The British Library; Bromley Museum; Centre for Kentish Studies; Church Archives, St Mary the Virgin, Hayes; Commonwealth War Graves Commission; Guildhall Library; House of Lords Record Office; Imperial War Museum; Lambeth Palace Library; London Metropolitan Archives; National Archives of Canada; National Archives, Maryland, USA; National Monuments Records; Royal Society Library; Religious Society of Friends Library; Sidcot School Archives; The National Archives and Wellcome Institute for History of Medicine Library.

The local newspapers, particularly the Bromley Mercury and Bromley Times and in more recent years the Bromley Borough News and News Shopper, have been a valuable source of information for the twentieth century.

Thank you to the many people who have provided memories, photographs, comments and helped in many different ways in the final preparation of the book, including: Mr C Atkins, Mrs Vera Bardgett, Mrs Elizabeth Barclay, Mr Colin Brook, Mr Charles Broughton, Mr S Carter, Mrs Nina Chamberlin, Mrs Clinging, Mr Gordon Collis, Mr Richard Cracknell, Miss Maureen Crowhurst, Mr Bill Dance, Miss Dorothy Dewey, Mr Richard (Dick) and Mrs Leta Frost, Mr Neville Gale, Mr Peter Gilbey, Revd David Graham, Mrs Marie Green, Mr Peter Groves, Mrs Jean Hadley, Mrs Joyce Hales, Mr David Hart, Mr Ron Holland, Mrs Sylvia Humphrey, Mrs Peggy Jackson, Mr Gordon

Johnson, Mr Tony King, Mr Philip and Ms Jennifer Lee Jones, Mr Martin E Lee, Mr Colin Legge, Mrs Josephine Lepper, Mr Gavin Martin, Mr Charles W. Mercer, Mr David Moxon, Mrs Beryl Neatby, Mr Bob Neville, Mr Bryan Nicholls, Canon W B Norman, Mrs Rachel Orr, Mrs Jean Partridge, Mrs Perrett, Mrs Brenda Petts, Mrs Shirley & Mr Alan Pettitt, Mr Peter Plant, Miss Christine Rees, Mr Tony Robinson, Mr Peter Rose, Mr John Ruler, Mr Roger Rowe, Mr David and Mrs Mary Rowedder, Mr Tony and Mrs Connie Russell, Miss Mercia Sansom, Mr Edward Searle, Flight Lieutenant Godfrey Smith, Mr Leonard Smith, Mrs Audrey Stanley, Mrs Margaret Stenning, Misses Dorothy and Winifred Timms, Mrs Christiana Timms, Mrs Una Tollman, Mrs Joyce Walker, Mrs Wendy Weaver, Mrs Mary Whytock, Mr Charles Wimble, Mrs Joy Wimble, Mrs Rhoda Witcombe and Mr Gordon Wright.

The Hayes Village Association has also always offered assistance and encouragement and particular thanks are due to Mrs Beryl Grimani Harrold and Mr Peter Harrold, Mr Michael and Mrs Shirley Savage.

There will be omissions and for these I apologise, particularly to those friends who helped Trevor Woodman with his research.

The book could not have been completed without the support of my wonderful family. My son David worked hard to prepare the final book layout and advised on the photographs. My daughter Elizabeth and her husband Mark spent a long time taking modern photographs of Hayes, proof reading and reproducing the maps, which were drawn by my husband Barry. He has been very involved with the book's production over many years in many different ways. His support has been vital to the successful publication of a book which we hope will be of interest to all who in the future wish to find out more about the history of Hayes.

Jean Wilson
Hayes, December 2011

# Abbreviations

| | | | |
|---|---|---|---|
| AA | Anti-Aircraft | LAA | Light Anti-Aircraft |
| ACF | Army Cadet Force | Lt | Lieutenant |
| AFS | Auxiliary Fire Services | MC | Military Cross |
| AGM | Annual General Meeting | MP | Member of Parliament |
| AIF | Australian Imperial Force | NFS | National Fire Service |
| ARP | Air Raid Precautions | NCO | Non-Commissioned Officer |
| ATC | Air Training Corps | PCC | Parochial Church Council |
| ATS | Auxiliary Territorial Service | POW | Prisoner of War |
| Bn | Battalion | RA | Royal Artillery |
| BRDC | Bromley Rural District Council | RAF | Royal Air Force |
| Bty | Battery | RAFVR | Royal Air Force Volunteer Reserve |
| Capt. | Captain | RAMC | Royal Army Medical Corps |
| CB | Companion of the Order of the Bath | RASC | Royal Army Service Corps |
| CMG | Companion of the Order of St Michael and St George | RAuxAF | Royal Auxiliary Air Force |
| Col | Colonel | RCS | Royal Corps of Signals |
| DCM | Distinguished Conduct Medal | RE | Royal Engineers |
| Div. | Division | Regt | Regiment |
| DSC | Distinguished Service Cross | RFA | Royal Field Artillery |
| DSO | Distinguished Service Order | RFC | Royal Flying Corps |
| ETU | Electrical Trades Union | RM | Royal Marine |
| EWS | Emergency Water Supply | RNVR | Royal Naval Volunteer Reserve |
| FAA | Fleet Air Arm | RWKR | Royal West Kent Regiment |
| Flt Lt | Flight Lieutenant | SRN | State Registered Nurse |
| F/O | Flying Officer | TUC | Trades Union Congress |
| GLA | Greater London Authority | UXB | Unexploded bomb |
| GLC | Greater London Council | VAD | Voluntary Aid Detachment of the British Red Cross |
| GP | General Practitioner | V1 | flying bomb |
| GPO | General Post Office | V2 | long range military rocket |
| HAA | Heavy Anti-Aircraft | WAAF | Women's Auxiliary Air Force |
| HCC | Hayes Community Council | WI | Women's Institute |
| HPC | Hayes Parish Council | WO/AG | Wireless Operator / Air Gunner |
| HVA | Hayes (Kent) Village Association | WRNS | Women's Royal Naval Service |
| JP | Justice of the Peace | WVS | Women's Voluntary Service |
| KCC | Kent County Council | | |

# Introduction

At the start of the First World War Hayes remained a small village of under 1,000 people living in about 200 houses. Volume 1 explained the changes in the parish of Hayes as it moved from an agrarian economy to one where much of the employment was based on the large homes that had been built in Victorian times. The opportunities for more clerical work and the easier access to London provided by the railway began to change the village structure. The increasing desire of people to move to the countryside and yet remain close to London encouraged some landowners to sell their estates for residential development. At the same time the increase in population, nationally and locally, put pressure on the infrastructure and created political and administrative changes.

These trends had a relatively limited effect in Hayes before 1914 but were accelerated both economically and socially by the effect of the First World War. In the interwar years there was a rapid growth in the size of the village. Volume 2 explores how the people of Hayes adapted to the changing situation, particularly as some of the main mansions, such as Hayes Place and Pickhurst Manor, were demolished. The population increased greatly. New societies and organisations were formed to meet the needs of an altering community with diverse interests. The parish council was abolished and Hayes became part of an enlarged Bromley Borough. The Second World War brought further challenges as the inhabitants coped with the dangers and difficulties. With the return of peace the process of rebuilding the community began.

The last two chapters outline the main developments in Hayes from 1951. It is impossible to do justice to the history of the schools, churches and all the organisations that exist in Hayes – many warrant a book in themselves. It is hoped, however, that the summary will help to bring the records up to date and provide a basis for further exploration by later historians.

The ancient parish boundary, much of which still defines the ecclesiastical parish of St Mary the Virgin, Hayes, has continued to be the area of study, although political changes have greatly altered the civil boundaries.

My very grateful thanks go to all those who have provided me with information. Without your assistance this history would not have been completed.

Jean Wilson
December 2011

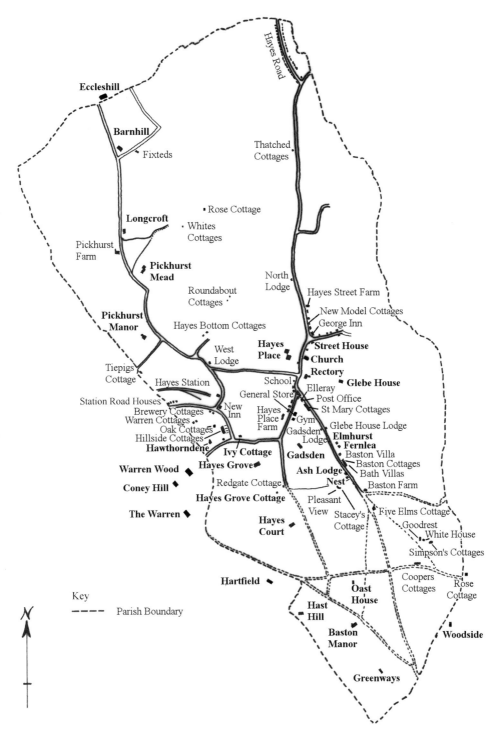

**Eccleshill**

**Barnhill**

· Fixteds

Thatched
Cottages

Hayes Road

· Rose Cottage

**Longcroft**

· Whites
Cottages

Pickhurst
Farm

**Pickhurst
Mead**

Roundabout
Cottages ·

North
Lodge

Hayes Street Farm

**Pickhurst
Manor**

Hayes Bottom Cottages

New Model Cottages

George Inn

West
Lodge

**Hayes
Place**

**Street House**

**Church**

Tiepigs
Cottage

Hayes Station

**Rectory**

School

**Glebe House**

Elleray

General Store

Post Office

Station Road Houses

New
Inn

Hayes
Place
Farm

St Mary Cottages

Brewery Cottages
Warren Cottages ··
Oak Cottages
Hillside Cottages

Gym

Gadsden
Lodge

Glebe House Lodge

**Elmhurst**

**Fernlea**

**Hawthorndene**

**Ivy Cottage**

**Gadsden**

Baston Villa

Baston Cottages
Bath Villas

**Warren Wood** ◆

**Hayes Grove** ●

**Ash Lodge**

**Coney Hill** ◆

Redgate Cottage

**Nest**

Baston Farm

**Hayes Grove Cottage**

Pleasant
View

Five Elms Cottage

**The Warren** ◆

**Hayes
Court**

Stacey's
Cottage ·

· Goodrest

White House

Simpson's Cottages

**Hartfield** ◆

**Oast
House**

Coopers
Cottages

Rose
Cottage

**Hast
Hill**

**Baston
Manor**

**Woodside**

**Greenways**

Key

N

- - - - Parish Boundary

**Map 1:** *The Parish of Hayes in 1914*

*The Upper Village*

***Many men, including those seen here clearing out Husseywell Pond for Sir Everard Hambro of Hayes Place, would soon be asked to fight for their country**[a.]*

# Chapter 1
## Village life and sacrifice: 1914-1921

The year 1914 was to become a very significant one, not only for Hayes but for all of Europe. January began very quietly. Most of the house building begun in the village in the 1880s had ended. Life had settled into its routine. A concert was held to raise funds for the Cricket Club. Charles Wood of Glebe House, Miss Winifred Gann and Captain Andrew Webb were among the soloists. A few days later, the marriage of Marjorie, the eldest daughter of Horace Devas of Hartfield, to Ralph Campbell, son of the Earl of Cawdor, was attended by several local people. Mrs Angus Hambro, who had been married for seven years and was a member of the most significant Hayes family, sadly died, at the age of 28, on 18th January. She was buried in Hayes churchyard.[1]

Hayes Parish Council (HPC) continued to be concerned mainly with problems of roads, sewerage and rubbish collection. In March, HPC agreed to pay Edwin Price £35 a year to collect 'dust' and appointed a representative to consider a sewerage and drainage scheme for the parishes of Hayes and Keston.[2] In April, Bromley Rural District Council (BRDC) was concerned with flooding caused by blockages in a culvert along Hayes Road and with surface water problems at Pickhurst Manor. HPC wrote to BRDC about the best way to clean and sweep Station Road, which had become muddy because of the haulage of manure from the railway station in bad weather. Not everybody agreed that cleaning was needed. Sir Henry Lennard, chairman of BRDC, used the road every day and said that there was nothing wrong with it.[3] For a little while longer life in Hayes was normal.

Nationally, Andrew Bonar Law, the Tory Opposition leader, warned his party in January that the country was 'drifting inevitably to civil war' in Ulster. Internationally, King George V and Queen Mary had a successful visit to Paris that highlighted the improving relationship between Britain and France. In June Archduke Franz Ferdinand, heir to the Austro-Hungarian Empire, was assassinated, an incident that quickly led to the outbreak of war in Europe. On 1st August Germany declared war on Russia; on 3rd August it declared war on France. The following day Britain declared war on Germany, as the latter had invaded Belgium.[4]

These world events were received in the village with mixed emotions. Since the assassination in June there had been speculation and rumour. Some people anticipated the worst but on most people's minds was the success of the harvest; many inhabitants did not expect the new war to impinge on their lives or the community. Events, however, unfolded at great speed with some 70,000 British troops of the British Expeditionary Force in action at Mons on 23rd August. The battle was a disaster and foretold what was to follow. Many thought the war would be over by Christmas, yet the call by Lord Kitchener for another 500,000 men for the army, bringing its strength to 1.2 million, signalled that the country was in for a long struggle.

## Volunteers from Hayes

At the beginning of August an advance guard of soldiers left Bromley Drill Hall for Dover and the Continent. The Liberal Prime Minster, Herbert Asquith, was unwilling to introduce conscription and a powerful recruitment campaign was started to persuade men that it was their patriotic duty to enlist and defend their country. In October whole page advertisements appeared in the *Bromley & District Times* calling for 300,000 men to volunteer. Initially, men between the ages of 18 to 30 were eligible but the upper age limit was soon raised to 38.

How did this affect Hayes? About 130 Hayes men fell within the volunteer age range and it is a significant sign of the wave of patriotism that swept through the village and country that half had volunteered their services by the end of 1914.[5] Many of those enlisting were married or living at home and contributing to the family income, so their decision was likely to cause financial as well as personal hardship to their households. Volunteers were not confined to any one social class.

One of the first to enlist was seventeen-year-old Harry, son of railway signalman Harry Bowles, from Hayes Bottom (later Bourne Vale). He became a signalman on *HMS King Edward VII*. George Beavis of Coopers Cottages was a signalman on *Torpedo Boat No.88*, part of the Mediterranean Fleet based at Gibraltar, and another naval recruit was Brian Mahon. John Mills became a stoker aboard the light cruiser *HMS Boadicea* and his brothers, James and Ernest, joined the army.[6] James became a gunner with the Royal Horse Artillery and Ernest a private with 5 Battalion Northampton Regiment. Most volunteers joined the army and many enlisted in the local Royal West Kent Regiment (RWKR). Friends and neighbours joined up together, such as bank clerk Simon Keech and Edward Meade of Spilman's Grove who enlisted in the Honourable Artillery Company. Several families had to face the worry caused when all their sons volunteered.

George Batten, a carter, and his wife Elizabeth had moved to Hayes in 1898 and lived in one of the Hayes Street Farm cottages. When their sons were old enough they worked on the Hayes Place estate. The Batten brothers, Walter, Albert and Ernest, and their adopted brother, Robert Mills, left to serve with the RWKR within the space of three months. The inhabitants of Rose Cottage, Croydon Road, also rushed to offer their services. Mrs Mitchell became a Red Cross worker and her husband Richard volunteered as a special constable. By the end of 1914 their three sons, Richard, Alfred, who was a former golf professional at the Regents Park Club, London, and William, who worked at Hayes Post Office, were in the army.[7]

A number of Hayes men were already in the armed services when war was declared. Harry Granville Lee-Warner, the 32-year-old son of John and Blanche Lee-Warner of Hawthorndene, was commissioned in 1902. He became a lieutenant in 1905 in the Royal Field Artillery (RFA) and had become a captain by October 1914. He had a distinguished war career, was wounded five times and twice mentioned in despatches. In 1915 he was awarded the Distinguished Service Order (DSO) 'for conspicuous gallantry and devotion to duty during the operations near *Rue du Bois* from 9 to 19 May'. Although wounded on the first day he remained in command of his battery, was twice shelled out of his observation station but continued to do excellent work under heavy fire. He was awarded the Military Cross (MC) in 1916 and ended the war as Brigade Major of 8 Division, Royal Artillery (RA).

Another 'regular' was Percy Garrard of 24 Battalion City of London Regiment who was attached to the 2/4 Kings Royal Rifles. He first volunteered for the army during the South African War (1899-1902) and took part in operations in the Orange Free State. He was mentioned in despatches and awarded the Queen's Medal for Distinguished Conduct. At the beginning of the First World War he served as a lieutenant with the West African Frontier Force and by 1917 had risen to the rank of major in the King's African Rifles and then the 4th Nigerian Regiment. He went missing on 24 August 1918 and died in Malawi, while in German hands, on 18th September. His home was 'Alpha' in George Lane and he is commemorated on both the Hayes and Keston War Memorials.[8]

Thomas Basil Duncombe Mann, whose father was a barrister and lived at Hayes Grove Cottage, was a stockbroker's clerk before he joined the Regular Army in 1912. By the time war broke out he was a Captain Instructor of Musketry with 10 Battalion London Regiment and was promoted to major and posted overseas in July 1915.

Local newspapers listed the volunteers and those who were decorated, wounded or killed. Julian Martin Smith, the youngest son of Martin Ridley Smith, was born and lived in The Warren, until his father's death in 1908. He was probably the first officer to enrol. He joined 9th Queen's Royal Lancers as a second lieutenant as soon as war was announced and was the first volunteer officer to be killed in action when he was wounded during the withdrawal from *Mons* on 5 September 1914. He died two days later at *Nangis*, near Paris, aged 27. He is commemorated on the Hayes War Memorial and by a wood in the north-east corner of the grounds of The Warren called 'Julian's Wood'.[9]

**Memorial in St Mary the Virgin, Hayes, to Norman Harris, aged 16**

Another early casualty was midshipman Norman Harris of The White House. He was born in Hayes in 1898 and, from the age of eleven, was trained as a seaman at Osborne Royal Naval Junior College. He progressed to the Royal Naval College at Dartmouth and at the beginning of the war his parents received a telegram saying, 'We are mobilized'.[10] The Navy was short of naval officers and the older boys from Dartmouth became midshipmen. On 4th August Norman Harris joined the old battleship *HMS Bulwark*. On 26th November the ship blew up when it was loading ammunition at Sheerness, Kent, killing 738 of its 750 crew, including sixteen-year-old Norman Harris. The huge explosion was probably caused by black powder charges being mishandled. His distraught mother never recovered from the loss of her son, which was said to be contributory to her early death in 1916.

Village life soon changed. In early August, the Hayes Branch of the West Kent War Clothing League held a meeting in the Gymnasium, situated in the upper village; the Kent County Fund was set up and the Rector announced that an additional Holy Eucharist service was to be held on Wednesday evenings for the duration of the war. The Soldiers' and Sailors' Families Association met in Bromley and the Rector's niece, Miss Eileen Clowes, became its secretary. At the same time a call went out for men to enrol as special police constables (Specials) to help fill the gaps caused by military service. Men from all walks of life enrolled; 28 were from Hayes, twelve of whom were Sir Everard Hambro's staff and estate workers.[1] The Specials' appointments were initially for six months but some, such as Wilfred Hawkings of Greenways and Walter Cole from Coopers Cottages, Hayes Common, very quickly volunteered for the fighting services.

## Help from the Home Front

News began to arrive from the battlefront and it was not long before some of the horrors became evident to the people of the village. Many women from the wealthier families had already joined one of the Voluntary Aid Detachments of the British Red Cross (VAD) that had been set up to provide medical support in the event of war. Kent 52 was the earliest to be formed in Bromley in 1910 and was supported by a few women from Hayes, particularly those living in the new houses in Hayes Road. Most, however, were involved in two detachments. Kent 50, started in 1912, covered Bromley Common, Keston and Hayes; Kent 82, West Wickham, was formed in 1913. Kent 50's quartermaster, Miss M Clowes, was another of the Rector's nieces. Catherine Harris from The White House and Louisa Hawkings of Greenways were early members. Kent 82's commandant was Gillian Lee-Warner of Hawthorndene and her sister Blanche was also in the group.

The women received wide-ranging training. They experienced camping and working under conditions approximating to those they might face if the German Army invaded Britain. They learned to cook, how to construct and use field-ovens, the need for good drinking water, proper sanitation and the disposal of waste. It was a far cry from their genteel life in Hayes. Training had intensified the year before war broke out. On 2 August 1913, Kent 82 camped at Herne, Kent, competed against fifteen other detachments and won the Yolland Shield competition. In September 1913, a VAD exercise was held on Hayes Common where a mock battle took place. The Boy Scout 'casualties' were taken from the 'battle ground' to the clearing station, set up at the village school, and then transported in cars and wagons to a temporary hospital on Mason's Hill, Bromley. Kent 82 held an inter-detachment competition in April 1914 to test home nursing and first aid skills. Gillian Lee-Warner came first and Blanche was second. In June and July 1914 a field training camp was organised at Rolvenden in Kent for all VAD units.

*VADs at Hayes Grove* [b.]

On the declaration of war the VADs came under the control of the Kent County Territorial Association. The aim was to assist any mobilized units by replenishing stores and drugs and by supplying hospital and general comforts. Members of Kent 50 worked for a time at Bromley Cottage Hospital and all groups visited local residents to discover what they would be prepared to lend in the event of an emergency. That emergency came on the evening of 13 October 1914 when, at about ten o'clock in the evening, a telephone rang in the headquarters of the Kent organisation. A telegram was read out instructing them to mobilise their hospitals at once because 'large numbers of wounded arrive tonight'. Miss Grace Lennard of Kent 82 later recalled that she was working at the Bromley Homeopathic Hospital, where she had gone on a short nursing course. She was telephoned in the early hours of the morning to report to The Warren as soon as possible. Everyone laboured through the night making ready temporary hospitals for the wounded soldiers due to arrive the next day.

The Warren, owned by Sir Robert Laidlaw, was one of three private houses that had been offered to Kent 82, if needed. In addition, Sir Robert had promised £25 per week and the produce of the garden, together with the use of five servants. This hospital would have 55 beds and an operating table donated by Mr Gurney Preston, who also supplied two tables for dressings. Coney Hill was made available by Mrs Elizabeth Hoskier. Sir Everard Hambro lent Hayes Grove for one year as an additional hospital for 20 patients, supplying the equipment and giving £5 per week, although initially it was only equipped to receive refugees. The money was gratefully received, as the War Office paid an average of just under three shillings per head per night. Everything else - food, heating, lighting, equipment, medicine, beds and bedding, was provided by the Red Cross.[11]

Kent 50 had three hospitals available: one at Bloomfield Road, Bromley Common, loaned by the trustees of the Primitive Methodist Schools, the Rookery, Bromley Common, where Mr and Mrs A C Norman provided three large rooms for eighteen beds and Lodore, Mason's Hill that was suitable for seven patients. Mrs Knowles, whose novelist daughter Mabel Winifred was a member of the Red Cross, also provided a number of beds at Hast Hill, five initially, for the reception of convalescent and wounded men.[12] In addition, Kent 52 had four beds at 88 Hayes Road.

The wounded soldiers and Belgian refugees arrived at Bromley South Station and were allocated to their respective hospitals. By 17th October there were 50 at the Warren and seven at Coney Hill. Most of the soldiers were suffering from rheumatism, some had bullet wounds in their legs and one was suffering from shrapnel wounds. Miss Maxwell, a trained nurse, was matron at The Warren and there were two nursing sisters, Sister Burke-Close and Sister Haugh. One of the nurses at Hayes Grove was Miss Fuller who lived in Oak Cottages, Hayes.

A few Belgian refugees were housed at Street House and on 2 November 1914 the first Belgian refugee child, Renée Zaman, was admitted to the Infants' School. By April 1915 the hospitals were dealing not only with Belgians but also with wounded soldiers from the West Kents, the Seaforth Highlanders, a number of Yorkshire Regiments and Canadians who had been involved in horrendous fighting at Hill 60 near Ypres. Seventy motorcars waited on 25th April to take 224 wounded men to the hospitals; 25 patients were allocated to The Warren. Two days later a further 227 invalids reached Bromley South and were quickly conveyed to a number of places, including to Hayes.[13]

In May 1915, A C Norman opened a 50-bed hospital at Oakley, Bromley Common, equipped with an operating theatre and x-ray apparatus. Another 20 beds were added a year later and this hospital replaced the three used by Kent 50. In the same month, Canadian Army Medical Authorities opened a convalescent hospital for their wounded soldiers at Bromley Park Hotel (now Bromley Court Hotel), one of the first opened by them in England. Initially, accommodation for about 100 patients was provided inside the building. During the summer it was increased to 185 with 75 under canvas in the grounds and a further ten in the 'annexe' at Hast Hill, which had been offered to the Canadians in June 1915 by Mrs Emma Knowles. In a report the Commanding Officer outlined the benefits of the house in Hayes. He said:

> The rooms which Mrs Knowles offers as small wards are two large bright apartments, one with a northern and one with a southern exposure. They are on the ground floor divided from each other by a corridor, leading off which is a lavatory and bath accommodation. They each contain five beds with a square footage of about seventy feet per bed. The rooms are suitably furnished and each bed provided with a

locker bedside table. In one [room] there is a dining table for the use of patients, in the other a large glass cupboard furnished with surgical dressing, etc. The kitchen from which patients will be provided is near at hand. The house is well situated on high land and is surrounded by pleasant grounds, which patients would be allowed to use. It is a little over three miles from this establishment [Bromley Park Hotel] and about two and a half from Bromley South station, from which point our ambulance could easily take patients.[14]

Houses like Hast Hill became military hospitals all over the country and this report gives a good description of how they were utilised. The Canadian soldiers who convalesced here and at the other local centres were involved with local events. Football matches with the Bromley Police and with other military units were all part of their rehabilitation. Some patients attended a recruiting rally in Bromley in October 1915.[15]

Many events were held to support the activities of the Red Cross, to raise money for Belgian refugees and to entertain wounded soldiers. One of the first was in November 1914 when William Plant organised a concert at the school, which was decorated with flags of the allies. Seventy schoolchildren took part and sang the various National Anthems and 'spirit-lifting' songs.[1] It was realised that the war would not be over by Christmas. By the end of 1914 the village and its people had become fully involved, whether through a family member being at the frontline, working in a VAD hospital, enrolling as a Special or providing funds and entertainment for the refugees and wounded. Even the schoolchildren's help had been enlisted to knit gloves and socks for the soldiers.

In December, another 100,000 volunteers were needed to replace the losses that had occurred in the first few months of the war. More advertisements appeared, for men 5ft 2in tall 'without boots'. A week later the West Surrey, Middlesex and Sussex regiments stated they would accept men of 5ft 1in and above. The recruitment drive began to move from one of patriotic duty to one of conscience with posters and placards depicting the non-volunteers as people to be pitied. Posters appeared declaring, 'Women of Britain say – GO!'

## 1915

The New Year brought more evidence of the horrors of war. In January 1915 the first Zeppelin raids occurred with bombs falling on King's Lynn and Yarmouth. The next month the blockade of Britain by U boats started and women were encouraged to work in factories to help the war effort. It was the year of the Gallipoli campaign, the sinking of the *Lusitania* and the death of the poet Robert Brooke while on active service.

During 1915 at least another 34 men from the village volunteered for service in the armed forces, including Henry Timms from Hillside Cottages and William George Clibbon, who worked in the gardens of Hayes Place.[1] Thus, within the first seventeen months of war, three-quarters of the eligible men of Hayes had enlisted.

As the war progressed, the pressure on those still at home became more intense as accounts from soldiers and sailors and their mixed fortunes filtered through from the various theatres of war. William Henry Pascoe, a policeman born in Hayes, joined the navy in May 1915 and was on the training ship, *President II*, before serving at sea. He was later mentioned in despatches, wounded and became a patient in Gunston Cottage Hospital, Lowestoft from July 1917 until April 1918 when he was retired.

*Henry Timms, his wife Mary and daughter Winifred, 1917* [c.]

*Alfred Harold Arnold enlisted in the Royal Artillery* [d.]

In 1914, George Cogger, an assistant cowman at Hayes Place Farm, married Amy Evelyn Mills, the youngest daughter of widow Mary Mills who lived near the George Inn. He became a temporary porter at Hayes Railway Station. His decision to enlist was probably prompted by his discovery of the body of Henry Hope on the railway line, a few yards from the viaduct bridge between West Wickham and Hayes stations. The inquest in November 1915 revealed that the unfortunate individual was an insurance clerk from Sydenham, who had suffered a nervous breakdown and who, a few days before his body was found, had been in hospital during a *Zeppelin* air raid when bombs had fallen, showering glass over his bed. The jury returned a verdict of suicide. Shortly afterwards George Cogger joined the East Surrey Regiment and was posted to Belgium where he died of his wounds on 8 June 1917.[16]

Another early volunteer was Frederick James Robbins, the son of James and Lucy Robbins of Tithe Cottage, who joined up in November 1915. He worked for the Post Office in Beckenham and enlisted in 8th London Regiment (Post Office Rifles) but was killed in action in France on 15 September 1916, aged 20. Mr A T Mylles, the Postmaster of Beckenham, in his letter of condolence wrote: 'Fred's unassuming manners endeared him to all his comrades, and his conduct was such as to earn the highest respect and confidence of his superior officers. His loss will be felt throughout the office.' His brother George was also in the army, but he survived.

By the end of 1915 at least 99 men had volunteered from Hayes. Almost half were from established families living in the district, the rest were mainly single men employed on the farms and estates or as carriers for Edwin Price. During 1915 several lost their lives. The first, on 25th April, was John Oswald Payne, a lieutenant attached to 1 Battalion Royal Warwickshire Regiment. His battalion suffered very heavy losses in the second battle of Ypres when, for the first time, the Germans used gas as a weapon on the Western Front. The battalion attacked a wood near *St Julien* at 4.30am but, because the German trenches were insufficiently shelled and no support could come up the line, they retired at about 7am to consolidate their position. John Payne was one of the seventeen officers killed in the action.

Charles Goldsmith, a Private in the Royal Marines Light Infantry, was killed in action on 30th April at Gallipoli. He was born and brought up in Hayes and was 25 years old. It was a terrible shock to the Goldsmith family, whose three other sons were also in the services, but thankfully they returned safely.[8] On 22nd July, Edward William Rust, aged 21 from Elleray, Baston Road, died in the Flanders trenches. He was a private with 6 Battalion Queen's Own RWKR, whose war diaries record the action:

> *Despierre Farm* – 12 noon – Ruse to tempt enemy to put his head over the parapet met with some success.
> 4.15pm Relief in trenches by 6th Buffs commenced.
> 11.5pm Relief complete. Casualties; Pte Rust killed and four others wounded.[17]

September 1915 was a tragic month for Hayes families with several men losing their lives. They included 19-year-old William Abel Tulett, son of William and Agnes Caroline Tulett, who died on 17th September whilst also serving with 6 Battalion RWKR.[8] He was born in Hayes and his family had lived in the village since his grandfather Abel arrived as a gardener in about 1870.

On 25th September Frederic George Plant and Arthur Colin Frost died. Frederic, the youngest son of the schoolmaster William Plant, joined 1 Battalion Artists Rifle the first week after the declaration of war. He trained at Lords Cricket Ground, after which his unit relieved the Scots Guard at the Tower of London; he moved to Waterdale and eventually to Flanders in October 1914. The regiment was converted into an Officers' Training Corps and Frederic Plant was gazetted on 23 April 1915 as 2nd Lieutenant, 1 Battalion Royal West Surrey Regiment (The Queens). He was home in April for four days and in September for a week, during which time he became engaged. Appointed as a bomb officer, it was while fulfilling that duty that he met his death during the battle of Loos. His commanding officer Major L M Crofts wrote:

> He was leading his men up a communication trench leading from the German first line trench, which we had captured, when a German bomb exploded and hit him in the head, and the men near say he must have been killed at once, though no one saw him afterwards … lack of bombs forced the men to retire to our original line, and all the wounded and dead had to be abandoned. Your son was killed leading his men in a gallant manner. His sterling qualities had made him a favourite with all and his loss will be deeply felt in the battalion.[18]

His loss was also felt deeply by his family and friends in Hayes, where he had been an active member of the cricket club and keen on tennis, football and hockey. Mrs Plant found it very difficult to come to terms with the death of her much loved youngest child, especially as nobody had survived who had witnessed the moment of his death.

The other officer who died on the same day was 2nd Lieutenant Arthur Colin Frost, known as Colin. He was born in 1896, educated at Sherborne and Rugby and enlisted in 1914. He obtained a commission in 11 Battalion Argyll and Sutherland Highlanders and was stationed at a number of camps in Southern England before sailing to France in July 1915. He was shot dead by a sniper while his unit was defending an important position on Hill 70, near Loos. Colin was just eighteen years old and the letters of sympathy written to his mother from his school, his Commanding Officers and friends survive. They reflect sentiments that other mothers and fathers were hearing in Hayes as news came through of the fate of their sons. Colonel Malcolm McNeil wrote, 'he was killed quite instantaneously and suffered no pain … You can have this consolation that he died a soldier in the execution of his duty.' Second Lieutenant Davidson said, 'I was by his side when it happened and must say he was behaving most gallantly and died a hero.' Mrs Frost's brother Frank wrote, 'the knowledge a proud one, that Colin gave his life for his country and for us does not mitigate the sorrow and fate has indeed been unkind in demanding the sacrifice of such a nice natured boy and so good looking.' Only those who experienced such bereavement could totally comprehend the grief and unhappiness created within the family. The letters remind us of the tremendous loss of young and promising lives and share the sense of tragedy that such deaths brought to families at home.[19] Colin's parents, Ellen and James Frost, did not live in Hayes until 1919 but it was agreed that his name and that of his brother Jack, who died in 1916, could be included in the Roll of Honour and on the Hayes War Memorial.

Another tragic death two days later, on 27th September, was that of 2nd Lieutenant Harold Evelyn Pennington of 9 Battalion Royal Sussex Regiment. He was not a native of Hayes but had married Ruth Lee-Warner of Hawthorndene just a few weeks before he was killed.[20]

Village life by now was geared to the support of the war effort and, in particular, to providing troops with extra comforts. The General Cigarette Fund was one such scheme to help those on the front line. Every shilling subscribed meant 50 large Virginian cigarettes could be sent to a soldier in the RWKR. In October 1914 Miss Nina Blick of Warren Nurseries donated 2*s.* and contributions, such as the sum of 2*s.* 9*d.* given by Miss A Hassell of Hayes Common in February 1918, were still forthcoming at the end of the war. Soldiers were appreciative of these comforts and Godfrey Marriage of Glebe House Stables received letters of thanks in March 1915 from two of them. 'They both seemed most grateful for smokes received, as they arrived just prior to the men going on duty in the trenches and were distributed among them.' Wealthy local inhabitants contributed far larger donations and, as we have seen, made their houses freely available for use as hospitals. In August 1914 Sir Robert Laidlaw gave £1,000 to the Prince of Wales National Relief Fund, two months later he donated £50 to the VAD and in February 1915 he and Sir Everard Hambro each gave £25 to the County War Fund. At the same time the collecting box at The Warren raised £1 15*s.* 6*d.*[1]

Village children played their part with smaller collections. In November 1914 children in the Infants were knitting for the soldiers and sailors. This was 'to replace other Kindergarten occupation as being more useful during the war'. Beatrice Russell, who attended the Village School until 1916, remembered knitting gloves, stockings, helmets and scarves, although she was never sure if the soldiers were able to make use of the end result. In 1915 many pupils were rewarded on Empire Day with an Overseas Club Certificate recording that they had 'helped to send some Comfort and Happiness to the brave Sailors and Soldiers of the British Empire, fighting to uphold Liberty, Justice, Honour and Freedom in the Great War.'[21]

*Pupil's certificate for support of the armed forces, 1915* [e.]

## The year of the Battle of the Somme

In 1916, the people of Dublin rebelled against British rule and proclaimed an Irish Republic, the battle of Jutland was fought and the secretary for war, Lord Kitchener, was drowned when the ship in which he was travelling was sunk. Lloyd George became Prime Minister. Tank warfare was introduced. The year, however, is mostly remembered for the terrible carnage of the Somme.

In January, the House of Commons voted overwhelmingly, after two days of impassioned debate, to introduce military conscription. The voluntary effort had not been enough to win the war and it decided that there must be compulsion on those of military age who were 'shirking their duty'. Conscription applied to all men between the ages of 18 and 41 but exemptions could be obtained on the grounds of continuing education, hardship, ill health or conscientious objection, providing the local tribunal approved the reason. Conscription caused great hardship to families and businesses, especially where their wellbeing was reliant on one man. The West Kent Military Tribunal met regularly from 1916 to the end of the war, deliberated on applications and tried to negate hardship, but was always under pressure to release men for war service.

No claims for exemption by Hayes men on the basis of conscientious objection have been found, although there were several applications for hardship and for medical reasons. The first Military Tribunal was held in March 1916 when Henry Charles Beavis, an insurance agent, applied for exemption because he was the sole supporter of his mother. By the time the Tribunal met he had heard that his mother would receive an allowance from his employer, the Prudential Insurance Company, and the Tribunal agreed that the company was very good at looking after dependants financially. Henry said that in the altered circumstances he had no objection whatever to serving his country and 'if it were possible he would like to join the aviation service'. During the same month the contractor Edwin Price applied on behalf of three carters who worked for him, 33-year-old Albert Harrington, Wallace James aged 27 and Ernest Russell who was 32 years old. In support of his application Mr Price told the members of the Tribunal that he employed nine men but should have 30. After consideration, the Tribunal said one man must be conscripted and Wallace James was chosen, presumably because he was the youngest. Robert Maidment, a 31-year-old cowman working at Hayes Place Farm, claimed exemption on domestic grounds because he had three dependants to support. The Tribunal said that an allowance would be paid to his dependants and his claim was dismissed. He survived and returned to work as a farm labourer after the war, although died in 1923.

In the case of John Staplehurst, a farm waggoner, the Tribunal delayed his enlistment by two months so that his employer, Thomas Marden, could look for a replacement. In contrast, Frank Holland, aged 27, was allowed only two weeks before he was called up. The same time was allowed to Frank Hold, a chauffeur from Hayes Lane, who applied on the grounds of domestic hardship. Both men survived, although Frank Hold appears to have been discharged in July 1916 with pulmonary tuberculosis.[22] The following month another chauffeur, Mr. Gilbert, applied for temporary exemption because of ill health and his case was referred to the Medical Board. Arthur George of Pickhurst Farm applied for further exemption on domestic grounds and was granted another two months. He again came before the Tribunal in January 1917 when his deferment was once more extended.

Miss Frances Sands, who ran the butcher's shop at 10 St Mary Cottages, was also able to obtain a deferment for her slaughterman, Reginald Hutchins, who was 18½ years old. The Medical Board examined him. His conscription was deferred for three months, with leave to apply again. Miss Sands, who also had a butcher's business in Downe, successfully reapplied for her employee until the end of the war.[1]

The optimism of some of the soldiers, or at least the desire to minimise worry for their loved ones, is illustrated by a letter written by Signaller Arthur Robson to his future in-laws, Mr and Mrs Lewis of Model Cottages, on 16 January 1916 from his camp at Shoreham:

> I really think I am going to make a move at last and it is splendid to think we are all going together. I only hope we shall all be attached to the same battalion and remain together … I feel quite certain that I shall be back safe and sound and equally certain that the war will end in victory for us, with a glorious peace to follow.[23]

***Signaller Arthur Robson*** [f.]

In February 1916 the Government asked 'well-off' families to release their male and female servants for 'more useful work'. It also suggested that parts of their homes should be shut off and that they should close labour intensive 'fuel hungry' greenhouses. Farms suffered from the loss of agricultural labour. In June 1915 schoolboy Thomas McRoberts asked for leave to help with the haymaking because of the shortage of labourers. In 1916 the Board of Trade and the Board of Agriculture organised a local meeting to promote a plan to employ women on farms. Sir Everard Hambro of Hayes Place chaired a meeting, which was held in the Gymnasium in May and attended by a large number of ladies. He stressed that married women's first duty was to their husbands and children. 'If a man had not a happy home and good food he would not do his work properly, and if the children were not brought up well … the race would deteriorate after the war.' Wives, however, should have spare time and unmarried women plenty of time to devote to the cultivation of the land. A Women's National Land Service Corps was to be set up to provide agricultural training and, at the end of the training, girls would be placed out in groups of four or five to work for farmers in various parts of the country. Mrs Eric Hambro of Pickhurst Mead agreed to become the local registrar for Hayes and to provide further information on the subject.[1] It has not been established how many, if any, Hayes women volunteered although several usually helped on the farms in Hayes at harvest time. Apart from the sacrifice of seeing their men go to war, Hayes women had already made great contributions to the war effort, particularly through the VAD. Individuals were still putting up wounded soldiers, such as Mrs Lewis of Model Cottages, whose patient was transferred elsewhere in March 1916.

One Hayes man to see action in 1916 was Arthur Robson, who was engaged to Jessie Lewis. His letters to his mother and fiancée hint at the terrible experiences that the men were suffering and also show that he was in contact with other soldiers from Hayes, such as Fred Bryant, Albert Batten and Douglas Skinner. In April 1916 he wrote:

> My 2 nights back in the village were spent in the snipers' billet and I had several long talks with Eva Batten's friend – for he is a sniper. He seems a very nice quiet sensible sort of fellow and I like him very much. Fred Bryant was also in the same billet.

The second half of the year saw an increasing number of casualties, both soldiers and airmen from Hayes. Not all the deaths were overseas. Air Mechanic 2nd Class William Bernard Bingham, Royal Flying Corps (RFC), who died on 5th July in a motor transporter accident, was buried in Chichester, Sussex. He was 32 and before the war was chauffeur to Sir Robert Laidlaw at The Warren and lived at the Lodge. His widow, Charlotte Jean, moved with their two young sons to 2 St Mary Cottages.[8]

The war on the Western Front intensified and the battle of the Somme began. James and Ellen Frost's eldest son, named James John after his father but known as Jack, was with 11 Battalion Northumberland Fusiliers. He was killed on 7th July leading a company of rifleman 'over the top' at *Contalmaison*. Mrs Frost found it hard to accept his death as his body was never found.[19]

Arthur Robson was more fortunate: 'I came through it all without a scratch, but I've never been in such an awful state in my life and I feel as if I could sleep for weeks on end. I'm only thankful to think that I've come out of that inferno alive.' He and Cyril Bower also came safely through the battle for Trones Wood, although 'the terrific noise and excitement sent little Bower into a sort of fainting trance for 5 hours.' Not so fortunate was Lieutenant Douglas Hilton Skinner who was wounded in the shoulder and later died. He was 24 and the eldest son of Hilton and Emily Skinner of Ash Lodge, Baston Road. Educated at Charterhouse he was a medical student at Oxford when war broke out. He enlisted in the RWKR and, when he died on 16 July 1916, he was acting as a temporary captain because his battalion had been reduced by a half through its losses. Fortunately, his younger brother Duncan survived the war.

A month later Charles Harald Wood, the twenty-one-year old son of Charles and Ellinor Wood of Glebe House, died on 25th August from wounds received the previous day. He was a 2nd Lieutenant in 8 Battalion King's Royal Rifle Corps and, while temporarily in command, led his company in the attack on Delville Wood.[24] After the war, on the expiry of their lease, Charles Wood and his family decided to leave Glebe House and Hayes, which brought back too many painful memories of their dead son.

Arthur Edmund Cassam, born in 1891 at Otford, Kent, was the son of William Cassam, a thatcher, who moved to Hayes from West Wickham about 1900. Arthur went to Hayes School, became a bell-ringer, was married in June 1914 and moved to Keston. In April 1916 he joined 1 Battalion RWKR as a private and saw service in France and Flanders. He was one of seven casualties when the enemy heavily shelled the RWKR positions on 10th September at *Leuze Wood*. He died the next day, leaving a young wife and child.[25] Four days later, Percy Arnold, a corporal in 11 Battalion RWKR, was killed during an attack on *Flers*, when tanks were employed for the first time. Percy was one of the eight children of Jeffrey and Sarah Arnold who lived at 9 St Mary Cottages.[26] Two of his brothers, Alfred and Walter, returned home safely after the war ended.

Arthur Robson was involved in a forward movement from 25th September in which four signallers were lost. He wrote home that Albert Batten was safe but Eva Batten's friend had been shot by a sniper and killed on the spot. Sometimes news and confirmation that a loved one had been killed took many months to arrive. William George Harris, the son of William and Elizabeth, at one time lived and worked at Hayes Court Stables. He married Sarah Bashford, a domestic servant, in September 1915 and moved to Lewisham. He joined 11 Battalion RWKR in November 1915 and was reported missing on 7 October 1916. His wife Sarah returned to Hayes with their only child to live with her father, a cowman at Pickhurst Farm. It was not until August 1917 that they were informed that William had been 'killed in action'. He has no known grave.[27]

On Sunday, 22nd October, 2nd Lieutenant Francis George Wake Marchant was killed when he was fatally struck on the head by shrapnel while flying with the RFC over the Somme at 8,000ft. His machine fell just inside the British lines and in the evening some Australian troops very bravely recovered his body. His flight commander wrote:

> He was a general favourite in the squadron. I could not have wished for a more skilful, fearless and cheerful pilot … His example had a great effect on the flight, as no weather was ever too bad for him to work in, or any work too risky to be cheerfully undertaken and carried out.

He was nineteen years old and the only son of Francis and Torfrida Marchant, who lived a few yards outside the parish boundary at Woodside, Commonside, Keston. They were active supporters of Hayes and its church.[8]

Torfrida's sister was Mildred Baldwin Wake who married Archibald Cameron Norman, one of the major landowners in Hayes. Their son, Gerald Wake Norman, served in the Royal Navy, took part in the Dardenelles campaign and the battle of Jutland and later received the silver medal of military valour from the King of Italy.

Two other members of the Norman family, sons of Henry John Norman who had lived at Gadsden until his death in 1905, were killed in action and are commemorated in Hayes churchyard. Major Harold Norman died at the Battle of Ypres on 10 November 1914 when he was commanding 1 Battalion Northamptonshire Regiment. His younger brother Captain Lionel Norman, MC, of 1 Battalion Scots Guards lost his life at the age of 35, in the battle of the Somme, on 15 September 1916.[28]

In August 1916 the village heard that Gunner George Boakes, who had enlisted in December 1915 and had been with the RFA as part of the Egyptian Expeditionary Force since January, had been captured and was a prisoner of war in Mesopotamia. He was from Spilman's Grove (George Lane) and was one of the fortunate ones eventually to return to Hayes after the war.[1]

In November 1916, schoolchildren were given a half day holiday to attend an 'In Memoriam' service for those in the parish who had been killed in the war, including six former pupils: Percy Arnold, Arthur Cassam, Charles Goldsmith, Frederic George Plant, Frederick Robbins and William Rust. Shortly afterwards, assistant school mistress, Miss Stone, was given a few days off to spend some time with her brother who was home from the Front where he had been wounded. At Christmas the schoolteachers and pupils sent a 'round robin' letter to all former pupils who were on active service.

> It is impossible to say how proud we all are of you and we think and talk of you very often … Now dear boy keep up your pecker, enjoy your Christmas fare and for a time at any rate banish thoughts of war, think of us at Hayes and of the happy times spent in your village homes.[23]

By the time he received this letter, one former pupil, Arthur Robson, was back in England. He had been admitted to hospital in early November with trench fever and repatriated to Yeovil Red Cross Hospital at the beginning of December. He was later invalided out of the army with heart problems and married Jessie Lewis in January 1918.

Memorial to Francis Marchant
in Hayes Church

Arthur Robson and Jessie Lewis,
married 23 January 1918 [f.]

Just before Christmas, Mrs Ann Torrens of Baston Manor was informed that her son, Major Atwood Alfred Torrens RFA, had been struck and killed by a piece of shrapnel while leading his men to safety on 8th December. He was buried in the British cemetery at *Pozieres*. He had been educated at Harrow and was a fine cricketer. He was included in the MCC tour of New Zealand in 1906 and sometimes played for Hayes Cricket Club. He was also captain of Langley Park Golf Club.[29]

The loss of so many able-bodied men from the village mostly occurred overseas and was hard on all concerned but tragedies and deaths still occurred at home. In May a fifteen-year-old boy, Stanley Gordon Tait from Penge, was found drowned in a flooded gravel pit at Furze Lane (Tiepigs Lane), by Florence Fisher, a housemaid from Pickhurst

Manor. The water was about 14ft deep and level with the surrounding meadow and was a place where boys frequently played. Sir Henry Lennard owned the land and at the inquest it was recommended that a caution board be erected.[1]

John Isdale Smail of Warren Wood, an Elder and the treasurer of Trinity Presbyterian Church, Bromley, died in January 1916. In August Michael Hambro, the three- year-old son of Angus Hambro and grandson of Sir Everard, fell ill. Nurse Lea, who had replaced Nurse Blundell as District Nurse in January 1916, nursed him at Hayes Place but sadly he died on 2nd September.[30] Ten people were buried in the churchyard that year.

The local newspapers continued to cover the war and its effect on the local population. Obituaries of those who had given their lives were well reported, often describing the actions and usually accompanied by a photograph. Other local news and notices relating to marriages, parish council meetings and sports events also featured although, with the shortage of paper as the war progressed, the coverage of less essential items of news reduced. The papers, however, performed a very valuable service to all communities; the broadcasting of national and international news on the wireless was still in the future.

# 1917

The people of Hayes experienced very little joy during 1917. The U-boat campaign was taking its toll and basic imports were not getting through. In May more than 100 ships were sunk. Britain introduced the convoy system to counter the threat. Two major international events were the entry of the United States into the war and the Russian revolution, with the rise to power of Lenin. Yet more troops were needed to replace the losses incurred in the various theatres of war. Military tribunals continued to be held, although it would appear that no new applications for exemption were made from Hayes in 1917.

The casualties continued to mount. The first in 1917, commemorated on the War Memorial, was Lieutenant Walter Holden Legge, son of the late Walter Bevington Legge and nephew of Henry Bevington Legge of The Nest. Lieutenant Legge at the age of 18, after the death of his parents, travelled to British Columbia, Canada and developed a fruit farming business. In 1914 he joined the Canadian RFA in Toronto and returned to Britain, where he was commissioned in the Royal Naval Volunteer Reserve. He was subsequently attached to the RFC. On 10 February 1917 he was testing a new aircraft over Solihull when he detected that the engine was not running correctly and he came down to have the problem resolved. On landing he hit a low greenhouse, the aircraft overturned and he suffered serious internal injuries. He crashed in the grounds of the VAD Hospital at Solihull, was unconscious when taken from the aircraft and died the following day.[31]

The next Hayes casualty occurred on 9th April when Corporal Walter Harvey Batten was killed by a sniper whilst in the trenches at Arras. He was in 9 Battalion RWKR, went to the front line in June 1916 and was wounded later that year. He recovered and returned to the trenches. Shortly before his death he was recommended for the Distinguished Conduct Medal (DCM) because 'with six others he threw many thousands of bombs [grenades] all day because of the difficulty in getting ammunition up' to the guns. On 25

April 1917 Thomas Alexander Manchip was killed. He was the son of Thomas and Eliza of Deddington and his wife Grace Lilian lived at 89 Hayes Road after the war. She was buried in Hayes churchyard in 1950.[8]

Two casualties, Percy Sands and Benjamin Potter, had joined the Australian Imperial Force (AIF). Percy Sands emigrated to Australia in 1911 but his mother Elizabeth continued living at 10 St Mary Cottages until her death in 1916. Percy enlisted in 1 Battalion AIF and, while serving in France, died of his wounds on 11 April 1917.[32] Benjamin Potter, who had emigrated in 1912, joined 18 Battalion AIF. He was wounded in 1916, the year that his parents moved to Brewery Cottages. He recovered, returned to the front, was wounded again and died in France on 3 May 1917. His brothers James and John survived the war.[8]

*Brewery Cottages, home of the Potter family* [ak.]

Just a few days later news came through that 2nd Lieutenant John Sheffield Holroyde had been killed in action on 10th May while flying with 55 Squadron. His family home was at 75 Hayes Road where his father, a solicitor, and mother Isobel lived. The family had come from Yorkshire and John had enlisted in the East Yorkshire Regiment but later transferred to the RFC.[33]

Mrs Lillian Williams, who was married in 1915, learned that her husband, Ordinary Seaman Herbert William Williams, of Mayes Cottage, Croydon Road, had been killed on 9 July 1917 while he was serving on board *HMS Vanguard*. This ship had taken part successfully in the battle of Jutland in 1916, as part of the 4th Battle Squadron, but blew up at Scapa Flow due to the spontaneous ignition of her cordite. Only nineteen of the 823 crewmen survived. Herbert Williams is listed on Hayes Cricket Club's memorial.

Herbert's parents, William and Amelia Williams, had to bear a second family tragedy when they heard that another son, Aircraftman 1st Grade Henry Valentine Williams, had died on 26th November whilst serving on *HMS President II*. He was in Yarmouth from 1 September 1916 to 26 November 1917 and died in the Royal Naval Hospital of 'chronic granular kidney'. He was buried in Great Yarmouth cemetery.[8]

On 20th August, Royal Naval Air Service pilot, Flight Sub-Lieutenant Cecil Barnaby Cook died when the *Sopwith Pup* in which he was learning to fly disintegrated and crashed. Cecil was eighteen years old and was interred in the churchyard following a full military funeral in which his coffin was conveyed on a naval gun carriage. He was educated at Dulwich College and was the son of Herbert and Laura Cook who lived at 60 Hayes Road.[34]

***Gravestone of Cecil Barnaby Cook who died in 1917***

Reginald David Lane was the second son of Thomas and Sarah Lane of Thatched Cottages, Hayes Lane. Educated at Hayes School, he worked as a gardener for Mrs Lee-Warner of Hawthorndene and for Mrs Austin of Wayside, Shortlands, Kent. He joined 17 Battalion Royal Fusiliers in February 1917 and served in France and Flanders. After the Battle of Cambrai, the first major tank battle, he was reported missing. He became a POW but died of his injuries on 30th November, aged nineteen. His eldest brother William served with the Coldstream Guards but was invalided out in July 1915. His younger brother Thomas, a sergeant in 14 Battalion Hampshire Regiment, returned home safely.

The last soldier connected with Hayes to die during this terrible year was Private Arthur William Tuson of 1 Battalion Welsh Guards on 1 December 1917.[35]

News of the war was brought to Hayes in many ways; a letter from a loved one at the 'front', a telegram announcing that a family member was missing or dead, the serviceman on leave and the many wounded that passed through the village. The war also manifested itself in other ways. In August 1917 three companies of 7 Battalion Kent Volunteer Regiment undertook a night exercise on Hayes Common. The plan was simple, 'on paper and in theory', with C Company taking up a defensive position and with A and B companies tasked to locate and attack:

> The manoeuvres demonstrated the difficulty of moving over country clad in gorse where every bush at a few yards looked like a soldier. In unfamiliar country small groups of men lost touch and became isolated and never engaged the enemy. Spies dressed as tramps managed to pass through enemy lines bringing valuable information.

Whether it was a great victory or defeat is not known but the exercise was said to have been very instructive.[1]

In June enemy aircraft bombed the East End of London for the first time, heralding a new and potent technique of attacking the country's infrastructure, well behind the frontline battlefields. One part of the strategy to combat these aerial attacks was to create anti-aircraft defences for the London region, which was divided into three sections. Bromley and the surrounding district were part of the East Sub-Command, which was equipped with 19 anti-aircraft gun stations supported by 36 searchlights and 38 observation posts.

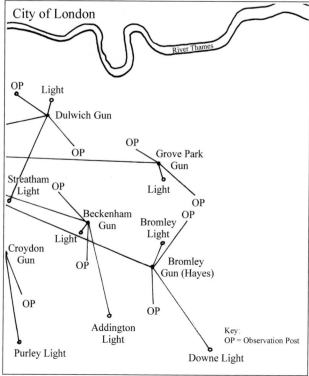

**Map 2: *Searchlights and Observation Posts for part of the East Sub-Command. The Bromley Gun was at Pickhurst Mead***

Pickhurst Mead was chosen as one of the gun stations. The owner of Pickhurst Mead at the time was Charles Eric Hambro, who was involved with the Central Intelligence Services. The gun was installed on an unmade road within the grounds and chosen because of its high elevation. The station was manned by an officer, two NCOs and 18 to 20 other ranks. It was served by two search-lights known as 'fighting lights', sited in fields adjacent to Hawes Lane, West Wickham (probably where the allotments are now) and at Hayesford Park.[36] The observation posts were at Keston and Sundridge Park, with the headquarters for the whole Command at Putney Heath.

Seven attacks were directed at London between September and November 1917. On 6th December a group of *Gotha* aircraft on the way to attack London entered the Bromley area in the early morning. One incendiary bomb fell in Station Road (Bourne Way) but failed to cause damage. A second incident occurred on 7 March 1918. On this occasion a *Zeppelin-Staaken Gigant* bomber dropped a 50kg bomb that fell in woodland near Hartfield house.[37] Again no damage was caused. Grace Willis née Knopp, who lived in Model Cottages, recalled the shells from the anti-aircraft gun going over the house and said that the noise was clearly heard all over Hayes.

## Self-sufficiency and rationing

Everyday village life, as in the rest of the country, was being continuously shaped by national demands as the war progressed. In 1914 there had been emphasis on self-sufficiency, stressing the benefits of effective cultivation. The Ministry of Agriculture provided a wide range of leaflets on many topics. Pig breeding and their management, rabbit breeding, feeding of poultry, cultivation of onions and fruit were just a few of the subjects. Mrs Smail of Warren Wood was on the local Food Control Committee throughout the war. Many villagers had a good practical knowledge of horticulture through their upbringing, work and membership of the Hayes Cottage Gardens' Association. At the school William Plant, who was a Fellow of the Royal Horticultural Society, continued to run the boys' gardening class. Each pupil had an opportunity to grow crops on the allotment at the northeast corner of what is now the junction of Pickhurst Lane and Bourne Vale. In 1915 the Inspector reported that:

> the ground is stony and some of the crops have suffered from drought but the plots
> are in good condition … The tools are stored in a small case which is inadequate for
> the purpose and they are in an unsatisfactory condition. A good shed is badly needed.

There is no evidence that one was purchased. In 1916 some 280lb of potatoes and 200lb of onions were harvested. Other crops were also grown including, in September 1918, carrots, beetroot, French beans and lettuce. The allotment also had a few productive fruit trees and bushes.[38]

While the boys were gardening, the older schoolgirls were encouraged to cook economically. In 1918, under the new assistant mistress, Miss Bache, they were making Cornish pasties when the Inspector visited:

> Miss Bache is evidently imbued with a keen desire to make the lesson of real
> practical worth to the girls and she recognizes the great value of gaining the
> cooperation of the mothers in allowing the children to practise at home what they
> learn at school. I should like, however, girls to recognize the importance of working

as neatly as possible as these lessons are a direct means of helping in the formation of good habits.

The schoolchildren were encouraged to pick blackberries and in September 1918 over 160lb of blackberries were combined with rhubarb, made into jam and sold to the parishioners.

As the war developed, the German U-Boat campaign against Allied merchant shipping created shortages in raw materials and food for Britain. Initially the Government relied on stressing the importance of eating less. Bread, in particular, was a major target of this campaign because, in 1916, the wheat crop failed and it seemed likely that there might be insufficient bread for the nation. At the time Britain only produced about one fifth of the wheat it needed, the balance coming by ship from the United States and Canada. Nationally, the situation deteriorated and, in 1917, the Flour and Bread Order was introduced fixing the cost of a 4lb loaf at 9d. The housewife was expected to ensure that each person had no more than one 4lb loaf or 3lb of wheat flour per week. The '*Win the War Cookery Book*' focused on the importance of beating the enemy in the larder. This policy was reinforced by Sir Arthur Yapp, Director General of Food Economy, speaking at a meeting in Bromley in December 1917:

> My message to you this evening is this. Although we cannot go out and help the men fighting at the Front, there is a warfare in which we can take part – the warfare in the kitchen, the war against waste of every kind.

Although Sir Arthur disapproved of rationing there were many in Hayes, and elsewhere, who were tired of queuing and who felt that the wealthy seemed to have an unfair advantage in obtaining items that were in short supply. There were several that were pleased when the Government was forced to introduce compulsory rationing. In January 1918 sugar became a controlled food and every householder was registered. On deposit of the 'Sugar Card' and vouchers, the retailer was able to apply for a sugar supply. Householders could only obtain sugar from the specific retailer against sugar vouchers and were limited to no more than 2lb per week. Meat restrictions followed the rationing of butter and margarine that was introduced in February. Previously the Government had introduced price controls on slaughtered meat and restricted the profit a retail butcher could make to 2d. a lb. By the spring of 1918, meat was rationed to 15oz. per person per week. Villagers were encouraged to have meatless days and to make use of cereals, pulses and nuts. Advertisements appeared for Foster Clarke's soups as a wholesome substitute for meat. 'Make them your daily food. You simply add water'. Bacon was restricted to 5oz. per head and in July 1918 tea was rationed to 2oz. per person per week.

National Ration Books were issued to everybody with details of the retailer with whom they were registered. These national requirements created additional work for Hayes shops. At the Walnut Tree the confectioner, Ernest Poynter, might have been pleased by the ruling of May 1918 that sweets could only be sold by shops where their sale formed 20% of the takings. While many basic foods were subject to rationing and the price of milk was fixed at 8d. a quart in 1918, there was still a fairly wide selection of goods in the shops, if you were able to afford them. Tinned red salmon was available at 2*s*. 4*d*.(about £5 today), pink salmon at 1*s*. 9*d*. and sardines at 10*d*. Baked beans were 5*d*. a tin and pork and beans, 9*d*.

Unlike the Second World War clothes were not subject to restrictions and, providing you had the money, there appeared to be a wide choice. With women undertaking men's jobs it is likely that more ladies in Hayes started to wear trousers as a practical garment. Many women wore black because their husbands or sons had died in the conflict.[39]

# When would peace come?

It was clear that 1918, even with the help of the Americans, was going to be difficult. There was no immediate sign of the war ending. There were, however, some successes. At the end of 1917, British forces captured Jerusalem from Turkish control and later Major Lawrence, 'Lawrence of Arabia', led an Arab army into Damascus.

More Hayes men continued to be killed in the fighting. Private Henry George Jarvis, who worked as a gardener for Sir Everard Hambro at Hayes Place, was serving with 37 Division Mechanical Transport Company, RASC, when a shell hit his lorry and he died of his wounds on 29 May 1918.[40] Private Percy Hardy of 10 Battalion Essex Regiment, whose brother Charles was killed in 1915, died on 23 August 1918. He was wounded at St Quentin in March 1918, returned to France in August and was killed in the attack on Tara Hill on the Albert-Amiens Road.[20]

Captain Harold Lewis Beeston of 5 Battalion RWKR died on 24th October from septic pneumonia, caused by trench fever. Prior to the war he was employed by the Prudential Insurance Company and was assistant secretary of Bromley Town Football Club. His parents lived at 76 Hayes Road. He enlisted in the London Rifle Brigade in August 1914 and, after basic training, was posted to France in January 1915. He was injured and buried by the effects of a shell blast. He returned home and spent two months in hospital. In August he was commissioned and the following January married May Slattery. In 1917 he returned to France and later served in Italy. Invalided home, he was attached to a depot in Tunbridge Wells and trained cadets at Queen Elizabeth's School, Cranbrook, where he died. He was 29 years old and was buried with full military honours at Hayes Parish Church.[8]

Private Edwin Arthur James, 7 Battalion East Kent Regiment, was killed on 23 October 1918 at the battle of *Selle*. He grew up in Hayes and was a chorister at the Parish Church. His family moved from Tithe Cottage to the Lodge, Wonersh Park, Surrey and he worked at the Chilworth Powder Works. He was 26 years old and married with a young daughter.[41]

Life in the village continued to be dominated by the war, with news from the 'front', lists of the dead, the wounded and also awards for gallantry. In February 1918 Sergeant Major William Mitchell, of Rose Cottage, attended Bromley Council Chamber to receive the DCM from the Mayor for organising a stretcher bearing party to recover the wounded of another battalion. As his medal was not ready at the time he was presented with the riband instead. In the same year, Geoffrey Charles Devas of Hartfield was awarded the MC for maintaining communications between the leading companies and battalion headquarters during a heavy enemy artillery barrage. Earlier in the war Bombardier Arthur Valentine Taylor, son of Charles Masters Taylor of Hayes Cottage, Station Road, was awarded the DCM 'for constantly setting a high example of courage and cheerfulness under fire, notably at *Hooge*, when, although wounded in the shoulder, he insisted on working his gun until utterly exhausted'. Before the First World War he had worked in Sumatra as a tobacco planter but returned to England to enlist. Private Albert Batten, of 7 Battalion RWKR, received the Military Medal for gallantry in sticking to his machine gun when he was the last man left from his section at Trones Wood.[42]

On the domestic front tribunals were still held. In February and April 1918, Farmer Marden successfully applied for renewal of the previously granted exemption for his eighteen-year-old son. As part of the justification it was said that the son was employed as a ploughman, shoeing smith and repairer of farm implements. The occasional social event was still held, usually to provide support for the war. In August the Girls Friendly Society held a fête at Glebe House, opened by Viscountess Margaret Goschen, to raise money for hostels, huts and canteens.[1]

## The war ends

*Victory Cup given to Hayes school children in 1918*

At last, the allies were successful and the war came to an end on 11 November 1918. The national newspapers reported the full terms of the armistice and the news brought relief and a hope that life would soon return to normal. At the Village School a half-day holiday was given. The pupils sang 'The National Anthem', 'The Star Spangled Banner', 'The Marseillaise', 'Rule Britannia', hoisted the Union Jack, saluted it and gave three cheers 'for the King, Queen, Navy, Army, Mr. Lloyd George, and Airmen. Then the children were dismissed'.[38]

Prisoners of war were to be repatriated immediately, although some like George Boakes did not return until November 1920. Many regiments were retained for occupation duties in the war-torn countries. It was some time before all Hayes' servicemen were back with their families and there were still tragedies, such as the death of Lieutenant Colonel Charles Douglas Clark of 5 Battalion RWKR. Born in Beckenham in June 1882, he was educated at Abbey School and joined his father in the Stock

Exchange. He became a member of the local volunteer Territorial Army in 1900 and by 1905 was commanding officer of the Bromley Detachment. With the reorganisation of the Territorial Army he was promoted to captain and by the start of the war was a major. He was mobilised on 4 August 1914 and served in India. In December 1917 he was posted to Mesopotamia where the regiment fought as part of the army of occupation and he was promoted to acting lieutenant colonel. By December 1919, their assignment completed, the regiment departed on the SS *Melita* for home. Unfortunately, Charles Clark died on 22nd January from influenza contracted on the journey. His body was conveyed on a gun carriage from his home in Shortlands, Kent, to Hayes Parish Church where he was buried with full military honours. Many remembered him commanding the parade for Lord Roberts in 1910 at the opening of the Rifle Range.[43] His parents lived at Eccleshill, Pickhurst Park, and his father died a few weeks later, an event possibly hastened by the shock of his son's death.

The last of the 40 men connected to Hayes to die as a result of the Great War was Lieutenant Harold David Williams of the Royal Engineers. He died on 20 December 1920 and was buried in Hayes churchyard in a grave registered by the Commonwealth War Graves Commission, although his name does not appear on the Hayes War Memorial. Harold was born in March 1894 in a cottage at 42 George Lane and was the only child of John Williams and his second wife, Clementina. She outlived her husband but was comforted in her grief by her stepsons, Isaac and Joe.[44]

Some men had to cope with injuries that affected their ability to work, or emotional scars which, in many instances, took longer to heal. In May 1920 Henry Brown, a 21-year-old labourer from 4 Baston Cottages, collapsed on the way home from work at Baston Manor. It was thought that he had a diseased blood vessel due to blood poisoning from boils that he had acquired at the Front.[45] Charlie Harrod, who fought with 8 Battalion Yorkshire Regiment, was wounded in the leg in France in 1917. He was sent to a convalescent hospital in Chester and discharged from the army in 1918 because of his disability. He always maintained that his life was saved by a farthing in his pocket that deflected the bullet. The lucky farthing is still retained by the Harrod family, although his daughter says that, because of his injury, the only employment open to him was odd-job gardening.[46] He lived with his wife, Florence, and two children in Spilman's Grove (George Lane) and died in 1965.

After the First World War employment was difficult to find and some villagers endeavoured to generate business through their own efforts. John Wood lived at Tiepigs Cottage which sat in just over an acre of land. In 1917 it was owned by the Lennard family and had a rateable value of £7 10s. 0d. Advertisements appeared in the local paper for 'Day-Old Chicks and Sittings, from pedigree poultry, Tyepigs Farm, Hayes, open for inspection to visitors, Orders booked at: Maison Rose Café, 4 Aberdeen Mansions, High Street Bromley.'[47] It would seem that John Wood, who had worked at Coney Hall Farm, West Wickham since he was a boy, was trying to run a poultry business from the cottage.

The effects of the 'war to end all wars' continued for some time and Hayes village life was never the same. During the decade, 1911 to 1921, the population of Hayes rose by only 85 persons, but the balance changed with five fewer males and 90 more females. The male population of Hayes had been steadily falling since 1851 when it was 48.4%

but the trend was aggravated by the war casualties and in 1921 reached 36.0%. The proportion of males took until 1931 to return to its 1901 level (42.9%).[48]

Some burials at the end of 1918 were the result of a dreadful influenza epidemic that caused a large number of deaths in the country. One was that of Canon George Clowes, who died on 18 November 1918, after a short illness. He had served the parishioners for nearly 32 years and during the war had often been called upon to provide personal help in moments of crisis. His curate, Revd Thomas Smylie, recalled that the Rector 'loved his people as he loved the village where they lived and the church where they worshipped'.[49] He was 78 when he died and was buried next to his wife in the churchyard. Many regarded him with great affection and wished to commemorate his memory. It was decided to convert the east end of the north aisle of the church to a side chapel to be used for weekday services.[50] It later became known as the Lady Chapel. Many villagers contributed to the memorial fund and the Bromsgrove Guild made the chapel furniture.

One of his most active supporters had been the sister-in-law of Sir Everard Hambro, Miss Clara Georgina Stuart of Ivy Cottage, who for 25 years 'visited the sick in Hayes, comforted mourners, taught and helped the young and promoted the cause of the Christian mission'.[51] She died in February 1918 and her family, including her younger sister Octavia who continued to live at Ivy Cottage, provided all the furnishings and fittings for the chapel, the cross, vases, candlesticks, altar book and linen. The Bishop of Rochester dedicated the memorial chapel to Canon Clowes and unveiled a tablet to Miss Clara Stuart after the morning service in July 1919.[52]

During his ministry Canon Clowes had witnessed many changes in the village. Most of the housing developments had taken place before 1914. The outbreak of war made it difficult to sell or find tenants as buyers were unwilling to purchase until the future was more certain. In July 1916, with his daughters no longer at home, John Lee-Warner tried to sell Hawthorndene. He died in May 1917 and his widow Blanche continued at the house until Major Basil Binyon bought it in 1920. Hayes Court also became vacant during the war. It had been leased by Reuben Preston who died in 1913. His widow Frances tried to sell the lease, which included nine acres of meadowland, for £350. The property was still for sale in 1918.

The Parish Council continued to play a role in matters such as roads, refuse, drainage and housing. There was an increase during the war in motor traffic through Hayes, particularly by the military authorities. Biggin Hill aerodrome was being established and many goods came to Hayes Station. In 1916, William Smith & Sons, the Bromley Common builders, were asked to collect a shed from Hayes Railway Station, transport it to Biggin Hill and assemble it for the new Wireless Experimental Station.[53] The Air Ministry was later, in 1919, asked to contribute £749 towards the cost of repairing the roads from The Fox to Hayes Station, no doubt due to military traffic to and from Biggin Hill aerodrome.

In August 1916, HPC considered the need for motor danger signs near the Village School and Rectory.[54] Towards the end of the war, BRDC recorded that army traffic through Hayes and Keston was causing a lot of dust. In November it assessed that £1,650 was needed to repair the damage to the highway caused by military traffic from The Fox,

Keston, across Hayes Common. The War Office contributed half of the bill. In 1919 the parish councillors were again concerned by the increase in traffic through Hayes and the advent of buses, for which many of the roads were thought to be inadequate. They proposed the widening of 'Beckenham corner' (the bend on Pickhurst Lane by Pickhurst Mead) and the erection of speed limit signs near the entrances to the village.[55]

In 1920 HPC considered the reinstatement of sixteen street lamps, turned off due to operating costs, and the equipping of the Gymnasium with a coin-slot operated meter for the gas supply.[56] HPC rejected a proposed drainage scheme for Keston and Hayes as inadequate. Also, after considerable discussion, it did not agree with proposals by BRDC for new housing in the village. This was in spite of a photograph that appeared in the local paper in 1919 showing a demobilised soldier and his wife living in a caravan.[57] In October 1919 the Council had debated the provision of housing for Hayes under the *Housing of Working Classes Act – 'Homes for Heroes'*. In November BRDC decided that ten houses were required in Hayes. Three possible sites were agreed:

1. south of and adjoining the railway station
2. at the bottom of Pickhurst Lane
3. land at the side of the Thatched Cottages in Hayes Lane (near the junction with Mead Way).

Six houses were to have three bedrooms, a living room and scullery, and four were basically the same but with a large parlour. The BRDC's proposal to build new houses in George Lane was emphatically rejected by HPC, due mainly to concerns about surface drainage water and the nature of the soil. BRDC, however, bought the land but the proposed construction costs seemed high and parish councillors considered that it would cause a great rise in the rates. They also argued that there was 'no real demand' for the cottages from Hayes people and that they should not be given to people working in Bromley.[58] Two months earlier HPC had received petitions from twelve people regarding the proposed houses, some of whom were not 'Hayes names'. The saga continued for some years before any council properties were built and occupied.

The contribution that women had made during the war resulted in 1918 in their eligibility to stand for national government and women householders over 30 received the vote. Although women ratepayers could stand as local councillors the first to be on HPC was Mrs Laura Smail of Warren Wood, who was co-opted in January 1921 and elected in April 1922. She had been appointed as a Guardian of the Poor during the war and Sir Everard Hambro was forced to overcome his reluctance to women in politics.

The year 1919 started with news of the appointment of Revd Henry Percy Thompson to succeed George Clowes as Rector. Revd Thompson was educated at Winchester School, Merton College, Oxford and Wells Theological College where, as a result of an accident with a cricket ball, he lost his sight completely. He achieved partial vision after two years of intensive surgery but managed to conceal this for most of his life. He relied almost entirely on memory for his sermons and services.[59] His first curacy was at All Saints Maidstone, then for eight years he was a curate in the crowded district of Battersea where he gained a deep understanding of all kinds of people and the conditions in which they lived. In 1895 he become Vicar at St Mary, Kippington, a church established by his father in 1878. He remained at Kippington for 24 years and made a considerable impact not only in the parish but also in the larger area of Sevenoaks where he became Rural Dean in 1909.

In 1890 he married Lilian Gilchrist Thomas, sister of Sidney Gilchrist Thomas, who with his cousin Percy Gilchrist had invented the Thomas-Gilchrist process in 1875. This was a method of eliminating phosphorus from steel produced by means of the Bessemer Converter. The process was licensed in many countries, making significant patent royalties that Lilian inherited on Sidney's death in 1885. She met her future husband whilst undertaking social work in South London. She continued her interest in that field and also in matters such as emigration, working class housing and movements connected with cooperation and co-partnership. She was opposed to sweated labour and worked for the freedom of women. The couple had three sons and two daughters. Canon Thompson, as he became, was to have considerable influence on the villagers of Hayes, helping them rebuild their lives and engendering a sense of pride in their community through his ministry and interest in local history.

After the end of the war the social life of the village began to return. In January 1919 a special concert was arranged for soldiers back from France and the concerts continued in subsequent years. Three months later the Social Club, which met every Thursday evening from October to April, had over 100 members. Singing and dancing classes were started and dances were held from time to time. The Church Social Club gave a concert at Easter but one of their main singers, Charles Frederick Wood, announced in May that he was leaving Hayes and held a farewell tea at Glebe House.[1] For a very long time he had been greatly involved in local affairs and organisations. The Social Club activities, however, continued and a fancy dress dance was held at the Church Schools in August.

After a twenty year gap, the local 'working-men' revived the 'Married v. Single Men's' cricket match, which was played on its traditional site, the old cricket ground on the common. 'The weather added to the attraction in a most delightful manner and a large number of spectators were present who thoroughly enjoyed the game.' The single men won the match by 68 runs and 'afterwards the players and their friends adjourned to the George Hotel where Mr. George Robbins, assisted by local talent, gave a most delightful concert.' Cricket Club members worked to revive the facilities on their pre-war ground at Baston Farm, leased about 1920 from Donald Campbell Haldeman. He agreed that the club could use the field every Saturday for matches, with the farmer having it the rest of the week to graze cows. The drinking trough had to remain in position, roughly at 'second slip'.[60] Bill Dance recalled that some matches were interrupted when the cows wandered across to have a drink!

In May 1919, at the age of 68, William Plant retired from the Village School after 45 years as headmaster. There were then 101 pupils - 68 in the Mixed School, the rest in the Infants. The war had stopped him retiring earlier and there had been several occasions when he had managed on his own. In 1918 the Inspector commented that 'Mr Plant has coped with the almost impossible task of teaching the whole school single-handed. I can only say that he has done so with wonderful success.' The Infants continued to be ably taught by Miss Morgan. In 1917 the Diocesan Inspector remarked that 'the little ones were bright and eager, giving thoughtful answers beyond the usual level'.[61]

When William Plant retired, a long article in the *Bromley & District Times* described his life and work. 'If ever a man can look back on his life's work proudly, and with the consciousness that it has been a life of real achievement, it must be William Plant.'[62] As headmaster his achievements were considerable and his influence on Hayes marked. For many years he was clerk to the parish council, as well as choirmaster and he took a leading part in developing the social club of which he acted as secretary. He was keenly interested in politics, very active on behalf of the Conservative party and acted as sub-agent for all elections in the Sevenoaks Division for about 40 years.

***William Plant, headmaster of Hayes Village School 1874-1919***[f.]

## Plans for a War Memorial

By the time William Plant retired progress had been made to commemorate those who had sacrificed their lives during the war. A public meeting was held at the Church Schools on Saturday 11 October 1919 to consider 'a suitable war memorial' for the village. The chairman, Revd Thompson, explained that a preliminary meeting had been held in the Rectory with families of the men who had been killed during the war, and said 'that they appeared to favour a memorial cross'. He observed that:

> they wanted something that would stimulate thought, enthusiasm and … devotion of those who would read the history of the Great War, and of all the self sacrifice that had taken place. They hoped their children and their children's children would by such means love their country and be ready if the need be to give themselves for their country as had been done by the present generation. They wanted something worthy of the very great events in the national history.[63]

Over the next few months, £463 19s. 6d. was subscribed by 335 local people towards the cost of the stone cross, bronze sword and base. The memorial was designed by Sir Reginald Blomfield and was the one chosen for use in many overseas' battlefield cemeteries and in many towns and villages at home. It cost £329 10s. 6d. to manufacture and erect.

The names of 34 men who died were inscribed on the stone base. The words on the Cross of Sacrifice were an adaptation of a dedication written by the late Canon Trevor, father of Mrs Smail of Warren Wood.

> HERE BENEATH THE
> SHADOW OF THE CROSS
> OF CHRIST BEHOLD THE
> NAMES OF OUR BRETHREN
> WHO SACRIFICED THEIR
> LIVES IN THE GREAT
> WAR 1914-1918. LET THOSE
> WHO COME AFTER SEE
> TO IT THAT THEY BE
> NOT FORGOTTEN

The memorial did not include all men with a Hayes connection who had been killed in the war. Several who had been born in Hayes, such as Captain Albert William McDonald MC, Private Frederick Calder and Gunner Arthur Croft, were omitted as they had moved away before war broke out. Nor did it mention some of the casualties whose widows lived in Hayes after the war. Major Linning of 1 Battalion Black Watch died in September 1914 and his widow lived at Glencarn in Pickhurst Lane. In the early 1920s, widow Elizabeth Devas moved to Hayes Grove Cottage to teach at the newly opened Hayes Court School. Her husband Bertrand Ward Devas, a barrister, had joined 2 Battalion Suffolk Regiment as a lieutenant and was killed in November 1916. The parents of Private Montague Frost, who is commemorated on the West Wickham memorial, moved to Ringwood, Station Road, Hayes after the war.[64]

On New Year's Day 1921, in typical wintry weather, the War Memorial was unveiled by Major-General A G Dallas, CB, CMG and dedicated by the Bishop of Rochester.[65] Major Dallas spoke movingly of the sacrifices that had been made by men who had been inspired by many ideas but above all by the sense of duty 'which prompted them to do what was right when the nation's call came'. The Bishop thanked God for the vision and courage of the young men and also for the heroism of those 'at home who hid an aching heart with a smiling face'. This act of remembrance brought the Great War to a close for many individuals, although none of the congregation could have realised that in less than twenty years Britain would again be involved in a World War.

The surplus money from the war memorial fund was used to install an oak tree trunk as a bench in the churchyard near the memorial, so that there would be a place near the Cross, 'for all who wished to sit quietly and remember those who had sacrificed their lives or who were buried in the churchyard'. Also, plans were made to rebind the Lectern Bible in which were written the names of 103 men who served during 'the Great War and by God's Providence returned home'. Mr Hilton Skinner of Ash Lodge, Baston Road, compiled and inscribed the names and completed the task by December 1922.[66] The list did not include the names of men or women who had served in the non-combattant services, such as Mr Sullivan Mortimer. He returned to Hayes as organist and choirmaster after spending three and a half years with the British Red Cross in France.

**Hayes War Memorial**
*The memorial bench (now enclosed) may be seen against the west wall*

Instrumental in the rebinding of the Bible was the new Rector, Percy Thompson, whose three sons, Sidney, Austin and Piers, had seen action during the war and who was very conscious of the anxieties and hardships that had been created during servicemen's absences. Piers had been captured at the first battle of Gaza and had been a prisoner for eighteen months before being invalided home. Sidney was awarded the MC.

The Bible survives but, unfortunately, the bench has succumbed to the English climate, although it is still positioned against the west wall of the church. Of the remaining money, £62 was given to the Sidcup Hospital Comforts Fund for victims of the war who were permanently disabled and the other £60 was placed in a special fund for the upkeep of the memorial.[67] In 1923 £100 of 2½% consolidated stock was purchased by the committee of the Hayes War Memorial Fund to be held by the PCC for the upkeep and insurance of the memorial. Any accumulation of income over £10 could be transferred to the Churchyard General Maintenance Fund.

Inside the church, members of wealthy Hayes' families erected separate memorials to record their personal loss. These include plaques to Norman Harris, Francis Marchant, Frederic Plant and Charles Wood. Although the Traill family sold Hayes Place in 1880, their family tablet in the north aisle of the church had three names added.

The memorial commemorates two sons and a grandson of James Christie and Julia Traill. Lieutenant Colonel John Murray Traill of 2 Battalion Bedfordshire Regiment was killed at Ypres, France on 30 October 1914. His brother, Major James William Traill, was not wounded in battle but died at home from pneumonia on 6 January 1917. Major James William Traill's son, Major Sinclair George Traill of 1 Battalion Cameron Highlanders, was wounded at the Aisne in September 1914 and at the battle of Loos in September 1915. He died on 23 November 1916 on active service in France, at the age of 26, as a result of a railway accident.[68]

**Traill Memorial, Hayes Parish Church**

As a result of the war, there was a change in people's expectations not only in Hayes but throughout the country. The village of Hayes would alter dramatically in the following twenty years. It became more difficult for wealthy householders to find domestic servants. Death duties, introduced in 1894, continued to make inroads into estates that had also been affected by the introduction of super tax on incomes over £100,000 during the war.

One of the main families to be affected was the Hambro family of Hayes Place. Sir Everard had come out of retirement during the war and returned to the bank, negotiating critical loans on behalf of the government. Like most of the villagers he had experienced great anxieties and heartache during the war as many of his sons and relatives were fighting overseas. His nephew Bertram Hambro, a Lieutenant-Interpreter with the Indian Expeditionary Force, died on 25 April 1915.[69] His second son, Harold, ended the war with the rank of Lieutenant Colonel and his youngest son Ronald, who was in the Coldstream Guards, was twice mentioned in despatches. Sir Everard's grandson, Charles Jocelyn Hambro, went from school to Sandhurst and by the end of 1915 was an ensign, also in the Coldstream Guards. He went to France in October 1916 and received the MC for conspicuous bravery in action. Charles Jocelyn's father, Charles Eric Hambro of Pickhurst Mead, worked in Intelligence during the war and, in January 1919, was made a Knight Commander of the British Empire in recognition of his services to the Ministry of Information. It was he who, on his father's death, made decisions that altered forever the traditional village of Hayes; decisions that were influenced by the changes in society and the economy brought about as a result of the war.

# Chapter 2
# A new beginning: 1921-1939

After the dedication of the War Memorial in 1921 villagers looked forward to a new era and those who had been affected by tragic events tried to rebuild their lives. Many villagers experienced poverty and economic hardship as a result of the war and were subject to the difficulties that affected the rest of the country in the succeeding decade. Employment opportunities changed as new owners or occupiers arrived at most of the 'big' houses. Baston Manor, Baston House (the farm), Gadsden, Glebe House, Hartfield, Hawthorndene, Hayes Court, The Nest, Oast House, Pickhurst Manor and The Warren had all changed hands by 1922. The staff who worked in these houses, some of whom lived in the lodges and stable blocks, were replaced and had to seek work and accommodation elsewhere.

Men demobilised from the forces returned to the village needing a job but some, because of their war injuries, had to find different occupations and others became dissatisfied with their home environment and moved away. At the same time there was a growing desire by many people, who lived closer to London, to move out to the countryside but still be near enough to maintain contact with their previous locality. Within a decade some of the 'big' houses and their estates had disappeared and the transformation of Hayes, from a quiet rural village into a larger community, had begun. The key to this was the death of Sir Everard Hambro in 1925 and the inheritance of Hayes Place by his eldest son Charles Eric Hambro, but even before Sir Everard's death change was happening.

## Hayes Parish Council and Early Housing Developments

Initially, HPC was slow to accept that change was needed. It was set in its ways and did not consider that there was any requirement for better working class housing in the village. It was concerned that any such activity would result in outsiders coming into Hayes. The composition of the council had changed during the war with the co-option of new members in 1917. The election in 1919 saw eleven nominations. The resulting show of hands resulted in a council whose social composition varied from a solicitor and stockbroker to a blacksmith and a carter. A poll was demanded in 1922 but it did not change the result. The Rector's wife, Mrs Lilian Thompson, and Mrs Laura Smail of Warren Wood, who had been co-opted the previous year to fill a vacancy, were amongst those elected. The change in parish councillors (Vol 1:Appendix 1), in particular the presence of Mrs Smail and Mrs Thompson, as well as supporters of the Labour Party such as Emmanuel Mansfield and Percy Jones, resulted in a different attitude. It was the start of considerable pressure on BRDC to provide houses.

*Hawkswood, 80 George Lane* [f.]

*Cheriton, 74 George Lane* [f.]

HPC's workload from 1921 to 1934 was largely concerned with new housing, both local government and privately sponsored, and with the provision and condition of the roads to deal with the rise in motor traffic. In 1922, with the fall in building costs, it was suggested that cottages should be built for the 'working man', providing he could afford the rent. Three years later applications were made to the BRDC. A key figure behind the proposal was Mrs Thompson who stressed the need for housing, pointing out in November 1925, for example, that two families were living in a large outhouse on a farm at Pickhurst and should be properly housed.[1]

Mrs Thompson was an important figure in a scheme to encourage working men to build their own houses. Six bungalows were constructed, Nos. 72 to 82 George Lane, on the south side of George Lane, on land purchased from the Norman family, by a co-operative, the Hayes Public Utility Society. The Society was set up with Revd Thompson as chairman and his wife as secretary. Under their auspices, six owner-occupiers built their homes each with a garden of ¼ acre. A C Norman sold the 1½ acres at the same nominal price as land that had already been bought by the BRDC for council housing. Each building plot cost £40, apart from a larger one that was £90. The bungalows were built and the owners moved in between 1925 and 1927.

The first residents were Henry Disdale at Weeting, 82 George Lane and Henry Lewis, who moved from Model Cottages in Hayes Street to Hawkswood, 80 George Lane. He lived there until his death, when he was over 90 years old. These men had always paid rent. It was a new concept for them to own property. Henry Lewis later commented that he decided to buy because of the uncertainties of tenure in his rented cottage, but he was surprised about the unexpected costs: £20 to connect to the cesspool, £17 a few years later to connect to the sewer and £80 for road charges. North View, 76 George Lane, was occupied in 1926 by Charles Harrod and in The Laurels, owned by Emmanuel Mansfield, were Frederick Charles Cox and his family. The last two utility houses to be occupied were Cheriton, 74 George Lane, by the Jordan family and No.72 by Herbert Shipp.[2]

To encourage the development of new houses HPC submitted plans to extend George Lane into the meadow where BRDC had earlier purchased building land. In January 1926, HPC, anxious not to lose the government subsidy available for the construction work, reminded BRDC that nothing had been done to erect houses on land bought five years previously. During that time BRDC allowed a Battery, 91 RFA, to bivouac on the vacant building land - probably as part of an army exercise. Construction finally started early in 1927 and by the end of the year twelve cottages had been completed and occupied by people previously living in Hayes.[3] The houses were 1 – 12 Hookfield Cottages (48 – 70 George Lane) and were sited on the southern side of the lane.

Canon Thompson wrote of the new residents in November 1927:

> Without exception they rejoice in their new homes. Some, because they have escaped from unsanitary dark, damp cottages; others because theirs has been insecurity of tenure; others have their furniture stored, and have been crowded in cramped surroundings … it is saddening to think of the 22 on the list of applicants whose names had to be put on the rejected list … One of the cruellest effects of the housing shortage is the number of young people who cannot marry.[4]

The first occupiers of Hookfield Cottages were:

| No.1 | William Amos Barnes* | No.7 | James T Gallacher* |
|------|----------------------|------|--------------------|
| No.2 | Frederick Tidbury* | No.8 | Albert James |
| No.3 | Henry Alexander Smart* | No.9 | Mark Friend* |
| No.4 | George Bailey | No.10 | Arthur Head* |
| No.5 | Harry Clacey* | No.11 | Arthur Taylor* |
| No.6 | George Harwood* | No.12 | Reginald Russell |

Many families, (those with *), still lived in these cottages at the beginning of the Second World War. George Harwood died in 1950. He was one of ten children, whose father came to Hayes in 1874. He worked for Edward Wilson at Hayes Place, married Eliza Killick and later became the churchyard gardener and sexton. On Sundays, wearing his best suit, he pumped the organ blower at church services and during the sermon, it is said, he would pop down to the George Inn for some refreshment.[5] Henry Smart, a bombardier with the Royal Artillery, married May, daughter of gardener Thomas Price, in 1918. Several occupants were sons of gardeners, such as William Barnes, who died in Hayes in 1973.[6] As a boy he lived at Hayes Court Lodge where his father Amos was a gardener for the Preston family. Harry Clacey's father was head gardener at Longcroft and Mark Friend was also a gardener. Frederick Tidbury's daughter Margaret still lived in the house until the 1990s and her neighbour Mrs Smart into the present century.

The unsuccessful applicants felt aggrieved and some protested that they had as much right to a home as the people who had been selected. Benjamin Saunders, whose home 1 Bath Villas was up for sale, said he had been a ratepayer for 27 years, had served 3½ years in the war and was in the same position as George Harwood who was allocated a house. Moreover, his daughter who was born, educated and married in the parish had also been refused a new home.[7]

To some extent George Lane was a twentieth century creation and the first part of Hayes to be developed for housing after the Great War. The road was essentially an extension of Spilman's Grove and was an unmade track leading to farm fields. The construction traffic and the occupation of the new houses resulted in the lane becoming a 'swamp' and throughout the 1920s the road had serious drainage problems, which HPC was continually trying to resolve. It was not until 1938 that the *Bromley and Kentish Times* could report that the lane was now a 'good road', having been surfaced along its length.[8]

Access to the road was restricted between Street House and the George Inn; a scheme to widen the entrance to George Lane by demolishing Street House and Blacks Cottages (42 and 44 George Lane) was abandoned. The Compulsory Purchase Order advertised in July 1937 caused such concern that an inquiry was announced in November. One view was that 'it was far better to demolish the dining room of the George Inn than Street House, one of the few period houses left in Hayes'. A C Norman, the owner of Street House, said 'it would be an act of vandalism'. In the end neither building was demolished.[9]

There was also considerable building activity along Hayes Lane and Hayes Road. By 1926 four more houses had been built in Hayes Road and by the early 1920s Norman land, along the east side of Hayes Lane, was being sold to construct detached houses and bungalows. In 1925 four new houses in Hayes Lane were added to the dust collection list and plans were submitted for 'Westfield', Hayes Lane. Later, the chairman inspected plans for houses along Hayes Lane to the north of Socket Lane, and between this track and the George Inn, although the latter were never built and the land continues to be part of Hayes Street Farm. Many houses in Hayes Lane were individually designed, built by W W Courtenay Ltd. and, to a lesser extent, by R Studman. By 1929 some 27 homes were erected, including four bungalows. One was Whiteladies, 145 Hayes Lane, whose land, referred to as part of the 'Hayesford Park Estate', was sold to Arthur Carlos in 1926 for £250 by A C Norman. Three years later Arthur Carlos paid a further £100 for a 20ft width of land alongside his new house. These houses in Hayes Lane were subject to restrictions that no trade or business was to be carried on from them and in particular they were not to be used as 'a hotel, tearoom, livery stable, public garage or beer shop'.[10] The location of the properties afforded easy access either by walking or bus to Bromley South Railway Station and then by train to London; few house owners had cars.[11]

Other houses developed in the 1920s included Gorsewood in Barnet Wood Road in 1924 for Charles Cubitt and a new bungalow, Lauriston, in Station Road (Bourne Way), for Laurence De Thier, the churchwarden.

*Lauriston, Station Road* [a.]

In 1930 BRDC reported that negotiations were in progress to acquire further land in Hayes for houses. HPC suggested a site between Brewery Cottages and Lauriston in Station Road but Bromley's surveyor reported that the land was unsuitable. After the Second World War, however, the land was used for council housing. In June 1930 HPC suggested an alternative two-acre site in George Lane, nearly opposite Hookfield Cottages, offered by A C Norman at £450 per acre.[12] The matter dragged on. Changes in local government in 1934 meant that decisions on housing in Hayes were transferred from BRDC to the newly formed Bromley Borough Council, whose Committee in October 1934 agreed to build 'working class' houses on 2.11 acres opposite the bungalows in George Lane. M J Colvin was appointed architect and eventually David Kenn & Sons of Bexley was awarded the contract at £8896. The first eight (Nos.37–51) were occupied in 1936 and the remaining sixteen (Nos. 53–83) by 1937.[13]

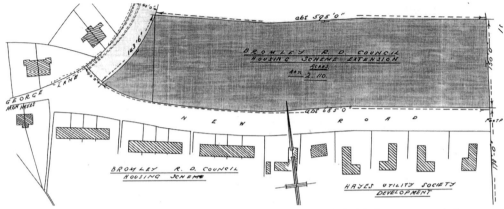

**Map 3:** *Plan of Utility houses 72-82 George Lane, Hookfield Cottages and the area for new council housing in 1934* [aj.]

*37-43 George Lane* [g.]

This was the only local government housing to be erected between the wars in Hayes, apart from the caretaker's house at George Lane School. It was built in 1937 for £865, half of which was paid by Kent Education Committee. It was occupied by war veteran Alfred Harold Arnold, who in 1935 married Ella Knights, daughter of Charlotte Knights who ran the Pleasant View Tea Rooms. He lived there until his death in 1951.

## Hayes Village Hall

With the end of the war and the return of village social life the number of venues where groups could meet was limited to the 'Iron Room' in the Rectory Garden; the Parish Room at St Mary's Cottages; the School and the Gymnasium. The Gymnasium was the only true 'village' hall in Hayes but was small, lacked facilities and was coming to the end of its life. Despite these drawbacks it was used by the Hayes Brass Band for band practice, for the occasional dance, for drill by 5 Battalion RWKR on Monday and Thursday evenings, by HPC and other organisations.[14]

Discussions about the need for a modern meeting place started shortly after the unveiling of the War Memorial. Canon Thompson recognised the importance of providing a suitable hall to meet the demands of the changing community:

> In the past, country people were satisfied with country quietness; they are not satisfied today, and all inevitably drift into the towns unless there is a life in the village that will meet the needs of which they are now conscious. Our young people want to dance; they want to act, they want to learn. A well run Hall in each village, which will give the opportunity for the expression of the life of the village, will do much to restore the balance between Town and Country, which at the present time is in real danger of being destroyed.[15]

By the beginning of 1923 an embryonic scheme to build a Village Hall for Hayes was in place and by 1924 the funds stood at £350. In his monthly letter the Rector asked whether the proposed hall should be linked to a village sports ground, where it should be sited and how it would be managed. A public meeting was held in the Gymnasium, in October 1924, to discuss these questions – could the old rifle range be used or could the Gymnasium be expanded? As HPC did not have the powers it was suggested that some form of limited company should be formed to manage the hall. The meeting was not very successful and Canon Thompson commented that he had 'found no general agreement as to where it should be, of what plan, size and materials, in whom it should be vested or how it should be managed or maintained'. Despite this, the fund reached £500.[16]

Eventually, it was decided to follow the example of the Kent Community Council and form a Village Community Council, with committee members drawn from the many Hayes organisations, to build and subsequently manage the hall. It was created at a public meeting just before Christmas 1925.[17] The Hayes Community Council (HCC), as it became known, held its first meeting on 3 February 1926 at the Rectory with seventeen members in attendance. The chairman was Canon Thompson and the secretary Mrs Kate Burman, the school headmistress. Several possible hall sites were mentioned, including land beside Mr Hack's shop in West Common Road, next to the Gymnasium, behind the Iron Room in the Rectory Garden, land beyond George Lane, the field at the back of Street House and an area between the Walnut Tree and the churchyard. The favoured site was behind the Church School with an entrance next to the forge or on to Beckenham Lane (Pickhurst Lane).[18]

Edwin Preston of The Warren had offered to pay for Mr Hack's land and agreed to do the same for the new site, up to £300. Negotiations started with the landowner, Sir Eric Hambro, and plans were drawn up for the hall whose standard was to be the same as the one built at Hayes Court for Miss Cox's new boarding school. HCC moved quickly, was ready to agree and sign the contract for the land when it was discovered that they could be liable for additional costs to cover road charges. As this might amount to several hundred pounds the committee decided that the Forge site should be given up.[19]

By this time HCC had raised £1,383 towards the £2,000 target for the Hall. Fund raising continued. Mr and Mrs Frost organised a tennis demonstration at Glebe House in July 1926 and a balloon race produced 22 postcard replies from the 113 despatched. The winning card, sent by a man from Keston, reached Cologne in Germany.[20]

At the next committee meeting the Rector reported that the land between St Mary's Church and the Walnut Tree, owned by the Norman family, was available and that a member, who wished to remain anonymous, was prepared to buy a little more land for hall amenities. Mr Norman's agent, Mr Hunt, was asked to look after the interests of the HCC and supervise the planning and construction of the hall.[21] The land was sold to Mr Preston and the anonymous donor, on 3 August 1927, and the following year the two men transferred ownership of the land to 'several persons who represented Hayes organisations, and the National Council of Social Services which became the Permanent Trustee'. The land conveyance reveals that the anonymous person was Arthur Collins of Greenways, who later became Mayor of Bromley.

The Permanent Trustee was to hold the premises for the purpose of:

physical education and mental recreation and social moral and intellectual development through the medium of reading and recreation rooms library lectures classes recreation and entertainment or otherwise as may be found expedient for the benefit of the inhabitants of the Parish of Hayes ... without distinction of sex or of political or other opinions.[22]

The Hayes' organisations that were party to the agreement were:

| Organisation | Named Representative |
|---|---|
| The Parish of Hayes | Canon Henry Percy Thompson |
| Parochial Church Council | William Owen Hamborough Joynson |
| Hayes Church Choir | Sullivan Dean Thornton Mortimer |
| Hayes Parish Council | Percy Jones |
| Conservators of the Common | Edwin Mumford Preston |
| Men's Club | Charles Frederick Wood |
| Cricket Club | Frank John Keech |
| Football Club | Arthur Spinks |
| School Managers | Mrs Gertrude Preston |
| School Staff | Mrs Kate Burman |
| Mothers' Union | Mrs Caroline Adini Carus-Wilson |
| Women's Institute | Mrs Honor Joynson |
| Nursing Association | Dame Margaret Payne |

| Organisation | Named Representative |
|---|---|
| Girls' Friendly Society | Miss Vera Gilchrist Thompson |
| Industrial Association | James Grandfield |
| Hayes Band | Arthur John Robjant |
| Social Club | Mrs Elizabeth Carter Hamlyn |
| Boy Scouts | Wilbury Edwards |
| Girl Guides | Miss Margaret F Harris |

Work on the new hall started in July 1927 when the building contract was given to Messrs William Smith & Sons of Bromley Common.[23] The foundation stone was laid on Monday 25 July 1927 by Dorothy Gumbrill, aged 13, and Mark Russell, aged 14. Revd Thompson addressed the assembled villagers, estimated at 250 people, thanked Mr & Mrs Preston and said he had received a radiogram sending best wishes from Arthur Collins who was on the *SS Arundel Castle*, en route to South Africa.

**Laying the Foundation Stone of the Village Hall, 25 July 1927**[h.]

Canon Thompson reported that the cost of the hall was £1,720 and about £200 more would be needed to furnish it.[24] Whilst the hall was being built HCC planned its décor and arranged for the supply of chairs, stage and window curtains, fire buckets and a piano. Many people helped; the Women's Institute made the hall curtains and Arthur Robjant painted the fire buckets scarlet with 'Fire' in black lettering. George Gray of 6 St Mary Cottages and Mr Emery were appointed joint caretakers at 10*s*. a week plus 1*s*. for a day letting and 2*s*. for a night letting.[25]

Lieutenant Colonel Fulcher, chairman of HPC, opened the Village Hall on 19 November 1927. The short ceremony was followed by a whist drive and a dance accompanied by the Hayes Brass Band.

By April 1928 the hall had been hired 47 times, a good indication of what might be expected. With the opening of the new hall the Gymnasium, having served Hayes for sixteen years, was no longer required. HPC decided to sell it through Baxter Payne & Lepper, with a reserve price of £100. It was sold to Mr Windross of Keston and the proceeds went to the Village Hall fund.[26] The last council meeting in it was held in November 1927. Subsequent meetings took place in the Parish Room or the School.[27]

*Hayes Village Hall* [i.]

HCC formed a Building Sub-Committee to oversee matters regarding the hall and this became the Hall Management Committee, the group that manages the Village Hall to this day. In April 1928 it suggested that a room for small meetings should be built on the north side of the main hall. No action was taken as the hall still had a small debt. Summer fêtes were held to raise funds and in 1930 Sir Eric Hambro allowed the use of the grounds of Hayes Place for a summer show. The profit of £183 was divided equally between Hayes Church School and the Village Hall funds. The extension and a potential grant from Kent County Council (KCC) was considered at the end of 1930 but postponed because there was still a lack of funds. Mrs Thompson wanted to buy a piece of land at the rear of the Village Hall and build a cottage on it. She asked HCC for a right of way along the side of the hall to the site and offered HCC or the Parochial Church Council the option to buy or rent the cottage for the hall caretaker or church verger. HCC agreed but the proposal was not taken any further, probably because Canon & Mrs Thompson left Hayes in 1933.[28]

A further matter that concerned HCC was its wish to remain independent from interference and to exist solely for the benefit of Hayes organisations. Local political parties were allowed to use the hall and facilities but were not able to appoint representatives to the Community Council Committee. Constituent organisations that formed HCC changed with time. The first of note was the resignation of Mr Spinks in 1929 because the Football Club was wound up. The gaps were filled by the new groups in existence by 1933, such as the Hayes Village and District Association, Hayes Players and Toc H. Although some clubs ceased to function, their representatives were sometimes co-opted onto the committee because of their skills or specialist knowledge. The growth and expansion of Hayes was reflected in 1936 when HCC welcomed ten newly formed organisations including Hayes Free Church, The Religious Society of Friends, Hayes Orchestral Society, Crusaders, Hayes Bohemians and Hayes Juventus Youth Club.[29]

The number of young children in Hayes grew as more houses were built and in 1932 Dr Hopton, the local GP, started an Infant Welfare Clinic at the Village Hall on Tuesday afternoons. Later, the Medical Officer of Health for Bromley wrote to HCC to ask if a pram shelter could be built. The cost of the shelter, built by William Smith & Sons in 1935, was £34 10s. 0d., to which Bromley Council contributed £25. It still survives, although put to another use as a store for dustbins.[30]

HCC decided that the village should mark the occasion of King George V's Silver Jubilee in 1935 by the ceremonial planting of a tree on the common opposite Ivy Cottage. It took place on Sunday, 12th May and was preceded by an interdenominational service. The plaque recorded:

> *This oak tree was planted by Roy Grandfield a scholar of Hayes School*
> *on 12 May 1935 to commemorate the Silver Jubilee of their Majesties*
> *King George V and Queen Mary.*[31]

Roy Grandfield was the son of James and Florence Grandfield of Hayes Gardens Nursery, West Common Road. Railings protected the tree for many years.

In May 1936 the villagers learnt from Revd McClintock that the Duke of Kent would make a brief visit to Hayes, during a private informal visit to West Kent to see the work of Kent Council of Social Services (Kent Community Council). On 10th June he visited the Village Hall and saw an exhibition of produce and handicrafts by the West Kent Federation of Women's Institutes. He stayed in Hayes under fifteen minutes. The Duke's visit was not without criticism:

> A large number of patriotic people turned out to watch his arrival and cheer the Royal visitor. But … right up to the day no one seemed to know what the arrangements were or anything, while it was felt that not enough stress was being laid on the fact that the Village Hall was a village achievement built and paid for by the people of Hayes. As one person expressed it: "there's too much Kent Council of Social Services about the whole thing – after all it is our hall and not theirs".[32]

The matter of an additional room was still under discussion. By April 1936 the cost of the extra facility was estimated at £386 15s. 0d. and plans were approved by Bromley Council on 12th May. The Annexe, as it is called, was built by William Smith & Sons, finished at the end of 1936 and opened in February 1937.[33]

*Visit of Duke of Kent to the Village Hall, May 1936*[j.]

HCC decided not to organise or provide funds for the celebrations for King George VI's Coronation in May 1937, feeling that it should be left to the local authority. The Rector was asked to arrange for a peal of bells on the day and the shopkeepers undertook to brighten up Station Approach themselves and it presented:

> a gay and colourful appearance. Strips of bunting across the street in several places and almost every shop ... carried out some decorative scheme in red, white and blue. The private residents ... are playing their part ... with many houses gay with flags and banners or coloured shields.

The Chamber of Commerce held a Coronation Eve Ball at the New Inn and the Bohemians a Carnival Gala at the Village Hall.[34] Hayes people entered into the spirit of the occasion.

## Change in the Air

By 1937 the population had increased. Eleven years earlier, a columnist in the *Bromley Times* wrote, 'so Hayes too, is suffering from the twentieth century disease of "not enough houses", and our prophecy that this little beauty spot would not be allowed to remain beautiful for many more years seems, unfortunately, to be correct'.[35]

In the early 1920s the inhabitants of Hayes had very little idea of what was to come and the impact it would make on their lives and community. The houses along Hayes

Lane and the George Lane development – 36 houses, 6 bungalows and the school caretaker's house – were relatively few compared with some of the schemes for private housing, which planned more than a thousand homes for the village. Houses were being constructed in the neighbouring villages of West Wickham and Beckenham and moving towards the parish boundaries. Hayes was seen as ripe for housing development in the same way that the railway promoters viewed it as desirable in the 1860s. To understand the dramatic change that was to confront the village, it is appropriate to review the fortunes of the large houses and estates.

## Fate of the Old Estates

**Pickhurst Manor** for a few years continued to be occupied and have a small dairy farm until Ronald Campbell, who succeeded Mrs English, moved to Sevenoaks after the death in 1928 of his wife Ivy. She had been very active in local women's organisations and in her memory he gave £100 to the Village Hall fund. In June 1929 he married Mary Grace Hallam Lennard, eldest daughter of Sir Henry and Lady Beatrice Lennard of Wickham Court.

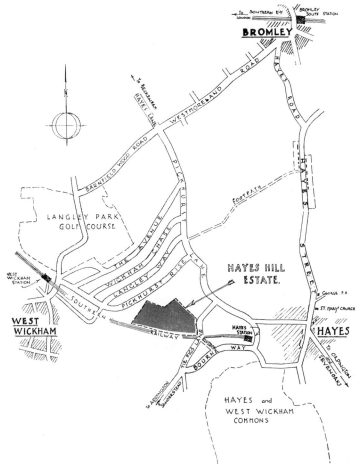

**Map 4:** *Hayes Hill Estate, built on part of the land of Pickhurst Manor* [q.]

The owners of Pickhurst Manor were the Howard family who sold a portion of the estate in 1926 to Captain Sidney Gilchrist Thompson, the Rector's eldest son. Captain Thompson went into partnership with Mr Ellis, forming Ellis Thompson & Co. Ltd. The land they bought was just in the parish of West Wickham and on the west side of the estate between the railway and parish boundary. It was used as a pig and poultry farm until planning approval was given and James Fabb, who worked there, then became the foreman for the builders. The plots were sold from 1927 for superior, freehold and individually designed houses that in time collectively became the Hayes Hill estate. It comprised Hayes Hill, Hayes Mead (later to become Hayes Mead Road) and Pondfield Road. The roads were laid out from 1928 with Hayes Mead Road added in 1929. Sidney Gilchrist Thompson lived in The Bungalow, Hayes Hill. Alderman Bertram Pearce, Mayor of Bromley 1922-23, moved to Hayes Hill in summer 1929.[36]

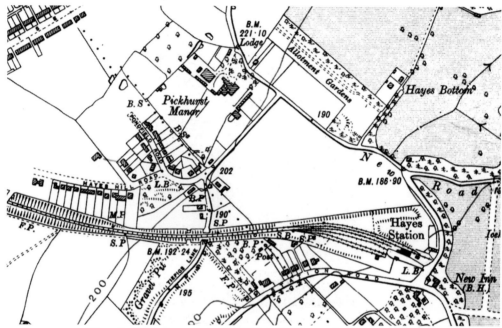

**Map 5:** *Development of Pickhurst Manor lands by 1931* [k.]
*showing Hayes Hill Road, first houses in Hayes Mead and Pondfield Road.*
*Pickhurst Manor was demolished in 1936*

As the demand for this type of property slowed, Ellis Thompson & Co. Ltd diverted their energies to less expensive and more standardised houses in Addington Road and Courtfield Rise; thus the Hayes Hill estate had unsold plots that were not completed for many years.[37] It seems that Ellis Thompson ran into difficulties as a notice of a creditors' meeting appeared in the paper in 1936.[38] Only thirteen houses were finished in Pondfield Road and about six in Hayes Mead Road before the war.[39]

George Ernest Spencer, a local builder of some repute, took over most of the remaining plots. By the time he purchased them he had already bought the rest of the 31 acres of the Pickhurst Manor estate from the heirs of Eliot Howard, who died in 1927. It took some time for Eliot Howard's sons, Francis and Geoffrey, and the latter's daughter

Elizabeth, to settle affairs but eventually the manor house and farm were sold to George Spencer in July 1931. In 1935, 'For Sale' notices were erected in the grounds and unsuccessful attempts were made to sell the house as a potential school, hotel or hospital. The old Georgian manor house and buildings were demolished in early 1936, the event reported as, 'Yet another landmark passes' and 'Another historic building razed to the ground'.[40] Although Tithe Cottages (Hayes Hill Road), Pickhurst Manor Cottages and the Lodge (Pickhurst Lane) were kept, little remains today of Pickhurst Manor or farm, except a chimney used as a sundial in the grounds of Hayes Free Church, a small section of wall and part of the Victorian greenhouses in the rear gardens of 2 to 6 Hayes Hill Road.

*Sundial in the grounds of Hayes Free Church,*
*formerly a chimney from Pickhurst Manor*

Spencer developed the rest of the Pickhurst Manor estate and used Killick & Knight for sales in the Hayes Mead Estate, formerly owned by Ellis Thompson. They offered three styles of house ranging in price from £1,075 to £1,225, each with a brick built garage. Baxter, Payne & Lepper, who were sole agents for the Hayes Hill estate, offered six house styles; a four bedroom house cost £1,455.[41] It was a very competitive market.

**Hayes Place** was owned by Sir Everard Hambro until his death in 1925. At the age of 78 in 1920, he became the first chairman of Hambros Bank Ltd, a bank created by the merging of C. J. Hambro & Son and the British Bank of Northern Commerce Ltd.[42] He remained a director of the Bank of England but always found time to take a close interest in village life. In 1924 he suffered a heart attack. He recovered but was forced to rely on an electric wheel chair that was often seen around the estate, particularly in the areas now called Knoll and Husseywell Parks, then part of the ornamental grounds of the mansion.[43]

*Aerial photo of Hayes Place, St Mary the Virgin, Hayes Church and George Lane* [l.]

*Hayes Place in the 1920s* [l.]

On 26 February 1925 Hambro died and was buried at Hayes Church on 2nd March. His coffin was carried by pall bearers from his house to the church for the funeral service.[44] Many people attended to pay their respects and celebrate his life and achievements. His and his family's influence and effect on Hayes cannot be understated and lasted for many years.

Before the First World War the house and gardens were valued at £55,000, which is over £3,000,000 today.[45] The estate passed to Sir Everard's oldest son, Sir Charles Eric Hambro (known as Eric) who lived at Pickhurst Mead until 1924. He also inherited Milton Abbey and became the second chairman of Hambros Bank Ltd until 1932. Hayes Place sat in 24 acres of grounds with about 272 acres of pasture, meadows, woodland and arable that, in total, represented about a quarter of the land area of the parish.[46] At the time of Hambro's death the estate included Pickhurst Mead, Glebe House, Hayes Place Farm and its three cottages, Fixteds Farm, Fernlea, the George Inn, the Forge, Brewery Cottages, the New Inn, a number of lodges and 53 other houses.

Ownership of The Grove and Ivy Cottage had previously been transferred to Everard's second son, Harold Hambro. By 1927 there were reports that Eric Hambro had decided to dispose of the Hayes Place estate for housing. His motives were varied but he did not intend to live there himself and like many landowners at the time he was influenced by the effects of death duties etc. on his father's estate, which was valued at over £2,000,000. It was a time when farmers were encountering difficulties in getting an adequate return on their land and it was clear that developers would offer a good price for the estate. Whilst he was considering the options he took out a mortgage on the property for £40,000 in July 1927 and started to prepare for an eventual sale. Everard's widow Ebba remarried at the beginning of the year. In December 1927 Eric left his wife Sybil and married his step-mother's sister, Mrs Estelle Elger, in 1929, after his divorce was agreed. He moved away from his roots in Hayes.[47]

Developing the Hayes Place estate for housing required the approval of BRDC. Agreement was reached on 31 December 1928 and the first plan showed the initial layout of roads, shops, houses and open spaces stretching from Pickhurst Lane in the south to the northern side of Mead Way, a road that was yet to be built.[48] The local paper reported that the development would take about twenty years to complete and would consist of 1,100 houses, 150 shops and five miles of roads and sewers.[49] The plan included shops on what is now the open space area of Bourne Vale. Provision was made for the social life of the community with land set aside for a club with grounds in the area that later became Kechill Gardens. After the Second World War it became the home of the Victory Social Club.

In November 1930 it was reported that the estate had been sold to a person 'who resides locally; and it is said that he intends developing it as a garden suburb, thus linking up with the development of West Wickham'.[50] It was later confirmed that William Edward Agg-Large had bought Hayes Place Estate. By 1931 the plan used in the agents' and builders' sales literature showed 901 houses, omitting most of the scheme on the west and north of the estate, which was scheduled as Phase II. At that time the total number of houses in the parish was fewer than 350 and it was clear that the proposals would change the nature of the village. Both early plans illustrated Hayes Place, suggesting that it was to be retained, but by 1932 the mansion was omitted and replaced by houses.[51]

The impact of the proposed developments on the people of Hayes started to sink in. HPC wrote to BRDC and pointed out that seven cottages would be destroyed in the course of building the new estate and that provision for rehousing the displaced families could not be found; nor were there any plans to provide a similar class of cottage property. It also expressed alarm at the meagre numbers of cottages in the village within the means of the 'working man' to rent and wished to know if the owners of the estate contemplated any cottage property in their estate plans.[52]

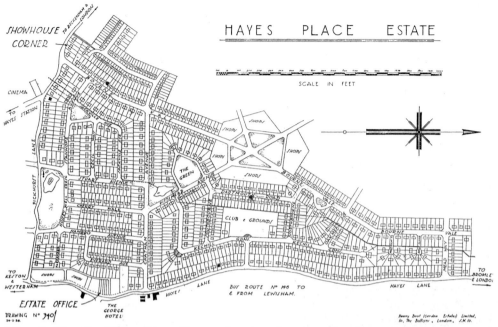

**Map 6: *Plan for Hayes Place Estate showing the areas for shops and open spaces*** [aj.]

William Agg-Large sold a large part of the estate, including Hayes Place, to the housing and construction company, Henry Boot & Sons Ltd of Sheffield. The families in the Hayes Place lodges were given notice to quit, although it was not the intention to demolish the cottages immediately. Henry Boot & Sons Ltd stated that, when it became necessary, sympathetic consideration would be given to alternative accommodation for the tenants.[53] Villagers became concerned about their future.

William Agg-Large arranged for many of the remaining properties on the estate, 27 lots, to be auctioned at the Bell Hotel, Bromley, on 29 May 1931. These included Bank Cottages, Hillside Cottages, Model Cottages, the New Inn, Pickhurst Mead, Staple Cottage, St Mary Cottages, Whites Cottages, Wood Cottages and four plots of building land.[54] It was an important auction, not only for the owner, but particularly for the families who lived in the properties for sale. The *Bromley Mercury* reported that 'many anxious people gathered at the Royal Bell … when portions of Hayes Place Estate not previously sold were put up for auction'. The large room at the inn was packed and 'many of the tenants, who were unable to make offers for themselves waited and listened patiently to learn the identity for their [new] landlords'.

Questions were raised about the validity of the sale of the Parish Room, 3 St Mary Cottages, since it had been given for the use of the church 'for all time'. The auctioneer said his client had a valid title and wanted a bid of £150. He received one of £50 and the property remained unsold.

Mrs Lilian Thompson, the Rector's wife, bought Lot 1, a small field on the southwest corner of Station Hill, for £425 and her daughter Miss Vera Thompson purchased the three Whites Cottages at Pickhurst Green for £270. Mr C Fisher, who lived at Crescent Farm, Sidcup Kent and leased Hayes Street Farm, bought Wood Cottages in Hayes Street for £695 to house his workers. Mr Banfield of Eden Park, Kent, paid £300 for 4 St Mary Cottages and the same amount was offered for 6 St Mary Cottages, which was bought by a consortium from Hampstead. The other lots failed to reach their reserve prices and were withdrawn. Subsequently, they were sold privately. Walter Foat, a butcher from Biggin Hill, bought 10 St Mary Cottages, the slaughterhouse and outbuildings on 20 July 1931 for £950 and it remained in use until the late 1970s. Thomas and Frederick Marks of Bromley purchased Bank Cottages for £750. The New Inn and some of the other building plots were sold before the auction.[55]

Some cottages, such as Rose Cottage, which was occupied from 1924 by PC George Walters and his wife, Roundabout Cottage, cottages in Hayes Bottom and Thatched Cottages in Hayes Lane, were excluded from the auction but later sold to Henry Boot & Sons Ltd.

*Rose Cottage, Pickhurst* [m.]

At the time of the auction Roundabout Cottage was occupied by Frank Price and his wife Rose. He died in April 1935. He detested motorcars and on the day of his funeral was conveyed by six horses to the church where he was buried in his white smock. The cortège travelled from Roundabout Cottage, Bourne Vale, along the route of the old footpath into Pickhurst Lane, instead of going along the new road into Hayes Lane to Hayes Church. Thereby he avoided the modern housing estate, to which he objected.[56] The cottage was demolished about 1936.

*Frank Price of Roundabout Cottage* [a.]

George Wheatbread and Harry Bowles, both railway signalmen on the Hayes branch line, tenanted two cottages in Hayes Bottom (Bourne Vale), at a weekly rent of 4s. 6d., for over thirty years. The cottages were vacated in 1930 after the men's retirement and demolished within the year. The third cottage, Bourne Cottage, built by Everard Hambro, survives to this day.

Albert Gilbert had lived with his family in No. 2 Thatched Cottages (Hayes Lane) for many years. Gilbert rented the cottage for 4s. 6d. a week, although in 1923 he let a bedroom and the use of the kitchen for 2s. a week to his newly married son Leonard Douglas Gilbert.[57] Albert Gilbert died in 1934 and his wife a year later, after which there were no more tenants. James Luxton was the last occupant of No. 1 Thatched Cottages from 1925 until 1930, when a possession order was granted to Mr W Skilton, as Luxton's employment had been terminated.[58] It is probable that both cottages were demolished within a year or two.

To add to the speculation and rumour in the village the *Bromley Mercury,* in 1932, reported that the South Suburban Gas Company had applied to Parliament for an Act allowing them to build a gas works for the manufacture or conversion of residual products from coal gas. These works were to be built on the old gravel pits between Tiepigs Lane, Bourne Way and the railway line. Although just outside the parish, Hayes would have been seriously affected by the scheme to which HPC was opposed and it endeavoured to protect residents' interests. Opinions were strong and residents held a protest at the site against the scheme.[59] The application did not materialise, although the

Gas Company installed a small gas governor unit at the western corner of Tiepigs Lane, Bourne Way and Addington Road. It was removed after Heydon Court was built in 1987.

The changes in the village created many stories for the local papers. They interviewed older villagers about life in Hayes and their opinions on events. Soon rumours started that 'Pitt's House' was to be demolished. BRDC wrote to HPC to ask whether steps should be taken to preserve the mansion in view of its historical associations. HPC formed a sub-committee and Mrs Lilian Thompson prepared a report. The National Trust was approached to save the house, but to no avail. A suggestion that Hayes Place should become a branch library and museum also came to nothing. More support came from Mr Waldron Smithers, Bromley's MP, who wrote to *The Times* asking for somebody to save the house for the nation. Henry Boot, the builders, responded by saying that if anyone came forward with a plan for preserving the house the firm would consider it. Later another HPC sub-committee was asked to advise on the trees on the estate that were worthy of preservation.[60] All efforts to save the mansion failed and in January 1932 part of the wall around Hayes Place (it ran from Pickhurst Lane to the North Lodge) was demolished for new shops in Hayes Street opposite the church. In March 1933 Hayes Place was pulled down.[61]

*Hayes Place Gates at entrance to Concord Park, Sheffield* [n.]

What remains of Hayes Place in 2011? Very little: the Coachman's House, the North Lodge, West Lodge and part of the ornamental gardens of the mansion, Husseywell and Knoll Parks, are still in existence. The parks were granted to the Council to remain in perpetuity as Open Spaces. It was suggested in 1934 that the Council should sell them for building plots, however, pressure from Lieutenant Colonel Fulcher and Percy Jones persuaded it not to take action. Many of the local gardens have rockeries that include pieces of dressed stone that probably came from the old house. Some modern road names such as Alexander Close, Chatham Avenue, Pittsmead Avenue, Everard Avenue and Hambro Avenue, emanate from Hayes Place and its past owners. The pedestrian gate of Hayes Place opposite the church is now the gate into the churchyard extension. The beautiful wrought iron gates from the main entrance still survive. Charles Boot, the head of the firm that bought the estate, presented the gates to Sheffield Corporation who re-erected them, in May 1932, at the main entrance to Concord Park, Sheffield. They are still there and in good working order.[62]

**Pickhurst Mead** was also sold for development. Charles Jocelyn Hambro occupied it in 1925 after his father Sir Charles Eric left in 1924. In 1927 Edward Thomas John and his family leased the property for five years at a rent of £300 a year.[63] He had followed his father into a steel works in South Wales and ultimately rose to become Managing Director of Linthorpe-Dinsdale Smelting Co Ltd. He promoted the idea of Welsh home rule and became MP for East Denbigh from 1910 to 1918. He joined the Labour Party in 1918 but was defeated in the 1918 election.

He continued to campaign for Welsh self-government but his efforts were unrewarded and on 16 February 1931 he committed suicide 'by hanging himself whilst of unsound mind'. He was buried in Hayes churchyard. He was the last tenant of Pickhurst Mead. The furniture and household effects were auctioned in April and the house, which had been bought by William Agg-Large, was included in the Hayes Place Estate auction in May 1931. It failed to reach the reserve price of £6,950, was withdrawn and sold privately to a developer, Bleach and Skipper.[64] Pickhurst Mead was demolished in March 1934 and nothing remains of the house or its lodge.

**Glebe House,** with its beautifully kept gardens, was also affected by development. James Frost, a steel rope manufacturer, leased it in 1919 and six years later bought the estate from Sir Eric Hambro. The estate grounds covered some seventeen acres encompassing rose gardens, shrubberies, woodland, a lake and boathouse, and four tennis courts. James Frost was always a keen sportsman. Whilst playing in the finals of the Leeds Tennis Tournament in 1884 he was approached by Mr Slazenger who wanted to look at the racquet that James had modified by inserting a piece of lead to give it a better balance. Slazenger was most impressed, copied the idea and offered James Frost a 50% discount on all his Slazenger purchases for his lifetime. On several occasions celebrity tennis matches were held on his courts, including the appearance in 1926 of the Ladies' Wimbledon Singles Champion, Kitty Godfree.

The entrance drive to the house was from the Lodge on Baston Road, situated close to where No. 81 exists today. The drive was about quarter of a mile long, lined with yew trees and after reaching the house it continued on to the Coach House.[65]

James Frost was an active church member and keen supporter of village activities. He and his wife, Ellen Katherine, lent their house and gardens for village events and fetes on a number of occasions.[66] He died in March 1930 at the age of 64 and the house and the grounds were sold. The contents were auctioned in December 1930 and raised nearly £1,000.[67] His wife, who died in 1950, and son Richard moved to Bencewell Orchard, Barnet Wood Road.

*James Frost and his son Richard in the grounds of Glebe House* [p.]

Glebe House's grounds were bought and plans submitted for 120 houses. In 1933 approval was given to convert Glebe House into six self-contained flats, but this did not materialise.[68] In 1935 the trustees of the Church School seriously considered purchasing the house for a new school, as the existing school buildings were too small. The financial implications, however, were too great and the plan was not supported by the Bishop. Glebe House Lodge, occupied by Frederick Evans the gardener, was pulled down when the estate was developed for modern housing.

Glebe House survived for another 30 years and the Coach House and Stables remain, much altered, at 80 Hayes Wood Avenue.

**The Nest,** further south on Baston Road, was lived in by Henry Legge and his family from 1913 until 1921 when he moved to Baston Manor. Sir Henry Arthur Payne, with his wife, two sons and a daughter occupied the old house from 1921 to 1931 and renamed it Redgates. Sir Henry, the son of Robert Payne of Chislehurst, was a joint Permanent Secretary at the Board of Trade from 1919. He played a valuable role at the Paris Peace Conference as one of the economic experts of the British Delegation and in 1923 was able to win the confidence of the Turkish negotiators. In 1925 he was created a KBE and at the end of the 1920s became an advisor to the department of Industry and Commerce in Cairo, from where he returned to Hayes for the summer months. He died suddenly at home in October 1931 from an illness he had contracted in Egypt.[69] Hayes resident, Bill

Dance, who worked as a gardener at Redgates, recalled that Sir Henry was very keen on his garden and insisted that he mowed the lawn, which went slightly uphill to two cedar trees, so that the stripes appeared in the shape of the Prince of Wales' feathers.[70]

The next occupier of Redgates was Mrs Lucy Annesley, a dog breeder from Didcot, Berkshire, who specialised in breeding and selling Golden Retrievers. She infringed the Town and Country Planning requirements and HPC wrote to the BRDC on the matter in September 1932. William Courtenay wanted to purchase Redgates to develop an exclusive estate and he arranged with Mrs Annesley that he would build her a new house, suitable for her dog breeding, and that she would leave Redgates. In May 1935 an appeal was heard against the refusal by Bromley Town Council to allow the building of a bungalow and kennels on 3½ acres of Baston farmland owned by A C Norman. It was argued that the establishment of kennels in this residential area would constitute a serious threat to the amenities of the area. Mr Norman's agents, however, argued that it would be less injurious than the 42 houses which could be erected on the land in accordance with the town planning scheme. Finally, on 21 June 1935 permission was granted for its use as a kennels on condition that the dogs were limited to the breed of Golden Retriever and not more than twelve dogs were kept. On 1 January 1936 the site was sold to W W Courtenay Ltd for £1,000 and on 23 July Mrs Annesley moved to the new house at 83/85 Baston Road for which she paid £5,170.[71] The property was known as Glenaffric Kennels and the veterinary surgeon Mr H Jackson held a regular clinic there.

*85 Baston Road* [m.]

With Mrs Annesley's departure, W W Courtenay Ltd became the owner of Redgates. The potential development of land so near to the common led the Conservators to take a close interest in the scheme. They were particularly concerned about the boundary, access to the common and the track between West Common and Baston Roads. In

November 1936 the Ranger reported that the house was being demolished and the Conservators arranged for the crescent shaped lawn area in front of the house to be restored as grassland by January 1937. A few months later it was suggested that some of Redgates' land should be bought as an addition to the common but the Council's Recreation Committee decided to take no action.[72]

A year later Redgate Drive was laid out. Bromley Council granted the first planning permission for houses Nos. 2, 3, 4 and 6 in 1938 and for 14 Redgate Drive in 1939. The houses were designed by the architect, J C Colvin, built by Messrs W W Courtenay and all occupied before the outbreak of war. Like so many other developments the Redgate estate was completed after the war.

**Longcroft** had been empty for a long time when its owner, John Thomas Hedley, died in April 1937 whilst living in Windermere, Cumbria. He was a wealthy man, owning most of the Royal Crescent at Margate and Westcliffe Lodge at Ramsgate, Kent, coupled with the family coal mining and other business interests in northeast England. His estate was valued at over £650,000, the bulk of which passed to his brother Edward's son, Oswald Hedley. Furniture and plate was left to another brother George and to his sister Margaret. His will stated that he was to be cremated and his ashes scattered by the actress and dancer, Miss Phyllis Broughton, to whom he left 'jewels and trinkets'. For many years he had remained in contact with Phyllis, who had rejected his earlier offer of marriage. She married Doctor Robert Wright Thompson of Margate during the First World War but she died in 1926.[73]

*Longcroft House* [o.]

*Longcroft Gardens* [o.]

By early 1938 interest was being expressed in the estate. Mr E F Bates of Shirley, Surrey, considered it for a housing development and submitted a plan of a proposed crescent shaped road and sewer layout with access on to Pickhurst Lane. The scheme encompassed the whole of the grounds with housing.[74] Nothing came of it and Baxter Payne & Lepper put Longcroft up for sale in May. By September the estate was sold, the roof of the house had been removed and the stable block taken down for new houses. The majority of the house was demolished by October 1939 when the local Air Raid Precautions' units used the site for training.[75] Nothing tangible remains of Longcroft, although the major part of the grounds forms Pickhurst Schools' playing fields.

Housing development took place fronting the east side of Pickhurst Lane just before the war, but building was curtailed after only about 12 semi-detached houses had been built.[76] Work on the small estate resumed after the war.

**Warren Wood** was also sold for development. Mrs Laura Smail moved from the house to Anglesey in the early 1920s. Mr & Mrs Hugh Wylie occupied the house in 1934 when they and their neighbour at Hawthorndene, Major Basil Binyon, were approached by developers to sell their properties. By the following year it was confirmed that Warren Wood estate had been sold for housing but Major Binyon refused to sell and remained at Hawthorndene until the 1960s.[77]

**Hartfield** was sold by Horace Devas, after his wife Edith died in 1924 and he bought a property in Hildenborough, Kent. The new owner, William Owen Hamborough Joynson, son of E H Joynson, took over in 1926. He and his father were partners in the papermaking firm of St Mary Cray Paper Mills. In 1931 William's father retired and the company was sold in 1933 to Wiggins Teape Ltd, who continued papermaking until 1967. William Joynson left Hartfield in early 1930. A sale of furniture and household effects took place in May 1930 and the freehold was sold for residential property development, with about 40 acres of land.[78] It was bought by Godfrey's (Properties and Flats) Ltd. who built 'the finest houses ranging in price from £750 to £4,000'. The land of Hartfield became known as Hayes Park (Sun Trap) Estate. Initially the fate of the large house was uncertain and it was rumoured it was to become a nightclub, 'The Queen of Clubs'.

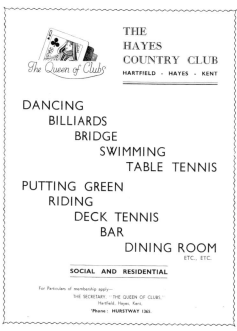

*Advertisement for the Country Club at Hartfield* [q.]

Godfrey's estate brochure waxed lyrical that:

> It is an old house ... and has now been skilfully converted into a splendid clubhouse for the use of residents and visitors. ... Set amidst fine lawns, gardens, and great banks of rhododendrons ... There are tennis courts; some rough shooting is available and a magnificent swimming pool.[79]

Not a great deal is known about the success of the club as ultimately the house was demolished. By 1936 Hartfield Crescent had been built. The original stables were retained and are now 5 Hartfield Crescent.

## Saved from Speculative Housing

Houses such as Baston Manor, Hayes Grove, Hast Hill, Hayes Court, Gadsden, Barnhill, Coney Hill and The Warren survived the housing development onslaught in the 1930s. By the beginning of the Second World War, however, all except the first three had changed their role from large family homes to institutions.

**Baston Manor**, once the most important estate in the parish, was empty for four years after Mrs Ann Torrens moved to the Grove. In 1921 Henry Legge and his family arrived and stayed until January 1934. Henry Legge and his sons Philip and Geoffrey, who played cricket for England, made occasional appearances for Hayes Cricket Club. He enlarged the house and built a squash court. The old pond by the front gate was part of the common and caused concern in the 1920s to the Conservators who asked him not to put surface water into the pond. Subsequently, the pond was filled in although the depression can still be seen.[80]

*Baston Manor from the rear 1929* [r.]

*Baston Manor drawing room 1929* [r.]

In 1934 Arthur Collins moved to Baston Manor, having previously been resident at Greenways. He had grown up in Bromley, attended Beckenham and Penge Grammar School in 1905 and graduated with a BSc from London University. In the First World War he was a lieutenant with the Durham Light Infantry and was wounded in France in 1916. He transferred to the Royal Engineers and served in Palestine and Syria. He became president of the Institute of Municipal Treasurers and Accountants in 1922, the year in which he resigned as city treasurer of Birmingham.[81] He set up a private practice in Westminster. His background and experience enabled him to play a very important role from the late 1920s in local affairs. In particular, he recognised the importance of Hayes Common and worked hard to ensure that it remained for the residents' enjoyment.

**Hayes Grove** also avoided redevelopment, although some of its land was sold. It was owned by Colonel Harold Hambro, second son of Sir Everard Hambro and leased by Mrs Ann Torrens. She died at the age of 81 in February 1924 and was buried, alongside her husband, in Hayes Churchyard. She left an estate of £7,403 and probate was granted to her sons Matt and Charles.[82] Matt, his wife Lillian and three children, stayed on at Hayes Grove. From 1925 to 1930 he was a member of HPC, a Common Conservator, chairman of the Hayes, Keston and West Wickham branch of the Chislehurst Divisional Constituency Association, member of the Hayes Flower Show Committee and Hayes Cricket Club. He worked as a clerk at the Bank of England and was a member of the London Stock Exchange.

Several Hayes' inhabitants attended the marriage of his daughter Betty to Randle Baker Wilbraham of Rhode Hall, Cheshire, at St Martins in the Fields, London in 1930. In the same year he moved to Limpsfield, Surrey, and died in February 1931 at the age of 61. His widow, Lillian Torrens, married Gerald Wainwright from Bournemouth, Dorset, in 1934 and survived until 1965. Like her first husband she was involved with local politics, was a founder member of the Hayes Women's branch of the Conservative Association and its president and chairman from 1922 to 1931.[83]

The house was advertised for sale freehold for £3,950 in 1930 and had eleven bedrooms, three reception rooms, a large garage with service pit and 2½ acres of pleasure grounds. It was considered suitable for a residential hotel. Despite this suggestion, the Grove remained a private house and was bought in 1931 by Dorothea, wife of Henry Wilding of Gadsden, for £2,500. By 1933 it had been resold to Henry Seymour Guinness for £3,500, and he was still in occupation in 1940.[84]

Henry Guinness's youngest daughter, Heather Seymour Guinness, known in her professional life as Judy, came second in the 1932 Olympic Games in the women's fencing competition and was British champion in 1933 and runner up in 1934. She married Clifton Penn-Hughes a racing driver who had competed at Brooklands and came second in the *Mille Miglia* race in 1934. He was also a pilot and in August 1935 landed his aeroplane in George Lane so that he could visit his fiancée at the Grove. Penn-Hughes clearly enjoyed fast sports but died in an aeroplane crash at Lydd, Kent, in July 1939; his daughter was born in January 1940.[85]

**Hast Hill** saw the death of Mrs Emma Knowles in February 1924. She had lived there for almost thirty years and had been an active supporter of Hayes Church. Her daughter Mabel was very involved with their joint efforts for the disadvantaged in the East End of

London and after her mother's death became a full-time church worker at St Luke's, Custom House.[86] From her study in Hayes, under her pseudonym May Wynne, Miss Knowles continued to write popular books, 16 romances and 35 children's stories between 1918 and 1924, that provided an income for her charitable work.

Within a month of Mrs Knowles' death the furniture, and a 'handsome Rolls Royce car' were auctioned at the premises, and by the end of the year the house had been sold to F H Rogers.[87] A year later Hast Hill was bought by the racing driver and businessman Granville Ramage McAlpine, the fifth son of Sir Robert McAlpine, who became one of the shareholders of the family's civil engineering business, Sir Robert McAlpine & Sons (London) Ltd, in 1926. Granville McAlpine's responsibilities included the construction of the Daventry wireless station, the new Dartford road and Farnborough by-pass road. He became vice-president of Keston Football and Cricket Clubs. He died in October 1928, aged 45, and by the following May the house had been purchased by Howard King.[88] Mr and Mrs King soon became involved in local activities and the house was often the venue for meetings of the Conservative Association or Hayes Nursing Association. In 1937 the house and gardens were used for the wedding reception of Elizabeth Hamer of The White House and Lieutenant William Batten. The Kings continued to live at Hast Hill until the mid 1950s.

For the moment, therefore, Baston Manor, Hayes Grove and Hast Hill remained large family homes. Four houses - Baston House, Gadsden, Hayes Court and Barnhill - either became schools or scheduled for a school in the inter war years. Their educational influence is considered in chapter 4 but the situation prior to that event is considered below.

**Baston House** was home to Katherine Morris, widow of Thomas, until her death on 14 August 1920 at the age of 94. The house effects and farm stock of 9 cows, 8 heifers, 22 pigs, 70 poultry and some prize rabbits were put up for sale.[89] Baston House was leased to Donald Haldeman who was born in Pennsylvania, USA, in 1860. He was the second son of John Haldeman, who owned an 'Iron Business' and who brought his wife and six children to England and in 1881 lived in Lewisham.[90] Donald Haldeman's occupation was recorded as 'Private Secretary'; he took British citizenship and by the time of his death in early 1930 he had been a JP since 1918, chairman of the Kent County Police Court Mission and Bromley Probation Committee, member of the BRDC, fellow of the Royal Horticultural Society, and Master of the Worshipful Company of Gardeners. He was a very successful farmer and breeder of pedigree cattle and in 1921 also leased Hayes Street Farm. Bill Dance recalled that if the village lads saw Mr Haldeman as he rode around on horseback, doffed their caps and opened a gate for him, he would give them a shilling.[91] Mr Haldeman stayed at Baston until 1925 when he moved to Gadsden. He was followed by solicitor Reginald Garrould Barnes, senior partner of Collinson, Prichard & Barnes, who moved from Fernlea and remained until 1932.

A new era for Baston Farm began in 1933 when Archibald Cameron Norman leased 'the house, cottage, cowsheds, granary, greenhouse and pleasure gardens' to Mrs Jane Smith, widow of Henry, and her daughters Marian and Margaret Stafford Smith, on a 21 year term at £200 a year. They started Baston School.[92] The surrounding farmland continued to be owned by Mr Norman and was leased to Reginald Fisher.

*Miss Marian Stafford Smith*
*Founder of Baston School, 1933* [s.]

**Gadsden** was another estate destined to become a school. James Railton continued to own the property and there were a number of tenants before Donald Haldeman became the occupier in 1925.[93] Donald Haldeman left Gadsden and Hayes in 1927 and died in 1930 at his home in Portland Place, London. James Railton put the estate of just over 13 acres up for sale in December 1927, including the lodge on Baston Road and the area of the stables described in the sale catalogue as 'garage for three small cars, two stables, harness room and loft, large workshop and storeroom, chauffeur or gardener's quarters comprising sitting room, kitchen, scullery and three bedrooms'. It was sold to Kent County Council (KCC) in August 1928 for £8,600.[94] The Education Committee of KCC planned, in the first instance, to establish a boys' school, then a school for girls and later a regional college. None of these schemes materialised before the war. The last person to tenant the house, between 1929 and 1930, was Henry Wilding who by 1931 lived at the Grove where he died shortly afterwards. Lady Margaret Payne of Redgates rented the squash rackets court until 1932 at £12 per annum.

The grounds were meant to be used as a sports ground or for grazing cattle, horses or sheep but in October 1935 the HVA reported that it had received complaints from residents in Hayes Street about the smell and noise of pigs kept at Gadsden and had contacted the pigs' owner who promised to remedy the situation.[95] This situation remained until the Munich Crisis of 1938. War looked possible and the empty house began to be used for local Air Raid Precautions (ARP).[96]

**Hayes Court** in 1918 was occupied by widow Frances Margaret Preston. The owner Mrs Louisa Lee died and the executors put the estate up for sale. It was bought by Professor John Cox whose daughter Katherine opened an exclusive school on 8 May 1919.[97]

**Map 7:** *Hayes in 1930* [k.]

**Barnhill,** at the northern end of the parish, also changed its role from a family home and became a school. In August 1931 Thomas Gillespie Chapman Browne, who had lived in the house from the time it was built in 1898, died at the age of 85.[98] His executors were his sons Hugh, a Westminster surveyor, Walter who became archdeacon of Rochester, Archibald of Queen's College, Cambridge, and his daughter Dorothy who moved to Beckenham. By January 1932 they had agreed a 21-year lease with Robert Hilary Smith who planned to convert the house and open a boys' school.

**Coney Hill** was lived in by widow Elizabeth Hoskier, her daughter Coralie and son-in-law Alexander Boord to whom the property was transferred after Elizabeth's death in 1916. Alexander Boord died in June 1925 and left £133,670 to his wife and children. Mrs Coralie Boord continued to live at Coney Hill until November 1928 when she 'reluctantly moved from her home of 46 years' to live at Eastbourne, Sussex. Eight years later she committed suicide at Beachy Head, Sussex at the age of 65.[99]

In 1928 Coney Hill was leased to Basil Jones who stayed about two years, after which it was sold and became a home for 'crippled children'. Mrs David Greig of Beckenham opened the home in June 1935. It catered for children between the ages of eight to eleven, and was managed by the Shaftesbury Society. At the opening ceremony it was described as a beautiful gift of anonymous donors.[100] The property continues to operate as a residential school for disabled young people.

**The Warren** was occupied by Lady Laidlaw until 1920 when it was sold to Edwin Mumford Preston for £19,500.[101] He was the nephew of Reuben Thomas Preston, formerly of Hayes Court, and during his fourteen years in residence he played an important part in the affairs of Hayes. He was a Common Conservator, churchwarden from 1930-33, president of the Hayes Horticultural Society and the generous benefactor of land for the Village Hall. His wife was on the Parish Council, leader of the Women's Institute and president of the local Girl Guides. His daughter Joyce married the Bishop of Gibraltar's son in 1924 and his second daughter Phyllis played an active role in the development of the Girl Guides.

*The Warren* [l.]

In 1934 The Warren was sold to Gordon Ralph Hall-Caine CBE, MP, for £14,500.[102] His circumstances changed and he wanted a quick sale. He put the house, lodge, three cottages, stabling and 22 acres of land on the market for £17,500. The sales catalogue suggested that the estate could be used for a housing development, as the restrictive covenant that allowed only one house had been removed in 1931. The other restrictions that remained were that the house could not be used as 'a lunatic asylum, non-residential public house or manufactory of an objectionable nature'. Hall-Caine refused an offer of £15,000 but accepted £15,500. Mrs Margetson, wife of Major Sir Philip Margetson Assistant Commissioner of the Metropolitan Police, who lived in Chislehurst, paid the original deposit. The Warren's proposed use as a police clubhouse was then made public. A further £200 was paid for the fixtures and fittings that included a billiard table.[103]

In April 1935 the police told Beckenham Borough Council that they were exempt from submitting alteration plans for the house for approval but that they were happy for the Council to inspect them. At the time the Council had plans to widen Coney Hill Road (Croydon Road), which would require part of the land of The Warren and the Lodge. Considerable controversy followed regarding the road and the old oak trees, a photograph of which appeared in *The Times* in October 1934. The Metropolitan Police Receiver refused to allow the widening to go ahead. This is one reason why the road is still so narrow at that point.

More difficulties arose regarding vehicles using the roadway at the rear of The Warren. To eliminate this traffic the Common Conservators erected notices at each end saying 'accommodation road only' and the ranger, Mr Drake, stopped lorries from going along it. The police continued to argue for public access, but eventually a compromise was reached in which they had a key to the gate across the road for use by private motor vehicles only, the rest had to use the Coney Hill road entrance.[104] The Clubhouse and facilities were officially opened in 1935 by Lord Trenchard, Marshall of the RAF and Commissioner of the Metropolitan Police. Since then the police authorities have developed and maintained the estate.

The changes in the 1920s and 1930s to the properties that escaped demolition had a marked effect on Hayes and its people. Fewer servants, footmen, and grooms were needed. Thus, the opportunity for villagers to find such work within the parish diminished. Other occupations expanded; for instance, more teachers were needed for the new schools but people from Hayes did not necessarily fill these jobs. One effect of the arrival of new people in the village was to increase the diversity of political opinion.

## Politics and Local Government

It was mainly after the First World War that people of every walk of life started to take an interest in party politics. All men over 21 received the vote in 1918 but it was a further ten years before women were given the same right, although female householders over 30 could vote from 1918.

Miss Margaret Stafford Smith, youngest daughter of Henry Stafford Smith a foreign stamp importer, stood for election in 1919 as a councillor for Martin's Hill Ward. She was unsuccessful but then stood for Bickley Ward and was elected. She became a successful local government councillor, serving on housing, health and education committees. In 1933 she moved to Hayes to set up Baston School with her sister, continued to be very active in politics and became the first female Mayor of Bromley from November 1938 to November 1940.[105] Mrs Louisa Smail, Mrs Lilian Thompson and Mrs Sarah Preston, became Hayes Parish Councillors in the 1920s and played an important role in raising issues, particularly on health and welfare matters.

*Miss Margaret Stafford Smith, co-founder of Baston School and Mayor of Bromley 1938 - 1940* [L]

There had always been a division of political opinion between the Conservatives and Liberals but by the 1920s the ideas of socialism were growing. In 1921 Mr Alfred Barnes, chairman of the London Co-operative Society and a Director of the *Daily Herald*, gave two lectures in the Rectory garden for the Bromley branch of the Independent Labour Party on relations between 'Co-operative and Labour movements'. A later speaker said, 'It was very kind of the Rector to have them there. It was a grand thing to find broad-minded men in the good old Church of England.' Revd Thompson replied that:

> it was a pleasure … to welcome them in that old parsonage garden, where grew honeysuckle and roses and lavender and thyme … to welcome those who were taking an earnest interest in Co-operation and the work of the Labour Party. He believed that the movement had a very important part to play … He was convinced that the party had much great work before it in the immediate future … They did not all think alike, but every man had the right to be considered and had a duty to impress their needs upon the whole of society. He would not like to see everybody a member of the Labour Party just as he would not like to see everybody in the kingdom a member of the Conservative Party.[106]

The Labour Party frequently held public meetings in the Village Hall covering topics such as 'The Need for Social Ownership', 'Why Rates?' and the 'Co-operative Movement'. In the 1930s the local prospective candidate, Mr W T Colyer, was invariably in attendance as were sitting MPs such as Dr A Salter, James Chuter Ede and Lady Noel Buxton, whose husband was a Cabinet Minister. The chairman of the Hayes branch from 1929 to 1934 was Emmanuel Mansfield of George Lane and the secretary was Percy Jones of Redgate Cottage. Both men gained sufficient support from the villagers to become parish councillors and were very active on matters relating to Hayes and its development. By 1938 the Hayes branch had increased its membership by 100% and was contemplating starting a women's section.[107]

Concurrent with the growth in the Labour Party was the increased activity of the trade unions. It was during 1926 that Great Britain experienced its first General Strike when talks between the owners and coal miners broke down. The Trades Union Congress (TUC) decided to support the miners, which on 3 May led to the start of the strike and confrontation with the government of Mr Stanley Baldwin. The TUC called off the strike on 12 May but during those few days the country suffered manufacturing and transport turmoil. Many middle-class people helped to keep essential services running, much to the anger of the strikers, and it had the effect of dividing people in Britain. Bromley was affected; the railway stations only had one member of staff on duty with the stationmaster but with a number of local volunteers they were able to keep two stations operating with about 100 trains running a day. The village of Hayes seems to have been unaffected by the strike although those using public transport experienced some disruption and inconvenience. Referring to the events in his June letter, Canon Thompson commented:

> All our thoughts, and matters of more local interest were put in the background. We were thankful for the spirit of good temper, and readiness to be useful, which was manifested on all sides, and herein we have a sure foundation for hope that the difficulties that still remain will be overcome.[108]

Bromley also had a small but dedicated Communist Party that was active during the late 1930s. One of its original founders was a young man, Kenneth Bond, who was born in Middlesex but came to Hayes in 1931 and lived with his family at 75 George Lane. When he was seventeen years old he worked as a 'milker' on Hayes Street Farm and lodged at Wood Cottages. He joined the Hayes Labour Party and Bromley Labour League of Youth and was keen to promote socialism and the improvement of the conditions of the working classes. He is said to have taken part in every London demonstration promoting the cause and sold the *Daily Worker* every Saturday in Bromley High Street. In 1936 he was one of six people who founded the Bromley Communist Party and was chairman of the Bromley Council Tenants Association. He volunteered to fight in the Spanish Civil War on a number of occasions, was finally accepted and joined the International Brigade in the early part of 1938. He left for Spain in March, stayed near Barcelona and in July took part in the *Ebro* offensive, the last major campaign by the Republican forces. He was killed in action on 28th July at the age of 23. A description of his time in Spain, written for the *Bromley Mercury*, was published after his death and a tribute by the Communist Party a week later.[109]

The activities of the Communists were of concern to the Conservative Party in Hayes, which was well established. In the late 1920s the president of Hayes Conservative Association was W. O. H. Joynson, the paper-mill owner who lived at Hartfield. In 1927 he presided over the annual meeting and 'Smoking Concert', held in the loggia of the

George Hotel, when Roy Wilson, MP for Lichfield, spoke on current political topics including the need to curb the Communists in their midst. The Conservative Men's group grew in numbers reaching 270 by the beginning of 1939 but their social events tended to be less well supported than those run by the women. The meetings were very varied. On one occasion Mr Waldron Smithers, MP for Bromley, called for the support of Mr Stanley Baldwin rather than Mr Beaverbrook and at a garden party at Greenways in 1934 he spoke to 120 people to encourage them not just to sleep and eat in Hayes but to take an active interest in local affairs.[110]

By 1930 regular reports appeared in the local papers about the Young Conservatives' 'jolly dances', surprise nights and rambles led by their secretary Miss Edna Grandfield. In January 1931 Miss Patricia Torrens resigned as president, as she was leaving the area. Philip Legge took on the role with Greta Collins as vice chairman and Miss Tidbury as treasurer but two years later the Young Conservatives' group decided to disband through lack of support. More successful was the Women's Conservative Association, which was active from 1923 and organised conferences and social events including dances, outings, garden parties and whist drives. Its members increased from 128 in 1932 to 258 in 1938. Many meetings discussed Conservative policies, such as an explanation in 1933 by a Central Office representative of the Budget and the 'dangers of the Indian White Paper'.[111]

In the 1920s the Rector and his wife encouraged the cause of the Liberal party. In 1924 the newly formed Hayes Liberal Association held a meeting at Hayes Church Schools and arranged a series of popular concerts to stimulate interest in Liberalism. Canon Thompson gave the vote of thanks to the artistes who supported these concerts.[107] His son, Piers Gilchrist Thompson, who married Hester Mary Barnes of Fernlea, Baston Road, at Hayes Parish Church in April 1932, was a member of the Liberal Party, became MP for Torquay in 1923 but lost his seat in 1924. To some extent the Liberal impetus disappeared when Canon Thompson retired and moved away. In 1936, however, about three years after he had left Hayes, a public meeting was held to discuss reforming the Liberal Association in Hayes, West Wickham and Keston.[112]

All local political parties benefited from the increase in the number of people living in Hayes, who came from different walks of life, with a wide range of views. Many played an active, but often unseen, role in local affairs. In the 1920s some sought election to HPC. Many voters considered the candidate's integrity and concern for local matters more important than an individual's political persuasion. On most matters parish councillors could only advise or seek action from BRDC although two issues were solely under their control, the agreeing of the Common Rate and the administration of Hayes Common and the running of the Gymnasium until the Village Hall replaced it in 1927.

As the 1920s and 1930s progressed, the workload of HPC and BRDC increased as a result of the housing developments. This state of affairs was not unique to Hayes and Bromley; it applied to many cities, towns and villages with an expanding population. In the late 1920s central government was aware of the economic problems this created and enacted the Local Government Act of 1929. The Act required County Councils to review, consult and create new and bigger Urban District Councils, to be in place by April 1934, that would absorb the duties of the Parish and Rural Councils. These were anxious times for all and Keston Parish Council wrote to Hayes suggesting that they combine to protect their mutual interests.[113] A special meeting was held to discuss the implications of the new Act; it was chaired by the Clerk to BRDC, Mr Wall. A major concern was Hayes Common. If BRDC was integrated with Bromley Borough Council a new Order would be required from the Ministry of Agriculture to protect the common. In September 1929 more issues were discussed and BRDC asked whether HPC was prepared to consider amalgamation with the new Bromley Borough Council. HPC called a special meeting to consider the proposed merger and in the end the majority preferred to support a move to be amalgamated with Bromley rather than with Orpington or Beckenham, although most were unhappy with the proposed demise of the Parish Council.[114]

When BRDC suggested that Hayes Ward be known as Pitt Ward, HPC asked to be involved in such matters. Representatives were invited subsequently to attend a conference at Maidstone on new local government structure and organisation. Meetings continued during the first years of the new decade and the parish councillors tried to safeguard the electorate's interests, protect the environment and make arrangements for the smooth transfer of power. This was not helped by the death of the retired schoolmaster, William Plant, on 21 December 1931 after he had been knocked down by a motorcycle on his way to a meeting of the HPC in October. He was 80 years old and had been the clerk to HPC since its inception in 1894. Mr Sullivan Mortimer, the church organist and choirmaster, took his place at a salary of £18 a year.[115]

HPC ceased to function on 31 March 1934 and its records and minute books were transferred to Bromley Council, which remained within the administrative area of Kent County Council. Surprisingly, the last entry in the minute book makes no mention of the change but simply records that the omnibus timetable was to be fixed to No.5 lamp post at the junction of Hayes Lane and Hayes Road. At the final meeting, however, the chairman, Lieutenant Colonel Fulcher, outlined the history of HPC since he joined in 1910 and was presented with a silver propelling pencil to mark the occasion. The last committee members included Mrs Alice Cowan, Mrs Sarah Preston, Arthur Carlos, Dr. Colville Barrington, Laurence DeThier and Allan Foster. In April the minute books and other official documents were officially handed over to the Mayor, Councillor W D Gibbs. A young oak tree was planted at the spot of the former boundaries of Hayes and Keston at the junction of Croydon Road with Commonside, known as Grace's Corner.[116]

The transfer was not straightforward as the majority of Hayes parish and Keston went to the new Bromley Borough Council but West Wickham and a small part of Hayes came under Beckenham's control. The changes to the parish boundaries were considered sensible and designed to make administration simpler. A small area of the north-eastern part of the parish, that was being developed as part of the Langley Park Estate, extended towards West Wickham and as the natural fall for drainage was to the north and west it would best be drained to Beckenham or West Wickham. This change amounted to the transfer of 145.9 acres and meant the eastern ends of Pickhurst Rise, Langley Way, Wickham Chase and The Avenue were no longer in the parish of Hayes. Another correction was where the boundary previously cut through 5 Station Road (Bourne Way) and required that rates had to be paid to two authorities. It was also proposed to take the sewer that took drainage to the West Kent Main Sewer into the area of one authority and this resulted in the transfer of 9.7 acres to Hayes. A third change concerned Fox Lane and Gates Green Road on the extreme southern edge of the parish. Again, it related to sewers and resulted in a transfer of land from West Wickham. The changes reduced the area of Hayes parish to 1136.3 acres, encompassing a population estimated at 1174 persons and yielding a rateable value of £12,093.[117]

**Map 8:** *Proposed boundaries of new Bromley Borough 1934, showing the effect on Hayes*

Changing the administrative boundary was only one part of the adjustments to the parish. The ecclesiastical boundaries also needed realignment and the Rector wrote to the Diocese of Rochester asking for advice as the part of Hayes transferred to West Wickham meant it would fall under the diocese of Canterbury. The opportunity was taken by the church authorities to introduce other changes and to create new parishes that affected the parishes of Beckenham and Bromley.[118] The most northerly part of the parish to the west of Pickhurst Lane became part of the new parish of St Barnabas, Beckenham. The area to the northwest, comprising Wickham Chase, Langley Way, Pickhurst Rise and The Avenue, was transferred to the new parish of St Francis of Assisi, West Wickham. The small section containing Barnhill and Eccleshill was transferred to the parish of Bromley, as was the part to the north of Mead Way.

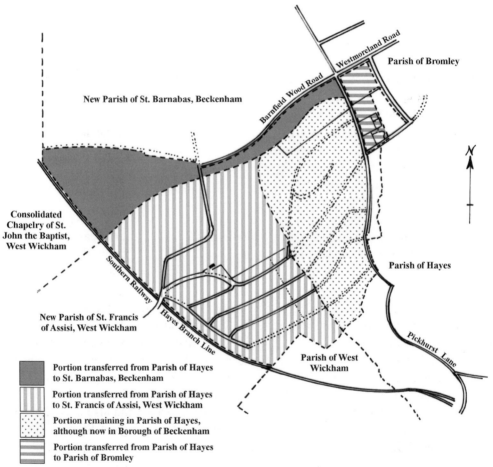

Map 9: *Ecclesiastical Parish Changes 1938*

The void that would be left by the outgoing HPC, and the sense that Hayes was one of many local villages being swallowed up by the seemingly remote new Borough Council, was recognised early on. Old villagers and newcomers alike needed and wanted to establish some form of voice and influence with the new Council. There was, of course, opportunity for Hayes people to become Bromley Borough Councillors and some residents were candidates. These included Lieutenant Colonel Fulcher of Hayes Road; William Hughes, a bank official living at 75 Hayes Wood Avenue; Percy Jones, a gardener of Redgate Cottage; John Barry of 36 The Knoll and George Evans of Hayes Street.[119] George Evans and Lieutenant Colonel George Fulcher were the successful candidates. However, some form of non-political representation was needed.

## Hayes Village Association

HCC had never needed to be involved in village matters because HPC was able and efficient in representing the inhabitants. With the demise of HPC and the decision of HCC not to fill the void, the need for an organisation to represent the village became urgent. William Hughes spoke to other neighbours under a lamppost one evening about forming a ratepayers' association to protect their interests.[120] The men quickly drafted, printed and delivered 200 handbills around the village calling a meeting in the Parish Room to discuss the need for such an organisation. On 9 November 1933 the little room at 3 St Mary Cottages was packed with about 30 residents. Agreement was quickly reached and the Hayes Village and District Association (Kent) (HVDA) came into being. The meeting appointed a steering group to administer the Association's affairs until a public meeting could be held on 7th December.

The December meeting held in the Village Hall and chaired by the new Rector, Revd E McClintock, was a great success with about 180 residents attending. Many of the audience expressed their concerns; these ranged from builders' advertisement hoardings, school facilities and tree planting to railway fares. The formal election of officers and committee members took place. Arthur Collins of Greenways, who was not present, was proposed as chairman but he later declined and Revd E McClintock was subsequently elected. William Hughes became Hon Secretary and R W Rosser Treasurer, supported by Messrs Atkinson, Barnsley, Evans, Hookway, Jeffery, Kanaar, Shirley, Stevens, Walford, Wyatt, Dr C Barrington, Dr J Hopton and Misses Harrod, Page and Mrs Place.[121]

The next public meeting was held in January 1934, the rules of the Association were discussed and with a few changes were ready for approval at the April AGM. Apart from protecting residents' interests, suggestions were made to form debating and drama sections and to develop a social side of the Association. Again this meeting was well supported with 150 attending out of a membership of 300. It was reported that a milk-bottling depot might be built in a Hayes residential area and that the newly formed Hayes Players was now affiliated to the Association; a Whist Drive had also been held. Four more committee members were elected: Councillor Miss Margaret Stafford Smith of Baston School, Dr Katherine Barrington, and Messrs Hickman and Knight.[122]

In the early days Coney Hall was seen by many to be allied to Hayes and a number of residents from the estate became members of HVDA. In January 1934 the committee received a letter from West Wickham Residents Association (WWRA) which pointed out that, as Coney Hall Estate would eventually be under Beckenham Urban District Council, the WWRA would represent the residents living in Coney Hall. This brought a strong reaction from Mr Jeffery, the Coney Hall representative on HVDA Committee.

He said:

> WWRA had not approached the Coney Hall residents in any way whatsoever and …
> there had been … a proposal to form a separate Coney Hall Association.

With the formation of the new Coney Hall and District Residents Association, HVDA transferred details of their Coney Hall members to the new organisation, bringing the matter to an end and to some extent lessening the closeness of the two areas. The reference to 'District' in the Association's name had been brought about by the representation of Coney Hall residents but in 1934 it was apparent that its use might lead to confusion of the geographical area of influence. To overcome this it was decided to change the name to Hayes (Kent) Village Association (HVA), which is the title still used today.[123]

During the early days the HVA was, in the opinion of its chairman, instrumental in obtaining improved postal services, better street lighting, the planting of trees, a more frequent bus service and was wholly responsible for the formation of the Hayes Common Rangers. Social activities included dances, concerts and also the promotion of the Horticultural Society, Drama Study Circle and Swimming Club events. In 1937 a local newspaper reported that, 'the HVA have continued to do good work' and its membership exceeded 1,000 households.[124] Throughout the first six years HVA concerned itself with many neighbourhood problems and the active promotion of the Hayes culture and spirit. It made a significant contribution to the modern history of Hayes.

# Chapter 3
## The end of the village?

A journalist called 'Hugo' wrote about a visit to Hayes in 1927:

> ... I like Hayes. I like it for lots of things, but I don't like it as I used to like it. I hate the changes and Hayes is changing. ... You don't see the changes so much as feel them. I should like to shove the village a little further out; it seems to have come too near Bromley. The 'buses have done that and the builder. True he's built some delectable dwellings this side of Socket Lane, and much as I envy the dweller in *Chef d'Oeuvre* and in the pretty pergolated cot this side of it with crazy paving, trim lawn and rambling roses – yet I wish the old lane had been left as it was in years gone by. Still beyond these dolls' houses there still stands the weather worn brick wall of Hayes Place and I want it to stand there forever. But I feel it won't.
>
> ... I dread the coming of the Hayes Place Building Estate – with its big board, and its big letters proclaiming the agent's name and the wisdom of buying a labour saving house.
>
> ... Still let us enjoy Hayes while we may ... A board outside the station proclaims the six minute proximity of the George (Inn as it used to be) Hotel it is now. And what a dear old inn it was, even if you didn't like the beer ... There are still a few quaint things to see to remind us of the old days. There's a timbered cottage with an old rusty fire plate [mark] still upon it; there's a seat outside the Rectory with its admonition to the despoiler. Near too, is printed the procedure to be followed in case of fire. "You ring up the Fire Brigade, Orpington; no number necessary: Tell them the address of the fire and then notify Captain Thompson at the Rectory." I like all such reminders of the still existing rural circumstance, but it is not for these things I like Hayes. It is for the people. I'm sure they are a happy community...[1]

This is one person's view but it reflects the mood of many at the start of the extensive changes.

The year 1931 was the turning point in the life and history of Hayes. A significant portion of the parish was in the ownership of developers and builders and within a few years over 1,000 houses had been built, drains laid, roads constructed and named, shops erected and opened for business. This change had been foretold in 1927 and the message repeated in 1928, although the timing was wrong. The *Bromley Times* reported:

> slowly, but surely, building operations are creeping along Hayes Lane and although there is no immediate danger of the picturesque little village of Hayes losing its beauty by the encroachment of new bricks and mortar, it needs no stretch of the imagination to foresee such a catastrophe within the next decade.

Yet in 1931 the same paper wrote:

> one thing should be remembered: those people who are coming to live at Hayes Place will probably enjoy their new surroundings, even if, to old residents, their coming seems to be something in the nature of an intrusion.[2]

An advantage for developers and estate agents was that Hayes had a ready-made railway connection to London. An added benefit was that the West Wickham & Hayes Railway was electrified in September 1925 as part of the Southern Railway network electrification scheme; the first major rail improvement since the line was opened in 1882. For some months it was used to convert train drivers from steam to electric traction and by 1926 a limited service operated, despite some power supply problems.[3] Thus, the conditions were right for the development of Hayes.

*Hayes Station, 1930*[4]

Railway trains and horse drawn coaches had met the needs of villagers since the 1880s. Motorbuses came to Hayes after the First World War and were provided by the London General Omnibus Company using open top deck buses made by Tilling Stevens. In 1921 route 136A went from Lewisham to Westerham Hill via Hayes. But in December 1924 the route became the 146 and then in 1933, at the height of housing development, it was split into 146A and 146B to Downe and Westerham Hill respectively, when the London Transport Executive took over the management of bus services. The service was daily every 20 minutes and every 15 minutes on Sunday.

At first the only service from Coney Hall to Hayes Station was provided by a coach run by the builders, Morell Brothers Ltd. In 1937, Route 232, using single decker Ts, was introduced to replace it and ran from Bromley North to Princes Way, Coney Hall. In 1940 the route number was changed to 138. The last route to be introduced before war broke out was in 1939 when West Wickham and Hayes were linked by bus route 119 which went from Bromley North to Barclay Road, Croydon.[4] When the original bus services started some people were concerned at the loss of rural peace. One person wrote to *The Times* deploring the 'Invasion of Hayes … That this quiet neighbourhood should be suddenly, on Sundays, turned into pandemonium by motor buses passing and re-passing every 7 minutes … is intolerable.'[5]

# Roads and Traffic

The roads of Hayes were neither designed to take the increase in numbers nor the physical size of cars, lorries and buses of the time. The road widths needed to be increased and dangerous bends, corners and obstructions removed. Conflict between motorist and horse riders frequently surfaced. 'A plea that us old fogies with our horses should be considered as well as the lunatics in motors' was made by a gentleman who complained to BRDC of the state of the main road at Pickhurst Green. The *Bromley Mercury* reported a complaint that 'the road which had been recently tar-painted, was covered with large pebbles rendering it absolutely dangerous and liable to make one use all sorts of language.' Another wrote:

> the pebbles were so slippery that horses could not stand, and suggested that to repair a road in such a fashion was not the way to spend ratepayers' money. It shows a complete lack of consideration for those who used the road …

Mr W O Joynson said a lot of large round gravel had been used on the roads and it was unsuitable for the horses but the highway surveyor reported:

> that he had inspected the road and could find no cause for complaint. The gravel used for the surface was the best obtainable for the purpose and was procured from the Hayes gravel pits.[6]

HPC records are full of road related activity. An early scheme to make a by-pass road across Hayes Common, known as the Central Common Road, brought many protests.[7] A few months after Sir Everard Hambro's death, HPC wrote to Sir Eric Hambro to thank him for removing trees and shrubs at the corner of Beckenham Lane (Pickhurst Lane) and Hayes Street, thus reducing the danger to road users. At the same time it was announced that the plan to build a new road from Bromley Common across the fields to the rear of the George Inn had been abandoned. HPC proposed that the land should be scheduled for allotments and recreation.[8]

As motor transport increased and became integral to normal village life, the pressure on local authorities to deal with roads and road safety grew. The number of accidents rose. Pedestrians, drivers and other road users were all vulnerable. In 1924, for example, two motorcars collided at Hayes Common and two years later there were two further accidents on the common, one at the intersection of the Croydon and Baston Roads where RWKR Cadets gave assistance. At the same time there was a fatal accident in Hayes Lane and another in Baston Road where 68-year-old Charles Church, a gardener who lived at Baston Manor Lodge, was knocked down by a motorcyclist and died. The Rector in his monthly letter complained that the road from Coney Hill to the Fox Inn was being used as a race track.[9]

In 1927 there was a call to white line and widen the junction at Hayes Lane and Hayes Road as there was no room for buses to turn and it was a most dangerous corner. In 1929 HPC applied to the Ministry of Transport for the classification of Hayes Road. It was deferred until a traffic census had been taken. In 1931 there were requests for white lines at the junction of Tiepigs Lane (Hayes Hill Road) and Beckenham Lane (Pickhurst Lane) to be marked with the word 'Slow'.[10]

In the next decade, with the growth in population and transport, the number of accidents increased. Another crash on the common led to the death of a woman; excessive speed was blamed. A lorry driven by James Cook of Meadow View, George Lane, knocked down a lamp-post opposite Beckenham Lane. He managed to stop the escape of gas from the lamp by plugging the leak with a rag. To cater for greater volumes of traffic, plans emerged to widen the road to Hayes Common at Keston Mark, which meant a 60ft wide road across the whole of the common.[11]

One of the first concerns of Bromley Borough Council, when it replaced BRDC, was the decisions on road widths that had been made and implemented, particularly those concerning Hayes Lane, Hayes Street and Station Approach. By 1933 many of the building sites along the eastern side of Hayes Lane had houses whose owners opposed Bromley Council's plans to widen Hayes Lane by as much as 60ft in parts. The extent of the scheme became public in the Council's 'Compulsory Purchase Order' of 5 June 1935, which listed 55 properties and parcels of land that would be affected, stretching from Hayesford Farm, leased by George Hoeltschi Snr, to Hayes Rectory. Virtually all the properties were on the eastern side of Hayes Lane and would lose part of their gardens and frontage.[12]

Householders were angry and at a Public Inquiry, held in October, Mr B Waddy objected on behalf of fifteen residents. Mr Arthur Bolton of 107 Hayes Lane said his front garden would be cut in half. He was the builder of four houses that had been constructed according to the original 40ft wide road plan. He considered a 5ft pedestrian path was sufficient. Mr Forster of 89 Hayes Lane had built his house on an assurance from the Town Clerk that the road would probably be 40ft. He felt that there was no need for wide footpaths as there was little pedestrian traffic. The Inquiry lasted three hours, after which the officials inspected the properties affected. The objections were noted but the widening went ahead. Road widening did not make roads safer; a magistrate remarked: 'sorry to have so many speed cases from Hayes Lane. The fact that it has been widened and modernised seems to have created an appetite for speed'.[13]

Further fatal accidents at the junction of Baston and Croydon Roads resulted in a proposal for traffic lights to be erected at a cost of £649. KCC agreed to pay £130 but the Ministry of Transport favoured a roundabout, a plan deplored by HVA and the Common Conservators who said that traffic lights would assist pedestrians to cross the road and could be installed without taking common land. Throughout 1937 and the first half of 1938 there was much correspondence between the interested parties. HVA asked Bromley's MP to intervene. He reported that in the last eighteen months there had been 27 accidents resulting in two deaths, eleven people seriously and many slightly injured. To support the case for traffic lights the HVA conducted a traffic census on Croydon Road over a weekend 23/24 April. The results for travellers from Coney Hall towards Hayes were:

|  | Saturday | Sunday |
|---|---|---|
| Cars | 963 | 1413 |
| Motorcycles | 97 | 181 |
| Commercial Vehicles | 149 | 30 |
| Buses | 1 | 5 |
| Cycles | 160 | 268 |

The total number of vehicles on Sunday passing the crossroads in all directions was 6,257; 1,356 used the Baston Road from Hayes and 1,151 from Keston, 1,897 the Croydon Road from Coney Hall and 1,853 from the direction of Farnborough.[14] The figures clearly showed the interest in cycling and motoring for pleasure on Sundays. The argument continued but the protests were eventually successful and, in October 1938, Bromley Council advised the Conservators that lights were to be installed. A year later they were working. This was the first major campaign to be organised for the community jointly by the Hayes Common Conservators and HVA.

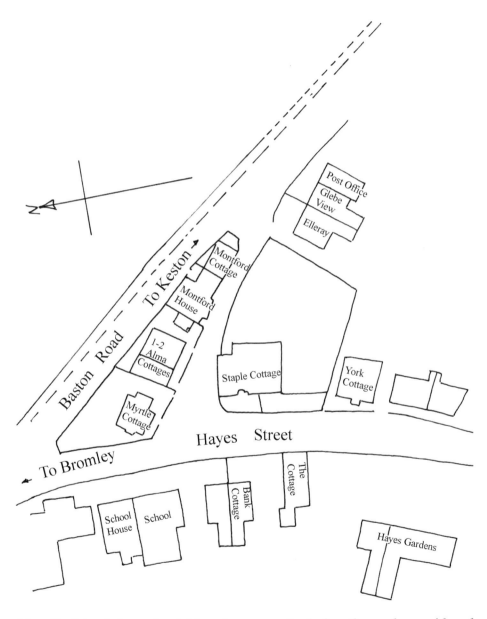

**Map 10:** *Island site and neighbouring properties before the road was widened*

Another widening scheme that was to have a dramatic effect concerned the 'upper village'. Baston Road and Hayes Street (later West Common Road), where they passed either side of the Island site near the Church School, were very narrow and inadequate for modern traffic. Late in 1934 it was reported that the Island site was to be bought by the Council and demolished to enable the roads to be widened. On 3 April 1935 Bromley Borough Council published Compulsory Purchase Order No.3 covering the acquisition of Myrtle Cottage, 1 & 2 Alma Cottages (William Banfield), Montford House and Cottage (Mrs Mary Ann Russell), a parcel of land near Elleray (Albert Collard) and a portion of the front garden of York Cottage (executors of James Fabb).[15] Staple Cottage, previously owned by Albert Collard and occupied by Ralph William Smith, was not listed in the Compulsory Purchase Order because it had already been bought by Bromley Council for £2,500 on 23 November 1934.[16] By September 1935 the cottages that featured on so many postcards had been completely demolished. The road works were finished and pavements and a green made by February 1936. The scheme later needed adjustment as larger vehicles had difficulty turning out of West Common Road as the exit was still narrow.[17]

*Robert Pearce, Postmaster 1894 - 1934*[z]

Naming the new roads generated the interest of the villagers during the redevelopment period. In 1930 a local reporter wrote 'In Hayes they don't go in for anything so old fashioned as street names', after a letter was delivered to 'Mr Mark Friend No.1 The Village, Hayes'. Mark Friend was living with his wife in Wood Cottages just by the George Inn at a time when the postman, Robert Pearce, knew everybody. He had been the postmaster since 1894 and when he retired at the age of 81, in 1934, he was reputed to be the oldest postman in England. It was estimated that he had walked 110,000 miles in the course of his duties. Elinor Harrold recalled that he 'was a small apple cheeked man with a Father Christmas beard, always smiling, but very difficult to understand as he muttered into his beard.' His daughter Amy ran the Post Office in Baston Road and, perhaps in preparation for the coming changes, a bay window was installed in the sitting room of their adjoining home, Glebe View, in 1931 and the room converted into a shop selling cakes and bread, sweets, chocolates, cigarettes and later ice cream. Six years later, Miss Pearce was presented with a clock when the Hayes postmen were transferred to the control of Bromley. On her retirement in 1940, the sub Post Office at Baston Road moved to 20 Hayes Street under Mr S W Freeman.

*Postmen in 1937 toasting the health of Miss Amy Pearce outside Hayes Post Office, after the presentation of an eight-day striking clock to her* [z]

With all the changes in Hayes, West Wickham, Beckenham and Bromley, some existing road names had to be altered to prevent confusion. One example is New Road, which derived its name from the 1760s when William Pitt, Earl of Chatham, moved the road to Beckenham further to the south of Hayes Place. New Road ran from the junction of Hayes Street and Pickhurst Lane to Hayes Hill Road. It was also known as Beckenham Lane. By early 1932 it had been renamed Pickhurst Lane throughout its length, from Hayes Street to Westmoreland Road.

In 1931 Lawrence De Thier of Station Road asked whether his road name could be changed as the postal authorities often confused it with Hayes, Middlesex. He said on one occasion he was stopped and asked where the (EMI) 'gramophone works' were. Station Road became Bourne Way and the part of the road in front of the Station became Station Approach, so as not to confuse it with Station Road in West Wickham. Hayes Hill Road, an extension of Tiepigs Lane, constructed in 1931, was for a period known as Furze Lane.[18] Other roads were named as the housing estates were developed (Appendix 3).

## Hundreds of New Houses

*'For Sale' boards start to go up. The Station fence is on the left and on the right the land to be sold for building some of the shops in Station Approach.* [1]

### Hayes Place Estate

In July 1931 Henry Boot Ltd received approval for 29 pairs of houses, probably at the east end of Mead Way and west side of Hayes Lane.[19] The following month the company gave its London District employees a party at Hayes Place and announced that plans for the whole area might be ready in two to three months.[20] The ambitious scheme for about 2,000 houses was approved by Bromley Council on 4th August although by the outbreak of the Second World War only 900 houses were completed. Some of the proposed estate roads never materialised.

Tracing the growth of the estate is difficult, as records have not been kept. Definitive house numbers were slow to be allocated so that early residents gave names to their homes or used plot numbers in their postal address.[21] Plot 550 in Bourne Vale, for instance, became No.3 in 1935 and the house named 'Little Gables' was No.5. This situation applied to most of the early roads on the estate and must have caused problems to the postal authorities.

As soon as Henry Boot Ltd received overall approval for the layout it quickly applied for blocks of houses in various roads. From 1931 onwards BRDC's records list many such applications: for example, February 1932, two pairs of houses in Pickhurst Lane and in November 1933 six pairs of houses in Bourne Vale and Hayes Lane. An application of particular interest was made in May 1934 and affected 2 and 4 Mead Way. The plans were to an 'International' design, inspired by Bauhaus, with flat roofs. After seeing these two properties and others in Gates Green Road, Coney Hall, the Council decided not to allow any more flat roofed houses.[19]

Henry Boot Garden Estates Ltd was set up to market the properties through well-illustrated brochures that showed photographs of the railway station, shops and newly constructed houses in Stanhope and Sackville Avenues, accompanied by the phrases 'Come to Hayes for good health' and 'no less than 11 acres of this beautiful estate ... are reserved as open spaces'. In 1937 Henry Boot offered to dedicate, free of charge, three plots of land earmarked as open spaces that remain to this today - The Green, the areas at the junction of Stanhope and Sackville Avenues, and off Bourne Vale.[22] The brochures also mentioned the railway train times and that a monthly season ticket between Hayes and Charing Cross, London, was £1 14s. 0d. Boot advertised the houses in the national press under the banner 'semi-detached freehold £595- £5 secures' and used estate agents, Messrs Summersell & Wadsworth of London, the company that had conducted the auction of the estate on behalf of Sir Eric Hambro.[23]

The company initially offered eight styles of houses, including a bungalow, with prices from £665 to £995. Later an additional seven designs were added to the portfolio. Mortgages were available from the Halifax Building Society against a deposit of about 6%. Repayment was over 23 years at, typically, £1 per week, an amount equal to about two days wages for a skilled worker in the building trade. Two, three and four bedroom houses, catering for all needs were built and, if required, a garage could be included for an additional £45.[24] Until the beginning of the war Boot had an office where prospective buyers could visit and obtain information, first at 'Show House Corner' in Pickhurst Lane, 80 – 90 Pickhurst Lane and later at a shop, 24 Hayes Street.

The first occupied houses were at the Hayes end of Bourne Vale, Husseywell Crescent and Stanhope Avenue during the latter part of 1932. By the following year families were moving into Chatham Avenue, Cherry Walk, Pickhurst Lane and Sackville Avenue. The pace of construction increased and more roads and houses were built to satisfy the demand. Cecil Way, Hambro Avenue, Everard Avenue and Stuart Avenue soon followed and the houses along the western side of Hayes Lane took from 1932 to 1937 to complete.

By about 1938 Dartmouth Road, Southbourne, Northbourne, and Kechill Gardens were developed, although the start of the war curtailed some house construction and completion.[25] Work on a number of houses was forced to stop and in many instances these were left as just foundations or shells. Others remained unsold.

TYPE "A" £850 FREEHOLD

TYPE "D" DETACHED £1,125 FREEHOLD
INCLUDING GARAGE

FRONT ELEVATION

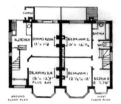

PRICE £850.    £10 SECURES.
£44 8s. ON OCCUPATION.
REPAYMENTS 25/6 PER WEEK.

FITTINGS.

All fittings and equipment are similar in every house
except where otherwise stated. The "A" Type house
differs only in that it has a bathroom whose walls are lined
to picture-rail height in Marbpanel.

POINTS THAT APPLY TO ALL HOUSES.

Average size of Plots : 35 ft. by 112 ft.
CAVITY WALLS.
ELEVATIONS : All differ ; monotony entirely absent.
GARAGE : Every plot has space for garage, which may be
erected if desired at a cost of £50.

GROUND FLOOR PLAN        FIRST FLOOR PLAN

PRICES AND TERMS.
PRICE £1,125          £10 SECURES.          £93 4s. ON OCCUPATION.
REPAYMENTS £6 11s. PER LUNAR MONTH.

TYPICAL KITCHEN (TYPE "D")

DINING ROOM (TYPE "D")

### Boot's Houses [q.]

Inevitably, the overall plan for the Hayes Place Estate changed from those published in 1930 and 1932. In February 1936 another version appeared showing part of Constance Crescent with 64 houses and more of Chatham Avenue with 10 homes. The new plan showed for the first time the retention of Bourne Cottage and two lodges but deleted two groups of three terraced houses planned for Chatham Avenue and Everard Avenue. Trevor Close was not shown and was probably an afterthought and included in the scheme after 1936.[26] It has been suggested that by 1938 Boot was feeling the effect of competition from other Hayes builders and finding it financially difficult. As a consequence, the company reduced the construction rate and devoted their main energies to new estates at Selsdon and New Addington, Surrey.

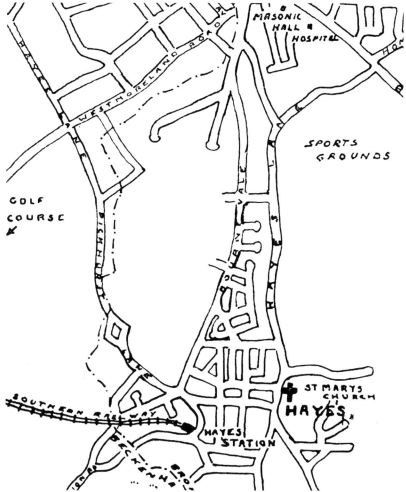

**Map 11:** *Development of Hayes Place Estate by 1935* [q.]
*The new Bromley boundary in the north west is shown.*
*A large area of the parish was still undeveloped.*

In spite of this, they were still advertising Hayes Place Estate houses six weeks before the outbreak of war at prices from £655 to £925 for 3 or 4 bedroom semi-detached houses with a garage. It was stated that 'only a few remain'.[19]

## The Bourne and Sewers

A necessary part of any housing development is the disposal of sewerage and the supply of water. These were major issues for the developers. In 1924 a sewerage scheme was finally agreed for Hayes. Three years later discussions started about the sewerage scheme for the Hayes Place Estate. Work on laying three miles of sewer pipes started in August 1929 and finished the following February.[27]

The Bourne, which for centuries had meandered across Hayes Bottom and Hayes Place, normally had a trickle of water but had the reputation of rising and causing localised flooding, as occurred in 1916 and 1927.[28] The original 1928 plan for Hayes

Place estate showed the Bourne following its natural course across the estate and it would appear that no decision had been taken on how to treat the stream. When Henry Boot & Sons produced their estate layout they planned that the Bourne would be diverted and put in a culvert from Tiepigs Lane to the south side of Southbourne and then flow by open watercourse to the north side of Mead Way. Initially, it would follow Sackville Avenue, part of Stuart Avenue, across the open space at Pittsmead Avenue, along the back of the gardens of houses on the east side of Dartmouth Road where it changed to an open channel. It proceeded via the gardens on the east side of Bourne Vale to the north side of Mead Way. The scheme was approved by BRDC. Bromley Town Council wanted the stream to be in a culvert throughout its length and the Ministry of Health asked for comments. The main reason for an open culvert was to guard against storm water from the whole area being suddenly concentrated into the Ravensbourne, which at the time was not capable of handling it.[29] BRDC's view was that an open watercourse would allow for soakage in flood times, but it acknowledged that the channel would soon be filled with rubbish and the sides would cave in if it was accessible to the public, particularly boys. Agreements were reached and work was undertaken to culvert the Bourne in 1934-35.

## Bromley Vale and Bromley Manor Estates

The first phase of the development of the Hayes Place estate mainly covered the roads to the east of Bourne Vale. Henry Boot Ltd, however, decided not to proceed with the remainder of the estate, the west side of Bourne Vale, and put the land on the market. The area was referred to in 1936 as Bromley Vale Estate but, later in the year, the name appears to apply to Bourne Vale (Nos.47 to 99) and Trevor Close only. The name Bromley Manor Estate was given to Constance Crescent, Chatham Avenue (high numbers) and the top end of Mounthurst Road. The houses in these roads were built by Williams A Phillips Ltd and T & H Estates Ltd; the latter were successors to Tysoe & Harris of Petts Wood who had been involved with building on land sold from the Hayes Grove Estate.

The agents did not restrain themselves when advertising their £650 houses:

> Bathroom Sensation! Bromley Manor was crowded out again last Sunday and potential purchasers were "pixyled" over the Coronation Bathroom – panelled out in opaque coloured glass. And this is only one of the many 1937 features incorporated in these modern homes which have been causing such a sensation at Hayes …

Most houses built in these roads were of the 'Suntrap' design with curved window panes in the front bay although many have now been replaced with flat double glazed panels. Constance Crescent and Chatham Avenue houses were built and occupied in 1937 and 1938; those at the top end of Mounthurst Road were mainly occupied in 1936 and 1939.[30]

Towards the end of the decade the remaining unbuilt areas of Hayes Place Estate changed ownership again and W L Cook & Company of Beckenham bought the area at the northern border of the parish. The company built the eastern end of Mead Way (Nos. 9-47 and 26-72) in 1938-39 and in September received permission to build houses in Hazelmere Way and Heath Rise.[31] When war broke out the plan was delayed.

## Hayes Garden and Hayes View Estates

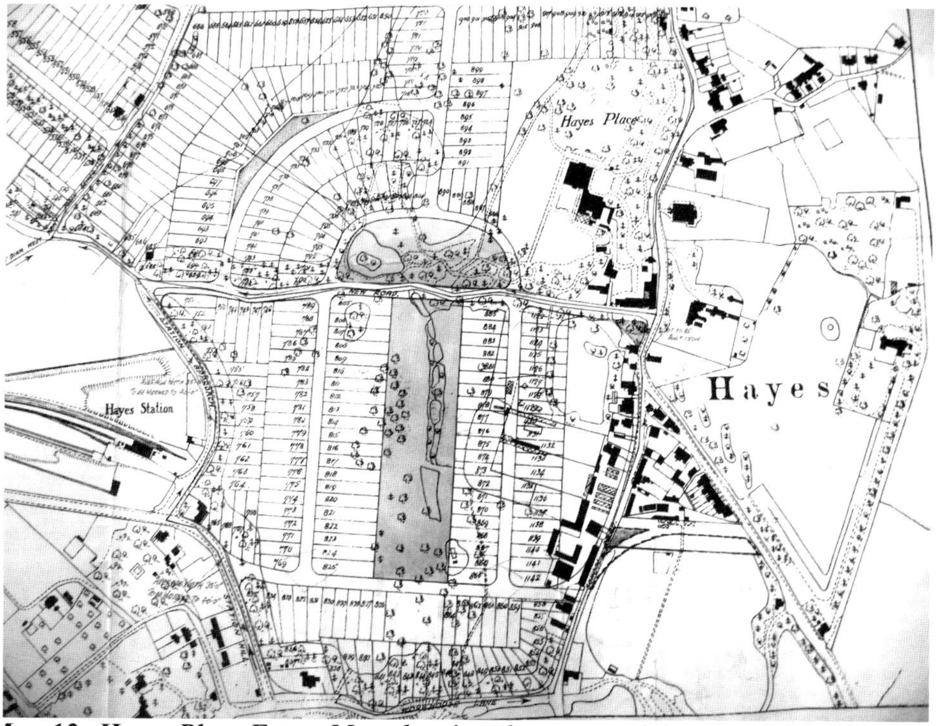

**Map 12:** *Hayes Place Estate Map showing the proposed development of the Knoll, Hayes Garden and Ridgeway* [aj.]

Hayes Garden and Hayes View Estates were developed on land that was part of Hayes Place sold in 1931. In May of that year the surveyor Hugh Thoburn developed plans for three new roads, Ridgeway, The Knoll and Hayes Garden. James Grandfield, proprietor of Hayes Gardens Nursery, was unhappy about the choice of name for the latter road and protested on the grounds that it would be detrimental to his business. HPC agreed and suggested to BRDC that an alternative be chosen but nothing happened.

Four builders were employed, Bleach & Skipper of Thornton Heath, J C Derby & Co. of Croydon, Keen & Sons and W A Jones. The southern side of Ridgeway was the first part to be built with 14 semi-detached houses occupied by 1932 and the remaining houses inhabited in 1933-34.[32] Two Hayes Place Farm cottages, near Gadsden, were demolished for the south side to be finished. The Knoll Park side of Ridgeway was completed during the following year.

In late 1931 Keen & Sons received Council approval for 60 houses, including some facing Pickhurst Lane. The sales brochure referred to this part of the estate as Hayes View. At the same time W A Jones received the go-ahead for 16 houses in The Knoll, although the majority in this road were built by Derby & Co. The other builder, Bleach & Skipper, built at the bottom end of Hayes Garden and at the Gadsden end of Ridgeway. Development proceeded quickly. The houses in The Knoll were all inhabited by the end of 1933 and in Hayes Garden by the beginning of 1934.[33]

The Derby & Co houses in Hayes Garden sold for £950 and the four styles of houses in the Knoll were advertised by Hugh F Thoburn Ltd at prices from £1,075 for a three bedroom house with garage to £1,195 in the case of four bedrooms. Hayes View Estate houses (Keen & Sons) were priced from £985 to £1,140.

*Ridgeway under construction, Hayes Place Farm buildings on left await demolition* [L]

## Glebe House Estate

Glebe House grounds were not immediately developed, because the area was almost completely surrounded by other property. The first plan for the estate by T Spencer Bright, who was involved with development of the Langley Way area, failed to materialise, as did a scheme by Baxter Payne & Lepper, the Bromley based company. By 1932, however, the grounds of Glebe House were bought and developed by Morrell (Builders) Ltd, a locally based firm, with an office in Bromley High Street. It was a difficult site to develop as road access was problematic since there was no access from the northern end where the estate bordered the gardens of Street House owned by the Norman family. Entrance from Baston Road was through the Lodge entrance opposite Gadsden. Soon Burwood Avenue was constructed, part of an unrealised plan to build a road from Baston Road to Oakley Road, Bromley Common. The houses in the two estate roads, Hayes Wood Avenue and Glebe House Drive, were of a standard style and were erected very quickly. It was reported that the houses were all sold within three weeks and occupied by 1933.

Miss Dorothy Dewey, who still lives in her parents' house in Glebe House Drive, recalled that her father was a gas engineer and involved with installing the gas in the new Morrell houses. He decided that they would buy one of the houses, as the monthly cost to buy was not much more than the rent on their existing property. They moved to Hayes in May 1933 along with other young families. The road was still unmade, the front gardens unfinished and a significant feature for those with prams was the deep step to the front door. Householders had a long walk to the shops and in 1933 a group of Glebe House Estate residents, helped by Lawrence De Thier, put their case for access to Hayes Street via George Lane to HPC. It agreed to approach the landowner but HPC's life was nearing its end and the situation was not helped when the developers went into liquidation. At one time residents used a short cut through Village Hall land but HCC objected and erected a gate and warning notice.[34] Access to the estate was not resolved until after the war.

*Glebe House Drive* [1.]

Within a few months of their purchase, some houses were advertised for sale in the local press. In August 1934, a semi-detached two bedroom house, 46 Hayes Wood Avenue, was on offer at £700 and surprisingly in 1937, No.71, a three bedroom house was offered at £625.[35] Once residents had moved into their new houses they very quickly expressed concern at the drainage problems and delay in surfacing the two roads. At a meeting organised by HVA, C H Morrell, one of the owners of the building company, assured residents that surfacing work would commence within two weeks. He explained that the problem arose because there was no surface water sewer available in which to discharge the water and his company had declined to surface the roads until Bromley Council provided one. The plan was to connect the sewer to one in George Lane but, as neither Bromley Council nor the builders owned the land between the north end of Hayes Wood Avenue and George Lane, nothing could be done. Until then the surface water was discharged into a nearby pond. HVA was approached to see if it would take over ownership and responsibility for the pond's care and maintenance. Wisely it declined. The quality of the estate roads remained a source of complaint for at least nine months but the work was finished in early 1935.[36]

In 1930, 900ft of Glebe House land fronting Baston Road was advertised for sale and by 1933 plans had been prepared for a parade of shops to be built opposite the post office in Baston Road. This scheme failed to materialise but the ground, which ran from the Rectory gardens to Elmhurst Villas, was used to build maisonettes in 1938. The first maisonettes in Hayes had been built in Burwood Avenue in 1934. HVA members had complained and written to the council, 'deploring the ugly flats in Burwood Avenue particularly the massing of front doors and asking that such unsightly elevation will not be approved in the future'. The council replied that the maisonettes to be built in Baston Road would have two doors at the front and one door on either side. The houses built on the west side of Baston Road, just south of Gadsden were built about 1938–39 by L T Pryor and others.[37]

The building of the Glebe House Estate was followed by the much larger development of Coney Hall, West Wickham, where Morrell's brochures made great mention of Hayes and its train service to London. In 1933, when Morrells started work on Coney Hall, the competition between builders was fierce and their estate was isolated from public transport and not necessarily seen as attractive to prospective house owners. To overcome this situation Morrells, prior to the introduction of a bus route in August 1937, operated a private service running from Hayes Station to Coney Hall about every 12 minutes 'for the use of residents and visitors, free of charge'.[38] Morrells were prevented from charging fares by the statutory monopoly of London Transport but ran the service with one Leyland Cub single deck, 25 seater, bus from January 1934.[39]

## Pickhurst Manor Estate

Local builder, George Spencer, not only bought the Pickhurst Manor estate but also purchased from the Southern Railway Company the land where Hayes Railway Station was originally to have been built in Station Approach.

The first 'Spencer' houses were built in Pickhurst Lane nearest to Station Approach and 31 to 53 Pickhurst Lane received approval on 9 June 1932. These were aimed to compete with the houses of Henry Boot & Sons Ltd and those sold by Hugh Thoburn. George Spencer offered about five different designs, all but one was semi-detached, and they were sold through Hayes estate agents Killick & Knight at prices ranging from £710 for a two bedroom house, £810 for three bedrooms to £895 if it was detached.[40] As with Boot's, Spencer houses were of sound construction and well finished and the estate roads were completed, unlike the Glebe House, Hayes Garden and Bromley Manors estates where they were a major problem. Spencer built all the houses in Hurstdene Avenue, Hurst Close, Dene Close, Hayes Hill Road, Courtlands Avenue and Hilldown Road. Occupation of the estate started in Hurstdene Avenue in 1933 and finished in Courtlands Avenue about 1936.[41]

In 1935 the Company's attention was turned towards 'up market' houses and the vacant plots in Hayes Hill were completed by 1939. Some of the houses in Briar Gardens were to Spencer's design but were built for him by small local builders, typically R I Aitchison, and each took five to six months to complete, once local authority approval was secured. George Spencer did not build 55 Pickhurst Lane, on the corner of Hurstdene Avenue, but sold the plot to H & D Winn Ltd. who obtained approval in June 1933.[42]

Two plots within George Spencer's Pickhurst Manor estate were not developed for houses. They were the lower part of Station Approach that became the cinema and the manor house frontage along Pickhurst Lane, including the Lodge that was used by the Free Church authorities.

# The Smaller Estates

## Hayes Grove and Hayes Grove Estate

When Harold Hambro sold The Grove in 1930, eight acres of the grounds were purchased by the builders Tysoe & Harris Ltd. Herbert W Woolidge of Catford announced that he had been 'appointed the sole selling agent for properties to be erected on this magnificent estate'.[43] The new estate was built as Grove Close, Hayes Close and Hayes Avenue, the latter becoming West Common Road. Within a month advertisements appeared: 'magnificent estate now being developed 3 minutes from station and adjoining the common, prices from £1,250'. In fact, the prices ranged from £1,395 to £2,500 for a detached 3, 4 or 5 bedroom house. The purchaser paid an additional £100 for plots overlooking Hayes Common or Hayes Grove House. The agent received 2½% commission. The houses in Grove Close were erected quickly; No.1 was used by Herbert Woolidge as the estate office and others were occupied in late 1930.[44]

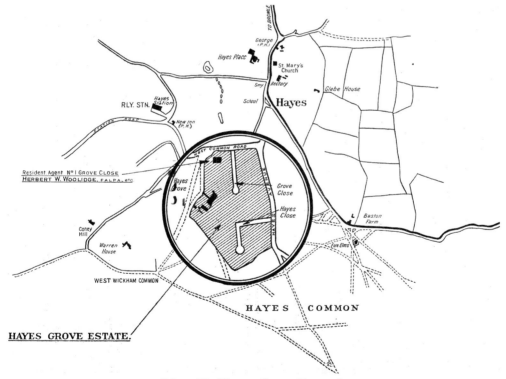

**Map 13:** *Hayes Grove Estate* [q.]

Tysoe & Harris also built nineteen well designed houses on the Grove's land in West Common Road during 1933 and 1934 (Nos. 68 to 104). Spinsters Laura, Marian and

Minnie Newport from Bromley bought 102 West Common Road on 29 October 1934.[45] Some houses in this road were built by Bleach & Skipper.

## Pickhurst Mead, Pickhurst Green and Crest Road Estates

By 1933, with most building land in the centre of Hayes being developed, some builders started to acquire sites that were some distance from the church and railway station. Bleach & Skipper bought the Pickhurst Mead Estate that consisted of Pickhurst Mead and the corresponding strip of Pickhurst Lane. Crest Road was also developed by the same builder who sought council approval for the plans in April 1934.[19] The houses in Crest Road, which were sold by Hugh F Thoburn Ltd., ranged in price from £785 to £840 depending on their position and whether they had a garage or three double bedrooms. They all boasted a 'Bright and modern Kitchenette, fitted tiled recess with "Wizard" all-mottle enamelled domestic boiler'.[46] In Pickhurst Mead the houses were generally to the same specification but, probably because of the location, were priced at £895 to £940. The Crest Road houses were completed by 1938 with Pickhurst Mead about a year later.[21]

As the name implies, Pickhurst Green Estate was bounded by the southern edge of Pickhurst Green. The houses were built by the Beckenham concern of W L Cook & Co. Ltd and occupied before 1937. They were marketed by Hugh F Thoburn Ltd and were of similar design and price to those in Pickhurst Mead.[47]

In 1937 a scheme to develop land adjoining Pickhurst Lane that was in the Borough of Beckenham went to public inquiry. The appellant wished to increase the density from six to eight houses per acre and to include the erection of sixteen shops and a petrol station, but the area had been designated for residential use. Hugh Thoburn claimed it would be uneconomic to build houses at six per acre when close by houses could be bought at £695. It was, however, alleged that Mr Sautoy who had bought the land in 1935 wished to sell it for a development that would 'turn the town planning schemes of Bromley and Beckenham upside down in order to make a success of a rather unfortunate speculation'. The inquiry reported that 632 residents had petitioned against the scheme. By the end of the year the Ministry of Health had dismissed the appeal on the basis that shops were within a reasonable distance and there were four petrol stations within a mile radius.

Another similar application, covering 83 acres of Hayes Place Estate, requested that the area be zoned from eight to ten houses per acre instead of the six to eight laid down by Bromley Council. Again, this was the subject of an inquiry. Over 550 residents from Bourne Vale, Mead Way, Pickhurst Green, Pickhurst Mead and Pickhurst Lane petitioned against the scheme as they had bought their houses on the understanding that the planned density would not increase. If it changed, their property value would decrease. The appellant argued that Bourne Vale had houses at twelve per acre and that the proposed development would not adversely affect the adjoining houses. He said that houses built at six per acre did not readily sell in this part of the borough, except for Pickhurst Mead where the Green was an attraction.[48]

## Warren Wood Estate

By 1935 it was confirmed that Warren Wood Estate had been sold and would be developed for housing by Durable Buildings Ltd. Hugh F Thoburn Ltd were the surveyors and sole selling agents and obtained approval from Beckenham Council as the majority of the land was in the parish of West Wickham. In spite of this the estate has always been thought of as a part of Hayes by most residents. The first road on the estate was originally Newlands Road but this name was never used by residents. By 1935 the builders obtained approval for it to be called Holland Way, a name that it has been suggested was chosen as the builders were Dutch.[49]

Initially, the estate consisted of Holland Way, Sandilands Crescent and the east section of Westland Drive; the latter was to be called Dale Rise. The houses were mainly detached with three, four or five bedrooms in ten styles and prices ranged from £1,025 to £1,700. The quality of these houses and their setting was recognised later by the London Borough of Bromley when the area was designated an 'Area of Special Residential Character'. Later Thoburns expanded the estate to the west and advertised it as 'Warren Wood (Extension) Hayes Kent'. The area included Abbotsbury Road and the remainder of Westland Drive. The houses cost from £1,125 to £1,375 and were completed and occupied by 1940.[50]

## Bourne Way Development

Like Warren Wood, Bourne Way is largely in West Wickham but was considered by the estate agents, and subsequently the residents, as part of Hayes. The development was handled by Thoburns and the houses erected on the south-side of Bourne Way were built by W Arthur & Son. Described as 'Artistic Modern Homes', the semi-detached, three bedroom houses were priced at £995.[51] A total of 31 houses were built and occupied between the beginning of 1933 and 1936. Nine were in the parish of Hayes.

## Shops and Commercial Developments

The original 1930s Boot's scheme envisaged a ring of shops around roads, named after the points of the compass, centred in Bourne Vale around green open space. This would have had a dramatic effect on Hayes moving the hub of the village to the north by a third of a mile towards Bromley (Map 6). Plans for these shops were dropped but South and East Way and Pittsmead Avenue were laid out and approved by Bromley Council in February 1938. The reality that shops in Station Approach were already trading was a factor influencing Boot's decision not to proceed.

A second parade of shops was planned by Henry Boot Ltd for the west side of Hayes Street, running from the junction of Pickhurst Lane to near the telephone exchange. Henry Boot Ltd, however, only built twelve shops known as Premier Parade (18 to 40 Hayes Street). The council approved the first nine units, with flats above, in April 1932. The first trader was C A Smallbone Ltd, a wine and spirit merchant, who opened for business about 1933 (No.38). By the next year a grocer, fruiterer, boot repairers and ladies' hairdresser all started business and at the beginning of the war all but two shops were occupied; No. 32 was empty and No. 24 was used by Henry Boot as their estate office.[21]

Premier Parade was not the only shopping area. The east side of Station Approach was considered for housing development in the initial plan of 1928. The west side was Southern Railway property and not part of the scheme, although HPC suggested in February 1930 that the land around the station should be used as a shopping area. In fact

***Premier Parade under construction. Hayes Place is in the background*** [l.]

the railway authorities had already written to BRDC explaining that they wished to dispose of the land.

George Spencer bought a strip of land in Station Approach from Southern Railway that was surplus to its requirements with plans to erect nineteen shops with flats above (Nos. 12-48). Such was the rivalry of builders, that Hugh Thoburn, whose offices were opposite, lodged a formal objection to Spencer's plans. This objection came to nothing and Spencer erected the shops from late 1931. The first (No.48) was occupied by Killick & Knight, his estate agents. The shops matched the Spencer houses – a Tudor style with large bargeboards and Tudor lintels for the porches. The exception was 12 Station Approach, which was said to be in neo-Queen Anne style, complementing the Osborne & Sons' off-licence opposite at 29 Pickhurst Lane that was designed by the Whitbread brewing concern.[52] Some of the companies that moved in had been supplying products to Hayes for sometime. Mac Fisheries Ltd made daily deliveries to Hayes, Keston and West Wickham as early as 1926, thus it was natural they should open a shop in Station Approach.[53]

When the Station was rebuilt and the Station Master's house demolished, further shops were built and continued into Bourne Way. The lease of the land for 50 to 58 Station Approach was made on 24 June 1932 and for 68 to 72 Station Approach and 2 to 12 Bourne Way on 24 February 1933. In April 1935 Hugh F Thoburn Ltd auctioned the shops. The sales brochure referred to 14 'Capital Shop Premises' for investment that could initially yield £1,150 per annum. The individual shop rents varied but ranged from £75 to £100 per annum.[54]

*Station Master's House, Station Approach* [j.]

*Station Approach west side*
*The Station Master's house has been demolished* [j.]

The land on the east side of Station Approach was also sold for shops. In May 1931 Thoburn's plan for the shops included a vehicle 'standing bay', as did the plan for the shops on the other side. From the outset BRDC recommended that the Station Approach carriageway should be 40ft wide with 20ft building lines and the shops on both sides were built in accordance with this requirement.

***Pickhurst Lane end of Station Approach awaiting development*** [j.]

When Bromley Borough Council assumed the responsibilities of BRDC they were very concerned at the general speed of development in Hayes and strongly protested that building work had overtaken the provision of local services to an alarming extent. The Council considered the best method of dealing with Station Approach to make it an attractive shopping centre and concluded that it was not in everybody's interest for the road to remain of 'byway width' with large forecourts owned and used by the shop keepers. The Council, therefore, proposed that Station Approach would be a dual carriageway 25ft wide with a central reservation and 12ft wide footpaths. The majority of the shop owners supported the scheme but a small minority were not prepared to lose part of their frontage even after protracted negotiations. As a result the Council made a Compulsory Purchase Order in 1936. Because of the objections the Ministry of Transport held an inquiry, after which the scheme was approved. In July 1936 tenders were requested to undertake the construction work, which was started in late 1936.[55]

The shops on the east side were begun in 1931, progressed down the road and were completed about 1938. The shops had flats above. Nos. 5 to 27 were built by Messrs Bovis and 29 to 57 by Bleach & Skipper.

*Station Approach east side. The station fencing can be seen on the left* [j.]

*Making up the road in Station Approach* [j.]

In late 1936 the ground floor of 4 St Mary Cottages (24 Baston Road) was converted into a confectionery shop that later became known as the 'Tuck Shop'.[56]

From 1931 to about 1938 eighty shops and businesses had opened in Hayes, the majority of which were retail outlets geared to support the new community of Hayes. The original village shops such as The Walnut Tree (Hayes Street), Hayes Village Stores (West Common Road) and Walter Foat, the butcher, in St Mary Cottages continued to survive and were patronised by both old villagers and newcomers.

The list of shops (Appendix 2) in Station Approach and Hayes Street shows that Hayes was well covered for everyday living. This was important as most houses did not possess a refrigerator or a car and family shopping was often undertaken daily.

## Business

The first businesses to trade were the estate agents Killick & Knight and Hugh Thoburn who were almost opposite each other. Thoburn initially traded from temporary offices next to the New Inn until No.57 was built.

*Thoburn Estate Office, Station Approach* [L]

H C Enright, the confectioners and newsagents, also traded from a temporary building located on the site of No.55. It was on 1 June 1933 that the Post Office opened in Enright's shop. Interestingly the Post Office retained the original name of Station Road and did not change to Station Approach.[57]

Land behind the shops on the west side of Station Approach was also used. Express Dairy built a milk distribution depot and made deliveries to Hayes using horse drawn milk floats. The other company to use this land was M A Ray & Sons who had their yard and stores just behind their shop.

In June 1933 rumours started that Hayes was to have a cinema, to be built on land at the north end of Station Approach, surplus to George Spencer's needs. By November the following year hoardings appeared on the site announcing that General Cinema Theatres Ltd. were to build the cinema and in November 1935 construction work commenced. The foundations were laid by Pitchers of Holloway and the builders were C H Gibson of Croydon, who also built the New Inn and the Plaza Cinema, West Wickham, that opened in September 1933. Construction proceeded quickly and the Rex Cinema opened on 6 August 1936, just ten months after the start.[58]

*Rex Cinema, opened August 1936* [j.]

The cinema, designed by Mr Cecil Masey FRIBA, consisted of a vestibule with pay kiosk and a large foyer with three distinct entrances into the rear of the stalls where all seats had an uninterrupted view of the stage. The balcony was a single span reached by a staircase, which opened into another large foyer with entrances on either side. It was built with red bricks, white concrete and had a corrugated asbestos roof. Originally there were to be 1,500 seats but that was reduced to 1,077 and, with the agreement of the Bromley Licensing Committee, 48 people could stand inside the auditorium at the back of the stalls, 60 people might wait for admission in the inner vestibule and 70 could wait against the wall in the circle foyer in a line two deep.[59] The Rex's café was well patronised by Hayes organisations and families for wedding receptions and parties and at the rear of the building there was a free car park.

The cinema projection equipment was by Ross with a British Thompson-Houston sound system powered by 'National' oil engine generators.[60] Some months before the cinema opened objections were voiced about the smell and noise that the proposed power generation system would cause. Bromley Council refused to grant permission for the powerhouse. HVA were pleased and wrote 'thanking them for the action'. The cinema company appealed to the Ministry of Health who gave consent and work started. It was understood that the noise would be eliminated. A month after the opening of the cinema residents close to it complained that they had 'been troubled by noise from the generator, glare from the lights' in the car park and the 'ugliness of a series of cooling tanks'. The HVA wrote to the company and to the Ministry of Health who replied 'that the Minister has no jurisdiction in the matter'. The Town Clerk of Bromley Council said that if it was asked for its views he would inform the Minister that it sympathised with the residents. The cinema company took measures to improve the situation and at HVA's General Meeting in January 1937 it was said that 'the only steps which could be taken, if there were a nuisance, would be court action'.[61] HVA approached the Anti-Noise League for advice and held meetings with the affected residents over many weeks, although no major changes appear to have been made to the installation.

*Hayes Telephone Exchange* [m.]

Telegraphs and telephones had been in use in Hayes from before the First World War but, in the case of the latter, only in the houses of the wealthy. By 1926 some tradesmen had them installed and the first to appear in the *Hayes Street Directory* was Edwin Tidbury, a taxi driver. His number was Ravensbourne 0172 from the Bromley Exchange. It was not until the beginning of the 1930s that telephones started to be installed in any great numbers and became a selling point for houses; for example, an advertisement appeared in September 1931 for an 'Artistic modern detached house, three bedrooms, two reception rooms, telephone, five minutes from station - £1400'. With the growth of telephone usage the authorities decided in 1929 to switch Hayes telephones from the Ravensbourne Exchange to a new exchange called 'Hurstway'.

Growth continued with no signs of abating and private numbers started to appear in the street directories. Plans were prepared and construction commenced in September 1934 for the Hurstway Exchange to be located in Hayes Street. It was built to a fairly standard GPO pattern, brick constructed, two storey, with a pitched roof, and was completed, equipped and opened on 5 December 1935.[63] All Hayes telephone subscribers were allocated new numbers and Edwin Tidbury's became 'Hurstway 1013'.[62] In May 1935 a telephone was installed in the Village School.

To meet the needs of the growing motoring community a motor garage with servicing facilities was built on a plot of land at the north end of Station Approach. Known as 'Surridge's', it opened about 1932 but changed in 1933 into Hugh K Campbell's ownership and was called 'Campbell's Garage'. It survived well into the late 1960s as a service and repair garage after which it became a self-service petrol station.

The last blacksmith at the forge was Mr Thomas Collins who started in Hayes in 1914 and retired in June 1931. The old building and land were sold as part of the Hambro estate and demolished in July 1931.

The loss was lamented by many:

> The whole world has shaken and shuddered but the forge has stood firm and unmoved – until the unquenchable force was directed towards it. Modernisation, progress will leave nothing alone; everything must go … On the spot where thousands of horse shoes were made and hundreds of horses were shod, motor-cars are going to be tyred, and have their tanks filled.

Part of the land was used for road widening when the Island site was demolished. The remainder was used to build another garage to sell petrol and service cars. It traded as Hayes (Kent) Garage Ltd.[64]

The Railway Station had served Hayes for nearly 50 years but by 1931 it was apparent that, with the influx of so many people, many of whom worked outside the district, there was a need to improve the facilities. Southern Railway's General Manager, Sir Herbert Walker, visited Hayes in 1931 to assess the practicalities of redeveloping the station. By 1933 villagers knew that it was to be rebuilt with an arcade entrance to a concourse, a 200ft long platform roof, a special loading dock and parcels' office. The new scheme incorporated a block of ten shops known for many years as Station Buildings. Work started on the £14,000 scheme in March 1934 and was completed by 22 March 1935 when the new station was opened.[65]

*Hayes (Kent) Garage* [l.]

*Hayes Station taken from the Goods Yard, Whit Monday 1935*

Southern Railway's decision to undertake the modernisation scheme was fully justified as passenger traffic dramatically increased between 1925 and 1935:

| Passenger Tickets Issued | | Season Tickets Issued | |
|---|---|---|---|
| 1925 | 1935 | 1925 | 1935 |
| 21,856 | 177,424 | 159 | 5831 |

# Inns and Public Houses

**The New Inn**, which until the 1930s had been fairly isolated, drew much of its business from people using the railway. It had a private and a public bar, coffee room, parlour, kitchen, two sculleries and larder. On the first floor were three bedrooms and sitting rooms. In 1931 it was an attractive proposition as it was considered that the Hayes Place development would bring an 'Enormous Increase of Trade'. It was sold prior to auction to the Midland Brewers, Messrs John Davenport & Sons of Birmingham.[66] Mrs Edith Davey, who had been the publican since her husband died in 1913, left the New Inn in December 1932.

The new owners had the licence transferred in January 1933 and employed Mr Frank Clarke as the publican. Davenports wanted to build a £25,000 hotel on the site and applied for a 'full' licence instead of one just for a 'beer house'. Its application was opposed by Joshua Fifield, the publican of the George, and by Canon Thompson, but the council gave approval and Messrs C H Gibson Ltd of Croydon started work on a new building the following year.[67] Apparently the Brewers owned land opposite the New Inn and rumours surfaced that it was to be used for an open-air swimming pool; nothing further came of it. By 30 November 1934 advertisements appeared in the local paper announcing that the 'new' New Inn would open on 1 December. The old building was demolished, just 36 years after it was built.[68]

*The New Inn* [1.]

Architecturally, the new building designed by Messrs Batemans of Birmingham, was quite out of character with the district. Mr S P B Mais wrote in 1935:

> I saw Hayes Station, terminus of the Southern Electric. And then I saw one of the most astonishing things I have ever seen. Rising proudly above these red roofs, which

look as if they had been put up in a tearing hurry to keep up with the pace with a quite impossible demand for homes, I saw a pure Cotswold stone inn. The brewers and bankers presumably have money to put into building. I would have every brewer and banker in the land go to Hayes to pay homage to Davenport's New Inn. What it cost I do not begin to think. It is beautifully designed. Its yellow stone glows. Its six tiny dormer windows wink out of the roof of glorious flecked grey tiles. The projecting plain oak beams are upheld by finely carved wooden figures. The pipes are of decorated lead. But I needn't go on.[69]

The inn had a popular large function room on the first floor. It was often used for dinner dances and wedding receptions, such as the marriage of Rosina Corby of Hurstdene Avenue, Hayes and Edgar Taylor in August 1937.

**The George Inn** was taken over by Maurice Lloyd and his wife Elizabeth at the beginning of the First World War. He originally came to Bromley in 1872 and ran an ironmonger's business. He married Elizabeth Lowndes, daughter of the proprietor of the White Hart Hotel, Bromley and when her father died he took over that business which he sold in 1901. After the death of his wife he handed over the running of the George to his eldest son Maurice in 1921. In 1923 Maurice's son, Sidney, assisted him when alteration plans were laid before the justices and there were objections about a proposed Darts' Room. Maurice continued to manage the George until 1926, the year before his father died.

Joshua John Fifield, a publican from Blackheath, took over the licence and Watney Coombe Reid Ltd bought the Inn from the Hambro estate. Joshua Fifield remained the publican until 1939 when he retired and his place was taken by Stanley Winkworth Poole, who was the licensee of the Red Lion at Rotherhithe, Surrey.[70] The George was one of the focal points of Hayes. It prospered as a result of the changes and influx of new residents, the formation of the clubs and societies and from the custom of the hundreds of workmen building the houses.

## Pickhurst Green Hotel

One of the casualties of the changes was Pickhurst Green farmhouse and farmyard, which were sold in 1928. Messrs Crescent Estate Limited applied, in October 1935, to build a hotel on the site. A large number of local residents lodged objections but the scheme was approved on appeal. Interestingly, the farm had been included in a scheme for the Langley area in 1912 by Beckenham Council, even though it was situated in the parish of Hayes but BRDC would not sanction the Hayes portion of the scheme. Technically the site was now just in the parish of West Wickham and the developers had to gain permission for it to be de-zoned from the residential development that had been granted by the Ministry of Health in early 1936. The licensee of the Railway Hotel, West Wickham, opposed the application.[71] The necessary approvals, however, were obtained and by October the *Bromley Mercury* reported that good progress had been made on the erection of Pickhurst Green Hotel, which was in the style of a Tudor building with dressings of white Portland stone. In February 1937 the builders, Western Construction Company, announced that it would open on 4th March. The owners were the brewing concern Truman, Hanbury, Buxton & Co and the first licensee was A R Stack. On the opening night of the Pickhurst Green Hotel many of the local objectors were in the pub enjoying themselves and when asked why they were there, having been against the development, they responded 'well the drinks are free tonight'! The disused cattle pens in the meadow remained the only sign of the area's former use until they were burnt down in 1938.[72]

*Pickhurst Green Hotel* [it.]

Thus, within a short period of time Hayes had two new large inns which, with The George, met the needs of the expanded village and the eastern part of West Wickham. It would be some years before another public house appeared in Hayes.

# Farms

Pickhurst Green Farm had gone but what happened to the many other farms that existed at the beginning of the 1920s? At Fixteds Farm Edward Cook was replaced by James Haygreen, who rented the land for £100 per annum and continued farming until about 1934. Fixteds was sold for development and became a building site, although most of the land was not built on until after the war.

In 1921 Donald Carmichael Haldeman took over the lease of Hayes Street Farm from James Marden and employed Leonard Powell as farm bailiff. The farm suffered a disastrous fire that was started deliberately. Hay stacks valued at £1,000 were destroyed. No culprits were found.[73] In 1923 Edward Mortimer managed the farm but in 1924 Sidney Herbert Cator Rose was appointed bailiff and he stayed until 1961. At the change-over, sales were held at the farm, in which 80 Middle White pigs plus pig huts and feeders, and 55 Guernsey cattle were auctioned.[74]

Sidney Rose had been employed as bailiff by Donald Haldeman but about 1925 the lease was taken by Reginald C Fisher, a farmer from Sidcup, who owned or leased fourteen other farms in North West Kent. The farm was referred to as 'Guernsey Farm, Hayes Street' as it specialised in Guernsey cattle. In 1929 it won the Silver Challenge

Cup for Grade A milk for the third time.[75] During Sidney Rose's tenure the farm had some 60 cows, 70 calves and 150 pigs. At that time Hayes Street Farm also collected milk from other farms in the district including from Pickhurst Manor and Fixteds until they were sold.

*Mr and Mrs S Rose - Hayes Street Farm, 1936* [v.]

*Hayes Street Farm, 1930s* [v.]

*Harvesting, Hayes Street Farm 1938. In the distance the self binding corn cutting machine is in action* [v.]

Change often brings difficulties. For instance, dairy foreman William Piper of Meadow View, George Lane, was given notice in December 1926. Nine months later, Mr Fisher was granted a possession order as he urgently needed the cottage for farm employees. William Piper applied for an extension in October 1927 but it was not granted and he subsequently moved to Model Cottages in Hayes Street where he stayed until 1931. Wood Cottages, Hayes Street, which Mr Fisher bought at the Hayes Place auction were also used to house farm workers. In 1913 they were 'in poor repair' and by 1935 they were declared not fit for human habitation.[76]

The Norman family owned Hayesford Farm, occupied by market gardener William Walter Wood, and Hayesford House lived in by Samuel Pedley. By 1925 the market garden business was in the hands of Walter Thomas Bruce Wood who went into receivership with debts of £1,200. The farm was taken over by Daniel Dutton who stayed until 1933, his wife Jessie having died in 1930.[77] After Daniel Dutton left, Hayesford Farm was managed by George Hoeltschi (Senior) through the Second World War until 1962.

Much of the land of Hayes Place Farm was taken over by the developers. The farm cottages, one occupied by the bailiff Henry Small and the other by the head herdsman George Jones, were demolished when Ridgeway was developed. James Grandfield and his family continued to occupy the farmhouse. He had come to Hayes about 1904 to work as head gardener for Sir Everard Hambro. At the time he was said to be the youngest head gardener in the country and was in charge of some 20 under-gardeners. In 1908 he married Florence Edith Dawson of Eastbourne and had six children, the last was born in 1922. James was a talented horticulturalist, a pioneer in growing alpine plants, and at one time secretary of the Hayes and District Horticultural Society. On the death of Sir Everard Hambro he acquired the old farmhouse and greenhouses and set up a nursery called 'Hayes Gardens'. He was successful, became a Fellow of the Royal Horticultural Society, won a number of show medals and was a show judge. His business was well established by the time Hayes was developed. Many gardens of the new houses were the result of work undertaken by him.

The whole Grandfield family was involved in village life. James' eldest son Jack became secretary of the Chamber of Commerce. His second son Roger, who married in 1936, was an outstanding cricketer, played football for Hayes Football Club and was a member of Hayes Table Tennis Club. His only daughter Edna, was married at Hayes in 1934 to Christopher Harler, a member of the editorial staff of the *Bromley Mercury*. They were also an unlucky family. In 1928, fourteen-year-old Cyril Maurice Grandfield was accidentally killed at Bromley South. In September 1937 a bad thunderstorm left a trail of havoc through Bromley, flooding garages in Bourne Way, breaking the glass bulb on a petrol pump in Hayes Garage, and James Grandfield's nursery lost 150 panes of glass that were smashed by large hailstones. In September 1938 their son Roy had a fishing mishap at Marlow but fortunately managed to scramble out from the river.[78] Even worse was to happen in the Second World War when the Nursery sustained a direct hit killing several members of the family.

The only significant part of Hayes Place farm to survive is part of the premises of Stevenson Heating Ltd, which was used by Hayes Common Riding Stables in the 1930s, run firstly by Miss S Bird and then by Eric Sharp from about 1931 to 1939.[21]

*The surviving part of Hayes Place Farm buildings in West Common Road*

Charles Blick, owner of Warren Nurseries, died in 1919 and his widow Annie continued to live in 1 Warren Cottages until evicted in 1923 by the new owner Arthur Savill, a bottle merchant from New Cross. She moved to Model Cottages. John and James Percy Moss, market gardeners from Willesden, Middlesex bought the nine acres of land and the other two Warren Cottages. They wanted Joseph Goldsmith's cottage, 3

Warren Cottages, for an employee and he had to leave in December 1920. He could not get a council house and moved to 1 Thatched Cottages and then Elleray in Baston Road.[79] In 1922 Arthur and Oscar Gilbey, took over the Nursery and introduced different stock. By 1925 they occupied Cottages Nos. 2 and 3 and when Arthur died in 1945 at the age of 78 his son, also named Arthur, carried on the business. The nursery had a small orchard of 62 trees including Cox's Orange Pippins, Grenadiers, late Russet and root vegetables, such as onions.[80]

Thus, by 1939 only Hayes Street Farm and Hayesford Farm, and to a much lesser extent Hayes Gardens and Warren Nurseries, were used for pasture, arable, cereal, fruit or livestock production. Some of the land from the other farms that had not succumbed to housing would be brought back into use, as a temporary measure, during the Second World War. There were still large areas of the parish that were not yet built on but the housing estates constructed over the past decade had radically altered the traditional village which had existed for many centuries. It could no longer be viewed as a farming community.

Key

- - - - - original Parish Boundary

- · - · - adjustments to Parish Boundary 1934

N

**Map 14:** *Hayes in 1939*

# Chapter 4
## Response to change: 1921-1939

The dramatic changes that took place in Hayes in the inter war years, particularly after the 1931 sale of parts of Hayes Place Estate, affected the villagers in many different ways. The families of Harry Bowles, George Wheatbread and Albert Gilbert, as we have seen, had to leave their homes because their cottages were sold to builders who needed the land. Others, such as William Piper of Meadow View, Annie Blick and Joseph Goldsmith of Warren Cottages, were typical of those forced to move, either through employment changes or because new owners wanted the cottages for their staff. It is not difficult to imagine what these and other older residents thought of the changes and they knew that they would soon be in the minority.

In 1921 there were 364 males and 646 females in Hayes, a total population of 1,010 living in 222 separate homes. Ten years later the number had increased to 1,678 (720 males and 958 females) in 452 dwellings and the balance of males to females showed signs of recovery to the pre First World War level. From 1931 to the beginning of the Second World War the population of Hayes expanded greatly and by 1939 there were about 6,500 people in 2,150 dwellings, almost ten times the number of homes in 1921.

The whole infrastructure of the village, which for centuries had been based on a rural economy, changed. Employment was found predominantly outside the village. Welfare, education, leisure and entertainment all developed to meet the needs and aspirations of the new Hayes.

### Welfare - Nursing and health

In the 1920s most villagers still relied for their health needs on the community nurse, who was funded by the subscriptions of individual members and voluntary donations. Her activities were overseen by the Hayes Nursing Association set up in 1909. In 1920 its committee consisted of:

> President: Mrs Ann Torrens, Treasurer: Lady Hambro, Secretary: Mrs Thompson
> Committee members: Mrs Barnes, Mrs Frost, Mrs Matt Torrens, Mrs Legge, Mrs Joynson and Mrs Haldeman.

Nurse Lea received the fees for school nursing, health visiting and maternity work and in July 1919 her salary was £100 a year. When it was increased to £120 in December 1921 the committee had to find ways to raise the extra money and also to pay for repairs to the Nurse's cottage. Lady Hambro allowed Hayes Place to be used for an open-air entertainment that raised £203 1s. 8d. and Mr Haldeman organised a concert party of musicians and singers from London.

The number of visits made by the nurse continued to increase and by 1927 had reached 970 with 97 subscribers. In that year Nurse Lea had a severe attack of sciatica that hindered her activities. With funds still scarce and a balance for the year of 3*d.*, committee members decided to open their gardens to the public to raise money. Funds were helped in 1928 by a £25 donation and the Pickhurst Cricket Club donated its balance of £7 8*s.* 4*d.* when it was wound up.

The Nursing Association's Annual Report in 1930 stated that the good health of Hayes village people was due largely to the preventative work done by the local Public Health Service, and by the District Nurse under its direction. In the eleven years since 1919 only five children had died under the age of five, compared with eight children under five who died in one year in 1887. The total number of visits in the year 1929/1930 was 1,304. Several were chronic cases.[1] The April Church Magazine reminded its readers that, for a yearly payment of five shillings, subscribers had the right to the services of a qualified nurse for themselves and their families. The District Nursing Association cards were an insurance against sickness:

> It is not only that many homes in Hayes are blessing nurse for unselfish kindness and help in sudden illness or accident, but also by the constant supervision of our children's health epidemics are checked and little ailments discovered which if not seen early might lead to ill health or some crippling disease later in life.

It is unclear why Nurse Lea was given notice the following year. It may be linked to the decision to join with West Wickham and form the Hayes and West Wickham District Nursing Association. Her successor, Queen's Nurse Elizabeth Jane Twort, soon made changes. The expenses incurred in meeting the requirements of 'modern nursing' meant that the financial year ended with a deficit of 2*s.* 7*d.* Seventy-seven subscribers did not renew their subscriptions, as they were unhappy about Nurse Lea's dismissal. Nurse Lea started her own nursing club from York Cottage, but in February 1933 was rushed to the isolation hospital with suspected diphtheria.[2] She recovered and continued to nurse until her death in 1939. She was well liked and a memorial tablet was placed in the Village Hall.

The rising population led to the appearance of several doctors in Hayes. In the Church Magazine in March 1932 Canon Thompson commented that, as far as he knew, there had never been a practising doctor in Hayes but 'now in the same week three doctors had arrived'. Dr Coville and his wife Dr Katherine Barrington moved to Husseywell, 7 Pickhurst Lane, and Dr Jack Hopton was at 18 Ridgeway until 1933 when he set up his practice at Forge House, Pickhurst Lane.

The increase in the number of young families in the 1930s resulted, at Dr Jack Hopton's instigation, in the setting up of an Infants' Welfare Centre for West Wickham and Hayes. A clinic was held at the Hayes Village Hall on Tuesdays. The Nursing Association assisted in the clinic's formation and funds were raised by dances and other events. By the end of 1934 there was an average attendance of more than 50 at the clinic.[3]

In September 1934 Nurse Twort resigned to take up a post in Dover, but rumours that the Nursing Association was about to close proved untrue. Nurse Collins was appointed in a temporary capacity until Miss White, a fully qualified hospital nurse and midwife, who lived in Bourne Way, was selected. She left in May 1935 and was replaced by Nurse Dobson from Coney Hall.

The Association's membership in 1935/1936 increased from 186 to 378 and the number of visits from 1,948 to 3,807. A permanent second nurse was appointed, Nurse M Crichton of 8 Dene Close, Hayes. The additional nurse meant the need to raise more funds and in 1937 a Saturday Market was held, attended by two film stars, Peggy O'Neill and Michael Hamilton, and achieved a total of £78. Nurse Crichton left in December and was replaced by Nurse Hocking.[4]

On 1 July 1937 a new Midwifery Act came into force, which placed all midwifery under Bromley Borough Council and KCC. The Association's nurses could now only deal with general nursing and Nurse Hocking left to take up a post as a tutor at Queen's Training College for Midwives in Cheltenham. The growing numbers in the rapidly developing areas of Hayes and West Wickham meant that Nurse Dobson had plenty to do, making 4,378 visits between April 1938 and April 1939 when there were 1,460 members. Nurse Finnemore was appointed in February 1939 and Nurse Goad in July. Nurse Dobson used her motorcycle to assist in making her visits promptly but concerns were expressed about the danger and it was felt that she should have a car. Fund raising remained one of the main functions of the Hayes Nursing Association.[5]

# Education between the Wars

## Church School

*School pupils celebrate Empire Day, 1921* [ab.]

In the immediate post war period there were changes in teaching methods at the Village School but it was not until the 1930s that the rising population had a serious effect on the use of the school buildings.

The new headmistress was Mrs Kate Burman whose black and white spaniel Pat accompanied her to school, to the delight of the children but to the disapproval of some parents. When Miss Annie Morgan, head of the Infants, retired in 1922 the two departments were combined as the school roll was low, totalling only 85 pupils. Mrs Burman stressed the importance of art, literature and music, although some School

Managers felt that she should concentrate on 'more practical subjects'. Favourable comments were made about her new methods in the Inspector's report:

> The head teacher has recently organised a very interesting experiment of group work combined with private study ... The children are thus encouraged to develop habits of independence, industry and each can progress at his own rate. The teaching given to the older children is in some subjects more of the nature of coaching or tutoring ... the school is characterised by a spirit of progress and life.

The long benches that had previously been used by the children were replaced with chairs and double tables. Colonel Scott gave an electric lantern for use in geography and other lessons. The Chief Justice of Ceylon, Anton Bertram, visited the school and was very impressed. 'I was astonished at the proficiency displayed in the appreciation of literature and music. To hear a village boy repeat Browning's *O to be in England* with such obvious sympathy was an experience I shall never forget.' Work from the school was shown at an Imperial Exhibition of Work of Elementary Schools in London, for the benefit of delegates from the colonies. In 1925 the Diocesan Inspector reported that pupils 'have been taught with the greatest care and insight. If the psychological theory is correct that children will retain what has interested them then these children should certainly retain their teaching all their lives.' Religious instruction remained important. In the same year, pupil William Mayhew of Baston Manor Lodge came first in the diocese in the Bishop's Prize Scheme examination.

After the death of his father, Sir Eric Hambro gave to the school the land originally leased in 1911 from Sir Everard to build the kitchen. He made the transfer on condition that 'the Christian religion, the love of the British Constitution and the Monarchy be fostered at the school – that if proof is found of the above not being done or any revolutionary ideas against the country are being fostered the land shall revert to him or his descendants.'[6]

Pupil numbers remained low and in 1926 there were insufficient seniors (pupils over twelve years old) to run the cookery classes. Four older boys, however, went to Keston School on a Wednesday afternoon for woodwork, an event recalled by Bill Dance who enjoyed the lessons but not always the walk to Keston or the punishment if they arrived late! In 1927, Mr Haldeman paid for the children and their parents to go to Eastbourne for a school treat, and an anonymous donor gave £26 for electric lights to be installed in the school buildings to replace the gas mantles.

After nine years, in 1929, Mrs Burman decided it was time to move on as the school would soon be only for children under 11 and she needed a bigger school. She did not foresee the enormous changes that were to take place in Hayes in the next few years. Miss Dorothea Page became the new head with a salary of £318 a year and the use of the schoolhouse, for which she paid an annual rent of £36. She was rather large and regarded by some of the pupils as a formidable lady, with Eton-cropped hair but 'rosy cheeks and a kindly smile'. Her bicycle had to be specially strengthened to take her weight. Many former pupils recall with fondness two teachers who assisted her and who each spent forty years educating the young children of the village, Miss Nellie Barnes 1927-1966 and Miss Doris Kiely 1929-1969.

Within a few months the Diocesan Inspector reported 'the tone of the school excellent' and in 1931 the School Inspector commented:

> This little school is conducted on bright and sound lines. An open-air class room has recently been built from funds largely raised by the pupils' own efforts; the practice of dramatisation has been greatly extended; the Handwork is a valuable feature of the instruction; use is made of wireless lessons, and the method of individual work by the older pupils is being more thoroughly developed.[7]

In January 1936 the elder children listened to Commander Stephen King-Hall speak on the wireless on 'the King and his People' after the death of King George V.

It did not remain a 'little' school. Miss Page had to deal with the influx of pupils created in the 1930s by the housing developments. By 1934, when local government changes meant she worked with Bromley Education Committee rather than Kent Education Committee, there were 159 pupils. Due to the increase, pupils who lived in the Beckenham area were not allowed at the school after January 1935.[8] The Inspector's Report for June 1935 stated that 'since the date of the last report this school has more than doubled in size and it now contains 200 children, a number that is considerably more than the premises will conveniently hold.' Every available space was used. A lean-to was built onto the Infants' cloakroom in December 1934 and the Infants used the cookery room. In addition, temporary accommodation was found in the Rectory Hut (Iron Room) opposite the school. All pupils over 11, who had not gained scholarships to the Grammar Schools, were transferred to other senior schools. The girls went to Princes Plain School and the boys to Raglan Road School, Bromley.[9]

As pupil numbers became too many for the old school buildings, the Managers looked at the options for additional space. With the increase in the population of Hayes it could not continue as an Infants' School nor was it sufficiently large to be accepted as a Senior School. If the old building was sold there might be sufficient funds to provide a bigger school elsewhere and the Managers felt strongly that it should remain a Church School. The Rector commented:

> If we are able to keep a Church School going we will know that definitive religious teaching will be given … even if they [the pupils] do not profit by it much now, it does form a foundation to build on later … I am anxious to maintain the religious teaching and atmosphere which an efficient Church School has ….[10]

The Managers were aware that Bromley Council had set aside land at the back of Hookfield Cottages in George Lane for a school for Hayes and Keston that would take 400 pupils. In April 1935 the Church School Managers hoped to raise £1,700 from the sale of the Church School to buy Glebe House from the builders, Morrell Brothers. They needed about £4,000 to adapt the house as a school and thought this was a reasonable target. There were, however, dissenting voices, who felt that the costs of running such an undertaking would be very high. Mr Arthur Collins said, 'we would do better to conserve all the funds we could obtain ... for the extension of church work, and for a curate.' When the bishop forbade them from making any appeal to the church people of the diocese the Managers realised that they would have to close the school. In June, Thomas Stiles wrote to Bromley Education Committee reluctantly agreeing that the Church School would cease as a day school when the new Council School was ready:

> The [Bromley] Education Committee will realise how much we shall regret having to close our Church School where such good work has been done for 150 years. To break the continuity of the school would be a great loss to Hayes and so to the Borough. If, however, your Committee will retain the present efficient headmistress, Miss Page with her staff as at date of transfer, for the new school, we feel the traditions of the present school (so far as it is compatible with Education Acts) and its excellent spirit will be effectively carried over to the new school. We hope also that the Rector of Hayes will be added to the panel of visitors for Religious Instruction.

Bromley Education Committee agreed and built the new school in George Lane.[11]

The Church School Trustees rejected a suggestion that the existing premises should be turned into a branch library and planned to use the building for Sunday School and other church activities. The last school session took place on Friday 4 June 1937. A cheque was given to Miss Page by the Managers and in her letter of thanks she wrote, 'I shall always remember with pleasure the interest you have taken in the school and your kindnesses on many occasions.' An era had ended.[7]

## The New Council School, George Lane

The following day, Saturday 5th June, a large number of parents and friends watched the Mayor of Bromley unlock the north door of the new Council School with a souvenir key handed to him by the architect, W A Forsyth. The school hymn, *Father, hear the prayer we offer*, was sung by the choir and then there was the chance to explore the new building. On Monday 7th June school began with 248 pupils in a building able to accommodate 400 students in eight classrooms. In October 1937 the Bromley Education Committee agreed to the experimental establishment of a canteen to provide a mid-day meal for pupils.[12]

*Hayes Council School, George Lane, opened in 1937* [m.]

One pupil to experience the changeover from Church to Council School was Hugh Burnett, who was at Hayes School from 1935 to 1941. To him

> it did not seem to make much difference as the teachers were the same. It was, of course, much larger and I recall the massive long corridors – ideal for running down, although that was not allowed! Everything was new. We had a kitchen where we stayed for dinner, indoor toilets and large playing fields.

The staff welcomed more room. The numbers continued to grow and by April 1939 there were 296 pupils.[13]

# Private Education

Not all local children went to the Council School. In and around Hayes there were families who wanted a private education for their children and schools were set up to meet this need.

### Hayes Court School

One of the most remarkable was Hayes Court School founded in 1919 by Miss Katherine Cox. Her father, Professor John Cox, had worked with Professors Rutherford and Callendar on radioactivity at McGill University, Montreal. On his retirement in England Professor Cox continued to lecture and published a book '*Beyond the Atom*' in 1913. After the war he bought Hayes Court and moved there with his daughter. Her pupils recall her with fondness but she was undoubtedly an unusual headmistress, whose ideas on the education of girls were well ahead of the time. 'She was memorable. Extremely tall, ugly but striking, angular but elegant.'[14]

It was an exclusive girls' boarding school and only a few day pupils were allowed from the wealthiest homes in the area, such as Margaret Binyon from Hawthorndene and Peggy Preston from The Warren. The names of the original eleven pupils were inscribed on a brass plaque on a chair in the grounds that was given to the school on the first anniversary of its opening on 8 May 1920.[15] The school was successful and grew to 60 pupils by 1925 and then to its maximum of 72 girls. Originally the uniform was a pale grey with a fringe of green but this was replaced in the 1930s by a grey pinafore dress over a green sweater.

Pupils recall two outstanding teachers. One was the medieval historian Miss Eleanora Carus-Wilson who taught at Hayes Court from 1926 to 1936. She headed the intelligence branch of the Ministry of Food during the Second World War and later became a Professor at the London School of Economics. The other was Miss Marion Richardson who played a pioneering role with her child-centred approach to the teaching of art in schools. The author Winifred Holtby also taught there for a short while until her first novel was published.

A number of pupils who attended Hayes Court achieved significant positions in English life. Ruth Cohen became an economist and Principal of Newnham College, Cambridge, Betty Behrens was a fellow and tutor of Newnham, while Kate Bertram (née Ricardo) became part of the 1930s 'Cambridge school' of biologists and later became President of Lucy Cavendish College, Cambridge. Honor Croome became an economist, Hildegard Himmelweit (née Litthauer), a university teacher and social psychologist,

Joanna Kelley (née Beadon) a prison administrator and Margaret Amy Pyke (née Chubb) was a campaigner for family planning and secretary of the National Birth Control Council.[16] The beautiful gardens, tended by Percy Jones, who lived at Redgate Cottage, were an inspiration for many pupils. Valerie Finnis, who died in 2006, was encouraged to follow a horticultural career and became one of the few people to hold the Victoria Medal of the Royal Horticultural Society.[17]

*Hayes Court School Pupils. 1935* [w.]

*Hayes Court School from the tennis court* [d.]

Katherine Cox was on the fringe of the 'Bloomsbury Set' and encouraged artists, actors and musicians to Hayes Court. Virginia Woolf discussed 'How should we read a book?' The Mohawk Indian Chief, Oskenonton, talked about Indian customs and traditions and Roger Fry spoke about art. Trips were made to London to hear Yehudi

Menuhin play a Beethoven violin concerto or Myra Hess give a piano recital. The young Alec Guinness directed the school's performance of *Merchant of Venice* and John Gielgud gave guidance to the VI[th] form on their play *Uncle Vanya*.

Perhaps the event that shows Miss Cox's more enlightened approach was that, on hot evenings, the girls were allowed to drag their mattresses downstairs and sleep in the open, although they had to keep their dormitory order.

By 1925 an extension was needed and William Smith & Sons built a range of classrooms with dormitories above. Later, another form room was constructed at the end of the wing with a bridge linking the sickroom and isolation room to the rest of the upper floor. The stables and outbuildings were converted to provide a science room and music block. A library was provided in 1933 and a comfortable Common Room in 1936. The staff lived in Hayes Grove Cottage and the girls used the swimming pool, which was close by and built in 1926 by William Smith & Sons (now the site of Deep End). The girls played lacrosse in the nearby field that in the 1950s became Courage Sports Club and is now used by Hayes Common Bowls Club. It is situated to the north of Redgate Drive. Bill Dance recalled spending a long time as a young man trimming the holly hedge that marked the border between Redgates and the playing field. It gave him the opportunity to watch the girls playing hockey and lacrosse, until reminded by his employer Lady Payne that he had other work to do![18]

On the outbreak of war in September 1939 Miss Cox tried to move a nucleus of girls to Gordonstoun School. Negotiations broke down, and Hayes Court closed, although some equipment was transferred there.

People saw the opportunities created by the growing number of young families moving into the area and attempted to set up private schools. Several preparatory schools started in Hayes in the early 1930s, usually in private houses and for a few pupils. Aston House run by Mrs Constable in Pickhurst Rise was in existence in 1931 and had pupils mainly from West Wickham. Chatley House School opened at 1 New Road (Pickhurst Lane) on 4 May 1932. It was for girls aged 5 to 12 and boys 5 to 8. The first Principal was Mrs Timewell from Hampstead and Miss Jolly took over in May 1933. The uniform was green and beige and the girls wore Panama hats. The school had a special interest in music and many former pupils recall the percussion band. As the numbers increased there was insufficient room in the house to give concerts to the parents and, at Christmas 1935, the children's performances of action songs, recitations, dances and a play were given at Hylda and John's Café in Station Approach.[19]

## Barnhill School

The financial difficulties of one of these ventures is shown by the early history of Barnhill School that was opened in May 1932 by Robert Hilary Smith, son of Mr and Mrs W R Smith of 217 Pickhurst Lane. He was educated at Leicester House, Surrey and Barrow Hedges School and became a housemaster at King's College, London. When Thomas Browne of Barnhill died, 27-year-old Robert, with the help of his parents, leased the property and in January 1932 notified HPC that he planned to start a boys' preparatory school.[20]

He had insufficient funds to run the school and during the first few years his mother gave him about £600 to purchase furniture and equipment. The number of pupils increased to 75. By 1935 he was unable to cover all the costs and had an annual loss of at least £160 on hiring cars to collect boys attending his school. He borrowed money and by the time of his marriage in July 1935 was in some difficulty, although newspaper reports on the school continued to be very positive. As captain of Hayes Cricket Club he was well known in the area and the school cricket team benefited from his experience.

*Barnhill School* [m.]

A friend loaned him £1,000 and then a further £1,000 when he agreed to turn the school into a limited company. He became a director and was paid a salary of £129 a year plus his board and use of a car. Two years later the friend was unhappy with the financial management and asked for the return of £1,000. He could not meet the request and transferred his shares to his friend. In July 1937 he appeared for the last time as headmaster at the fifth annual sports day when Mrs Eric Davies of Brackendene presented the prizes.[21]

In September 1937 C E Colbourne became headmaster. There were 83 pupils and secondary education was now provided for boys up to 16. Sir William Waldron, one of the governors and a former sheriff of London, presented the prizes in 1938 when there was a display of model aeroplanes made by the boys. On 27 May 1939 the executors of Thomas Browne sold the property to Barnhill School Ltd for £3,600. The money was provided as a mortgage by Dame Elizabeth Waldron. By the outbreak of war three new classrooms and a science laboratory had been built and new playing fields acquired. By July 1939 there were 112 pupils but ambitious plans for further expansion were shelved when war came.[22]

## Baston School

Another school that opened in September 1933 was the only local private school from the 1930s to survive into the 21st century. Baston School for 'girls and little boys' started in Baston House with 11 pupils. Its founder and head, Miss Marian Langley Stafford Smith, had always wanted to run her own school. Born in Brighton in 1877, she read classics at Girton College, Cambridge, taught at Leeds Grammar School and was head of Durham High School 1911-1932. Her father, Henry, died in 1903 and her mother, the daughter of S P Webber, president of the Bromley Photographic Society, and younger sister Margaret moved to the family home in London Road, Bromley in 1909. Miss Margaret assisted her sister Marian in the plans to open a school in Hayes.[23]

*First pupils at Baston School, 1933* [s.]

One of the earliest pupils, Mary Place, who then lived at 14 Husseywell Crescent, remembered that Miss Margaret had long auburn hair worn in a bun and that they were all in awe of Miss Marian who had short, wavy, sandy hair. She wanted the girls to enjoy Latin and they soon performed their own Latin plays dressed up in togas:

> She taught us as if we were older than we were – and it brought out the best in us. She read us poems and we absorbed her love of words. I have never forgotten how she read us Tennyson's *Ode on the Death of the Duke of Wellington*. After she finished she sat quite still and there was an intense silence. The gong sounded for the end of the lesson. Looking at one another, we crept out. "She was crying!" said someone in awestruck tones. It showed us that a grown-up could be moved by poetry – a new dimension for us.[24]

Pupil numbers steadily grew, a school hall and gymnasium were built and two new classrooms were added to the original two rooms used at the front of the house. By 1939 there were over 100 pupils.

## St Mary the Virgin – The Parish Church

At his first Annual Parochial Meeting in 1919 Revd Thompson made it clear that he had no plans to make any changes but, inevitably, there were alterations during his ministry.

The ancient Early English window in the west wall was renovated in memory of William Richardson Kettle, formerly of The White House, Hayes who died in 1918. By 1924 ventilation had been restored in the roof and the window in the tower had been re-hung. Its modern coloured glass was replaced with diamond panes. Old oak altar rails found in the Rectory stables were cleaned and repaired. They replaced a deal desk at the east end of the north aisle. Mrs Torrens donated a replica of one of the banners carried at Lord Chatham's funeral. A music cupboard, made from wood from the old pulpit, was installed by the organ. Blue hand-woven curtains were hung to make a setting for the reredos and the fine organ screen was relined with the same blue material.[25]

In 1925 A C Norman gave land to extend the churchyard. Five years later, £100 of 2½% consols (British government securities) were given for the upkeep of the churchyard by the sons of Mrs Carden on her death. She had been notable for her work with the Women's Police Force. She was buried alongside her husband, George, who had been interred in 1894. The churchyard was well managed by the sexton, George Harwood, who was given an armchair on his retirement after 40 years' service in January 1937.[26]

By 1919 Revd Thompson was on the Diocesan Board of Finance, Diocesan Committee of the Church of England Temperance Society (of which he became chairman in 1929) and honorary secretary of the Diocesan Branch of the Queen Victoria Clergy Fund.[27] In 1921 his services within the parish and diocese were recognised when he was appointed an Honorary Canon of Rochester Cathedral and Rural Dean of Beckenham. For 40 years he was also a trustee of the Gilchrist Thomas Trust for the Thames Police Court Mission and supported the activities of the Mission to the Kent Hop Pickers, where his daughter, Vera, spent some time each summer.

Support continued for Miss Knowles in her mission work at St Luke's Parish, Victoria Docks. In 1921 a party of 50 girls from her mission was entertained to tea and games at the Rectory. In September 1924 Canon Thompson visited Miss Knowles in St Luke's Parish and wrote:

> one half of the world does not know how the other half lives … No gardens, no grass, no flowers, nothing green or growing. Swarms of children shouting and running in the dusty streets, their play grounds; … If we even realised what silent pitiful tragedies of embittered life are happening at our elbows, owing to the housing shortage, we should each of us be sacrificing some of our money, either in building even one 'home' for someone else or invest in one of the many housing schemes to decentralise the population such as Welwyn Garden or Letchworth Garden cities.[28]

Revd Thompson soon started to delve into the history of his new parish and was convinced that it was important to foster the feeling of community. He wanted

*Miss Mabel Knowles, known as the 'Angel of Custom House'*

parishioners to reflect on their past as well as look forward to their future. Social activities were encouraged and when he discovered the existence of the *Hayes Portfolio*, compiled by Charles Kadwell in the 1830s, he felt it should be acquired for the village. Numerous fund raising activities were held including a fancy dress party organised by Mrs Hamlyn. 'From the opening waltz until the hour of midnight chimed, there were scenes of great merriment in the prettily decorated schoolroom. Then Old Father Time made his departure and Cupid came tripping in to herald the dawn of the New Year.'

The portfolio was purchased for £65 and joined the copy of Kadwell's manuscript *History of Hayes*, written in 1833 that had come to the church during Revd Reed's rectorship.[29]

For over fourteen years Mrs Elizabeth Hamlyn, founder of the Hayes Social Club, was the primary organiser of many of the village's social activities and manager of the annual carnival. Canon Thompson became chairman of the Social Club, whose activities were well supported. In the 1930s he persuaded the playwright Ben Travers to write two of the 'playlets' performed at the church fête in aid of Hayes Church funds.[30]

During his ministry, the *Parish Magazine* became an effective source of local information for the village, covering more than church activities. It recorded HPC meetings and gave details of local organisations, including those not affiliated to the church, such as the Women's Institute (WI) and the football and cricket teams, whose fortunes could be followed in detail. Canon Thompson became treasurer of Hayes Cricket Club and his wife was president of the WI.

One result of his interest in the local history of Hayes was the realisation that there was no memorial within the church or village to two significant Prime Ministers, Pitt the Elder and Pitt the Younger. Early in his ministry in Hayes, he welcomed Edwin J Van Etten, a theological student from Pittsburgh, USA, who came to see the place where William Pitt the younger was baptised and took back with him a piece of stone from Hayes Church to install in the Calvary Church of Pittsburgh.[31]

*Fancy Dress Party 1923* [z]
*Front row: Mr S Mortimer (Cupid), Mrs L Smail (A Welsh Lady),*
*Canon Thompson (Revd John Till) and Dollie Price (the newly formed 'Social Club')*

*Young Mothers meet in the Rectory Garden, 1920s* [d]

In 1928, the 150th anniversary of the death of William Pitt, Earl of Chatham, a campaign was mounted to install an appropriate memorial in the church to the Pitts. A committee was set up comprising the Lord Lieutenant of Kent, Lord Camden; Lord Stanhope whose family was connected by marriage to the Pitts; Lord Stanley, the owner of Holwood which was developed on the site of the house bought by the younger Pitt; Sir Mark Collet, Miss Flora Fardell, A C Norman, R G Barnes (the PCC's representative) and Canon Thompson. Contributions were received from across the country, including from five former Prime Ministers - Lord Rosebery (a descendant of the Earl of Chatham), Lord Balfour, David Lloyd George, Stanley Baldwin and Ramsay MacDonald.[32] A sum of £439 16s. 3d. was collected and the British sculptor, Revd Allan Gairdner Wyon (1882-1962), was commissioned to create an appropriate memorial in marble. It was unveiled on 30 September 1929 by Lady Stanhope.

*Pitt Memorial, north wall*
*St Mary the Virgin Hayes* [h.]   *Blue Plaque unveiled in 2009*

In 1930 a second replica banner was made to portray the arms of the house of Grenville, the family of Hester Pitt, and was hung above the memorial with the earlier Pitt banner presented by Mrs Torrens in 1920.[33] It was not until 2009 that a further memorial to the Pitts was set up. A blue plaque was erected above one of the shops in Hayes Street (No. 52) near the former site of Hayes Place.

The 1930s also saw the provision of a harmonium, the replacement of rotten wood in the spire and the overhaul of the bells and chimes. When she retired from the New Inn in 1932, Mrs Davey gave a clock for the vestry and seven years later the tower clock was repainted.[34]

By October 1928, Canon Thompson was concerned about the future as both he and Mrs Thompson were now 70 years old and although 'still full of health and vigour' they did 'not wish to outstay their welcome'. The parishioners were keen for them to remain.

In November 1930 Canon Thompson referred to the changing nature of the parish:

> Hayes will soon be suburban. Hayes Lane, which a short time ago was a beautiful country road, along which one walked under leafy trees, has lost most of its trees, and these have been replaced by houses. Along Workhouse Lane (West Common Road) a row of houses will soon be commenced on the fields of 'The Grove'. That part of Langley Park which is in the Parish and has been from time immemorial open fields, is already cut across by four roads with others in contemplation. New houses seem to spring up every day and the population of this part of the Parish alone will be many times greater than that of the whole Parish in former times.

On a similar theme, in August 1931, he referred to the many newcomers settling in the northern part of the parish that extended from the Sports Ground (Bromley Football Club ground) in the east to Eccleshill, Westmoreland Road, in the west. As Hayes was expanding so rapidly he could not cope alone. Deaconess Mabel Rolls was appointed in January 1932 to assist with the work and she soon became a familiar figure.[35]

***Canon and Mrs H P Thompson*** [f.]

In 1933, at the age of 75, Canon Thompson decided that the time had come to hand over to a younger man. At the farewell fête in May, he and his wife received many gifts, including a casket made from wood from the 1602 tenor bell frame that was removed in

1900. Mr Thomas Stiles, churchwarden, spoke for many when he said of Canon Thompson that:

> looking back over the past fourteen years many of them felt that the life of the Parish had been very much enriched in his care, not only in the matter of the Church but also the general social interest of the Parish. His name would be associated with many things, to name three – the recasting of the bells, the repairs to the spire and the memorial to the Pitts … Mrs Thompson won the hearts of all from the earliest days and her activities in the interests of the Parish had been so numerous that it would be quite impossible to enumerate many. Three of the many things with which her name was associated were the building of the village hall, the inauguration of the Community Council and the building of much needed cottages due to her energy and persistence.[36]

It was difficult to find a replacement. In June 1933 Canon Thompson wrote:

> The Dean and Chapter have not yet been able to find the fit person who would take on the responsibilities of the Parish. The main difficulty lies in the smallness of the income and the size of the Rectory and grounds. When the cost of maintaining these has been met there is nothing over for the other necessities of life; it would be a tragedy for the whole neighbourhood if the Rectory were to become a building estate, but it is difficult to see how this can eventually be avoided.

At least one possible candidate from Liverpool turned the position down when he saw the amount of repair the Rectory needed.

Eventually, Revd Edward Louis McClintock, the organising secretary of the Church Missionary Society for the diocese of Oxford and Coventry, was appointed. He was born in Northern Ireland but went to school in England. He married a great great granddaughter of the prison reformer Elizabeth Fry, became Vicar of Haltwhistle, Northumberland in 1914 and joined the army as a temporary chaplain in 1917. At the end of the war he was appointed Rector of Frinton until he took up his appointment with the Church Missionary Society in 1925. He had three daughters. Rhoda, his youngest daughter, remembers that the house was in a very bad state with rickety stairs and an incredible number of black beetles in the kitchen and store rooms; beetle traps had to be laid every evening.[37]

The problems of the accommodation were not solved until 1936 when the Rector persuaded the Diocese that a new rectory should be built on the land between the church and the existing rectory. The architect H W Grant FRIBA prepared plans for the new building with five bedrooms and two attic rooms, a drawing room, dining room, study, kitchen, larder and maid's room. The Rector was said to be a little disappointed with the size of some of the rooms but it was a considerable improvement on the previous accommodation.

The question then arose as to what would happen to the existing rectory and grounds. There was a general feeling that it would be a calamity if the greater part of the grounds was sold for building development. In that case there would arise a cluster of small houses each with their own garden and the existing grounds and trees would be destroyed forever. A petition, signed by more than 1,550 residents, was sent to Bromley Borough Council asking it to buy the Old Rectory and gardens and adapt it for use as a branch library.[38] Eventually the Council agreed and negotiations proceeded. Various conditions

*Revd Edward Louis McClintock [y.]*

*The New Rectory in the snow, 1937 [y.]*

were made upon the sale that was finally settled at £3,000. On 12 February 1937 the agreement was signed by the Rector and the Mayor and Town Clerk on behalf of the Mayor, Aldermen and Burgesses of the Borough of Bromley. The sale realised £312 less than the cost of the new rectory. Plans were drawn up to transform the ground floor of the house by creating a library and reading room 32ft by 24ft, with stores on one side, a changing room on the other and a caretaker's flat above. The mulberry and fig trees were to be preserved and the old bricks saved and used to build a low boundary wall to Hayes Street.[39] Syme and Duncan Ltd of Beckenham's tender of £1,895 was accepted. They pulled down the old observatory and other outbuildings but were forced to stop work with the outbreak of war when it was used as a Damage and Casualty Centre and Auxiliary Fire Station. It was not until after the war that it was converted and opened as a public library in April 1946.

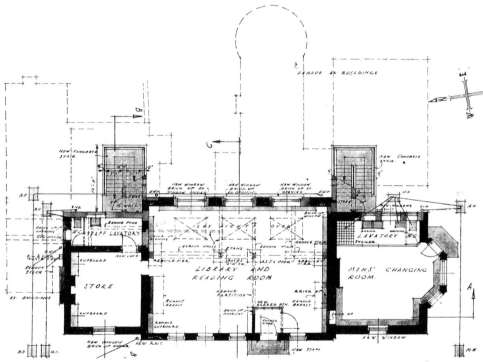

*Plan for the conversion of the Old Rectory to a Library, 1937* [aj]

The sale of the rectory and plans for the new one caused one set of difficulties for Revd McClintock. Older members of the congregation were also upset by his alterations to the traditional way of worship. Members of the Oxford Group, followers of Frank Buchman, a controversial American revivalist minister, came to give 'testimonies'. The churchwarden, Lawrence De Thier, complained to the bishop about:

> the many unauthorised actions and prayers which are introduced as well as mutilations and omissions from the prayer book services to which the congregation have been accustomed and to which we are entitled.[40]

On 8 March 1934 Arthur Carlos wrote to the Rector setting out similar objections and also referring to the curtailment of the musical portions of the service, which was against the wishes of the organist and choir:

> I thought the altered services might appeal to a number of newer residents but seeing the services are becoming more and more extreme and really a travesty of the orthodox prayer book service, I feel bound to utter a protest.

He resigned as treasurer and was replaced by Henry Guinness from Hayes Grove, who had previously been a member of the synod of the Church of Ireland and in the senate of the Irish Free State.

The next year Miss Octavia Stuart asked Laurence De Thier to ensure that the vases were replaced on the Memorial Communion table in the Lady Chapel and that the altar furniture, paid for her by her family, was not moved. She said it was 'all so painful and hurting to those of us who appreciate what hitherto has been treated with such respect and reverence.' It was clear, however, that the services were appealing to more people. A few weeks later she complained that she had not been able to sit in her normal pew, as the middle aisle was full. 'The Church was full of young people as it seems always to be … it is clear the majority prefer what now goes on and … we must just try and bear it.'[41] For some years Mr De Thier continued to be churchwarden, although he described himself as 'high church' rather than 'evangelical'. He resigned and moved away from Hayes in 1938.

*Hayes Church Choir, 1930s* [x.]
**Back row: Mr Lewis, Mr de Thier, Charlie Bingham, Ernest Russell, Mr Fairbrother,**
**Mr Godfrey, Mr Carlos, Eric Clancy, Mr Timms, Mr Whitehead, Bobbie Oakshott, Mr Preston**
**Middle row: Jim Harwood, Mr Greenwood, Mr Murphy, Mr Mortimer, Canon Thompson,**
**Mr Hamlyn, Mr Sexton, , Arthur Russell**
**Front row: Freddie Timms, Jimmy Ellis, Douglas Gray, Cecil Holwick, Fred Tidbury,**
**Willie Hall, Victor Bryant, Willie Barnes, Willie Cox, Alan Jones, Ralph Fairbrother**

By this year the electoral roll had risen to 552, although collections and donations were down. At the Annual Parochial Meeting in 1935, Revd McClintock said that he was aware that there were critics but he was pleased with the decided growth of the spirit of fellowship and friendliness in the church:

> The spirit had been helped by the Rectory 'at homes', the fellowship meetings in the Rectory Hut during the winter and by the people coming into the Rectory Garden after the Sunday evening services. The infant Sunday School numbers under Miss Robjant and Miss Jones had grown. A children's service was held in the Church on Sunday afternoons and the new Women's Meeting met a real need.

A Girls' Fellowship for those over 16 was started in September 1934 and in October 1935 a youth club, Juventus, was begun and became very popular.[42]

By this time Revd McClintock had the help of a curate, Harry Rooke. At first he lived with the family in the Rectory. Revd McClintock's daughter Rhoda recalls how the new curate had been theologically well trained at Wycliffe Hall, Oxford but had no practical experience. Before he undertook his first baptism he was shown how to hold a baby using the family's pet cairn terrier. Harry Rooke was an active member of the Oxford Group and meetings were held at Hylda and John's Café. In June 1937 he spoke at a meeting at Canning Town Hall and was supported by Victor Kent, Roy Hickman and Aidan Bacon from Hayes.[43] Visitors from Canada, Holland and Norway attended an Oxford Group meeting in the café at the end of June.

*Revd E McClintock (right) and Revd Harry Rooke (2nd right) in the Rectory Gardens* [y.]

In 1938 a 'goodnight service', lasting about twenty minutes, was instituted on a Sunday evening around the War Memorial for bikers and hikers on their way home from a day out. With the darkening clouds of war in 1938 there was considerable relief when Neville Chamberlain flew back from his meeting with Hitler promising 'peace'. The October Harvest Festival service was arranged as a thanksgiving service. The numbers were so large that the morning and evening services were relayed to the Village Hall where a further 150 to 200 people were able to listen.[44]

# Development of other Christian groups

Concurrent with the evangelising zeal was help for other Christian organisations that were setting up in the community to meet the needs of a changing population.

## Religious Society of Friends

Canon Percy Thompson supported the activities of the Religious Society of Friends (Quakers), who at first met for morning worship on the 1st and 3rd Sundays of the month in the Parish Room in Baston Road. Their Correspondent was Mrs Christina Yates (née Elliott) who had been educated at Sidcot, a Quaker school in Somerset. She had worked in Quaker Centres in Paris and Geneva and married Paul Yates in Switzerland in 1932, before returning to England to live in Queensway, Coney Hall. Dr Colville Barrington had been at school with Christina and he became a prime mover in setting up the Meeting House in Hayes.[45] He lived at 7 Pickhurst Lane and his Garden Room became the meeting place from the late 1930s until the Bromley Meeting House was established, largely as a result of Christina's efforts.

The Society of Friends held its first public meeting in the Village Hall at the end of April 1936 when the topic was about Quakers and their beliefs. As the political situation worsened their meetings reflected views on the importance of the Peace Movement. Speakers talked of their impressions of conditions in Europe, especially in Germany, and outlined the need to establish friendly contacts between Jews and Arabs in Palestine.[46]

## Methodists, Baptists and Congregationalists

By 1934 the need for an independent 'Free' Church was recognised. All denominations desired to establish some form of presence in Hayes and its environs. The London Mission and Extension Committee of the Methodist Church were keen to build in Hayes and wrote in March 1934:

> I understand that you have Hayes in mind ... The securing of a site need not involve the Circuit in any heavy liability. You are aware that the London Committee pays interest for a period of five years on sites. The question of building could be considered later. It would be a tragedy if all the sites in Hayes were taken up and there were none left for a Methodist Church.[47]

In the end no Methodist Church was built in Hayes but it was agreed that the three 'free' denominations – Baptist, Congregational and Methodist – establish a church in each of the main areas of housing development in Hayes and south West Wickham. This resulted in the building of Coney Hall Baptist Church, Hawes Lane Methodist Church (West Wickham) and Hayes Congregational Church in Pickhurst Lane. In 1938 the Bromley Strict Baptists moved to their new church in Hayes Lane, just outside the boundary of Hayes Parish, and continued to increase their congregations under their Pastor, G. Stanley Smith, gaining some members from the newer houses in Hayes.

Revd McClintock wished to help the Hayes Free Church (Congregational) group and offered the Rectory Hut in his garden as a place of worship. Stanley Sheppard, a student minister, became involved in the challenge of setting up the new church and 35 people attended the first morning service on 13 January 1935, which was led by Revd C J Barry, Minister of Emmanuel Congregational Church, West Wickham. Later 41 people signed as Foundation Members and Hayes Congregational Church was established. Revd McClintock, Harry Rooke, and Stanley Sheppard were frequently seen together visiting the new families. On 1 July 1937 Stanley Sheppard was ordained and became full-time once he had finished his training.

When Pickhurst Manor was demolished in 1936 the site was anonymously donated for the fledgling Congregational Church. The two-room Lodge, which still stood, was used as its first church. It was converted into one large room that accommodated 60 people. The room was used not only for Sunday services, the first of which was held on 28 June 1937, but also for evening meetings and all social occasions. There were no other rooms in the old Lodge that might be used as an office or vestry and when the minister arrived he left his coat on a chair, put on his gown and conducted the service from the lectern. A Women's Fellowship, Young People's Fellowship and Bible Reading Fellowship were organised.[48] The lodge was soon full to capacity and plans were made for a larger building on the site but a shortage of funds hindered progress and it had not been started when war broke out.

*Hayes Free Church, started in Pickhurst Manor Lodge in 1937* [m.]

## Hayes Brethren

After the departure of the Free Church to its new premises, the Rectory Hut was used for a short time by members of the Hayes Brethren who were keen to establish a Gospel Hall in Hayes. The founders included Mr & Mrs Walter Sivier who moved to 2, The Knoll in

1933 and, with a number of others, had continued to attend Clayton Hall, Peckham until a suitable place could be found in Hayes. Mr Joseph Williams, who lived at 42 George Lane, sold them a parcel of land in George Lane bought from the Hambro estate. The new hall was built by Mr L Skevington of Kemsing to a design by the architect, Mr George Soulsby RIBA of Maidstone. The total cost, including fixtures and fittings was about £1,000 and it was built between December 1938 and March 1939.

The Gospel Assembly Hall was opened on Saturday, 6 May 1939, when tea was provided for 120 people. In commemoration of the opening, special meetings were held each evening for a fortnight and were led by evangelist J Bennison from Stoke on Trent.[49]

### Roman Catholics

Roman Catholics in Hayes in the 1930s included Horace and Ada Crowhurst and Miss Coggan, who went to Mass at St Edmund's Beckenham. As the number of Roman Catholics increased, support for them was provided by the Bromley Roman Catholic Church but they did not yet have a building for worship in Hayes.

A few combined Church Services were held, although these mainly consisted of the congregations of the Free Church and Parish Church. A combined Coronation Service was to have been held on Hayes Common on 9 May 1937 but rain meant that it took place in the Parish Church. The Royal British Legion, Hayes Rangers, Guides, Scouts and Cubs, Revd Harry Rooke and Stanley Shepherd took part.[50]

When war broke out the leaders of the various Christian communities in Hayes, including the Society of Friends, sent a joint message to all its inhabitants offering support and extending a 'very warm invitation to their services'.[51]

## Sport, Leisure and Pastimes

The increase in population resulted both in the development, or revival, of older clubs and in the growth of new ones. These societies, groups and organisations generally flourished and provided an important outlet for all the residents, new and old. They generated a sense of community spirit bringing together all ages and backgrounds, a spirit that would be put to the test in 1939.

### Norman Park

The need to provide land for leisure activities led Bromley Council in January 1934 to purchase 56 acres of land, some in Hayes but most in Bromley Common, from A C Norman for £24,000. The land ran from the rear of the houses in Hayes Lane to Hook Farm, Bromley Common with access via Socket Lane and Hook Farm Lane. The area, still known as 'Norman Park', was to be used for recreational purposes with provision for organised games. Possession of the land could not be obtained immediately as the leases were held by the farmer, Mr Fisher, and did not expire until July 1939 (39.5 acres) and September 1951 (17 acres).

Most of the land was in the parish of Bromley and it is not clear how the new Hayes Lane residents viewed the creation of Norman Park. Some were against the use of Socket Lane as temporary access; others worried about noise but were pleased that the area had been protected from mass housing development. One advertisement for a four bedroom house in Hayes Lane, at £1,275, mentioned that it overlooked Bromley's new park. HPC approved but did not want it to affect the thirteen acres put aside for recreation and allotments and scheduled for acquisition elsewhere in Hayes Parish.[52]

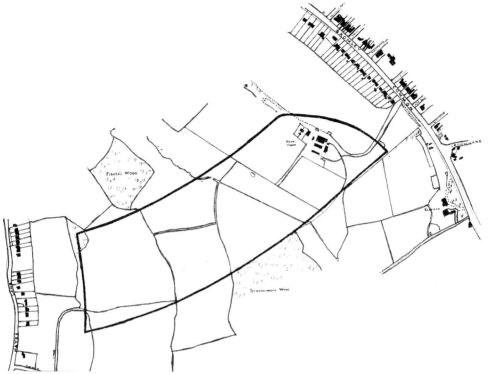

**Map 15:** *Plan of Bromley's proposed Norman Park 1934.*
*Hayes Lane and Socket Lane are on the left*

## Cricket Club

Frank Keech and Jimmy Dance were key figures in the revival of Hayes Cricket Club after the war. Frank Keech was made an honorary life member in 1936 for his efforts both as secretary and treasurer. Jimmy Dance was not only a good cricketer but also devoted most of his life to ensuring that the wicket was in the best possible condition. His younger brother Bill also became a fine cricketer and headed the Hayes bowling and batting averages in 1936. He recalled that, as a lad, from about the age of ten, he was expected to help his brother pull the heavy mower up and down the square in the evening. He hated it and often ended up crying but was made to continue and, at the end of the evening, his brother would give him 1*d.* for his efforts. There had earlier been an attempt to use a horse to pull the mower but it had proved an unfortunate experience since, when it was put in the shafts and ready to move, it dropped down dead.[53] Mrs Dance, who lived in Baston Cottages, helped with the refreshments. She used to get up at 6am to make the cakes for the tea and she provided the urn, full of hot water, which had to be collected from her stove and carted up to the Barnet Wood cricket field.

The ground at Barnet Wood was leased from Donald Carmichael Haldeman who, in 1921, became president until he left the district in 1927. A well-known cricketer was

Geoffrey Legge of Baston Manor who captained Oxford University Cricket team, Kent Cricket Club from 1928 and toured South Africa with the MCC in 1927-8. In September 1929 he married Rosemary Frost, the second daughter of James Frost of Glebe House, at Hayes Parish Church and the Kent Cricket team formed a guard of honour.[54] The marriage was timed to allow a few days' honeymoon in Paris before he joined the MCC on the tour of New Zealand. This was his last international appearance, although he occasionally played for Hayes Cricket Club.

*Wedding of Geoffrey Legge and Rosemary Frost, 1929* [r.]

The nature of the team changed as it no longer consisted predominantly of members of the gentry and became essentially a village side. By 1925 the Hayes side was struggling to find sufficient players to field a strong team for their Saturday matches. An appeal was made for 'good' cricketers at the annual meeting, when Bertram Plant was made captain and Frank Keech and Arthur Spinks became joint honorary secretaries.[55]

In the same year there was an attempt to start a Pickhurst Cricket Club. It played on a ground near Tiepigs Lane, but also had difficulty in fielding a sufficiently competitive side. Bill Dance remembered being invited to play for them as a young boy and it was the only time he could recall seeing underarm bowling used in a match. In July 1926 the team was bowled out for 12 runs in a match against South Hill, Bromley. In contrast a Hayes team a few weeks later beat South Hill, scoring 98 for 8 wickets.[56] The Pickhurst Cricket Club closed in 1928.

With the influx of newcomers in the 1930s a Hayes 'A' team was started, then an 'extra A' team and a Sunday team. In 1935 a Thursday Cricket Club was started, which used the playing fields of Hayes Court in West Common Road and was still active when the Second World War broke out. The working men's 'Married v Singles' match became an annual event on the old cricket pitch on the common and was held to mark the end of the season during the 1930s.

A major change took place at the Barnet Wood cricket ground. Worries about the lease, and fears that the ground might be sold for development, led the Cricket and Tennis Clubs to combine to form the Hayes Cricket and Sports Club, which secured a 21 year lease with an option to buy. Each club continued to operate as a separate organisation. It was hoped there would be sufficient support to form a Bowling Club but they could not attract 78 members to provide £10 each to cover the estimated cost of £780 to provide a bowling green.[57]

The cricketers were 'fortunate in having a beautiful ground and a playing pitch which was acknowledged to be second to none' but by 1937 finances were stretched. It was agreed to raise the subscription to 30s. for over 21s, keeping the 18-21s' amount at one guinea. A new pavilion was built, designed mainly by Reginald Busbridge of 20 Ridgeway and comprising a lounge, tea room, kitchen, large dressing rooms, lavatories and comfortable roomy verandah. It cost about £200 and was opened on Coronation Day 1937 by the president Richard Lowndes. After tea, members and visitors listened to the Coronation broadcast and heard King George VI's speech.[58]

When Arthur Collins took over the presidency in 1939 he said:

> Cricket is a glorious game and we who live in Hayes have a glorious place to play it in. I don't know of any ground within 20 miles of London that is so beautifully situated. Members of visiting teams, however, are not only impressed by the ground, but by the spirit of comradeship they encounter and the Hayes Club has a high reputation … It is a pleasure to see the new residents at Hayes furnishing their full measure of recruits to the club.[59]

## Racquet Games

Arthur Collins was also keen on tennis. He was a good player and had his own tennis courts both at Greenways and later at Baston Manor, to which he moved in 1934. The following year exhibition matches were held on his two courts, in aid of funds for Hayes Tennis Club of which he was president. His son was twice a junior Kent Champion and in 1931 reached the semi-final of the Junior Lawn Tennis Championship at Wimbledon.[60]

It was normal for big houses to have tennis courts and both Canon Thompson and Revd McClintock allowed the use of the Rectory's tennis courts by youth organisations. Dr J Hopton and Mr T Adamson became the driving forces behind the Hayes Lawn Tennis Club in the 1930s. The club initially had the use of the hut at the cricket ground where there was one grass court and Jimmy Dance became the groundsman.[61] After the acquisition with the Cricket Club of the sports ground they started to build hard courts and two had been laid down, in addition to the pavilion, by the time of the annual meeting in 1937. Dr Hopton, the chairman, reported a balance in hand of £21, compared with a deficit of £19 the previous year. By 1939 there were almost 130 members and a further hard court was planned to make a total of three hard and five grass courts. Electric lighting was installed in the pavilion.[62]

As a result of the improved facilities a badminton section was planned in 1936, although a badminton club had existed in Hayes from 1930 when Miss Vera Thompson asked for names of interested people. Muriel Adamson was one of the founder members of this club, which met in the Village Hall.[63]

Table tennis was another popular sporting activity and by 1934 took place in Hylda and John's Café on Tuesday and Friday evenings. The club's membership was about 30 and until 1937 they played only friendly matches. In that year, when William Mayer of 17 Glebe House Drive was the men's captain and Miss K Hood the ladies' captain, they decided to enter the Bromley and District League. They faced strong opposition and by April 1938 when they had played 21 matches they had lost 14, drawn 2 and won 5.

There was also the opportunity to play squash, after the Kent Education Committee acquired Gadsden and made its squash racket courts available to the public on two evenings a week.[64]

## Football

In 1922, at a well-attended meeting, it was agreed to set up a Football Club for those who lived or worked in the parish. Mr Haldeman, its new president, provided a football pitch at one end of the cricket field near Baston Farm. Frank Govier was appointed captain and the playing members' subscription was fixed at 5s. for the first season and 2s. 6d. in subsequent years. In the first season they played 11 matches, lost 4, drew 2, and won 5. In 1923 they ran a 'B' team and Edgar Barnes became its temporary captain but they only managed to win one match out of eight. They decided to continue with friendly matches and contributed £10 to buy, with the Cricket Club, the disused rifle range building for re-erection as a pavilion and dressing room. In 1925 they entered the Beckenham Cottage Hospital Cup Competition and the Bromley Charity Cup. A new pavilion was set up but some regular players moved from the district. In 1926 Frank Govier remained captain but travelled from Banstead, Surrey, to play. Club funding became a problem and although a number of dances were held to raise money they were not successful. In January 1929 it was agreed to disband the club because there were insufficient players, since the majority of likely young men had left the village to seek employment elsewhere.[65]

With the arrival of more newcomers it was decided in 1936 to restart the Football Club and some 20 players joined and used the old site at Baston Farm. In 1937 they entered the Bromley League and continued to do so although in 1938, as a result of the changes created by the Cricket and Tennis Clubs, they lacked a dressing room. This meant that every home match had to be played away at Goddington Park, Orpington, which was not satisfactory. By December they had played seven matches and lost six; four months later they had only won four out of fifteen games.

A Thursday Football Club was started in 1938 at Baston Farm by Fred Archer. The subscription was 10s. and the players wore red shirts and black shorts.

With so many clubs in the area, including the Bromley Football Club, it was always difficult to attract and retain skilled players but, at the outbreak of war, Hayes Football Club managed to remain in Division 1 of the Bromley League. Hayes was large enough to have a successful team although there often seemed to be a lack of interest and general support from people in the village.[66]

Park House Rugby Football club drew its membership from a wide area and met at its ground in Barnet Wood Road. Their games did not receive much coverage in the local press although there was a report of a match against Westcombe Park in 1936. In 1939 the Club hosted, for the third year, a seven aside tournament for Bromley and District Hospital that was won by London Scottish.[67] Rugby International and Oxford Blue James Richardson was often in Hayes and stayed with his friend Geoffrey Legge of Baston Manor, whose sister Esther he married in September 1931.

## Athletics and Cycling

Another opportunity for the sportsmen of Hayes was the arrival of Blackheath Harriers in 1926. This athletics club, now known as Blackheath and Bromley Harriers AC, had moved to Catford Bridge for its track meetings. It was increasingly difficult to find suitable land for cross-country running and from 1922 the club had journeyed to West Wickham. In 1926 it purchased the old buildings, formerly used by Edwin Price, at the rear of the houses near Hayes Station from Arthur Steer of Woodgrange, Station Road for £850. Steer was an engineer and part property speculator and had bought the land and outbuildings from the Lennard family three years earlier, with the idea of building one or two houses for profit. He retained for his own use a small triangle behind the cottage at the end of the garden of 2 Station Road (later 54 Bourne Way).[68] The club members were delighted since it meant that:

> they would be within 200 or 300 yards of a stretch of open country some 3½ miles long by a mile wide. The new headquarters would have a clubroom 60ft by 25ft with dressing room accommodation on the ground floor. In addition they would have a caretaker's cottage and about half-an-acre of ground for training.

In the succeeding years numerous competitive events were held around Hayes. The club started to organise an inter schools cross-country race over a four mile course for teams of seven from secondary schools. In 1930 the Kent Cross-Country Championship race was held at Hayes. By 1937 the club had prospered and members were pleased with its progress and position in the athletics world. Between 1930 and 1936, 294 new members joined, bringing the total membership to 724. In March 1939 the Blackheath Harriers finished eighth out of 29 teams competing in the Southern Senior Championship and retained the Camden Cup for the first Kent team of twelve runners to finish the course.[69]

On the athletics track Ernest Page was the fastest sprinter in the country in 1931, the same year that Sydney Wooderson became a member of the club at the age of seventeen. The club joined the Southern Amateur Athletic League in the third division but finished at the top of the first division in 1935. Sydney Wooderson represented Great Britain in the 1936 Berlin Olympics in the 1500 metres race. At club meetings he set world records of 4min 6.4sec for the mile in 1937, 1min 49.2sec for 880 yards in 1938 and won the European title for the 1500 metres in the same year. Harry Owens, who died in Hayes in 2005, was in the gymnastic team in the 1936 Olympics. He remembered clearly the impact of Hitler's appearances at the Games.

The 1930s saw an increasing interest in athletics and the concept of 'keeping fit'. Hayes Church Youth Club, Juventus, held keep fit classes for girls from 1934 and in September 1937 opened up the classes to non-members on alternate Fridays in the Old Church School Room. A branch of the Margaret Morris Dance Company, which combined dancing with physiotherapy and physical training, also started in the late 1930s. Winifred Ridings of Westland Drive organised the classes in the Old Church Schools.[70]

Others preferred the freedom of the open countryside provided by cycling. Cycling clubs became very popular and in 1936 Joan Hicking, whose father was a cycle dealer in Station Approach, held a meeting to consider forming a cycle touring club in Hayes. In April 1939 Miss Peggy Allin of 61 Bourne Way started on a cycle tour, to visit American and New Zealand youth hostels and to demonstrate the reliability of an English made bicycle; unfortunately the outbreak of war prevented the completion of her tour.[71] Dick Stacey's tearoom at Dreadnought Cottage on Hayes Common became a favourite stopping place for cycling clubs.

## Social Events

Alongside the participation in sport and physical activity there was a considerable interest in social events. The Village or Men's Club had existed for more than 50 years and was held in the Rectory Hut from October to April, every weekday except Saturday evening. The membership fee was 3s. and there was billiards, table tennis and darts. Women had the opportunity to enjoy regular meetings of the Mothers' Union, Women's Fellowship, and the very active Church Social Club. The latter had been formed before the First World War by the curate, Rev G Harvey, and Mrs Hamlyn of Sunningdale, Baston Road, with the aim of providing an opportunity for social gatherings. For members of Hayes Parish Church, who were over 14 years old, the subscription was 6d. a month. The first meetings were held in the small Parish Room at St Mary Cottages. The members played draughts, dominoes, ludo and similar games, and had weekly whist drives. The club grew and moved to the Gymnasium in West Common Road.[72]

When the curate, Revd Thomas Smylie, left Hayes to work abroad with the Church Army, Revd Thompson replaced him on the Social Club committee. A New Year's Eve Fancy Dress Carnival and a children's Fancy Dress Party, organised by Mrs Hamlyn, became annual events until the early 1930s. The local newspaper reported:

> how very far the social life of Hayes is from the state of dull stagnation which town dwellers so often seem to imagine exists in all villages. It might be argued that with Bromley only a couple of miles or so away, Hayes residents have not far to go for amusements and social relaxation. "We do not need to go at all," they would be justified in answering. "We are quite capable of providing our own." And on Tuesday's showing [the Carnival evening] Hayes does not need to look to its larger neighbour for originality, humour or effectiveness; in some directions, in fact, it might reasonably claim to be able to "give Bromley points".

Dances were usually well supported whether raising money for the Social Club or for some charitable activity such as the Hayes Nursing Fund in 1926. In 1927 the first Ball to be held in the new Village Hall was successful and attended by over 200 people, despite the difficulties of getting there in arctic weather conditions. Some couples were on a 146 bus that ran into snowdrifts in Hayes Lane but everyone helped to dig it out so they could continue on their journey. In 1928 the Church Social Club changed its name to the Hayes Social Club and met in the Village Hall. Mrs Hamlyn remained the main dance organiser until 1931 when she felt the task was too much for her, although she remained a member until she left Hayes for Sevenoaks in 1933. At the end of 1937 Percy Jones was president and there were 223 members, mostly from Hayes, enjoying weekly whist drives and dances.[73] Miss Mary Harrod, the secretary and treasurer, was also an active member of HVA, treasurer of Hayes Players and started to lead Sunday rambles that were well supported. She was joined on the walks by her future husband, Frederick Hassell of West Wickham. He later shared the leadership until their marriage in June 1936 when they left the district.

In October 1935 the Bohemians held their first dance in the Village Hall. It was aimed not only at 'those who enjoy dancing in jolly company, but also those who appreciate a spirit of sociability.'[74] Twenty dances had been held by July 1937. They were well attended with between 120 to 160 people.

## Horticultural Society

*Flower Show Committee 1926* [aa.]
**Back row: J Grandfield jnr, J Jordan, T Price, T Stevens, H Harrod, T Clarke, Timms,**
**A Collins (president), Jones, Winter, Goldsmith and Spinks**
**Sitting: H Lewis, E Turner, Rowbottom, Canon Thompson, Newman, Wooding,**
**J Grandfield (hon. sec)**

After the war various efforts were made to widen the appeal of The Hayes Cottagers' Garden Association. In 1920 its name was changed to the Hayes Village Industrial Association and handicraft exhibits were included in the July show. Sir Everard Hambro was president, James Grandfield secretary and Tom Price collector. In 1921 Miss Cox offered the playing fields of Hayes Court as the venue for the shows, which initially attracted many entries. Mrs C E Hambro offered a leg of mutton for the best collection of four varieties of vegetables. In 1924 an open sports' meeting was included and the event took place at the cricket ground at Baston Farm but numbers declined. Even the move from Wednesday to Saturday in 1926 did not ensure sufficient support. The show ran at a loss and in 1927 the society decided not to hold one.[75]

The following year E H Joynson called together a number of people to try to revive it and it was agreed to hold a show in October and change the name of the society to the Hayes (Kent) and District Horticultural Society, its present title. The society continued to encounter difficulties. There were fewer professional gardeners living and working in the parish, entries were relatively small and from 1929 there was always a deficit on the shows, which were now held in the Village Hall. The horticultural lectures were poorly attended and only 27 people turned up in December 1931 to discuss the Society's difficulties. The Social Club held a function to wipe out the deficit. The 1933 committee decided to hold a small show in the Church School during the summer for members and to hold the usual show in September. So poor was the support for the first show that they cancelled the Autumn Show.

Mr Arthur Collins said:

> the difficulty of maintaining the society in the altered conditions of Hayes was insuperable. The society had been kept alive by the zeal and patience of a few, and the more Hayes grew on its present lines the less he thought it was likely to be interested in a horticultural show which in the past catered mostly for the villagers and the gardening staff of the principal residences. He thought it would be best to recognise that they must give way to the modern movement for the extension of London and consider themselves no longer a rural community.[76]

A small committee of three was appointed to watch over affairs until the situation improved.

In April 1934 a resident suggested to HVA's secretary that a horticultural show should again be held and the secretary reported that he had learnt that the Horticultural Society, 'which had ceased to be active would most likely be only too willing to organise a show.' HVA arranged a meeting between members of the Association and Arthur Collins, Basil Jones and Percy Jones of the Society in June 1934. Theodore Perkins of 24 Hayes Garden was asked to act as secretary of the proposed revived Horticultural Society and it is probable that Mr Perkins had made the original request for a show. In July, HVA reported on the reformation of the Horticultural Society but two months later F W Atkinson told the HVA Committee that membership was disappointing.[77]

At the HVA General Meeting in October, Mr Atkinson, chairman of the new Society, referred to the 'resuscitation of the Hayes & District Horticultural Society by the Association.' and made a plea for members with the promise of winter lectures and a show for a subscription of one shilling a year. The first lecture, described as suitable for new householders, was to be held in November and entitled '*How to Plan a Garden*'. The revived Summer Show was set for July at Hayes Court.[78]

The Society was affiliated to the Royal Horticultural and the National Rose Societies and social events were arranged. Outings took place to Wisley and Kew Gardens. Dances and whist drives were held. The appeal of the show was broadened with the addition of a Baby Show and sideshows, including bowling for a pig.

The 1935 show was a success and made a £3 profit and it was decided to hold another in the Village Hall. In 1936 the Rector said 'we are doing our best to make Hayes beautiful and get it out of the chaos of a new district ... the Society's object is to encourage people to love their gardens and make the most of them'. Entries for the

Summer Show increased from 333 in 1935 to 600 in 1936 when large numbers also watched a display by 330 Anti-Aircraft Company Royal Artillery, TA. In 1937 there were 820 exhibits in the Summer Show and the Society agreed to hold three shows each year; a Summer Show in July, Autumn in September and Chrysanthemum in November. In 1938 the first Chrysanthemum Show attracted 190 entries.[79] Membership of the Society rose to 283 and there was a balance of £60. In 1939, in addition to the show, a varied programme was organised including children's sports, a physical culture demonstration by members of the Margaret Morris Movement, a display by the Bromley Auxiliary Fire Service and the Hayes Players performed '*The Master Key*' by Wilfred Massey

*Bowling for the Pig at Hayes Show*

## Hayes Players

The Hayes Players were formed in 1933 as a result of a conversation between Joe Merrill, who had just moved to Hayes, and Doreen Barry who lived in Hayes Garden. Joe Merrill contacted the Marjoribanks in Pickhurst Lane with whom he had been associated in a drama society in Dulwich. One of the first recruits was Sullivan Mortimer, the organist at Hayes Parish Church. For new groups, such as Hayes Players and HVA, it was important to become established and effective quickly. Some form of mutual co-operation seemed beneficial and Mary Harrod at an HVA meeting suggested that it should support an amateur dramatic society. The affiliation of Hayes Players to the HVA, however, had its problems. Initially, Joe Merrill of Hayes Players proposed that affiliation should be on the understanding that the finances would be separate and that they would be free to give performances outside Hayes and with people who were not members of the Association. He also offered to produce one play each year for the benefit of the HVA funds. There was general agreement, although the HVA thought that if the Players made use of their name it would be desirable that the play to be performed was submitted to the HVA for approval. The latter would pay the costs if it rejected a play. HVA would receive 25% of the annual profit and would help to sell performance tickets. Towards the end of 1934 the 'Rector reported that two plays had been submitted to him for approval and that he had turned one play down because it was full of sex.' As might be expected, HVA received a letter from Hayes Players stating that affiliation had served no useful purpose and ended the arrangement.[80] Despite their artistic differences both organisations flourished, worked together on many occasions, and celebrated their 75th anniversaries in 2008.

By the end of 1934 Hayes Players was totally independent and had freedom to choose its plays, which were generally well received, although the audiences tended to prefer comedies to tragedies. During one performance in October 1934 W A Cook who took the part of the 'corpse' made his fall from the cupboard too realistic with the result that he struck his head heavily and was stunned. The scene was cut short. Mr Cook was carried out semi-conscious but later recovered. The chairman and producer was Joe Merrill. Frank and Nadia Marjoribanks acted as secretary and assistant secretary and Bert Frost as stage manager.[81]

***9.45 performed by Hayes Players, October 1934 [at.]***

## Women's Institute

In 1926 the Hayes branch of the Women's Institute (WI), founded in 1920, formed a Drama Society and staged its first performance the following year. In 1928 it came fifth in the West Kent Drama Festival judged by Edith Craig, the daughter of Dame Ellen Terry. The members acted scenes from *Antony and Cleopatra* in the open air at Redgates, the home of Lady Payne.[82] It was a good performance but one made difficult by the noise of picnickers on the common! In 1930 both Elizabeth Montgomery and Audrey Harris, who were to become famous theatrical designers, took part in a WI production of scenes from *Quality Street* by J M Barrie.

The WI originally met at the Oast House but the venue was later changed to the Gymnasium because of members' difficulties in getting there in bad weather. Meetings were held every month, except August, and normally attended by between 30 and 40 women but, in 1929, some 80 members were present for its ninth birthday party that was presided over by Mrs H Lewis.[83] During the early years lectures were held on a variety of subjects, including Citizenship and Hay Box cooking. Members also raised money for the Village Hall Fund, to which in 1923 they contributed £25. They organized a Baby Show at Warren Wood in the 1920s and took part, dressed as druids, in the Kent Pageant for Women's Institutes.[84]

The 1930s saw the continuation of the successful drama group and also the development of a choir that, in January 1931, came first in its group at the Bromley Music Festival. In 1935 it won the community singing shield competed for by about 60 branches of the WI. The Institute continued to flourish and its membership increased to 171 in 1936. During the 1930s it entertained hospital patients, groups of old ladies from Docklands and arranged a Coronation treat for crippled children from Coney Hill.[85] The organisation met an important need for women in the 1930s and brought together established villagers and many newcomers.

## The Royal British Legion

In December 1933 the Hayes and District branch of the Royal British Legion, a national organisation founded in 1929, was formed under its chairman Major J Douglas-Henry. He resigned in June 1934 on his departure to Australia and Captain R L Hamer of The White House replaced him. In July 1934 the headquarters for the local branch was opened at 2 Hillside Cottages, Station Hill consisting of two large rooms, a bar and committee room. A competition was held to design a layout for the front garden and Mr Sharpless won £1 for his suggestion of a concrete forecourt, a tea-lawn screened by a rose bower, a rockery between two high and two low lawns. The old apple tree would have seats round it.[86] The branch organised socials, whist drives, children's parties as well the annual Poppy Day collection that normally raised about £100. The women were a great help with the collection and were often at the Railway Station at 5.30am to catch the first travellers to London. They were not allowed to form a women's section, a fact that was regretted by many who worked hard to gain funds. In 1937 'veteran' Poppy Day and Royal British Legion worker Mrs Edith Poston of 9 Cherry Walk, who lost two sons in the First World War and who had lived in Hayes for about six years, received a certificate from the Royal British Legion headquarters for all her work.

## Toc H

Hayes Toc H, set up in 1932, attempted to run a boys' club in 1933 and, at the end of the year, entertained 40 to 50 club members. In March 1934 a football match was held with the Waterloo Boys' Club. The Toc H movement continued to entertain groups from less fortunate backgrounds and almost their last activity before the outbreak of war was to hold a weekend camp at Hayes Court for children sent by church worker, Mabel Knowles, from the Customs House District, Docklands.[87] In 1937, when Toc H had 27 members, they were given branch status and they regularly held socials known as 'WISCAUMS', socials for wives, infants, sons, cousins, aunts, uncles and mothers.

## Library

For those who preferred less active pursuits there was the library. In the 1920s the village library was housed in the Parish Room at 3 St Mary Cottages and Canon Thompson's daughter Vera was the librarian. It opened on Mondays from 12 noon to 1pm and 8.15pm to 9pm but closed during the summer holidays. A subscription was charged of 2*d.* a month for adults and 1*d.* a month for children. In 1926 arrangements were made for a visit every three months from Kent Education Committee's Travelling Library. A hundred new books were provided and members were able to borrow one novel and one non-fiction book free of charge each week. At this time there were 32 adult and 36 juvenile borrowers. In 1928 the lunchtime opening period was reduced to 45 minutes but now all books were free to everyone. The number of borrowers increased to 101, one tenth of the population, and the number of books loaned by the county library rose to 260 volumes by 1930. In the same year Mrs Preston and Mrs De Thier donated a number of children's books. In 1933 there were 143 borrowers and over 2,000 books were issued.[88]

The following year, on 1st December, Bromley Borough Council's Library Committee started a library service at the Parish Room, and agreed a yearly tenancy of £26 inclusive of lighting, heating and cleaning with the PCC. The library now opened more frequently on Monday and Friday 2pm–5pm, Tuesday 5pm-7.30pm and Saturday 6pm-9pm. One of the youngest new users of the library was Dorothy Dewey of Glebe House Drive, who recalled that as she entered the room the books were kept on cupboard shelves along the left hand wall. The adult books were on the upper and children's books on the lower shelves. The cupboards were closed when not in use. The numbers using the library increased rapidly and in July 1939 1,062 adult books and 197 juvenile books were issued. It was realised that, as the Hayes population grew, the facility would be inadequate and a larger library would be needed. Various places were considered such as the Old Church Schools, Glebe House, a site in Ridgeway adjoining the New Inn and finally the Old Rectory was selected.[89] The Parish Room was used until the new library opened in 1946.

## Hobbies

There was more time available in the inter-war years for the development and pursuit of a wide range of leisure activities as hours of work lessened and, by the middle of the 1930s, people had more disposable income. Home based hobbies grew as people spent time in their gardens, kept racing pigeons, went fishing, or practised photography. Listening to the radio became a popular pastime and was one in which a Hayes man,

Basil Binyon of Hawthorndene, played an early part. He was an electrical engineer by training, helped to set up the BBC in 1922 and was a director until 1926 when it became a public corporation. In the 1930s Arthur Milne started to experiment with amateur radio and his tall aerial posts were very visible in his garden in Kechill Gardens. After the war he was in touch with similar radio enthusiasts all around the world.[90]

## Cinema

The cinema was another new experience for many in the 1920s and 1930s. The official opening ceremony of 'The Rex' (Station Approach) took place on Thursday 6 August 1936 by Miss Joan Gardner, the celebrated British stage and screen actress. Mr D Daniel, the manager of the Plaza, West Wickham was made general manager and Mr C E Bushnell was house manager. The first films shown were Ambrose and his Orchestra in *Soft Lights and Sweet Music* and Wallace Ford and Molly Lamont in *It Happened in Hollywood.* On 28th October the first of a series of Sunday concerts was started under the direction of Horace Sheldon who had been musical director at the London Palladium for fifteen years.[91] The end of the concerts was timed for 10pm to allow visitors from West Wickham and district to catch the train without having a long wait at the station.

Various other ways were found to entertain the local population at the cinema, including talks and talent contests. In February 1938 a 'prettiest child competition' was held and the winner presented a bouquet to the film actress Elma Slee. In July 1937 Mr Bushnell was made manager of the Plaza and Mr Daniel became manager of the Rex.

Meanwhile Hayes had its own film producer. At 22 years old, Norman Hope-Bell of Hayes Hill Road became the youngest UK film producer when he made a slapstick farce *Love up the Pole,* featuring Ernie Lotinga in 1936. *Song of the Forge* followed and in September 1937 the world premiere of *Rose of Tralee* was shown at the Rex. In 1938, *Old Mother Riley* had its first showing at Hayes, an event attended by the producer Norman Hope-Bell and various film stars.[92]

## May Queen

One activity filmed in Hayes for Pathe News was the traditional ceremony of the crowning of the London May Queen that took place each year on the old cricket ground on the common.[93] A large procession made up of May Queens and their retinues from communities around London walked through Hayes for a short service outside the Parish Church and then on to Hayes Common. The London May Queen was crowned, the Realm Queens presented to her and dancing took place around the Maypole. By 1922 there were 52 May Queens. Joseph Deedy had organised the ceremony since before the First World War.

In 1919 Marjorie Dodd was the May Queen of Hayes and, with all the other Queens and their attendants, in superb weather,

> made a pretty picture wending through the village, singing as they went ... In the rear came one who for many years figured notably in the May Day processions … This was Mr Frank Price of Roundabout Cottage who, seated on his horse, and wearing his picturesque garb, … was as full of the spirit of the whole proceedings as ever.[94]

He was still present in 1933.

> With his sun-browned wrinkled face and goatee beard, his grey green scarf, his snowy white smock, black leather gaiters and shepherd's crook, his patriarchal figure was a striking contrast with the fresh young faces all around him. He looks old but never older.

Frank Price made his last May Queen appearance the following year and died in April 1935 at the age of 74.

***Hayes May Queen, Margaret Friend, 1929***

Another familiar figure in the procession was William Robjant, of Nest Cottage, who conducted the Hayes Brass Band for 55 years until his retirement in 1927 when his son Arthur became the band's leader. After Arthur's death in 1934, his brother William led the procession until 1936 when the Bromley and Bickley Brass band took over.

In 1928 and 1937 the London May Queen flew from Croydon to Biggin Hill, flying low over the crowds and dropping a tiny parachute of flowers. In 1921, when Vera Tidbury was Hayes May Queen, rain caused everyone to rush to the schools to take shelter and in 1930 and 1931 led to the shortening of the ceremony. As the numbers became greater the difficulty of policing the event became apparent:

> From Abbey Wood and Addington, from Finsbury Park and Forest Hill, from Thornton Heath and Tooting, a hundred Queens with their retinues converge on the little Kentish village. On the day of days every 'bus and train' with Hayes as its destination has "standing room only". The roads in the vicinity are filled with charabancs, taxis, private cars, motorcycles, pedal bikes and pedestrians, whose enthusiasm stands the test, all other methods of transport failing, of a long walk in scorching sunshine.[95]

*Hayes Brass Band 1927/28* [ab.]

In 1933 the procession was restricted to the common and the ceremony of the Little Sanctum transferred from outside the church to around one of the large oak trees. The move was not popular and the following year the normal procession around Hayes was restored, although in 1939 the route was changed to go along quieter roads.[96]

Visitors to Hayes for the annual event noticed the considerable changes that were taking place in the village. In 1935 many 'seemed perplexed on their arrival by train to find a completely new railway station, their astonishment increased when they observed the arresting new premises of the New Inn and the new shops outside the station.' Fortunately, once they made their way up the hill they were back to the familiar sight of the common. The Common Conservators also became concerned about the crowds and in 1939 insisted that the organisers provide adequate temporary lavatories and first-aiders.[97] By the time the Second World War broke out there was no sign of any lessening in enthusiasm for the event. Each year the numbers in the different realms increased and to avoid any confusion a colour was allocated to each group. Hayes was given 'Madonna Blue'.

## Scouts and Guides

Uniformed organisations for the young began just after the First World War. In 1919 a meeting was held at the Gymnasium to start a Brownie pack and Guide company. Miss Thompson arranged for the enrolment at the Rectory of girls aged 9 to 11 into the Brownies and from 11 to 18 into the Guides. Two Guide patrols were formed and initially met on Wednesdays in Hayes Grove Stables with the permission of Mr and Mrs Matt Torrens. Later the girls moved to the garage at The Warren. In May 1920 the 1st Hayes Guides took part in a Bromley Guide Rally at St Hugh's School, Bickley. In 1925 the guides held their first dance. By 1927, Miss Thompson was assisted in leading the guides by Miss Peggy Harris of The White House and Miss Rachel Stiles of Barnet Wood

Cottage. Peggy Harris was already showing her considerable talent as a costume designer. In 1928 she made the costumes used in an entertainment by the guides that raised £8. In a Girl Guide rally at Bromley Palace in 1927, attended by 400 girls from nineteen companies, the most popular demonstration was the fire-fighting display by the guides from Hayes, West Wickham and Keston.

A Ranger group, 18th Bromley Rangers, was created for girls over 16 from the three villages and met initially in the stables at Hayes Grove and then at Baston House. It was led by Sybella Stiles from 1934 until she left the district in 1937. In 1933 the 1st Hayes Brownie Pack was formed under Brown Owl, Miss Audrey Penman of Ash Lodge, who handed over to Mrs Mayhew but continued as guide lieutenant until she moved away after her marriage to Revd John Downward in 1937.[98]

Hayes boys could join the scouts or cubs formed in the 1920s, although there were few members in the early days. One impetus for the boys was the arrival of 150 Danish boy scouts who were billeted in Kent in July 1923. Sixteen scouts from the Roskilde troop were lodged in Hayes and their scoutmaster commented on the warm welcome and good comradeship.[99] The scouts existed intermittently until January 1935 when they were reformed under scoutmaster Philip C Keen of 35 Chatham Avenue and numbered fifteen.

*Hayes Scouts on County Marathon 1939* [ac.]

At Barnhill School a 2nd Hayes Scout group was formed and by 1939 there were over 50 boys in the Cubs and Scouts. In 1937 a Rover group was established for the older boys led by Mr George Barber of 28 The Green and they met in the Den behind Mr Smalley's newspaper shop, the Walnut Tree.[100]

The Hayes Wolf Cubs for 8 to 10-year-old boys was started in 1923 under Mr Edwards and in 1925 won the cup for the most efficient pack in the neighbourhood, gaining 49 out of a possible 50 points. Their numbers declined as older members went up to the scouts and by December 1926 there were only five cubs in the pack. The following August, when only two were left, the pack was temporarily suspended until more boys were ready to join. By the mid 1930s there were sufficient numbers for the group to be reformed under Cub Master Henry Rye of 25 Bourne Vale and the Granary at Baston School was used as the headquarters. By 1939 they had grown in numbers to 28 with a waiting list of 6. Once again they won the Cubs' cup.[101]

## Hayes Common

The common was a favourite place for rambles and for children's activities. The Conservators continued to strive to keep it free from any development. Canon Thompson and his wife were members of the Metropolitan Public Garden Association and were very aware of the importance of open spaces and keen to enhance public facilities. The Conservators agreed to the installation of a fountain at the edge of the common by Warren Road, providing that Mrs Thompson was responsible for the water supply. She and the Rector arranged to have the fountain erected with a memorial tablet to their faithful companion Miss Mabel Parker, who died in June 1920. Unfortunately, vandals wrenched out the tablet, which had to be replaced. A few years later the water supply pipe was twisted and needed repair, but the fountain survived.[102]

The increase in visitors coming by car to Hayes resulted in successful negotiations between the Conservators and the Automobile Association to provide a free car park on the common. Some drivers, however, were reported in 1934 to the Conservators for driving their motorcars and motorcycles onto the common every night, parking under the trees and in the early hours leaving with a roar of their engines that disturbed the residents.[103] Posts had to be inserted in appropriate places to prevent this occurrence. Another car park was established and in 1938 the Conservators agreed to enlarge a reserved space near the Fox Inn.

Villagers capitalised on the visitors, set up stalls and tea gardens to help them enjoy their day out, although these were not allowed on the common. Whenever there was such a request it was denied. In July 1920 Mr L J Clifford of Camberwell, Surrey, wrote to the Conservators:

> I hope you will kindly excuse me writing to you but as I am unable to follow my previous employment owing to disabilities due to war service in Mesopotamia and my present circumstances are very bad and I have been unable to obtain work since last March would you kindly grant permission to stand on Keston or Hayes Common with a refreshment stall during the day only. I am quite willing to strictly abide by your rules and regulations and will even pay a small rent and I will promise to be of no inconvenience or nuisance to the Common or the public in any way whatever. Sir if you cannot grant me this would you allow me to stand there on August Bank Holiday Monday or on the roadside.

The Conservators' minute was to the point - 'refused'. In 1934 another Hayes trader, Horace Penrose, a baker and confectioner from Station Approach, wished to set up a 'tea table' at the top of Station Hill but he failed to obtain approval.[104]

Miss Ada Yeoman of Oak Cottages wanted to expand her tea garden and discussed with BRDC the possibility of having a refreshment stall on roadside wasteland near the

Railway Station, but the Council refused. In 1929 she applied to turn the shelter in her Tea Garden into a room. HPC approved the application, subject to satisfactory sanitation, but a few months later BRDC turned it down.[105] Miss Yeoman was protective of her position and complained to HPC about vans and traders being allowed to sell fruit and food at the top of Station Hill. In 1929 she wrote to HPC about other refreshment vendors using Hayes Common and the neighbouring roads. Her business appears to have been successful as it continued until at least 1935. Today the site of the Tea Garden is occupied by 3 Oak Cottages, Hillside Lane. The Conservators also ensured that Mrs Charlotte Knights, who ran a tea house at Pleasant View, Baston Road, did not encroach on the common.[106]

*Charlotte Knights with her daughters Grace and Ella in the tea garden at Pleasant View* [d.]

Next door to Pleasant View, Richard Stacey ran Dreadnought Cottage as a Tea Garden from the end of the First World War until 1936 when he died. The business continued under his wife Mary until 1939.

The increase in traffic to these two tea rooms convinced the Conservators that they should re-erect posts at the entrance of the track running between Dreadnought and Redgate Cottage. There were objections and Robert Pearce, who was 81 at the time and a native of Hayes, was asked about the track. He said he had:

> known the road that we call Stacyes Road all my life that runs past Stacye's Tea Rooms out to Redgates, opposite Mr. P. Jones, Hayes Court. I have never known a footpath to be fenced off or any posts only the three that is still standing. They were erected their by Mr. Edgar Jones about 25 years ago to stop people from running up on to the Common with their carts etc. it as always been rather a rough road.

William Robjant was also asked and added:

> Speaking back 60 to 70 years that I have known Stacye's Road I have never known any posts only the three that is still standing and had only known it as just a rough road leading through the Common for vehicle and foot traffic and at no time any footpath.

Richard Stacey said 'the closing of this road is liable to injure my trade which is my sole means of livelihood – been a public thoroughfare for at least a hundred years.' The Conservators decided to erect a notice, 'closed to vehicle traffic in case an accident should happen in the road'.[107] The new posts were erected and reduced the nuisance.

Owners of property bordering the common frequently needed the Conservators' permission. A good example is the Oast House, which was bought from A W J Cecil by Guilford Edward Lewis, a solicitor practising in Grays' Inn, London, in 1919.[108] He decided to convert the coach house and stables into a house and divide it from the garden with a separate entrance to Croydon Road. He asked permission to level the intervening ground. The Conservators agreed that he could make a track over the strip of common between the highway and his stabling, if he abandoned the right to wheeled traffic across the common to the gateway on the north side of his property.[109] The new building was called Turtons. In 1926 he planned to build a small cottage for his gardener near the north-east corner of his property and needed access. It was to be a single storey bungalow and in his application to the Conservators he said, 'although there is a roadway leading to the gravel pit the opening I would make [to the road] would be for foot passengers only'. The request was not well received by the Conservators who considered the opening to be trespass. Lewis responded a few weeks later stating that the ditch around his property was part of the Oast House land. At one time he suggested that the gate would be set back from the edge of his property so that when going through the gate he would still be on his land and therefore not trespassing. By June 1928 the gardener's cottage had been built but the argument between Lewis and the Conservators went on for another year and nearly ended in court. The Conservators obtained legal advice and sense prevailed. A compromise was agreed and permission was granted for the gate at a cost of one shilling a year.[110]

Guilford Lewis left the Oast House in 1934. The new owners were Ernest and Sylvia Hessenberg who, in 1935, sought permission to take gravel from the nearby pit on the common. The Conservators agreed but added that local users considered the gravel of little use for paths as it contained insufficient binding material. The Conservators also allowed the Royal Artillery at Woolwich in 1937 to purchase gorse to build fences for their point-to-point races.[111]

With the changes in local government and the demise of HPC, questions of the Common's management and the role of the Conservators were debated. Unlike most of the Bromley Borough Councillors, all the Conservators were local people with an intimate knowledge of the land that was protected by Act of Parliament. Realising the legal difficulties the Council decided in 1934 to retain the existing Conservators and allow them to continue to levy the Common Rate for the upkeep of the common. Arthur Collins remained Chairman of the Conservators. The Council decided to draw up a new scheme of management to include Keston Common that had been set up on a different basis. This required revoking the original scheme, approved in 1868, and the additional rules made by the Conservators in 1870, 1883 and 1890. The proposed new scheme was sent to the Ministry of Agriculture and Fisheries but followed the original format and sought the power to enforce the necessary bylaws to ensure the common was preserved.

The Commons have become a popular place of resort for a great number of people who reach them by public transport, private motorcar and motorcycle from London and neighbouring towns. They are much frequented by pleasure parties who if not watched often thoughtlessly or wantonly injure the trees, shrubs, turf and herbage on the Commons, and leave behind paper rubbish and other litter thereby greatly disfiguring the Common and destroying the rural aspect.[112]

Litter was a constant problem and in May 1938 the Conservators' Annual Report referred to it as 'an evil which the Conservators are always trying to reduce but never succeed in eradicating … there is still great room for improvement in the attitude of many visitors towards the preservation of parts of the countryside like the common.' A few months after its formation HVA expressed concern to the Conservators over the number of fires on the common and asked what they were going to do about it.[113] HVA also approached Bromley Council to obtain the help of the Bromley police in an attempt to prevent undesirable use being made of the common.

More patrols were needed, particularly at weekends. In 1934 HVA and the Conservators met at Baston Manor to consider a draft scheme for volunteers. HVA approved it, except for one point concerning the scavenging of the common, that it felt could be done by unemployed men and paid out of the Common Rate.

*Beating the Bounds* [ad.]

A Corps of eighteen Volunteer Rangers was set up to assist with 'dealing with fires, patrol the common and help Rangers in dealing with crowds'. Mr F W Atkinson, 3 Grove Close, from the HVA Committee was appointed 'Chief Assistant Ranger' to organise the rota. Each volunteer had to be over 21 and wear an armlet while on duty. The scheme started on Sunday 20 January 1935 and the Volunteer Rangers beat the bounds of the common. The following month 22 members had been recruited and requests were made for more volunteers.[114]

In the summer HVA suggested that volunteers should have first aid experience and that the St John Ambulance should attend Hayes Common on weekends and Bank Holidays. This was agreed and was implemented with HVA and the Conservators each giving a guinea to St John Ambulance' funds. The brigade members were stationed at the junction of Croydon and Baston Roads where most accidents occurred.

The work of the Conservators in maintaining Pickhurst Green and Hayes Common was often routine, yet they vehemently upheld the rights and by-laws. In 1934 they wrote to United Dairies to stop one of its milkmen from parking his float and allowing his horse to graze on Pickhurst Green. They rejected a proposal from Bromley Council's Coronation Celebration Committee to plant an avenue of copper beeches along Baston Road.[115] The Conservators were not against everything. In October 1935 they allowed Mr Guinness to top trees near Hayes Grove and in December 1936 John Hamer of The White House was allowed to attach an aerial to a tree just outside his grounds. In August 1937 permission was given to J & R Killick Ltd to lay a water pipe to the three Whites Cottages, Pickhurst Green at the request of the owner, Miss Vera Thompson. A few months later Killicks filled in the well formerly used by the three cottages.[116] These were probably the last cottages to draw water from a well in the parish.

***Pickhurst Green Pond***[1.]

It was about this time that the Conservators decided to fill in the pond on Pickhurst Green, which was unfenced, open to the road and considered an eyesore. They were concerned about whether the pond was filled from a stream. Bromley Council drilled three trial holes that proved inconclusive. However, Arthur Clacey of Longcroft Lodge reported that the pond did not have a spring. Beckenham Borough Council had put in a pipe to drain the water off the side of the Green and when Sam Price cleaned the pond in about 1907 he found that it had a puddled clay bottom. Bromley Council estimated that the cost of filling in the pond, erecting concrete posts and galvanised rails was £985 and it was carried out in 1939. While this was being considered Beckenham Council told the Conservators that they intended to widen Pickhurst Lane to 60ft and needed part of Pickhurst Green, which is why the depression caused by the old pond appears closer to the road compared with that shown on early maps.[117] Beckenham Council provided land abutting the Green in exchange.

Hayes Common, in the past, had many ponds, most of which were in old gravel pits that had fallen into disuse. One of the better known was Stacey's Pond close to Dreadnought Cottage filled in about August 1938 and another at the junction of Preston's Road and Warren Road that has recently been excavated and made into a feature. The latter was often subject to duckweed and smells from the stagnant water, which were dealt with by the Council's sanitary inspector.[118]

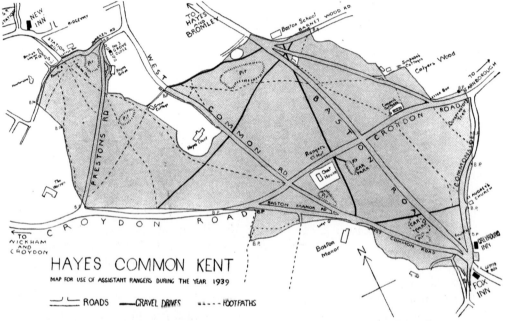

**Map 16: *Assistant Rangers' Map for Hayes Common 1939*** [aj.]

Although the common and Pickhurst Green survived under the continued policing by the Conservators, the approaching clouds of war brought new threats. Some military exercises had already taken place. In August 1937 the Conservators received a request from the Commandant of the School of Anti-Aircraft Defence, Biggin Hill to use Hayes Common for a mobile section of Anti-Aircraft guns. A year later the army at Biggin Hill arranged with the Conservators to deploy a searchlight battery on the common for a week. Afterwards the Conservators, ever guardians of the common, confirmed that the site was clear apart from a telephone cable which they asked them to remove.[119] When war broke out the Conservators were: Chairman Arthur Collins of Baston Manor, Major Basil Binyon of Hawthorndene, Lieutenant Colonel G A Fulcher from Hayes Road, Emmanuel Mansfield from George Lane and Percy Jones from Redgate Cottage.[120] It was through their efforts that Hayes Common was saved for future generations.

# Chapter 5

## Towards war

In 1919 few would have contemplated another world war yet, by 1933, some politicians had begun to voice their concern over the rise of fascism in Europe. By 1935 public opinion was divided over the likelihood of another European war. Events of the Spanish Civil War filled the newsreels, adding to the debate and apprehension about air attacks on Great Britain, should it ever be drawn into another conflict. Of all the weapons of war, the fear of gas attacks became the main preoccupation, largely supported by memories of mustard gas from the First World War.

In July 1935 the Government sent a circular to County Councils setting out the need for local authorities to form a Civil Defence organisation and in due course Bromley Borough Council began to implement these requirements. Throughout 1936 guidelines and instructions from the Home Office arrived at Bromley Town Hall and, via the various Council Committees, strategies and plans for air raid precautions (ARP) were drafted, which were soon to have an effect on the residents of Hayes.

HVA took an active interest in ARP arrangements. In July 1937, HVA's Minutes noted that Lieutenant Colonel E J Heilbron, a Vice President and representative of KCC, '… was uneasy with regard to the slow progress made by the [Bromley Council's] Air Raid Precautions Committee and suggested that the Association could handle many of the essential things which must be done'. Later in September, he said '… he was not satisfied from a county point of view of the example we were setting in view of the vulnerability of Kent.'[1] It was such opinions that goaded Bromley Borough Council to take more positive action in 1938.

Air Raid Precautions were never very far from the minds of HVA's committee members. A letter sent to the Council in January 1938 suggested that provision be made for an air raid shelter under the shops proposed for Station Approach. A second letter advised that a number of HVA members were willing to assist with ARP work and it was from this offer that a small sub-committee was formed to watch over the official ARP arrangements for Hayes. During January 1938 committee members inspected a gas mask. Over the next three years considerable efforts were made and money spent in arranging community gas attack precautions. In February 1938 the Borough Council created a new ARP committee with responsibility to organise the district's emergency plans. Under this new arrangement the HVA's representatives met the Chief Officer, Lieutenant Colonel Bird, and agreed that the Association's ARP Sub-Committee would be absorbed into the Council's ARP Committee.[2]

The 'Munich Crisis' in September 1938 brought new energies and political argument to both rearmament and civil defence in Great Britain. Mr C E Nash of 19 Cherry Walk gave an account of local ARP progress at the HVA's October 1938 General Meeting held in the Village Hall:

> An immense amount of work had been done in the last fortnight during the crisis, [including] the assembly of 60,000 gas masks at Gadsden in less than two days. He thanked the wardens, wardens in training and last minute helpers. 240 were now in training in the old school building. Fitting and distribution of gas masks was still necessary. Bags for babies will be re-designed before being issued ….

The Chairman said 'volunteers for decontamination were badly needed' and a member asked 'if the derelict Wood Cottages in Hayes Street could be used for demolition instruction'. They were not used but were demolished in 1943. Gas masks were distributed from the Old Church Schools during late September and early October 1938; 3,000, for instance, were given out on Wednesday 5th October, such was the fear of war. Other arrangements started to be made. The Hayes Common Volunteer Rangers, for example, divided up the common into areas for ARP coverage.[3]

Bromley Borough Council called for civil defence volunteers and prepared to train men and women for an unknown future. Halls and schools all over the borough were used for training sessions. In Hayes this activity centred on the Old Church Schools and the Village Hall, both of which could be made available at short notice. By November 1938 the borough had 220 male and 519 female volunteers in various stages of training, many attending first aid lessons in Hayes conducted by Dr McDonald in the Old Church Schools or Dr Hopton in the Village Hall. It was during this period that Bromley Borough Council chose the Old Church Schools for a First Aid Post and Gadsden, which had not yet been used by the Kent Education Committee, as a centre for other ARP activities. The third Hayes building to figure in the plans was the Old Rectory, recently purchased by the Council. Initially it was used to store gas masks but by December had been designated as a Damage and Casualty Centre, one of four established in the borough. In the event of the crisis worsening, the centre would be staffed by 2 sub-controllers, 2 plotters, 2 diarists, 2 message clerks, a supervisor, 4 telephonists and 8 messengers, making a total of 15 men and 6 women to provide 24 hour coverage.[4]

Bromley and Beckenham Auxiliary Fire Services (AFS) established a sub-fire station at the Old Rectory, one of a number in the district.[5] Opposite, at Hayes Street Garage, the owner agreed to allow a fire appliance - or rather a private car converted to carry ladders, hose reels, and fitted with a tow bar for a trailer pump - to be parked on his land. The nearest full time fire station to Hayes was the new station at Glebe Way, West Wickham, opened in July 1939, which with the sub-fire stations and central Bromley fire station were thought sufficient to provide the district with adequate fire cover.

The Old Rectory became the focus for ARP activities in Hayes. It was designated as a centre for decontamination and rescue parties, light clearance and demolition sections and to store ARP equipment. In January 1939, however, the Council moved the stores to Gadsden as the equipment was suffering from the effects of damp in the old building. Training and preparations continued. By May a Nissen hut had been erected in the grounds of the Old Rectory to provide sleeping accommodation for the staff.[6]

Despite all the precautions and growing uncertainty, Hayes continued to develop with neo-Tudor houses appearing on the various estates. Complaints about rail fares from Hayes to London and the local authority's general rates continued to keep the HVA Committee busy. Closure of the Old Church Schools caused problems for the Parish Church and the organisations that met in these rooms which, with the Village Hall, were well used by the growing local community during the first six months of 1939. During the year more and more ARP demands were placed on the village's accommodation.

At the February 1939 meeting of the men's branch of the Constitutional Association, held in the Village Hall, Sir Waldron Smithers, said that he was '1000 per cent behind the efforts of the Prime Minister in trying to avert war and called for everybody to give 100 per cent for the national service appeal.' Next month a photograph appeared in a local newspaper, captioned 'Somewhere in Kent - the first anti-aircraft defences'. A week later members of the 8th and 13th Companies, Women's Auxiliary Territorial Service, were drilling in Bromley, and in the subsequent edition photographs appeared of an ARP exercise held in Bromley. Yet with all this activity there was still dissatisfaction with Bromley Council's ARP preparations, a matter voiced by Lieutenant Colonel Heilbron at the April 1939 Annual General Meeting of the HVA. He complained of inefficiency, of senior air raid wardens not having the authority to issue orders to those wardens under them and that the organisation was not a cohesive force. He wanted the ARP organisation to be placed on a compulsory footing and, suggested that they should be organised on lines similar to the Territorial Army.[7]

During March 1939 the first tangible sign of air raid precautions appeared in Hayes. This was the Metropolitan Police air raid siren, which was erected on a tall pole at the junction of George Lane and Hayes Street, next to a blue police box. The police box has since gone but the siren remained for many years and was occasionally tested, producing a sound that no one who lived through the war will forget.

April 1939 saw a major exercise take place at the new school in George Lane. The drill was designed to test the first aid and communications teams and their equipment. It was a successful exercise despite it being a wet day. The following month the first night time exercise was held to test the men and women of the Borough's ARP organisation and their equipment. The success of this and other exercises led Kent County Council to declare that the ARP formations and structure were complete. Preparations continued and the Borough Council's minutes show that all except 1,400 gas masks had been distributed.

In June the Borough Council approved the expenditure of £2,000 to convert the Old Church Schools into a first aid centre. The main hall, which had been built in 1863, required the installation of a substantial false ceiling. This was approximately 8ft to 9ft above the floor, of wooden construction, and covered by sandbags to provide a measure of protection for those in the hall. Mrs Peggy Jackson of Hayes Street, who came to live in Hayes in 1940, volunteered to become a first-aider and was posted to the Old Church Schools. She recalled that the staff who manned the centre 24 hours a day used the south end of the hall. The main area was partitioned with curtains into cubicles, each containing a fabricated steel stretcher. The male toilets became the duty-office that was fitted out with a table and telephone through which the staff received the air raid 'alert state' - red, amber or green. The female cloakroom was used as the sluice, hot water being drawn from an Ideal boiler.[8]

Internationally, the outlook was very gloomy and in March 1939, Prime Minister Neville Chamberlain pledged to defend Poland. Britain was rearming as fast as she could with the Government budgeting to spend £1,322 million on defence. The Territorial Army planned to double in size to 340,000 men and local authorities were asked to build more drill halls. The expansion plans affected all branches of the services, armed and civil.

## IMPORTANT

# AIR RAID PRECAUTIONS

### Borough of Bromley.

(1) THE WARDEN OF YOUR SECTOR IS:—

*Mr C. H. Keller*

ADDRESS .............................................
*220*
.............................................

TELEPHONE *HUR : 1431*

(2) **RESPIRATORS**
allocated to your house.

Large *6* ... Medium ... *1* ... Small ... *–* ...
You **must** notify your Warden of any change in your household
Visitors **must** bring their respirators with them.
Servants engaged from outside districts **must** bring their respirators with them.

(3) YOU ARE RECOMMENDED TO:—
(1) Prepare a gas-proof refuge.
(2) Keep your respirator in order and ready for use.
(3) Have buckets of water and dry sand or earth ready in case of fire.

(4) ON WARNING OF POSSIBLE AIR RAID
Keep indoors.
Shut doors and windows.
Extinguish fires and lights.
Turn off gas (at main).
Take your respirator and retire to refuge room.

### AVOID PANIC.
[P.T.O.

(5) IN CASE OF A RAID with resulting damage to or near your house:—
INFORM YOUR WARDEN.
Let him notify the necessary authorities.

AVOID TELEPHONING Headquarters yourself, and avoid using telephone as much as possible to enable essential A.R.P. Services to use the telephone.

(6) WHEN SIGNAL " RAIDERS PASSED "
is given, make sure your neighbourhood is clear of gas before you leave your house or refuge.

(7) YOUR WARDEN is ready to give you necessary advice on all above matters ASK HIM.

(8) AIR RAID WARNING SIGNALS

" AIR RAID POSSIBLE WITHIN 5 MINUTES "

SIREN from Police Headquarters (intermittent).
Whistle Blasts by Wardens and Police.

" GAS DETECTED LOCALLY "

HAND RATTLES by Wardens.

" RAIDERS PASSED "

SIREN (continuous note 2 minutes) from Police Headquarters.

HAND BELLS from Wardens.

*Signature of Occupier*
.............................................

*Address*
*25 HAYES STREET*
*HAYES KENT.*

*Date*
*19/7/39*

*ARP Instructions issued to inhabitants of Hayes July 1939* [af.]

Farmers were encouraged to plough up grazing pastures to support a Government scheme to increase food production. All this furious national activity was repeated at local authority level, including Bromley, where it was directed at Civil Defence, the maintenance of Borough services and the accommodation of army units that were being deployed in the district.

Bromley experienced a mock air raid during June 1939. Various parts of the Borough were 'hit' including Gadsden. It was at a similar exercise that Alan Pettitt, a Boy Scout living in Pittsmead Avenue, was involved as a mock casualty. With a label tied to his coat, stating that he had broken his shoulder and was suffering from the effects of mustard gas, he was sent to Socket Lane, to await the rescue squad. Alan and the other scouts were duly rescued and taken to Gadsden where they were 'laid out' on the grass. Afterwards they went to the Old Church Schools for a bath.[9] The June exercise was fully reported and it is interesting to quote from the local newspaper, as wartime reports did not normally give such detail.

> The shriek of the sirens at Hayes brought people to their doors and quite a crowd collected around the Hayes garage, and ARP centre. The curious were not disappointed for there was a great deal of activity. Seven people were injured outside the railway station by a shower of small high explosive bombs, and civil defence first aid volunteers were called to attend their needs. The injured were stretchered out to the car park by the New Inn while details were taken and first aid rendered. Then they were carried on stretchers to the ambulance and whisked away to a first aid post. The ambulance services were also called to Gadsden where fragments of anti-aircraft shells fell on several people who were leaving the fête there. Rescue and demolition workers had a lot of work to do at the open space at Pittsmead and Chatham Avenue. A high explosive bomb partially demolished a hut and a local resident was trapped there. He was rescued and a 'sitting car' came along to take him for treatment. AFS men quickly answered a call for trailer pumps at Station Approach where incendiary bombs fell. All around the district the wardens seemed to be on the alert and we may safely declare that Hayes was adequately protected.

To add to the realism of the exercise two large planes of the Royal Air Force circled over Bromley.[10]

Although the common had escaped most of the changes brought about by the development of the village, the approaching preparations for war were to bring Pickhurst Green and Hayes Common into the frontline, the effects of which were to last more than a decade. The first approach by the War Office to use part of the common as an Anti-Aircraft gun site was made on 18 May 1939 to the Chairman of Hayes Common Conservators. The Conservators refused stating that the ground of the suggested site was too soft and to try a site near Keston School instead.[11] The Chairman met with representatives of the Lands Branch of the War Office, Office of Works and a Royal Artillery gunnery officer. The Army outlined their requirements for an anti-aircraft site for four heavy mobile guns to be situated near the south-east corner of the junction of Baston and Croydon Roads by the traffic lights. The guns would require concrete foundations, a prepared roadway and were to be deployed as soon as the work was completed. In addition, four to six army huts were to be sited just to the west of the proposed gun-site. The position of these, however, was temporary until a more permanent location could be arranged. The Conservators agreed to cooperate but expressed their concern over the possible permanent appropriation of the land, and reserved their rights under the Act protecting Hayes Common. The government's representative advised that he had all the legal powers needed to undertake the work and occupy the area and stated that the same was happening to Richmond Common, Barnes

Common and many other open spaces. The Conservators requested that the huts should be rustic in appearance.

The Hayes gun-site was one of 23 built to protect London and the southeastern approaches. The Conservators sought legal advice from the Town Clerk of the Borough Council, as they were concerned over the long-term issues regarding the Army's occupation of the common. Bromley Borough Council, as lord of the manor, and the Conservators joined forces to act in their mutual interests. These matters were resolved and by 20 May 1939 agreement was reached for the levelling, clearance and construction work to commence for four heavy guns, six huts and the use of the gravel pit on the south side of Croydon Road, east of the Oast House. Access to the site was from a new track, the entrance to which was on Croydon Road opposite Romany Cottage. By August 1939 the Conservators had written to the Land Agent of Eastern Command pointing out that the gun detachment had arrived and a search light crew had occupied another part of the common near Hartfield Crescent, without approval.[12] The local newspaper noted that Royal Artillery gunners were seen playing cricket on Hayes Common. This was the beginning of a long association between the army and residents of the parish.

On Saturday, 2 September 1939, Bromley Borough Council held a special meeting of the General Purposes Committee to discuss the national emergency.[13] Amongst the many topics considered was the creation of a Food Control Committee. The ARP Committee reported to the Council that a further 700 respirators were needed and these were duly assembled over the weekend at Gadsden, under the supervision of Mr S Wrathall, the storekeeper. Camouflage nets, some of which were used by local army units, were also made at Gadsden. Tenders were received to line the slit trench shelters that had been dug during the Munich Crisis in September 1938. Under the Civil Defence Act 1939 the Borough Council designated the basements of four shops in Station Approach, Nos.42 to 48, as public air raid shelters. Slit trench shelters were also dug in the grounds of the Old Rectory and Knoll Park, off Pickhurst Lane. Lighting restriction came into force and, to aid the movement of night-time traffic, white lines were painted everywhere and illuminated road signs were fitted with louvered hoods. The Government was concerned about the danger to large gatherings in cinemas, schools and similar places.

## The Phoney War – September 1939 to July 1940

Many inhabitants were at home, tuned into the BBC's Home Service programme, to hear Prime Minister Neville Chamberlain speak to the nation on the morning of Sunday 3 September 1939. He announced that Britain was at war with Germany. At approximately 11.15am, just fifteen minutes after war had been declared, sirens sounded all over the borough warning that an air raid was imminent. The morning service at the Parish Church was interrupted. The Rector had just read the banns of marriage for Charles Harvey and Joan Long, whose wedding was to take place that afternoon.[14] If the warning had been a few minutes earlier the couple's wedding might have had to be delayed. Older villagers remembered incidents in the First World War and shuddered at the thought that Hayes might again be bombed. The alert was a false alarm but it was an indicator of what might be coming.

Cinemas and schools were closed. Plans to build the Free Church on the old manor site in Pickhurst Lane were postponed and most house construction stopped for the duration of the emergency. Hayes was experiencing dramatic changes in line with many other communities.

More changes were on the way, not in terms of bricks, mortar and new houses but of people. Within a year there was an influx of military personnel who had to be billeted and refugees from the Continent to be housed. Other people left the village as they volunteered or were conscripted into the forces. The war and the prospect of combat brought considerable anguish to people with strong pacifist beliefs. Conscientious objectors appeared before tribunals to plead their case against being 'called-up' into a combat unit of the armed services. Wilfred Batten of Hurstdene Avenue, a member of Hayes Free Church, was dismissed by his employer when he registered as a conscientious objector. His case was heard by the London Tribunal who decided that he must do full time AFS, ARP or land work. Leonard Wilkes, an architectural assistant of Trevor Close and an ARP stretcher-bearer, had his case considered in July 1940 by the South-East Tribunal and he was registered for non-combatant service with a recommendation for service in the Royal Army Medical Corps (RAMC). Later that year, Charles Mcleod's name was removed from the list of registered non-combatants but he stated that as a member of the Peace Pledge Union he would appeal against the decision. The Central Appellate Tribunal agreed that another Hayes man, G A Treagus, should be registered only for non-combatant duties.[15] Dr Colville Barrington, a member of the Religious Society of Friends, enrolled with the RAMC and was sent to West Africa. Later he was one of the first doctors to render medical assistance when Belsen Concentration Camp was liberated at the end of the war.[16]

Most difficult of all was the evacuation of families to safer areas. Sometimes whole families moved but, in many cases, it was mothers and children who went, or children were evacuated on their own. Miss Mercia Sansom, who lived at 37 Pickhurst Mead, recalled several occasions when she and other local teachers were sent all over the country escorting children to evacuation homes in, for example, Leeds and Chester. She also escorted a group of children, each wearing a yellow armband, to Liverpool for embarkation to Canada. On one occasion a party of 321 children, including Derek and Doreen Fairhurst and Michael Brooker from Hayes, were embarked on *SS Volendam*, which sailed from Liverpool for Halifax, Nova Scotia, on 29 August 1940 with 606 passengers and crew. The liner was torpedoed on 30th August but the children returned safely to the Clyde. Derek and Doreen, aged 13 and 10 respectively, came home to 47 Westland Drive. Derek described his experience at the time, 'I woke up to the sound of a big bang and thought it was a bomb. It was about 30 seconds before the bells began to ring, and by that time I had my clothes on. They put me into a lifeboat, and after half-an-hour they tied a rope around my waist and hauled me on to a collier.' Ten-year-old Michael Brooker, who lived at 189 Bourne Vale, did not return home because an unexploded bomb was still being dealt with and there was a possibility that his house might be destroyed. He travelled to Liverpool and was given priority on the next ship bound for Canada, *SS City of Benares*. This time he was not so fortunate. The ship was torpedoed on 17th September, the crew managed to launch the lifeboats but most, including Michael Brooker, did not survive.[17] The scheme for overseas evacuation was abandoned after this tragedy.

Many parents arranged for the private evacuation of their children. Some Hayes pupils went to Wales or Devon and others to Hereford. Miss Shirley Stevens and her brother stayed almost twelve months in Hereford. She recalled that her brother was most disappointed to be away from the action and wrote to his mother asking her to send all the shrapnel she could collect, as he knew 'a boy who would pay sixpence for a reasonably sized piece'. Keeping in contact was important but when a child had been evacuated overseas, as was the case of John Cushen (113 Pickhurst Lane), who was despatched to Weymouth Massachusetts, the problem was magnified. In February 1944, however, his father Leonard Cushen was fortunate to be able to send a message to him via the BBC's *Hello Children Service*.[18]

Those who remained became a close-knit community, working together and supporting each other in such tasks as fire watching, air raid precautions, or as special constables and auxiliary firemen. Social activities became an integral part of bringing everyone together and were instrumental in enabling villagers to cope during wartime.

From the outset it was clear that this war was different from the First Word War. Preparations continued and everyone awaited the expected aerial attacks. Many hundreds of Hayes people became involved with local Civil Defence and many duties were carried out in the evenings, after a full day's work. In September 1939 the ARP Committee reported to the Borough Council on the District Wardens' organisation. Hayes was in No 5 District and the District Warden was William Melville of 15 Hurstdene Avenue. He left to take a commission in the RAF in May 1940 and was replaced by Percival Nye of Prickley Wood. Under him were five Post Wardens and 81 Wardens and the posts (PD1-5) were situated at Socket Lane, Courtlands Avenue, Chatham Avenue, Knoll Park and Gadsden. In November, the Courtlands Avenue Post, PD2, moved to the garage of 126 Pickhurst Lane and later had 31 Wardens, drawn from surrounding roads, attached to it. Changes occurred when men were drafted, moved to another branch of the civilian services, joined the Home Guard or their employment took them away from the village. Mr Dewey, for example, who was in PD2 during the daytime and PD5 at night, was directed to Oxford in July 1942 to make aircraft wings.[19]

Fire watching was an important ARP task. The threat of fire by incendiary bombs was real and many hours of training were given to cope with these nasty but effective weapons. With their magnesium alloy casings, the bombs could become trapped in roofs, gutters and all sorts of crevices and would soon ignite, setting alight any building in which they were caught. Road and street fire squads were formed to detect and deal with these incidents using buckets, stirrup pumps, long handle shovels and sand. By January 1941 Hayes had 40 fire-watching parties, organised in squads of 10 or more, so that groups of three people were on duty each night. A surviving document details the fire squads formed to cover a small part of Bourne Vale and Trevor Close, where 28 people initially volunteered for fire cover duties. They were later organised in seven groups of three, the remainder acted as reserves.[20] Squad 7 was manned by Mr and Mrs Eland of No. 69 and Mr Phillips of 59 Pickhurst Lane. A near miss, while she was on duty in March 1941, resulted in Mr Eland refusing to allow his wife to undertake any more duties until she was provided with a steel helmet. Mr G Gell from 100 Pickhurst Lane took her place. By the end of 1941, Hayes had 150 fireguard squad leaders and deputies and 1,250 fireguards in 63 squads.

In addition there were the volunteers for the AFS, and the Light and Heavy Rescue sections of the ARP. Inhabitants were determined to safeguard their community. Local Boy Scout troops had helped on many ARP exercises and their support was not limited to training exercises. Scouts were attached to the Sub-Control Centre at the Old Rectory and to each Warden's post to act as ARP messengers. In 1939 two scout messengers were attached to PD2; one was on duty from 9am to 3pm and the other from 3pm to 9pm. An adult carried out the night duty.[21]

Dorothy Timms of 16 Mounthurst Road trained as a communications worker in the early part of 1939. On the outbreak of war she was assigned to the Old Rectory and afterwards to a room in Gadsden where she maintained contact with the local Wardens' posts. In 1941 she was deployed to the Borough ARP Centre with her sister, Nancy, and Mrs Haden, wife of John Haden, who was later Mayor and Alderman of Bromley.[22]

*Bromley ARP Control Centre* [c.]

In October 1939 Hayes experienced another ARP exercise centred on Longcroft, which had been partially demolished the previous May. This ruin provided the Gadsden based No.3 Stretcher Party and Light Rescue Sections with practical training in the recovery of realistic mock casualties from building debris. Equipment for Civil Defence units was adequate although there was a shortage of 'comforts'. A month later, No. 3 Stretcher Party asked, through the local newspapers, for easy chairs, card tables, curtains, carpets and rugs to make Gadsden more comfortable during the long hours of duty.[23]

***Bromley ARP Control Centre*** [c.]

In the same month Keston Ponds were used for a large AFS trailer pump exercise involving twenty brigade crews. Later similar drills were held at Kelsey Park, Beckenham. Natural water supplies would become an important source to fight fires if the mains supply was disrupted. Emergency Water Supply (EWS) tanks were built to supplement the natural resources. One such brick built EWS tank, holding about 100,000 gallons of water, was constructed at the junction of The Green and Pittsmead Avenue.[24]

In the first week of the war, a reporter wrote that he 'did not expect a time when such a landmark … as the Old Church School would disappear behind piles of sand-bags'. The use of the Schools as a first aid post seriously affected the village organisations that regularly used the halls; compromise and adjustment had to be the order of the day. By October 1939, the Juventus Youth Club, the forerunner of the Hayes Youth Fellowship and Challengers Youth Club, reported that it:

> had not been able to meet for the winter session on account of the school being used as a first aid post. Most young men were engaged in some form of war work; efforts were being made to find accommodation where the girls might meet from time to time.

At the same time the PCC was planning its forthcoming AGM and 'hoped there would be a full moon on the night', on account of the lack of street lamps and blackout.[25] A year later, Revd McClintock reported that practically all organisations had been hit by the 'commandeering' of the halls.

The war at sea started immediately but the air and land wars, as far as Great Britain was concerned, were some months away. The first recorded Hayes death was of Arthur James Davis, Petty Officer Stoker on *HMS Iron Duke*, a gunnery training ship badly damaged in a German air raid on 17 October 1939. The first phase of the war at home was a waiting time. Civil Defence members were ready to test their training, but there was little action until the start of the Battle of Britain in July 1940. This intervening period, known as the 'Phoney War', was unexpected but allowed Britain's civil, manufacturing organisations and armed services to continue preparations and training for total war and its consequences.

The great uncertainty was reflected in the activities of many local organisations. HCC carried on and reported at the AGM in May 1940 that despite the blackout the village hall had been in constant use. The management and hiring of the hall by groups continued, although public meetings were discontinued and not reinstated until 1943. HVA cancelled its October General Meeting but, as there seemed little immediate threat from air attack, held the January meeting and the AGM in April 1940 at which plans were announced about the organisation to be adopted if it was necessary to suspend the Association until the end of the war. An Emergency Committee was formed to conduct the Association's affairs as the need arose. It consisted of Messrs F W Atkinson, chairman; F W Walford, treasurer; A G Hancock, secretary; L Morton and Councillor Percy Jones. The items discussed at the April AGM reflected the changing priorities; there was less about developers and more on civil defence, war savings and allotments. The Secretary's report throws some light on the difficulties encountered by the HVA during the emergency:

> The past year has been one of difficulty for the Association ... Many new matters have been considered which have arisen out of wartime conditions such as the increases in the price of gas and electricity, allotments, dangers to pedestrians in the blackout ..., air raid precautions, public shelters, travelling conditions on the railways, ... national savings, war damage to property, and so forth ... your Committee has not met so frequently as usual and at one stage an emergency sub-committee was appointed ... in order to have in existence a body with the authority to act in the event of war developing in such as way as to give rise to the necessity for immediate decisions ...[26]

The minutes of this meeting were not confirmed until April 1945, the next time a General Meeting of the HVA was held.

The Council built a decontamination centre on the north side of the Old Rectory Gardens at an estimated cost of £1,865. The Old Rectory was said to be very 'war like'. Public shelters, slit trenches or surface structures, were constructed in Knoll Park (Ridgeway end) and the Old Rectory grounds for 200 and 150 persons respectively. The latter was not built until 1940 after it was reported that a number of Auxiliary Firemen stationed at Hayes had been using the cleansing station as protected sleeping quarters and had been joined by 30 members of the public 'owing to heavy rain'. A small shelter for 50 people was dug on land at the junction of Mead Way and Hayes Lane. These, with the basement shelters in Station Approach, provided protection for a few but with a population of about 7,000 it could not be expected that the local authority would, or could, cater for everybody. In July 1940 thirteen householders in Bourne Vale were allowed to erect a communal shelter on a grass reserve forming part of the highway. A public shelter was constructed in East Way at the request of local residents in October 1940.[27]

*Shelter sign outside Hylda & John's Café in Station Approach* ⁿ·

*Brick built shelter in Baston Road, later used as a garden shed*

Hayes and Baston Schools were provided with shelters for pupils and staff. Householders were encouraged to obtain Anderson shelters, at a cost of £6 14s. 0d., from Bromley Borough Council, who were inundated with requests during the first weeks of the war. The Council had started supplying shelters much earlier and by July 1939 had received 3,557 applications for free shelters from those who earned less than £250 per annum. Anderson shelters were partially sunk into the ground and covered with earth, which gave effective protection, but frequently became waterlogged if they were not lined. The problem led to many people suffering from 'shelter fever' similar to a sore throat.

Mr Alan Pettitt remembered that with the introduction of Morrison shelters in 1941 the Boy Scouts helped many elderly ladies assemble them. These shelters were steel fabricated and erected inside houses, usually in place of the dining room table, under which families slept. Canon Bill Norman, who as a child lived at Street House, remembers well the Morrison Shelter Table under which as many of the family as possible lay, if the enemy planes seemed near. His bedroom was on the top floor and the Morrison Shelter was in his father's study on the ground floor. It normally meant that he was woken from a deep sleep and he often felt that he 'would rather have stayed in bed and risked the danger from the bombs'.[28]

Many houses had brick-built shelters, some of which survive and are often used today as garden sheds. Mrs Vera Bardgett, a teacher at Hayes School from 1942, recalled that when war broke out a brick shelter was built in their garden at 66 Pickhurst Lane. It had a reinforced concrete roof and was entered down steps. It was well equipped with bunks and electric light. Mrs Bardgett, however, did not like sleeping in it, and after a couple of nights she and her husband decided that, as they had no dependants, they would not sleep in the shelter and returned to the house in which they slept for the rest of the war. Despite the many incendiaries that fell in their garden they were never injured, and sand and a long handled shovel were always kept nearby to extinguish them.

The gardens of the cottages of 182 to 200 Croydon Road were too small for air raid shelters and the Borough Engineer asked the Conservators for permission to erect steel shelters on the common at the rear of Nos. 194 and 198. This was granted on the understanding that, when removed, the ground would be restored to its original state.[29]

The Conservators purchased two steel helmets for the Rangers at a cost of 6s. each. It was a busy time for Conservators and Rangers with routine activities, plus the additional work brought about by the occupation of part of Hayes Common by the army authorities. This was compounded by the call-up of the third ranger, Williams, who was a reservist in the Scots Guards.[30]

## Military Preparations

Two elements of the defence of Great Britain affected the community; first the need to prepare for and neutralise the enemy's capacity to attack from the air and secondly, to organise protection on land against a sea-borne invasion. Anti-aircraft and anti-invasion defences were built and servicemen and women deployed in the parish.

Hayes Common Conservators worked with the Lands Branch, Eastern Command of the War Department, during the 'Phoney War' regarding the use of Hayes Common and

Pickhurst Green. Formal agreement to the army's occupation of Hayes Common was finally reached in April 1941. Initially, the agreed area was fairly small but the site expanded to encompass the whole of the common bounded by Croydon Road, Baston Road and Commonside. The Army also negotiated to mount a searchlight battery on the common near the junction of Croydon Road and Hartfield Crescent.[31]

To keep the public away and to provide a measure of security, Baston Road between Croydon Road and Heathfield Road was closed to all civilian traffic and bus route 146 was diverted via West Common Road and Baston Manor Road away from the anti-aircraft gun site. The Hayes name was removed from all notice boards and boundary posts in an attempt to mislead a potential invader.[32]

Bromley Council approved the laying of telephone lines between the gun site and Hayes Court, which had been commandeered by the army as an emergency measure. Another telephone line was laid between Baston Manor and the Battery headquarters at Woodside in Commonside, Keston, and electricity supply cables provided to the army huts.

By early 1941 military activity on the common increased. Some sites were abandoned, such as the search light station opposite Hartfield estate and the original temporary huts to the west of the Oast House, when new ones were completed to the south of the gun site. A machine gun post was sited opposite the Fox Inn for the Home Guard. More wooded parts of the common were taken over around Hayes Court and The Grove and military vehicles were dispersed under the trees along Baston Manor Road. The army indicated to the Conservators that it needed more land. For technical reasons it wished to erect a high fence, construct brick buildings, concrete foundation work and take in part of Baston Road for the installation of radar-controlled gun laying equipment. By this time Hayes Common was also being used by the Royal Corps of Signals (RCS) and a Canadian detachment of artillery had built huts near the Oast House and the Grove.[33]

Apart from construction staff, the first army unit to occupy the Hayes Common gun site, known as site ZS10, was 302 Heavy Anti-Aircraft (HAA) Battery Royal Artillery (RA) which, like most batteries, was manned by men of the Territorial Army. They were deployed on 29 September 1939 with two old naval guns, each of 3" calibre. The unit was part of 99 (London Welsh) HAA Regiment, which had its headquarters at Wickham Court, West Wickham. By 18th October the battery had been replaced by 303 HAA Battery, whose stay at ZS10 must have been difficult as 30 of the battery's troops had contracted gastroenteritis by 3rd November and were taken to hospital. This prompted an inspection the next day by the Divisional Commander. On 5th November an outbreak of scarlet fever was reported and 34 'other ranks' were taken to Orpington Isolation Hospital, destined not to return to ZS10 until 29th November. For the first few months the gunners were occupied setting up the local organisation, submitting to inspections by senior officers and installing communication systems, the latter being undertaken by 1 AA Division Signals Unit. From 303 HAA Battery's War Diaries, it appears that the first action happened on 20th November when the Battery Commander received a signal that a hostile aircraft was approaching Hayes. In the event the aircraft changed course and was not seen over Hayes. By early June 1940 the gun site was occupied by 263 HAA

Battery, who had established its headquarters at Hayes Court, which had been unoccupied since Miss Katherine Cox's school had closed at the end of 1939. Throughout the war, the units at ZS10 constantly changed for tactical needs, training and practice or when deployed on overseas duties.[34]

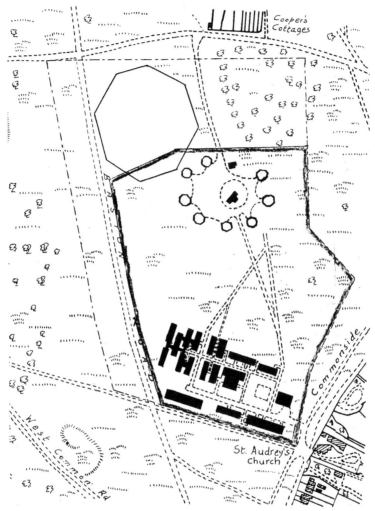

**Map 17: *Gun site and Army Camp on Hayes Common* [aj.]**

Land defence against invasion was very complex.[35] The Army's strategies and organisation to defend Britain evolved and changed many times, as military intelligence of the enemy's intentions developed. In May 1940 Hayes was in the Metropolitan Police area and part of the London Defence District, protected by the Army's 2nd London Division. Within the 2nd London Division, the formations included the 20th and 24th Brigades of Guards and the boundary between them ran from Leaves Green to Keston, then to Hayes Station and along the railway line towards Beckenham. Forming part of 24th Brigade, whose headquarters was at Addington Palace Golf Club, Addington, were 1 Battalion Irish Guards, 1 Battalion Scots Guards, 1 Battalion Welsh Guards, 2 Battalion

Warwickshire Regiment, 23 Field Regiment RA and 285 Anti-Tank Battery RA. Cover was provided for Hayes by 24 Bomb Disposal Section, Royal Engineers, which was based at 48 Wickham Road, Beckenham.[36]

The army unit at Hayes Court was 2 Artillery Signals Section, Training Battalion, RCS, whose orders in the event of invasion were 'to deny the area around West Common Road to enemy parachutists and to defend their base in Hayes Court'. No. 4 Air Formation Section later occupied Hayes Court to provide communications between the various army and air force units in the area. Throughout the war RCS were continually laying new cables across the common and installing communications equipment at ZS10. For some years after the end of the war telephone line insulators could be seen on trees.[37]

In May and June, with the growing threat of invasion, all road direction signs were removed and the Conservators placed all notices and signs from the common, including the tablet on the fountain, with J & R Killick for safekeeping.[38]

Army specialists surveyed the physical defences and proposed a linear defensive line, known as the 'Anti-Tank Line', that bisected the northern part of Hayes and included Pickhurst Green, for which the Conservators gave permission in July 1940. The Anti-Tank Line was designed to stop the enemy and made use of all available features; where houses were close together they would delay enemy armour advancing on London. The Army's Operational Order stated the defensive line must be defended 'to the last man and the last bullet'.

In the case of open spaces, anti-tank ditches were dug, usually 18ft wide by 9ft deep, or large concrete blocks constructed. For roads a series of sunken sockets were set into the carriageway in which bent railway lines could be inserted on the approach of enemy vehicles. One of these obstacles was constructed by the Lodge entrance of Hayes Free Church.

*Part of the road block barrier in Pickhurst Lane into which barricades were to be slotted to slow an approaching enemy [ag.]*

The anti-tank line was established in the later part of 1940 and a map prepared by the Royal Engineers in July 1942 shows its exact position. In Bromley it followed the railway line to Bickley and Bromley South where the defensive line followed Stone Road into Hayesford Park, which was then still open land. It crossed Mead Way to Cupola Wood and Pickhurst Green where a section of anti-tank ditch was dug, probably by 706 General Construction Company, Royal Engineers, based at Woolwich, assisted by the Home Guard. From Pickhurst Green the defence line crossed Pickhurst Lane, where road slots were sited for rails to be inserted when the need arose. At the corner of Crest Road a pillbox was erected in the front garden of 117 Pickhurst Lane.[39] On the west side of Pickhurst Lane the line ran behind Hilldown Road with the houses in Pickhurst Rise forming a long 'natural' obstacle. From here it moved to Hayes Hill and crossed the railway line just west of the footbridge where a single tank-trap was built that marked the eastern end of the anti-tank ditch cut across Hawes Down School playing field.

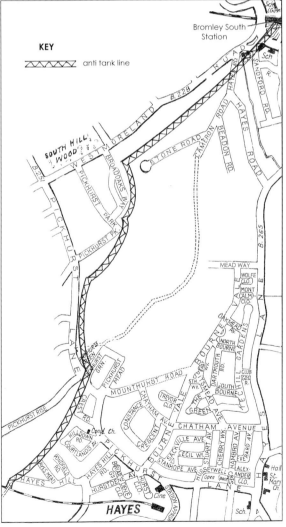

**Map 18:** *Anti-tank line set up in 1940*

There were two other strategic defence lines that, although important in the overall plan, did not affect Hayes. These were the inner defence line, which ran from the Thames at Woolwich around Eltham, Blackheath, Lewisham and westwards, and the other was the outer defensive line established a few miles south of Hayes that bisected the county. If the German forces had invaded and broken through the first defensive line, Hayes would have become the front line with all the horrors that that would have entailed.

1st Battalion Irish Guards moved their battalion headquarters to Sanderstead in November 1940 and covered the sector from West Wickham Railway Station to Chislehurst. The 1st Company Battalion was to occupy the line from the site of Hayes Place to West Wickham Railway Station and the 2nd Company from the site of Hayes Place to Bromley Common. The 1st Company's headquarters were designated as 4 Wickham Chase and 362 Pickhurst Rise, both just north of the anti-tank line.

The 1st Battalion was involved in a number of Brigade exercises on Hayes, West Wickham and Keston Commons, in order to familiarise itself with the area. In the event of an invasion barricades were to be erected at critical points including the junctions of Pickhurst Lane and Westmoreland Road, Hayes Lane and Masons Hill, and across the road opposite 206 Hayes Lane. These defensive arrangements continued well into 1942, with army units changing regularly.[40]

## The Home Guard

Men from the age of 18 to 40, who were not in reserved occupations, had been called up since 1939 but in May 1940 Anthony Eden, Secretary of State for War, announced the setting up of a Local Defence Volunteer Force for men between the ages of 17 and 65. The force became known as the Home Guard. Over 3,000 men descended on Bromley Police Station to register for service. The list of applicants was reduced to 200 from which the initial Home Guard unit was formed. 51 Kent Battalion, Bromley's Home Guard, consisted of four companies; B Company covered the Hayes area. Most of the fifteen men from Hayes selected at the first enrolment on 16 May 1940 had served in the First World War.[41] On 10 August 1940 King George VI, accompanied by the Home Guard Zone Commander, Colonel F W Chamberlain of Glebe House, West Wickham, inspected 51 and 52 Battalions at West Wickham Cricket Ground.

A further recruiting campaign opened on 9 February 1941 with a drumhead service, held on Hayes Common, conducted by a Canadian Army chaplain, Captain J McKinnie, and assisted by Home Guard Company Commander, Captain Harrison. The enrolling officer was Major John Haden and the first of several Hayes men to enlist was Reginald Stevens of 45 Chatham Avenue, who resigned from the AFS in order to join. Later he was commissioned as a lieutenant, demobbed at 'stand down' in 1944 and rejoined for the period 1952 to 1957 when the Home Guard was reformed during the 'cold war' period. Over 150 Hayes men joined and a number also formed part of a Mobile Home Guard unit.[42]

One of B Company's first tasks was to construct a 'strong point', rather like a small rectangular pillbox, in the front garden of 210 Hayes Lane, one of a series in the Borough. A second 'strong point' was erected at the entrance of Socket Lane but in this case it was constructed with sandbags. Another was built, by the Home Guard, on the extreme southern edge of the common and parish border, near The Fox public house and used to mount a machine gun to cover the road junction.

Gordon Johnson of 3 Redgate Drive joined the Hayes Home Guard in 1942 and took part when his employment, converting Thames barges for military purposes, permitted. He recalled that 'the "strong points" had to be manned all night' and that 'sticky bombs, guns and ammunition were buried in a big pit [probably the old farm pond] in the garden of the Pickhurst Hotel in case of an invasion'.[43] This arms dump was close to the anti-tank line that was to be manned and defended by the Home Guard. Towards the end of the war this cache of arms was retrieved and returned to the army ordnance authorities.

***Recruiting for the Home Guard in Hayes in February 1941.***
***The enrolling officer is John Haden*** [ah.]

The Hayes 'B' Company used the vacated Hayes Estate shop, 24 Hayes Street, as its headquarters and stored more guns and equipment. The men heard training lectures from First World War soldiers and during a typical month would be involved on at least 21 evenings on such activities as reconnaissance patrols, spigot weapon firing and night exercises. A mini rifle range was established on land at Baston School where they practised their skills with 0.22″ rifles. Drills were held in various parts of Hayes, including in the evenings the Village Hall and the main hall at Hayes Council School. In June 1941 the Hayes Village Hall Management Committee was very concerned about the hard wear on the drugget caused by the Home Guard's drilling. It decided that: 'should the Home Guard wish to book the Hall in future, an undertaking must be obtained that drill in heavy boots will not take place'.[44] During the summer months the common was used and on one occasion the Home Guard drilled along Redgate Drive, to the delight of the local children. Hayes Street Farm, Glebe House, Barnet Wood fields and most open land in the parish were used for exercises.

By 1942, 51 Battalion was well established in Hayes, manning the Anti-tank Line. Observation posts were set up at Mounthurst Road and Cupola Wood, both of which afforded a reasonable view of Hayes Bottom and the land to the southeast. 55 Battalion, which was responsible for the area to the west of Hayes, created similar observations posts at Hayes Hill Sports Club (now the Old Wilsonians), and at Hast Hill. Ammunition dumps and inflammable supplies were also established behind the Walnut Tree, at Baston School and a number of other sites.[45]

The operational boundaries between 51 and 55 Battalions lay approximately along a line from Pickhurst Lane via Crest Road to the railway-bridge in Tiepigs Lane. It crossed Bourne Way to Holland Way then along the eastern edge of The Warren to Croydon Road. In the event of an invasion 51 Battalion's Operational Instruction for 1942 stated that it had 'to prevent by every means and at all costs the occupation or penetration of the Zone Area by the enemy' and 'to hold every position to the last'. To bring the battalion to action stations the code word was 'Call Out The Home Guard', the air raid siren would be sounded or church bells rung for five minutes. Once the alarm had been given the battalion's tasks were to man the open spaces and the Anti-tank Line, to camouflage defensive positions, insert barrier rails into the road slots, distribute grenades and explosives and requisition houses required for operational purposes. At 'Action Station' the troops guarding the open spaces would be withdrawn to man the Anti-Tank Line, minefields would be laid and disruption parties deployed to undertake immobilisation activities. B Company would be deployed, initially, in the Crest Road, Baston Farm and Keston Mark areas. They would only withdraw from Keston Mark when relieved by 52 Battalion and then re-deploy at the Anti-tank Line.[46]

*Members of Hayes Company, Home Guard* [ai.]

*Hayes Home Guard* [x.]

The Home Guard had to be fed and each man was to bring rations sufficient to last at least 24 hours. Additional rations were to be requisitioned from local retailers. Meat would be obtained from P John, a butcher in Hayes Street, milk from R Bowyer & Sons, Wickham Road, Shirley, groceries from E Tidbury, Hayes Stores, West Common Road and bread from A J Wood & Son, Keston. All catering would be undertaken at the Company HQ at 24 Hayes Street. Fuel for motor transport would come from Campbell's Garage, Station Approach. Such plans demonstrate the involvement of local people in the event of an invasion force reaching northwest Kent.[47]

Throughout the war until the 'stand down' in 1944 the Home Guard undertook many tasks, including supporting the local authorities in cordoning off roads, guarding unexploded bombs and crashed aircraft. Home Guard troops, whether on sentry duty or manning the anti-aircraft guns, were at risk from enemy action. In 1941, for instance, two men of 'B' Company on duty at a company post were injured by a bomb falling nearby. One soldier had his trousers blown off and the other was knocked on the head, and both suffered from shock. When the Company Commander was asked what action he had taken, his reply was 'I took them along to The George, gave them a pint and put them back on duty'.[48]

In the last half of 1942 the requirement to release men from the Anti-Aircraft Command, in particular from the many HAA and LAA regiments, led to the transfer of 100 Home Guard men of 51 Battalion to 71 County of London HAA Battery. These Home Guard soldiers helped to fill the gaps when Territorial Soldiers were posted to other units.

Hayes Common Conservators also suffered from a loss of manpower. In July 1940 Mr J Harwood replaced Mr Williams as a full-time third assistant ranger at a salary of £2 15s. 0d. a week, but within the year he left to take up a full-time post with the ARP. Ranger Drake joined the Home Guard. During the same period it was proposed that the Volunteer Rangers formed in 1935 should be disbanded as the men were on civil and military defence work.[49] These staff changes affecting the Hayes Common Conservators were typical of those felt by many local organisations and businesses as they adjusted to a shortage of manpower. By 1940 many men and women from Hayes had joined up. Once again, as in the First World War, families waited anxiously for news of their loved ones although for most people at home there was not yet any sign of enemy action.

# Chapter 6
## Hayes at war: 1940-1945

The end of the 'Phoney War' was signalled by the collapse of the Low Countries when German forces overran them in May 1940. Many displaced families from these countries arrived in the district under arrangements made by the Ministry of Health. The Mayor of Bromley, Councillor Margaret Stafford Smith, co-founder of Baston School, formed a War Refugees Voluntary Committee to organise the refugees' reception and welfare. Hayes Councillor Percy Jones and Mrs E M Busbridge of 20 Ridgeway were also members. The refugees were supplied with identity cards, ration books and gas masks. Gadsden was chosen as the Reception Centre for northwest Kent and large marquees were erected to accommodate them while their needs were assessed and more permanent billets found. Local Scout groups, including the Hayes troop, were entrusted with making many of the preparations. The first group of refugees was from Belgium and Holland and was quickly followed by some from France. From Gadsden the initial group of refugees went to Keston Village Hall for dispersal in Burnt Ash and Shortlands. Others went to Beckenham, Bromley, Chislehurst, Orpington, Penge and Sidcup. In July 1940 the billeting officer for Beckenham reported that a refugee from his area was now working in Hayes as a companion-help. Individual families in Hayes also separately offered assistance. Wilfred Batten, for instance, gave shelter to a German refugee child.[1]

Hayes men were amongst those who safely returned from the evacuation from Dunkirk in May 1940 but some had dreadful experiences. Private Ivor Wells from West Common Road, who had been working in a forward dressing station in Flanders, had a terrible journey from Oudenarde to Dunkirk on a train that was bombed and machine-gunned. The person next to him was shot in the heart but Ivor finally reached Dunkirk where the injured men slept in the fields until they could be taken off on a hospital ship. He eventually returned to England and his parents were informed in June that he was in hospital 'somewhere in the Home Counties'.

Mrs E Eames of 21 Dartmouth Road heard that her husband, Despatch Rider A J Eames, was amongst those who had been taken prisoner. Others were reported missing, such as Peter Marchant of Hayes Road, a signalman with RCS who 'it was understood was in charge of a switchboard at headquarters in Calais when the town fell'. It was an anxious time for families until they received news. It was not until 1942 that Winifred Williams heard that her husband Moelwyn, who had been allowed seven days special leave for their marriage in September 1939, had been captured in May 1940 and was a POW at Stalag 20A, Poland. The Timms family heard that their twenty-year-old son

Frederick had died near Nantes, but it was many years after the war had ended before they knew the details. He was one of the unfortunate ones who had reached St Nazaire and with an estimated 6,000 people was on board the Cunard liner Lancastria on 7 June 1940 when it was bombed. He was killed in the resulting explosion. No mention of the event was allowed in the newspapers at the time.[2]

Until the start of the Battle of Britain on 10 July 1940, the air war against Great Britain consisted largely of reconnaissance flights and exploratory raids. Although the parish had been affected by air raid warnings, no bombing had taken place. The first bomb to fall on Kent occurred on 10th May and landed in the Chilham area, near Canterbury. A week later Revd McClintock preached at Hayes on 'God and the War' and on 26th May, a National Day of Prayer, his theme was 'Trust in God'. The Parish Church was packed and the service was relayed to the Village Hall, the Annexe, the pram shed and even to the surrounding trees, where people were sheltering from the rain.[3]

It was in July and August 1940 that the anti-aircraft gun site, ZS10, saw numerous changes in equipment and men. At the end of June the site was manned by 261 HAA Battery who left for Slough on 28 June. Their tasks were taken over by one troop of 317 HAA Battery who departed on 10 July. Two days earlier, 158 HAA Battery with two 3" guns, took over the responsibility but advised the Gun Operation Room, the command and control centre for all the local gun sites, that it was closing down leaving only a guard. It seems that, for a short period, ZS10 was without any operational guns. During this time 1 AA Division Signals Group made changes for new equipment and foundations were prepared for four 4.5" guns that had been allocated to ZS10 for late August. On 12th September, 162 HAA Battery came to Hayes in anticipation of the arrival of the new guns which were finally installed in the last week of October. To provide some measure of defence during this period two sections of 159 HAA Battery, with four 3.7" guns, arrived at ZS10 on 17 October but departed on 25th October.[4]

From July 1940 the air war started in earnest, often conducted above the heads of the villagers and to the rain of shrapnel that was a reminder to retire to a shelter. Air raid sirens sounded at any time. On 16th August, classes at Hayes School were interrupted from 12.10pm to 1.10pm when 43 children went to the shelter. The following Sunday the Evening Service was affected by a 35 minute warning. On Friday 30th the Parish Church's Intercession Service was disrupted at 11.30am. The cause was a raid of 100+ enemy aircraft whose targets were the airfields in Kent, including Biggin Hill and the London area. This time, however, matters were different as bombs were dropped, destroying 44 Baston Road and a small outhouse near Dreadnought Cottage in the same road. This was the first damage sustained by the village but fortunately no one was killed. It was the start of a very difficult period for Hayes people, a month full of terror, disrupted routines and tragedy.[5]

Some of the difficulties are revealed in letters written by Mrs Ellen Robson of 4 Simpson's Cottages to her son Arthur, who lived at Horsforth in West Yorkshire. His in-laws, Mr and Mrs H Lewis, lived in George Lane. The first letter was written on Wednesday 4th September:

> I haven't heard or seen anything of Mr & Mrs Lewis since they were up here for the day, but that is not surprising, they couldn't possibly come, no one goes out, only

young people who can fly on their cycles, their isn't time between the raids, they are so frequent, and last so long, 3 thro the day and three thro the night, I might say the last three weeks have been dreadful and each raid got worse than the last, but last Friday [30th August] was the day of days (its the aerodrome they have been working for) at 6 o c in the evening it was all in flames, for 3 weeks they have been trying to get it but our AF [Air Force] kept them back and the awful battle that was fought, and it was all over us and the more it went on the worse it got, the noise was terrible, the droning of the machines, the fighting in the air, the guns and the bombs, and the crashing of the machines as they fell, I couldn't describe it if I tried, it was nothing short of <u>Hell let loose</u> then last Friday evening was the climax, they had been over in the morning, over again in the afternoon, then again in the evening, it seemed as thought there were thousands of them, and the furiousness of the bombs being dropped, it seemed to us they would never stop, then on leaving they dropped 5 bombs in Stacey's old pit, smashed one of those new houses on the other side of the road from where Mrs Dance lives, 37 killed at the aerodrome and a good number wounded, the ambulances were flying top speed from 6 o c to 3 o c next morning to deal with the dead and wounded, we have had two raids today and three yesterday but only about an hour and they haven't been right over us since Friday, yesterday they were dropping time bombs and people were asked not to go out and all thro the night last night those bombs were going off and some have been today, it was all too dreadful here but it was worse for Keston especially up the old Church Way, now you can imagine what Mr & Mrs Lewis were going thro' but I know they are sharing a shelter with someone, but I haven't heard a word about anybody, as I have just said, no one goes out, they know they can come up to you if they want, but how could anybody travel times like these now you'll wonder what we are doing thro it all, to start with we don't dare be in these cottages when these raids were on they shake terrible and the earth everywhere shakes, the Hutchens [3 Simpson's Cottages] have a shelter, they sleep in it, they have all their meals in it, everybody sleeps in their shelters now, most of them have made themselves <u>bunks </u>to sleep in. Mrs Wynn has no shelter nor have I but we have been sleeping in our lavys [outside lavatory], we have fixed them up very comfortable with boxes and chairs, blankets, cushions something to make us comfortable, we pack ourselves in at bed time and there we stop, till morning, the raids come and go as they like of course we get a good shaking but we daren't be indoors. Rose [Wynn] is home now and she has to tuck in with her mother, and every time there is a raid we fly to the lavy until the all clear ... I am keeping very well but we are all worn out for want of sleep, but perhaps we shall be faring better now, their has been no possible chance to get any sleep between the raids, it has been a most lovely day today but I think everything in the garden is dead for want of rain, it can't rain, I can't write any more now, we have had 2 raids today, our third usually comes about 10 o c, last night it was 12 o c now I'll close this up and its 7 o'clock. I write again when I feel like it ... much love to you from your loving Mother

The following day she sent another letter

My dear boy, is it <u>possible</u> or <u>safe</u> you could come down and fetch me things are getting worse and worse, I feel I can't stand much more of it, I wrote you a long letter yesterday it was put in the post last night fierce raids thro the night and again this morning.

Mother

Arthur Robson sent the following telegram to his mother written on the reverse of the envelope she had sent to him.

WILL COME MONDAY PREPARE TO LEAVE TUESDAY MORNING Arthur

He drove to Kent as quickly as he could, collected his mother and also his in-laws Mr and Mrs Lewis. Arthur's wife, Jessie, later recalled that he had a nightmare journey there and back in the blackout and that the engine of his car, a green Morris 8, became extremely hot. The family was soon safe, squashed in the small bungalow in Horsforth but thankful to have escaped the noise of the air battles.[6]

***Mrs Ellen Robson standing outside 4 Simpson's Cottages**[f.]*

During the raid on 30th August a 500lb bomb fell in the back garden of No. 4 Redgate Drive causing damage to the back of the house and blowing out the kitchen. The whole of the lawn, which the owner Harold Kanaar had recently laid, landed on his neighbour's house. Mr Gordon Johnson of No. 3 returned from work, surveyed the damage, and immediately arranged for his family to be evacuated until the worst was over.

Such decisions were discussed in many homes as people tried to assess what they could or should do. Some chose to leave Hayes, if it was practical, but most had to endure the continuation of the raids.

Meanwhile, on 5th September, there were more raids, three craters were discovered in the woods near Hayes School, George Lane. During the evening, houses in Pickhurst Rise were hit and 48 Hayes Hill was badly damaged. Early next morning 101 Bourne Way was destroyed, killing sisters Vera and Nora Marfleet and Josephine Sullivan.[7] On Saturday, 7th September, a large bomb fell and destroyed 44 to 50 Mead Way and rendered another 35 houses uninhabitable; there were no casualties. A few days later a large enemy force attacked London and two stray bombs fell in fields near the school.

The experience of these events gave the Civil Defence organisation its first test under fire and appeals were made for more ARP wardens for the Baston, Hayes Common and West Common Road areas. On the day recognised as the turning point of the Battle of Britain, 15 September 1940, Hayes suffered its worst day. It started as a normal wartime Sunday with a Morning Service at St Mary's that was interrupted by an air raid warning. The sermon was appropriate, *Calm in Air Raids*. There was a fierce anti-aircraft barrage from ZS10 against the raiders and during this air raid two houses in Bourne Vale were hit, although there were no serious casualties. A second air raid took place during Evensong when a high explosive bomb fell in the middle of Station Approach, between the Rex Cinema and the off-licence opposite, causing a large crater and fracturing a gas main. The massive blast from this bomb hurled a paving stone through the roof of 66 Pickhurst Lane.

In another incident a bomb demolished the New Inn, the largest and most conspicuous building in Station Approach. The *Bromley and Kentish Times* reported:

> Apparently it was struck in the centre by a high explosive bomb ... there was an enormous fall of debris. The great roof with its matching stonework crashed into the forecourt carrying with it the front wall. Only the back wall of the main building remained standing. Stones and lumps of gravel were hurled a quarter of a mile, and some of these missiles broke windows of houses. The force of the crash and weight of the debris smashed down the outer boundary wall at the street side of the large courtyard. ... A motorcar could be discerned among the ruins.

***Damage caused to the New Inn, Station Approach, 15 September 1940*** [l.]

Rescue work at the New Inn was made difficult by the fallen masonry but the manager, who was injured, and his wife and children were brought out safely. Others injured included Mr & Mrs Grimble, who lived in Ridgeway, and A W Peyton, a vet, who subsequently joined the army. He was later part of Orde Wingate's second expedition in Burma, from which he failed to return.[8] Unfortunately, two people were killed. One was Frederick Scates, the head-waiter, and a father of two children, one only a few weeks old. The other fatality was 47-year-old Charles Hammond, the husband of a waitress, who had come to escort her home to Coney Hall, West Wickham.

The New Inn had been a popular venue for wedding receptions, club dinners and other social events. In March 1940, the manager and six villagers had formed a small committee and initiated a 'cigarette fund', which provided many servicemen and a hospital with gifts of cigarettes. The inn was extensively damaged but partially repaired and reopened for business in December 1941, just in time for Christmas.

The damage in the area was made worse by a third bomb that hit the railway station. The stationmaster's office, ticket office, south side of the concourse, shops and a lorry were all destroyed. The buildings were not restored for many years. During this period the railway station's Ladies' room was used as the ticket office. Shops and businesses affected included the estate agents next to the New Inn and Enrights the newsagents. Villagers were relieved when the proprietor emerged safely from the rear of that shop, a few minutes after the explosion. Killicks, the builders and undertakers, the coal merchants, opticians' and a shoe repair shop were also damaged.

*The day after the bombing of Hayes Station on 15 September 1940*[j.]

Many of the houses in Hayes Garden that backed on to the New Inn needed so much repair that the families had to leave their homes, some for as long as four weeks. In the same raid a delayed action bomb fell at the corner of West Common and Warren Roads which, when it exploded, damaged some of the nearby houses.[5]   Sunday, 15th September, was a long day for the Civil Defence forces and all the civilians affected by this raid.

*Bomb damage to Hayes Station, 15 September 1940. Workmen can be seen repairing the roofs on the buildings situated on the other side of the road* [L]

*Bomb damage to houses in Hayes Wood Avenue, 29 September 1940* [L]

The air raids continued unabated during the remainder of the month. Next day, during the early hours of the morning, a delayed action bomb dropped on the anti-aircraft gun site, ZS10. The weapon was defused and destroyed by the Bomb Disposal Section, Royal Engineers (RE). Only the month before the *Luftwaffe* had taken reconnaissance photographs of the site and whether this led to it being attacked is unclear.[9] On the night of 19th September three bombs dropped in the Baston Road area, one of which landed in the garden of No 42, creating a crater 30ft by 20ft. Five days later, at about 5am, a bomb destroyed 24 Southbourne, killing three men; Albert Goodenough, his brother Jack Goodenough, a Lance Bombardier in the Royal Artillery and Sydney Harper. Six other bombs fell on Hayes, one at the corner of Chatham Avenue and Hayes Lane, three in the grounds of Hayes School, one in George Lane and one hit 28 Dartmouth Road.[7]

On 26th September the anti-aircraft gun site was attacked again and three 250kg bombs fell on ZS10. One exploded within a few feet of the command post, the second approximately 50ft away and the third, at the time the Battery's War Diary entry was made, had not exploded. Two days later a further air attack took place on ZS10. Three oil bombs were dropped around the site.

> One fell outside the camp's fence and caused an outbreak of fire, which was prevented from spreading by the speedy action of the troops. The second fell a few feet from the command post and was dealt with adequately. The third, 1,000kg capacity, fell just behind the guardroom but failed to ignite and was defused by the Royal Engineers Bomb Disposal section on 5 October.[10]

Another 1,000kg bomb landed in the grounds of Baston Manor, just a hundred yards west of the house, luckily it failed to explode otherwise the old manor house would have been demolished.

The month of attacks ended with a night raid on Sunday 29th September when bombs fell behind 61 and 63 Baston Road; two people were injured and taken to hospital. A second bomb fell at the junction of Glebe House Drive and Hayes Wood Avenue causing extensive damage to Nos. 9 to 15 Hayes Wood Avenue, which were rebuilt after the war. A third bomb fell in the grounds of Gadsden.

Throughout this period villagers witnessed, at first hand, the air battles and dogfights from their gardens. On 27th September a Messerschmitt Bf 109 was in combat with a Spitfire from 72 Squadron, Biggin Hill, flown by Flying Officer Paul Davis-Cooke, a native of Cilcain, Flintshire. Flying Officer Davis-Cooke was forced to abandon his damaged aircraft, which crashed in Coney Hall destroying 70 and 72 Queensway, West Wickham. The 23-year-old pilot baled out but was dead when he landed in Prickley Wood, off Bourne Way. He was buried in the churchyard of his hometown.[11]

Three Hayes airmen were killed during this time. One was Pilot Officer Vincent Pattison, whose parents lived at 28 Ridgeway. His Bristol Blenheim Mk IV was shot down when escorting Royal Navy destroyers off the coast of Norway, on 6 July 1940. His brother Wing Commander Robert Pattison was also in the RAF but survived the war and received the DSO in 1944. A similar plane crashed on 2 August 1940 in Holland, killing Sergeant Observer Kenneth Roy Bryant, whose parents lived at 105 Chatham Avenue. On 9 September 1940 Pilot Officer John Lenahan, based at Tangmere with 607 Squadron was flying a Hurricane when he died. He was twenty-years old. Both Bryant and Lenahan were amongst the twelve men from Bromley included in the memorial service for Battle of Britain pilots in Westminster Abbey in 1947.[12]

Until June 1941 bombing continued unabated with numerous night-time air raid alerts and attacks.[13] On Monday 7 October 1940 aircraft attacking Biggin Hill dropped bombs that fell in the fields behind Hayes Lane, north of Bourne Vale, and just to the east of Pickhurst Mead opposite the Pickhurst Hotel, mainly causing damage to the roofs and windows of several houses.

The next attack took place on 15 October when a massive bomb, one of many that landed in the London area, fell in the back garden of 103 Hayes Lane. It made a crater 60ft by 30ft 'the largest seen in the district', so the local paper reported. Two people were buried in their garden shelter, eight-year-old John Sheridan Foster, who was killed, and his mother, who survived and was rescued by ARP personnel. Normally John's father would have been with them but on this occasion he had a cold and was in bed in the house. Both parents were taken to hospital where their injuries were treated. Four days later a bomb crater was discovered in the school playing field, off George Lane, and on 23rd October the school was badly damaged when a bomb landed nearby, bringing down ceilings in the playroom and two classrooms.[14]

Another difficult day was 24th October when 6 Cherry Walk received a direct hit. Ronald and Olga Bowman, and their relation Stanley Bowman died. Another inhabitant was badly injured. The house next door, No. 8, was also badly damaged but the occupants escaped unhurt. The blast damage from this bomb was extensive, with garage doors and windows blown out in many houses in Chatham Avenue. The next day a large number of incendiary bombs fell, mainly in the fields at the end of George Lane. Two of these small bombs landed on houses and were quickly dealt with. One of the houses to be affected was 80 George Lane, the home of Mr and Mrs Lewis who had evacuated to Yorkshire, but whose niece Kathleen and her husband John Hack had just moved to the house following bomb damage to their home, 8 Cherry Walk.

A letter John Hack wrote to his aunt, when they moved back to 80 George Lane on 11th November, shows some of the difficulties in dealing with the situation created by incendiaries, something experienced by many inhabitants of Hayes. The water, gas and electricity services had all been affected. John Hack unblocked the water pipe, arranged for the gas fire to be put right and transferred his gas stove from 8 Cherry Walk. The West Kent Electricity Company wanted cash in advance to rewire and so he did it with a neighbour's help. One of his greatest frustrations was the delay of the Borough Engineer in arranging first aid repairs to the roof. Eventually, with the help of local Councillor Percy Jones, it was done about ten days after the event and the rooms were no longer open to the sky. John Hack was then able to board up the spaces between the ceiling and joists where the passage ceiling was down and put boards over the joists where the roof timbers were burnt away. A side effect of their recent disasters was that his wife decided 'to have her hair shingled', stating it was impossible to cope with long hair when dealing with all the brick dust and plaster.[15]

On Saturday 26th October three high explosive bombs were dropped. One at the junction of Hambro and Chatham Avenues caused general blast damage, severe damage to 11 and 13 Chatham Avenue but no serious casualties. The second bomb badly damaged 18 and 20 Hambro Avenue, both of which were rebuilt after the war. The third demolished 216 Hayes Lane where three people got out alive but three were killed. This was the home of the Stoner family and David Stoner, then a young boy of four, recounted in 1990 that 'I was in bed at the time when I woke up suddenly and found that there was a heavy weight on top of me. I shouted to my mother and heard her answer, but she was buried further away'. It was some time later that he heard the reassuring voices of Owen Parsloe, superintendent of the Borough Council's works department and a member of the ARP, who with a colleague tunnelled through the rubble to rescue David and his mother. This was a particularly difficult recovery and for his action and gallantry Owen Parsloe was awarded the George Medal. Mr D Carlill was commended for 'his gallantry and devotion to duty' in the same incident.[16] By cutting out the springs of a bed he managed to lower David to comparative safety. David's sister, Mary, who was eight years old, seven-year-old Harry Brück, an Austrian Jewish refugee, and an elderly lodger named Albert Goody were the three people to die in this incident.[7] Harry Brück's father was a Jew. The family had moved to Vienna to escape persecution in 1938 but they were still in danger so Harry, an only child, was sent to England as a refugee through a scheme run by the Quakers. Mr and Mrs Stoner had taken him in as a foster child and he attended Hayes Council School. Soon after Harry's arrival in Hayes his father, along with other Jews, was put on a train in Vienna, transported east and never heard of again.[17]

By the end of October the four new 4.5" guns at ZS10 were ready and cleared for action. Gun-laying radar was installed and on 30 October a team arrived at the site to calibrate the system using a balloon. The anti-aircraft defences around London were all being updated with the larger calibre guns and new fire control technology and, as the battery War Diaries show, results improved. It recorded on '6 November – ZS10 engaged unseen target – Fired four rounds – aircraft believed to have crashed'. This was the first claim made by the Hayes gunners.[10]

The next time the village was attacked was on Friday 1st November when two bombs fell, one in the grounds of Baston Manor and the other at the junction of Pickhurst Lane and The Knoll where a 119 bus travelling down Pickhurst Lane narrowly escaped being hit. Bombs were also reported to have fallen in the Barnet Wood Road and Hayes Lane areas. Three days later two houses, Brackendene and The White House, both in Five Elms Road, were the subject of enemy attention when they suffered bomb blast causing roof, window and ceiling damage. Eric Davies, who was serving in the RAF, suggested that his rent for Brackendene should be reduced as 'the house has been bombed and windows broken thereby. The ceilings are coming down owing to gun fire … circumstances are exceptional. At present it is (nearly at any rate) unfit to live in and will continue to get worse.'[18]

German aircraft constantly flew over the parish and were engaged with heavy and progressively more accurate anti-aircraft gunfire. Only two other incidents occurred during the remainder of the month. The first was on 10th November when high explosive bombs were dropped in the fields off Hayes Lane and an incendiary bomb hit a house. The second incident involved a Hayes resident, although it occurred elsewhere. A 21-year-old AFS fireman, Reginald Knight, was killed on duty when a bomb hit an AFS station in a school at Invicta Road, London. He lived at 196 Croydon Road and is buried in Hayes churchyard.

Unexploded bombs (UXB) caused much disruption, often took many days to make safe and were usually dealt with by the army bomb disposal units of the Royal Engineers. Much of this work fell to the 720 General Construction Company, RE, which was based during the latter part of 1940 and 1941 in Beckenham. Two local examples illustrate the difficulty and dangers of their work. One bomb, probably dropped during the raid on 7 October 1940, landed in Hayes Garden and failed to explode. By 14th October, the soldiers had opened up a deep excavation to locate the weapon. Shuttering was erected and a few days later the road was closed. On 20th October the bomb, which could not be removed from where it lay, was ready for detonation. The War Diaries record:

> 15.00 hrs. bomb blown - very successful, no structural damage except one house which was cracked. Windows were broken by debris but not by blast. Blast mat [used to cover the bomb and reduce the blast] was almost destroyed by it and maybe it did some good.

In December 1940 another UXB was found in Hayes Lane. It had fallen close to the gas, water and sewerage services and was not made safe until the first week of February 1941. A month later the RE unit moved to York and was replaced by 692 and 695 General Construction Companies RE, who carried on the dangerous work.[19]

With the military activities on Hayes Common many bombs fell among the trees and bracken. The Common Rangers, who continued to work throughout the war, received special bonus payments - approximately 2s. per week - for the additional danger to which they were exposed. One task was to count the number of bombs that fell on the common. From the start of the war until 18 January 1941 they recorded 48 high explosive, 5 oil, 3 delayed action and numerous incendiary bombs.[20]

Hayes men and women continued to face great dangers overseas. Florence Goodall, who lived at The Green, heard that her husband Chief Steward Alfred Goodall had died on the Merchant Ship *Pacific President*, part of a convoy on its way to New York torpedoed and sunk by German U-boat, *U-43*, on 2nd December. At about the same time it was announced that Captain R L Hamer of The White House had been awarded the DSO for his gallantry in hunting down U boats.[21]

On Christmas Eve the Regional Commissioner sent a message of encouragement to his Chief ARP Wardens:

> Twelve months of training and watches and three months of intensive raiding have imposed tests which you have met brilliantly. London is grateful to you and encouraged by your example that has shown the world that come what may Britain stands fast. We greet you with pride and we wish you every success in the months of struggle that lie ahead.

The message from S Critchley Auty, Town Clerk and Controller of Civil Defence, Bromley, was equally positive:

> you have been faced with blitz and boredom but you have beaten them both. Each one of us in service is an essential part of civil defence, each one represents Bromley, Britain and Freedom … I hope that the New Year will bring a victorious and lasting peace.[22]

# 1941

The first action of the New Year started on 4 January 1941 when the guns of ZS10 opened fire on an enemy aircraft, for which the gunners made a formal claim. Three days later the air raid warning lasted from 1.05pm to 4.20pm and during this time the children of Hayes School remained in cold, unheated shelters, conditions aggravated by the freezing winter weather. An air raid occurred on the night of 11/12 January when a large number of incendiary bombs fell on fields at Hayes Street Farm between George Lane and Socket Lane, and also Kechill Gardens. No serious damage was caused; however, disruption occurred to the Hayes branch railway line when an unexploded 1,000kg bomb was discovered on the railway embankment at Elmers End.[23] Unexploded anti-aircraft shells landing in built-up areas often caused damage. Such was the case on 30th January when a shell landed and destroyed the garage at 18 Cecil Way, luckily no one was hurt.

On Wednesday 19th March, just before midnight and with a cloudless sky, enemy bombers attacked London. Damage was inflicted on many districts including Beckenham, Bromley and Hayes, where bombs fell around Bourne Way and Holland Way. Two 250kg bombs also fell on fields of Hayes Street Farm, about 250 yards east of 129 and 133 Hayes Lane, causing two massive craters but despite this there was no major damage or injuries to residents. This attack was the prelude to a more ferocious one that occurred over the next twenty-four hours, 20/21 March, when bombers flying towards East London docks released their weapons early. Dead-reckoning navigation was used as the whole area was cloaked in thick mist. Many bombs fell on Hayes and the neighbouring towns. At 8.55pm on Thursday, the first stick of four 50kg bombs fell around Tiepigs Lane, Hayes Hill and Pickhurst Rise. Another bomb fell near Hayes Station, but it failed to explode. (Two days later the 25 Bomb Disposal Company, RE. defused and removed it). Five minutes later a bomb fell on the lawn of 83 Bourne Way causing some damage to the houses around and yet another landed in the centre of Holland Way close to No. 28. Two more bombs fell, at 9.15pm, on the common near Baston Manor and West Common Roads, the second fracturing a gas main that ignited and was extinguished by the emergency services. Another 50kg bomb fell in the grounds of the Oast House and others landed, at 9.30pm, near the Oast House bungalow, Croydon Road, but caused no damage. A further two bombs landed, one on the allotments in Pickhurst Lane, and the other just over the parish boundary near 28 Hayes Lane and the tennis courts. One unexploded shell fell opposite 104 West Common Road causing a small hole in the carriageway.[24] The anti-aircraft guns mounted a fierce barrage against the planes but no claims were made.

The evening of Wednesday 16 April 1941 and the early morning of the next day was another night to remember for all the villagers who lived through it. The main *Luftwaffe* attack was directed against London and proved to be the heaviest raid against Britain up to that date. Under cover of darkness, cloud and rain, the bombers attacked London. The raid started at 8.50pm and lasted until 5.18am, when the 'all clear' was sounded. Ground mist over the designated target area made the location of specific targets difficult. Many bombers homed in on fires caused by bombs dropped, in a seemingly indiscriminate fashion, from aircraft in the vanguard of the raid. Beckenham, Bromley and most of the southeast boroughs suffered heavy damage and casualties.

For Hayes most bombs fell in the early part of the raid. Revd McClintock recorded that 'hundreds of incendiary bombs fell as well as many high explosive bombs, one land mine and many flares when the whole place was lit up like daylight'.[3] The sequence of events in Hayes started just after 9.30pm when a delayed action bomb fell near the ZS10 gun site. It self detonated nearly seven hours later. Another bomb landed near the first and a third made a direct hit on an empty Nissen hut. At 10pm a delayed action bomb fell on the bungalow at 154 Pickhurst Lane, opposite Hayes Free Church. It exploded the following morning killing James Stevens, an eighteen-year-old from Bromley and injuring two others. Between 10pm and 10.15pm two bombs destroyed 165 Hayes Lane and damaged twelve houses; another fell in the back gardens of 61 and 63 Pickhurst Lane and also badly damaged twelve houses; a fourth bomb fell in the rear gardens of 27 and 29 Courtlands Avenue and caused severe blast damage to these and sixteen other houses; a fifth, a large 500kg bomb, dropped close to 'Brambledown', next to Barnhill School, Pickhurst Lane.[25]

By midnight more bombs had fallen on the rear of 160 and 162 Bourne Vale, the front gardens of 167 and 169 Bourne Vale and the Tiepigs Lane area. A parachute mine landed in the rear of 167 Bourne Vale, damaging some 250 houses, over a radius of 400 yards. At the start of the new day three bombs were aimed at the gun site. No damage was reported but eighteen houses were affected when a bomb exploded in the front garden of Prickley Wood, Bourne Way. Minor damage was caused when a bomb landed in the grounds of Baston Manor. Many incendiary bombs and coloured marker flares dropped during the raid. A number of high explosive bombs also fell around the Prestons Road and Dreadnought Cottage areas of the common.[24] Eric Harold Strouts of 6 Redgate Drive was killed by an enemy firebomb while he was fighting the fires threatening Dreadnought and Pleasant View cottages.[7] He had only been married eighteen months and his wife Bunty, who later returned to work as a sister in Bromley Hospital, was also very upset when she heard that her brother Frank's ship had been torpedoed in the North Sea. He was picked up from his raft by Germans and became a POW until the war ended.

Over 16/17th April numerous incendiaries and at least four tons of bombs were dropped in nineteen individual incidents around the parish. Two people were killed, many injured, five homes destroyed and hundreds of others damaged to a lesser or greater extent. Utilities were severed and the many bombs that fell on the Hayes to Elmers End line disrupted trains. People's lives and possessions were destroyed and many had to find new accommodation until their homes had been repaired. Some houses were not rebuilt until 1947 or 1948.

Hayes ARP, AFS and other branches of Civil Defence were put under immense pressure during these months. The dangers of their work were illustrated on 19th March when, at West Ham, five Beckenham AFS fireman based at Coney Hall sub-fire station lost their lives through enemy action while travelling to Silvertown. One of the firemen killed was Charles Drew who lived in West Wickham and whose parents lived at 96 Hayes Lane. A month later, on 19/20 April, another 21 firemen from the same brigade were killed at Poplar, East London; ten of these were stationed at West Wickham, one of whom was Harry John Carden who lived at 7 Mounthurst Road, Hayes.[26]

For the next three months the guns and searchlights were very active, using their radar gun laying predictors that enabled them to engage unseen aircraft. One War Diary entry reads 'three targets were engaged using the new plotter, which allows a high rate of fire. Targets seen to take avoiding action - 78 rounds fired.'[27]

Despite the lull in the air offensive from June 1941 to April 1942 the fear of gas attacks was still present and the population was encouraged to continue carrying gas masks. Mobile testing vans toured the district to ensure masks were in working order, visiting the school and other places such as the New Inn on Saturday 27 September 1941.[28]

By the end of 1941 all men up to the age of 52 were conscripted and women from the age of 19 to 31. As the demands for fighting men grew, the Army instigated a policy of forming mixed anti-aircraft batteries manned by Territorial and Home Guard soldiers and women from the Auxiliary Territorial Service (ATS). This policy, which enabled some Territorial soldiers to be released for overseas and other front-line duties, affected most anti-aircraft gun-sites including ZS10. In January 1942 the site was manned by the all male 343 HAA Battery while the camp was converted to accommodate men and women of the new mixed batteries. Despite the fact that the conversion of the buildings for the ATS was running late, 343 HAA Battery was ordered to vacate the site on 9th February to make way for the first mixed battery. By 21st April the gun-site was ready for 493 HAA Battery of 141 (Mixed) HAA Regiment RA to take over. This was a newly formed regiment whose baptism of fire occurred on 28th July when the guns engaged an enemy plane and fired seven rounds at the target.[29]

By September 1942 the unit had changed to 565 HAA Battery, part of 163(M) HAA Regiment RA, the advance guard of which arrived at the site via Hayes Station. When fully deployed the battery comprised eight officers and 194 other ranks, more than half were ATS. The camp consisted of seven accommodation huts, washing block, cookhouse and dining room, Warrant Officers' and Sergeants' Mess, Officers' Mess and Quarters, Company offices and guardroom, stores and garage. In October and November 1942 some of the Home Guard started to man the guns at S10, the new code by which the Hayes Common gun-site and camp was known.[30]

Many single Hayes women joined up and 32 Service brides were married in Hayes Church between 1942 and 1945, including five WRNS, ten ATS and nine WAAFs. Several saw service overseas but only one is named on the Hayes War Memorial. Joan Ashburner of 4 Cecil Way joined the WRNS and trained as a radio mechanic. She was posted to *HMS Merlin* where aircraft radio sets were repaired. To measure the effectiveness of the radio from ground to air, a radio mechanic and a radar Wren went on test flights. On 9 June 1944, a Fairey Albacore took off with a New Zealand pilot Andy, Joan and another Wren, Peggy Bachelor. The plane crashed and the three were killed. The funeral took place in the Naval Church at Rosyth. Joan's parents travelled to Scotland and brought with them a wreath for the pilot, as they knew his parents could not be there. Joan, who was aged 20, had been due a fortnight later to marry a pilot who was returning from duty in the Far East.[31]

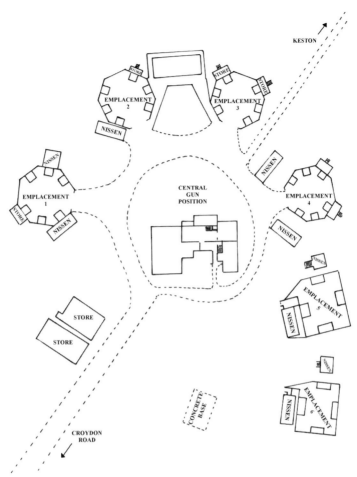

*Organisation of the Gun Site on Hayes Common*

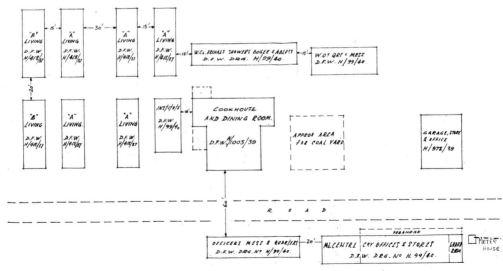

*Plan of Army Barracks on Hayes Common* [aj.]

# The Canadians

The 1st Canadian Division was part of the land defence forces for the south of England and was deployed to repel any invasion attempt. During 1940 and 1941 Canadian Army units used Hayes Common, particularly around the Oast House and Hayes Grove, where two huts were erected under the trees.[32] A Canadian detachment of artillery requisitioned part of Baston Manor in 1940 for transport repair and dispersed their vehicles between Baston Manor and Hast Hill. Three Canadian Army units were in the district between 1942 and 1944. No. 11 Detachment of the Canadian Postal Corps arrived in Coney Hall in November 1942, made its headquarters at 46 Kingsway and stayed until the early part of 1944. Men from this and other locally based units were billeted around Coney Hall and Hayes, many in empty houses. The second unit, 6 Canadian Light Anti-Aircraft Regiment Platoon, occupied Coney Hall during the first six months of 1943. The other unit was 82 Canadian Anti-Aircraft Brigade Company, which arrived in the district in August 1942.[33] Its War Diary records little enemy action but throws valuable light on its life in Hayes and Coney Hall and its relationship with the community:

> Hayes, Kent, 1 September 1942 - The weather is clear and warm. This is our third day in the new area and there is still a great amount of work to be done as regards cleaning, repairing, replacing, etc. The houses are quite comfortable but no beds are permitted for use by the men. It is apparent that this is a blitzed area from the visible scars on the buildings, houses, etc. Plumbers, carpenters, electricians are busy engaged in their own branch of repairs and replacement work … The lads are slowly becoming acclimatised and little in the way of complaints are heard. The evenings are spent in making acquaintances and in this respect the troops are living up to the tradition of all "Canadians". Beautiful girls are quite plentiful. Army life is not too dull at times.

Two more entries seem to confirm the bond between the local people and the Canadian troops:

> The people in this area are extremely nice to the lads and they are forever extending invitations to tea.
> The girls in these parts are unusually pretty on the average and many friendships have been created in the short space we have been here. No doubt marriage applications will make an appearance in force without delay. Previous Canadian units in this area apparently made a killing as is evident from the number of baby carriages in this area. Good lads to the families.[34]

This Canadian unit stayed in the Hayes area until the end of 1942 and the diary entry of 23rd December says 'there is not a tremendous amount of Christmas spirit in the air, but the neighbours in the district are very kind to the boys. Nearly everyone has an invitation out to dinner on Christmas [day].' Afterwards the unit moved to the Basingstoke area. It is clear that both Hayes and Coney Hall had made their mark as the diary entry for 12 March 1943 says:

> Better news. At 17.45hrs instructions were received for the Company to move back to Hayes. The unit was ready to roll in faster time than ever before, whether it is due to much practice or eagerness to see the girl friend again is a matter of conjecture.

Eleven days later it was reported, 'at least 12 men have filed papers for marriage'. During the war eight local girls married Canadian soldiers in Hayes Parish Church. Not all relationships flourished. In January 1944, a 'Hayes girl' summoned a sapper in the Canadian Army and alleged that he was the father of her child.[35]

## 1942 and 1943

1942 saw the start of the North African campaign in which many soldiers from Hayes were involved. Some, like Lance Corporal Bunn on 25th October and five days later 2nd Lt Thomas Morley, lost their lives. Both are buried in El Alamein War Cemetery.

Invasion of Great Britain was never very far from the minds of the War Cabinet and the Imperial General Staff. Based on military intelligence assessments of the German forces, it was considered possible that an invasion might soon be mounted and that existing plans should be reviewed and updated. Whilst this matter was largely a national concern, plans in the event of an invasion went far beyond the War Cabinet and affected many local organisations. Two contingency plans of this major review concerned Hayes and provide an insight into the complex planning and organisational aspects of fighting the war and protecting the community.

Mr Charles Broughton, a signalman at Hayes Railway Station, in June 1942 received 'secret' written instructions that, if an invasion should be launched against Great Britain, 65 steam locomotives from Ashford Depot would be transferred to and stabled on the 'down' line between West Wickham and Hayes stations. It was not intended to use the engines but to store them in the cutting under cover of the trees along the embankment.[36]

The other plan, dated March 1943, relates to the actions to be taken by the National Fire Service (NFS) in the event of an invasion. It included NFS Region 37F, whose area was Orpington, Bromley, Beckenham and Penge and straddled the anti-tank line. Preparations were made concerning the fire stations and sub-stations situated outside (south-east) of the anti-tank defensive line. The plan recognised that 'when the outer tank barrier is closed eleven stations [including Hayes] would be outside and mobilising would be greatly affected.' The affected stations would be self-contained and controlled from the Sub-Divisional Station. The fire pumps at Hayes Sub-Fire Station (at the Old Rectory) would, in the event of the tank barrier closing, be moved to the sub-fire station at Bromley Grammar School for Boys in Hayes Lane. 'If conditions deteriorated, appliances would be withdrawn to other areas.' Emergency feeding would be linked to the Borough scheme, whereby the NFS would purchase food locally and use field kitchens.[37] These are just two small parts of an anti-invasion scheme prepared but never put to the test. All public utilities, hospitals and services drew up similar plans.

During the period of the Baedeker raids, from April to October 1942, Hayes escaped serious damage from enemy action.[38] Air raid warnings still disrupted daily life and the guns engaged the enemy aircraft when they entered Hayes air space. Despite this, village life continued although the army wanted to make more use of Hayes Common. In March 1942 the authorities wrote to the Conservators seeking permission to park military vehicles in Preston Road. In August they asked to use the common for military training exercises that included the use of live grenades and in November they wanted to instruct army motorcyclists in fieldwork.[39]

From November 1942 to January 1944 enemy tactics changed to 'tip and run' raids, some of which were undertaken by single engine aircraft flying fast and low to evade the British air defences. To meet these tactical changes the Hayes Battery, along with other sites, was equipped with a 40mm Bofors gun for use against the low flying daylight raiders.[40] When the Battery went into action during the night, the Bofors gun was trained in the direction of Baston Manor and fired tracer rounds as a deterrent to any would-be attacker.

With the introduction of mixed personnel anti-aircraft batteries, Hayes seemed to have more female than male service personnel. In the December weekly return 160(M) HAA Regiment, which was deployed at S10, had 3 officers and 66 other ranks of the Royal Artillery and 2 officers and 85 other ranks drawn from the ATS, a total of 156 plus the staff of RCS and other units. The ATS clearly set a good example as they came second in the 48 Brigade's 'Best Barrack Competition' held in August 1943.[41]

October 1943 saw more bombing and destruction in the district. The increase in enemy activity is reflected in the records for 7th October: 'all sites open fire at 22.15 hrs … S10 fired 99 rounds … five aircraft engaged … no results'. The records of 26 Searchlight Regiment, which covered the Bromley area, state that this raid consisted of 22 enemy aircraft, which entered from the south. Searchlight illumination was excellent and it was possible to recognise many different types of German planes.[42] A few bombs fell in the borough although none fell on Hayes.

*One of the six Civil Defence Corps in Hayes in 1943* [i.]

The first bomb to fall on the parish in the new wave of attacks occurred on 17/18 October 1943 when the guns at S10 fired 96 rounds at unseen and illuminated targets with some measure of success, as the Battery lodged a claim of one aircraft damaged. The enemy aircraft released their bombs at 2.23am. The largest bomb was 1000kg and fell on the playing field at Gadsden, about 65yds from the junction of Baston Road and Burwood Avenue, wrecking the East Lodge, where a woman and four children survived unhurt. About 30 houses were made uninhabitable by falling ceilings and damaged roofs.[43] Hayes School and the Old Rectory also suffered damaged. The Bible was blown off the lectern in the church and two panes of glass were broken in the vestry. During the same raid three bombs fell in the Holland Way and Prestons Road area with only slight damage. Three bombs also fell on Sandilands Crescent, one on Westland Drive and another on Abbotsbury Road.

A few days later Major Binyon had a surprise when an aircraft 'drop-tank' landed in his garden at Hawthorndene. Major Binyon was Commandant of the south-eastern sector of the Royal Observer Corps and had played an important part in the air defences of London in 1940-41. Before radar was widely available he devised ingenious predictors based upon alarm clock mechanisms. His only daughter Margaret was a junior commander in the ATS and served in France and later Germany with the British Army of the Rhine; his sons Roger and Hugh were also in the services although sadly Roger was to be killed at Arnhem in 1944.

Arthur Gilbey, who lived at 2 Warren Cottages, Hillside Lane, was an ARP warden. His diary recorded 112 air raid warnings in 1943. Fifteen air raid warnings were sounded in October during the evening and night, eleven in November and eight in December.[44]

News filtered back of seven Hayes airmen lost in bombing raids over Europe.[45] The Grandfield family heard that their son Clifford, who joined the air force in 1940 and trained as a wireless operator/gunner, had died when his plane crash-landed in Malta on 8 December 1942. He had previously completed twenty successful operational missions but in April had suffered broken ribs and a fractured leg when his plane crashed in the Western Desert. He had only recently returned to duty and would have been 21 years old the following month.

The Allied Invasion of Sicily in July 1943 and the slow and difficult fight through Italy resulted in further casualties for Hayes soldiers, including Lance Sergeant Arthur Harris, Rifleman Leonard Stiles and Private Robert Renno. Good news was received in October by Mr and Mrs Nye of Prickley Wood that their son, who had been captured in Italy, had escaped and arrived in Switzerland. Another soldier, Captain Stanley V Sutton of the Pioneer Corps, was repatriated to his home in Husseywell Crescent. Lieutenant Colonel H J Thicknesse RA, an active member of Hayes Church, who lived at 107 Harvest Bank Road, received the DSO for a skilful four days' reconnaissance in his jeep of an unmapped part of the Western Desert. Unfortunately, he later died of wounds received in action on 23 October 1944 and is buried in Dordrecht General Cemetery in Holland.[46]

# 1944

The people of Hayes found 1944 another difficult year. By the autumn several, who had returned home because 'things were quieter', evacuated once again. The first alert came on Sunday 2nd January just after midday and lasted for eight minutes. The second occurred at 11.41pm and at one minute past midnight the local guns and searchlights engaged a small force of single and twin-engine enemy aircraft entering local air space. Six bombs were dropped on the western edge of the parish at two minutes past midnight. A cluster of four fell around Tiepigs Lane and the railway embankment, one of which hit

6 Tiepigs Lane killing Mrs Dorothy Robbins. Her two daughters and son escaped uninjured, as did the neighbours even though their home was also badly damaged. Mr Robbins was away on night work and was unaware of the tragedy until he returned home next morning. One of the other bombs fell on 'Burlings', Pondfield Road, where it penetrated the roof, passed through the ceiling and travelled out through the front wall into the front garden, where it failed to explode. The remaining bomb hit the rear corner of 38 Hilldown Road, partially demolishing the rear wall and destroying the garage of No. 40 and damaging Nos 36 and 42.[47]

Over the next three months there were 38 air raid warnings, most of which occurred at night or during the small hours of the morning. Not all the raiders passed over the village, although the enemy was engaged on at least nineteen occasions by the guns of S10 and their supporting searchlights.

On 24th March, Hayes experienced another bad raid from 143 aircraft aiming for London. The alarm sounded at 10.55pm and an hour later an intense anti-aircraft barrage opened as the aircraft approached. Just after midnight a 500kg container was dropped, showering incendiary bombs, some of which were the explosive type, over Station Approach, West Common Road, Ridgeway, Station Hill, Hayes Garden and Hayes Common.[48] Barclays Bank, at 49 Station Approach, was damaged, as were many other buildings including the railway station. The roof of one shop was burnt out and the contents of the upstairs flat destroyed. Customers, however, were still served next morning in the 'business as usual' fashion. The Women's Voluntary Service (WVS) centre, a few doors away, was also damaged.

Maureen Crowhurst, who was ten years old at the time, has recalled that she, her sister Patricia (Paddy) and Pamela Mote, daughter of the Barclays Bank manager, who lived above the bank, were sheltering in the Morrison Shelter at the back of the Chemist shop where her father was the Manager. They left the shelter to go to the basement shelters on the opposite side of Station Approach. As they were leaving a bomb came through the shop roof and killed four-year-old Pamela immediately. Maureen and Patricia were already outside but another bomb seriously injured Patricia and she was taken to Bromley Hospital where she died the following day. Dr Hopton treated Maureen's arm that was bleeding badly and it eventually healed. The Morrison Shelter was unharmed in the attack. The two dead girls were buried, side-by-side, in the churchyard, a few feet from the east window of Hayes Parish Church.[49]

The tragedy shocked everybody. Hayes Traders were moved to donate money to Bromley Hospital for equipment and a tablet was erected in the girls' memory. It said:

THE EQUIPMENT AND FURNISHINGS
OF THE CHILDREN'S WARD
WERE DONATED BY THE TRADERS OF HAYES
IN MEMORY OF
PAMELA ANNE MOTE,
AND
PATRICIA CROWHURST,
KILLED BY ENEMY ACTION ON THE NIGHT
OF MARCH 24th 1944.

The tablet remained at the hospital in the Wheeler-Bennett Ward until the building was demolished in 2003 and the memorial was salvaged.[50]

Several other people were injured during this raid, including some who were seeking cover in their shelters; some were still in hospital six days later recovering from their wounds. No. 15 Hayes Garden, home of Mr Stanley Deason, whose son Robert had died on service with the RAF in August 1943, was destroyed. Many houses were damaged, including 11 Hayes Garden, Ivy Cottage, Warren Road, 68 to 78 West Common Road and houses in Ridgeway and Grove Close. The fires from the incendiary bombs were quickly extinguished by the NFS, wardens and other volunteers, including the Rector, many of whom had taken part in a realistic ARP exercise that had been held in Hurstdene Avenue only twelve days earlier.[51]

The air raids against Britain continued during April, May and the first part of June but none affected Hayes. In June 1944 a major offensive, D Day, was launched when the Allied troops landed on the Normandy beaches. This resulted in more deaths for Hayes men such as Private Peter Rogers on 29 June 1944 and Corporal Harold Wilson on 21st August.[52]

## Flying Bombs

It had been hoped that after the D Day landings there would be rapid progress and that victory would soon be in sight. Hitler had other plans. On 13 June 1944 flying bombs (V1s) were launched against Britain and on that day S10 guns fired 46 rounds against these small, fast and deadly 'pilotless aircraft'. On 15th and 16th June, the first attack lasted six hours and the Hayes Battery opened fire many times with both heavy and light anti-aircraft guns expending over 1,000 rounds of ammunition. Hits were claimed by all local gun-sites. It was soon realised that the anti-aircraft guns were wrongly sited to protect Greater London against these weapons because when the V1s were shot down they often fell on built-up areas.[53] Permission to engage the flying bombs was restricted to four gun sites because of this problem. It included Hayes but the next day all gun sites were ordered not to open fire. A few days later the AA Command created a defensive gun and barrage balloon belt south of Hayes to minimise the damage to built-up areas.

The flying bomb attacks against the southeast built up quickly into an almost continuous barrage. Mr Gilbey's diary entry for Saturday 17th June illustrates the intensity. He recorded 'rocket bombs and gunfire' on eleven occasions.[54] The first V1 to crash on Hayes occurred at 12.30am on Wednesday 21st June, and fell in the rear garden of 133 Constance Crescent. The explosion caused considerable damage to nearby houses, to the extent that 129 to 135 had to be rebuilt. Fortunately there were no serious injuries. Mrs Luscombe and her son, whose home was at 133, had been evacuated some time before this incident. Dorothy Timms, then living at 16 Mounthurst Road, recalled that 'the blast blew out all the windows and broke many things inside'. Her family was safe in the Morrison Shelter in the back room. Four people taking cover in a brick-built surface shelter, only 51ft from the point of impact, escaped uninjured although the shelter walls were cracked at each corner. A semi-sunken Anderson shelter, 55ft from the point of impact, was undamaged. On the same day V1s fell on allotments just north of Addington Road and in Padmill Wood, Keston. The Rookery, just across the fields from

Hayes Street Farm, was the subject of two flying bombs that crashed in the grounds and exploded on the 18th and 22nd June. On the 23rd a flying bomb fell on the fields north of 52 to 58 Mead Way.[55]

26 Searchlight Regiment, which was deployed around Bromley, included 339 SL Battery at Hayes Common and logged the number of bombs to fly over Bromley. During July 1944 there were only two days, 25th and 29th, without bombs. During the other 29 days 705 flying bombs entered the district, the most in the first three days of the month when 142 were counted. The next V1 to hit Hayes dropped near the Lodge to Baston Manor at 12.57pm on 3rd July. The Lodge, which was uninhabited at the time, took the full blast and was destroyed. Damage extended to the Manor House and Oast House along Croydon Road. Many trees were uprooted by the blast. Three more flying bombs fell in the parish before the end of the war. The first, at 5.56pm on 11th July, landed in Barnet Wood near a potato field southeast of Barnet Wood Road. The next attack took place at 12.59pm on 2nd August, when the V1 exploded in the trees on Pickhurst Green; no major damage was caused although the roofs of Whites Cottages were hit, some tiles and ceilings were brought down and much glass broken. The last occurred at 4.39am on 5th August when a V1 landed in Bolds Wood, Hayes Street Farm, about 200 yards southeast of Hayes School; again no serious damage was caused.[56]

*Baston Manor Lodge, which was destroyed by a V1 on 3 July 1944* [r.]

As the flying bomb campaign progressed, the defences grew more proficient in destroying these weapons before they reached the capital. Despite this, and the capture of many launch sites, 34 V1s landed in the Borough of Bromley. Flying bombs were, in the end, successfully defeated but in September 1944 the V2 rockets appeared with their new technology and could not be stopped by the defensive weapons at Britain's disposal.

Only one V2 rocket landed on Hayes and that occurred at 5.25pm on Friday 9 February 1945. The rocket exploded on James Grandfield's nursery in West Common Road and was the 691st 'Big Ben' (as they were code named) incident to occur in Britain. A few days later the *Bromley & Kentish Times* reported:

> A V bomb which fell recently in the heart of a peaceful old village in Southern England destroyed an old farmhouse as well as picturesque old red-tiled stables that were used as a riding school. Actually the bomb fell in a nursery, completely wiping out all the greenhouses. Apart from the farmhouse some of the oldest cottages in the village - the village green is hard by - were seriously damaged, one of them being the house where the Parish sexton and his wife resided. This couple, by the way, narrowly escaped serious injury. Strangely, the old Church School facing the green did not appear badly damaged from the outside at least. For many years it has been used exclusively for ARP purposes and on this occasion it served as a first aid station. Apart from the old house in the vicinity of the village green considerable damage was done to new property farther away and some people were rendered homeless. A grocery store was put out of action. All concerned speak of the prompt arrival of the rescue parties.
>
> Mr and Mrs James Grandfield and their son, Mr Jack Grandfield, lost their lives. Mr Charles Pinhorn, who lived [at 24 The Knoll] in a modern part of the village, also lost his life. A number of people were injured including some passengers in a bus, which was passing the green at the time. The injured included the driver ... and a lady who had formerly been Mayor of her Borough [Miss Margaret Stafford Smith]. Fortunately, in most cases the injuries were slight, only two or three being in any way serious.
>
> A roadside cafe was damaged [now Mintoos] as well as the picturesque old house that served for many years as the village post office. Elsewhere damage was done to the roof of a British Legion Club. The former rector [Revd E L L McClintock] of the Parish, who visited the scene next day and called on several families, mentioned that he heard the bomb explode in his new house.
>
> A discharged soldier [Mr Edwin Tidbury], who had been working in the greenhouse, escaped uninjured, but complained of deafness next day. It is stated that he was about 40yds away from where the bomb fell. Windows in two shopping centres were broken. One of the first-aid posts which had been closed by recent cuts in Civil Defence personnel, and which had been badly damaged by the bomb re-opened, and within three minutes was staffed by volunteers. They treated people who had been injured and gave most excellent service. The medical officer of the district spoke highly of their work. A light rescue depot had also been closed, but men turned up and rendered efficient help.[57]

Four people were killed and some 70 others, including other members of the Grandfield family, were injured by the effects of the explosion. Twelve were taken to Bromley Hospital. Over the next few days several people from Baston Road, The Knoll, West Common Road and Ridgeway were treated in out-patients for scalp wounds and cuts to their face, arms and legs. David Walford of 36 The Knoll and Michael Byrne, both aged seven, were the youngest patients and 68-year-old Alice Morley, of St Mary Cottages, was the oldest.[58] Mrs Morley, the widow of a well known local artist, Thomas Morley, had already suffered the loss of her son, Thomas Jeffrey, in 1942.

*Memorial to members of the Grandfield family*

*Hayes Gardens Nursery and house were destroyed by a V2 Rocket on 9 February 1945 [1]*

*The Coal and Coke Office and Hayes Stores opposite Hayes Gardens Nursery [1]*

*The damage caused by the V2 on 9 February 1945 to the buildings shown above [1]*

This incident was the last occasion on which Hayes suffered from direct enemy action, although the anti-aircraft site on Hayes Common continued to be manned until December 1945.

## Hayes' Civilian Organisations

So many Hayes' organisations, clubs and societies gave support to villagers and troops stationed in the area that it is only possible to provide an outline of their role.

Ivy Cottage, which became vacant on the death of Miss Octavia Stuart in April 1940, was made available, through the generosity of Lady Estelle Hambro, for servicemen and women stationed in the area to use as a United Services Canteen. The HVA Emergency Committee requested volunteers in November and Ivy Cottage opened for business in December 1940 with dining, reading and writing rooms available for the soldiers.

A separate committee was formed to manage the canteen scheme with Revd McClintock as president and Mrs G E Hancock of 97 Bourne Way as secretary. The canteen remained open for four years during which time it served 91,467 hot meals, 173,407 hot drinks, 75,400 cakes and 81,925 cigarettes. This was achieved with 120 local volunteer helpers and numerous donations of equipment; the latter often sought through the pages of the local newspapers. An advertisement appeared in March 1941 and specifically asked for second-hand refrigerators. Money for the 'little extras' was raised through dances held at the Village Hall. Many ladies, who volunteered to cook for the soldiers and ATS girls stationed in the area, remember the canteen. They also formed a knitting circle that produced many pairs of mittens and Balaclava helmets. It became a focal point for troops billeted in Hayes and many parties were held, such as on New Year's Eve 1941. In May another dance was held to raise funds for the canteen and the organiser, Mrs Hines, said that she 'hoped to run one every two weeks'. The United Services Canteen closed in December 1944 and the staff held a final farewell meeting on 19 January 1945. During the four years it had only closed once, for a few days in April 1944, when a burglar stole the rations and prevented the canteen from operating until new supplies arrived.[59]

*Ivy Cottage used as a United Services Canteen, December 1940-January 1945* [9.]

The Ivy Cottage Canteen was very popular, as were the paths to it across the common. These were so well used that their surfaces were reinforced with bomb damage rubble so as to ease the passage of the troop vehicles to and from the canteen, searchlight and gun-site camps. These paths are still popular and retain many patches of this trodden down rubble.

Ladies also helped with meals and refreshments at the gun-site mess. Mrs Kelly remembers that her mother, with her friend Mrs Rothwell, worked there two or three evenings a week, preparing drinks and sandwiches in a small room at the end of one of the long wooden huts.

Troops were also supported through the NAAFI organisation and at least one woman from Hayes, 2nd Subaltern Kathleen Lander of 29 Pickhurst Mead, was one of 200 girls sent to France with the British Army of Liberation in late 1944.[60]

HVA carried on its emergency committee work throughout the war until April 1945 when it held its first AGM for five years. Mr Arthur Collins was elected President and Mr Vellenoweth reported that on the closure of the United Services Canteen the Committee was able to 'send handsome donations for the King George's Fund, Royal Navy, Merchant Navy, RAF and Army Benevolent funds, British Red Cross, St John's and St Dunstan's funds'.[61]

HCC did not hold AGMs in 1941 and 1942 but recommenced on 28 April 1943. Its work was mainly the routine one of maintaining the Village Hall through the Management Committee. The hall was well used, with approximately 450 bookings for the main hall in 1942 and 1943 with the annexe used 307 and 278 times in those years.[62]

The local branch of the WI continued to meet. In September 1939 it had a membership of 169, of whom 90 normally met every month in the Village Hall. By October 1944 they had 183 members and the average attendance was 106. They, like other groups, suffered from the effects of war. Meetings were cancelled in September 1939, 'owing to the use of the hall for national service', in 1940 'owing to the frequency of the air raids' and in July and August 1944 because of flying bombs. Their motto was 'Pull Together'. Knitting parties were formed to make garments for the troops and socks for Land Army girls. Needlework groups sewed hundreds of items for the Bromley Hospital Supply Depot and for the Soldiers Sailors and Airmen Association. In 1944 the members made 580 individual garments. In 1941 and 42 some members worked at the Fruit Preservation Depot in Keston. The *Bromley Times* recorded that 1,000 cans of fruit were preserved and 1,625lb of jam were made. In 1943 members took part in a National Water and Sewerage Survey and reported that two houses in Hayes still depended on pumps for water, 26 had no drainage and eight had an earth closet.

Another major activity for the WI was fundraising. The Red Cross, YMCA, YWCA, St Dunstans and many other organisations benefited from its money raising schemes. It also supported special campaigns such as 'Thanks Giving' and 'Wings for Victory' weeks. In addition, the WI encouraged its members to invest in National Savings to help fund the war effort. In 1941, their first year of savings, they raised £1,230 and the annual figure had risen to over £2,000 by 1945. They were encouraged in their activities by Miss Margaret Stafford Smith, who had been secretary of the Bromley Savings Committee for almost thirty years.[63]

*Raising Money for the Spitfire Appeal* [j.]
**Mrs W J Lofthouse, Mrs J A Holden, Mr H A C Crowhurst, Mrs Lockhart**

*Spitfire Appeal* [j.]

*The Mayor of Bromley indicates the target reached* [j.]

Advertisements encouraged employers, employees and private citizens to form National Savings groups and to save a portion of their income, which indirectly was used to finance the war effort. Everybody saved, even the very young. During War Weapons Week, Mrs Sunderland of Bourne Vale gave birth and, to mark the event, the baby received a National Savings Certificate from the organisers. Residents of Bourne Vale and Chatham Avenue had a flourishing savings group, organised by Mrs Reginald Stevens of 45 Chatham Avenue. Her group received a Certificate of Honour in recognition of special achievement during the 'Wings for Victory' campaign in 1943, as did many others in the parish.

Such campaigns were borough wide; in 1940 the Bromley Fighter Fund raised over £5,000, and by August 1941 had enough to provide a Supermarine Spitfire for the RAF.[64] In another fund-raising campaign for War Weapons Week at the end of February 1941, the people of Bromley donated over £440,000. Hayes contributed to these activities and often decked out Station Approach for these events.

The Red Cross provided invaluable service during the war in all theatres of operations. Its need for support was recognised by the Hayes and District Horticultural Society who maintained a Red Cross Agricultural Fund. One day, in July 1944, the Society's Treasurer, F W Atkinson, had a visit from four Hayes boys, all under ten years old, Colin Wilkie, Brian Rigarlsford, Raymond Finch and Edward Searle, who presented him with £1 16s. 0d. for the fund. They had collected the money by selling toys that they had made from scraps of old wood and a few months later raised a further £1 from a similar enterprise.[65] Local schools contributed to the savings campaigns, including 'Warship Week' which was held in March 1942. Hayes Council School aimed to raise £400 towards the appeal and the adoption of Bromley's warship, *HMS Broke*.

Many unofficial local ladies' groups were formed to provide comforts for servicemen. One was a knitting group started in 1940 by Mrs Nye of Prickley Wood, Bourne Way. This ladies' circle made over 1,200 articles of clothing in its first year. Four years later the group, despite the death of its leader, was still able to maintain the production rate. In January 1944 it was reported that during the previous year they had met at the WVS centre at 27 Station Approach and had completed 1,079 garments. Another knitting group was St Mary's Women's Fellowship who decided in 1941 that 'as it is now difficult to obtain wool without coupons ... a needlework renovations afternoon should be held once a month'.[66]

## Digging for Victory

The 'Dig for Victory' campaign applied to everybody. Private individuals, allotment and smallholders, and local farms all played their part in feeding the nation. At the start of the war Britain had an urgent need to increase home food production by bringing large areas of land back under cultivation. The import of food could not be relied upon because of the danger to merchant shipping travelling across the Atlantic and other oceans. County War Agricultural Executive Committees had the task and authority to increase home food production and could direct methods of cultivation, the type of crops to be grown, inspect properties, terminate tenancies and organise mobile groups of farm workers.

One of their first tasks, from June 1940, was to survey all farms, with the immediate purpose of increasing food production. The survey, which has been called a 'Second Domesday Book', categorised each farm or holding of five acres or more in terms of its productive state, managerial efficiency, condition of fields, building, fences and hedges.[67]

In 1941 Hayesford Farm and part of Hook Farm, both owned by the Norman family, were farmed by George E Hoeltschi with seven men, four women, three horses and two International tractors. He had 42 acres under cultivation with Brussels sprouts, cabbages, cauliflowers, beetroots, onions, runner beans, lettuces and rhubarb. Fifteen acres had potatoes, 20 acres were devoted to cereal, barley and oats, and a further 72 acres were fallow - a total of 149 acres. The inspector noted 'a decided improvement in cropping arrangements but more labour [was] needed for market garden crops'. He also reported that the farm suffered from an infestation of rooks and pigeons. Mr Hoeltschi had held the tenancy of Hayesford Farm for seven years and in March 1941 also took over 46 acres of Hook Farm, the condition of which was much the same as Hayesford Farm.[68]

Hayes Street Farm and Baston Farm were leased from the Norman family by Mr R Fisher, and from 1925 had been farmed by Sidney Rose. The survey showed that 111 of the 270 acres were used for cereal, 17 acres for mangolds, 18 for kale and 11 for clover. The remaining 113 acres were pasture, used to feed three bulls, 73 cows in milk, 18 cows in calf and 25 other cattle. There were also poultry, five horses, a tractor and twelve full-time men. Sidney Rose was rated a good farmer and the report stated that 'this farm has improved since 1940 and should become one of the best in the neighbourhood when the drainage scheme has been completed and the land feels the resultant benefit'. In 1956, when James Ellis received a Long Service Award at the Kent County Show, he recalled that he had worked for Fisher & Sons for 55 years, of which 30 had been at Hayes. 'I have seen plenty of changes … I was in the Civil Defence … and at the end of the war we had a party of German prisoners working for us on the farm'.[69]

Many of the old farms and smallholdings had been sold to developers. At the outbreak of war, however, not all of this land had been converted into roads and houses. One such farm was Fixteds and here D Hassell who lived in Bromley Common, brought back into cultivation some 35 acres of which 30 were oats and 3.5 were potatoes. He received a 'pat on the back' from the inspector who said 'this land known as Fixteds was a building site, ploughed last year [1940], now carries a good crop of oats (well done) - All ditches need attention.'[70] Not all farms and small-holdings received favourable comments. Hayes Court Farm, a smallholding, suffered from an infestation of rooks and rabbits and in the words of the inspector was 'neglected'. 'This holding can be improved by extra ploughing which the occupier has promised to do.'

With the increasing shortage of male farm workers, many of whom had been called-up or had volunteered for the armed services, the Government introduced conscription for women in 1941. Some women, like Winifred Timms who lived at 16 Mounthurst Road, chose to join the Land Army rather than go to a munitions factory in Birmingham. She went to Benenden, Kent where she was employed in planting out crops, hoeing and threshing. Agricultural work was not without its dangers as one Hayes woman found to her cost. Nancy Arthur of 24 Baston Road worked at Farthing Barn Farm, Downe, and in September 1944 during harvesting lost her right leg in a threshing machine accident. In a later court case she was awarded £2,500 damages for her injuries.[71] Six Land Girls were married in Hayes Church between 1942 and 1945.

Where possible, natural resources were collected to help the national drive to increase food production. School children, Boy Scouts, other youth organisations, and adult groups were involved in scavenging the common, fields, woods and hedgerows for acorns for pigs, and hips and haws for the manufacture of rose hip syrup. Many older residents have vivid memories of this and of collecting blackberries used for homemade jam, even though sugar was rationed.[72]

Inhabitants were encouraged to supplement their rations by growing vegetables and fruit in their gardens or on allotments. Any small area of land that could be cultivated was used. In January 1940, Bromley Borough Council agreed to provide allotments for residents on unused housing plots in Bourne Vale and Constance Crescent. By the first week of April, 84 of the 99 plots along Bourne Vale had been taken and all seven of the allotments in the Old Rectory grounds were actively cultivated. Demand grew; another 17 plots were opened in Redgate Drive and remained in use until 1948. Allotments were prepared in other parts of the district; 24 plots at Tiepigs Lane and 28 plots in Bourne Way. Nine of these were on the railway station side and were in use until 1950 after which the land became Bourne Way Nurseries run by Mr G Bellenie. On the south side of Bourne Way the Council had bought land for housing. Here nineteen allotments were opened which were still in use in 1949/50. Many of the open spaces on Hayes Place estate were used, such as the Green at the junction of Sackville Avenue and Stanhope Avenue, and land on the east side of Hayes Lane opposite Hayes Road.[73]

Allotments were also set out in November 1939 on the Glebe land behind the Village Hall. Plot holders were charged one shilling for the first year's rent and five shillings for subsequent years. After a few months the plot holders approached HCC to have access to the plots via the path alongside the Hall rather than passing through the churchyard. This was granted. At the end of 1941 they were warned that the land would soon be required for a graveyard extension. It was not until Saturday 6 May 1944 that the land was consecrated in the presence of many parishioners by the Bishop of Rochester, Rt Revd Dr C M Chavasse.[74] Even then, most allotment holders were allowed to continue using the land. Beckenham Council took over land in Pondfield Road for additional allotments in October 1943 and Wickham Park Sports Club's ground that backs on to Hilldown Road was also used.

The village had its pig club in Bourne Way and individual families kept chickens in their back gardens and grew vegetables in the front garden borders, all designed to eke out the rations. These actions were encouraged by the Ministry of Food, the Borough Council and local newspapers, which published recipes and household hints throughout the war.

## Rationing

As soon as war started, rationing and the ration book became a way of life for every family and person. By January 1940 meat, bacon, butter and sugar were on ration and the grocery shops in Hayes started to feel the effects of food distribution controls. Shops also suffered from a shortage of male staff as many were called-up into the services. Express Dairies began using women as milk float drivers in November 1940 at its milk distribution centre in Station Approach (where the public car park is now sited). At that time horse drawn milk floats were used and during air raids the milkmen and women, when out on their rounds, would seek refuge in the nearest public or private shelter but the horse was often left to fend for itself. In Pittsmead Avenue arrangements were different, as Alan Pettitt recalls that his parents would allow the horse to shelter in their garage, which afforded a measure of protection against shrapnel.[75]

As the war progressed, food rationing had its inevitable effect. Individuals and organisations found ways to eke out their meagre allowances. In October 1942, the Mothers' Union Committee requested members to bring milk for their tea at meetings. Many neighbours made arrangements to exchange items to suit personal needs, such as the sugar allowance for the bacon ration. Occasionally shops would sell large tins of American pork meat for half-a-crown. There was a layer of white fat that surrounded the meat that some people prized more than the meat itself. Meat and sausages were always difficult to come by. Mrs Jean Hadley (née Wilkins), then living in Harvest Bank Road, remembered that one high-class local butcher never seemed to have sausages. She asked 'why is it that when other shops have sausages you have none?' This drew the response that they only got 4lb a week and that was just enough for the staff! Many other outlets, such as hardware stores, were unable to obtain goods from their wholesalers.[76]

The shortage of all sorts of personal and household items led to the 'Make Do and Mend' slogan. People were encouraged to save waste paper, rags, aluminium and even old bones, anything that was capable of being collected and recycled, all to aid the war effort.

*An encouragement to the people of Hayes to hand in their aluminium pots and pans* [j.]

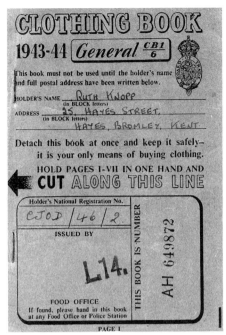

*Clothing Ration Book belonging to Ruth Knopp* [af.]

Clothes were rationed from May 1941 and a points system was introduced. Individuals had 66 coupons for the year (later reduced to 60). The number of coupons varied according to the item. A raincoat was 14 points, a woollen dress 11 and a skirt 7. Men's shoes were 7 and men's socks 3 coupons. The government also introduced utility garments to save material and control prices.

## Wartime Schooling

School life in Hayes, as elsewhere in the Borough, was affected from the first day of the war. Because of the threat of air raids the Borough Council decided that the children would remain at home with their families until shelter provision had been made. Schoolwork was undertaken at home with teachers visiting pupils to check on their progress. Edward Searle, a pupil of Hayes School, who lived at 18 The Green, remembers, 'Miss Irene Mearns [Hayes School teacher] holding classes in the front room'. Miss Mearns also had a group of infants in her house, 5 Burwood Avenue, and was helped by one of the pupils, Dorothy Dewey of Glebe House Drive, who had been due to go to Princes Plain Secondary School in September.[77]

In November 1939 normality started to return with pupils attending school once more but in one-hour shifts, so as to minimise the concentration of children at any one time. By March 1940 one of the shelters had been built and the three top classes now attended on a half-time basis; a fortnight later all juniors were taught in the same way. A start was made on the Infants' shelter and the closets were finally installed by the end of May. Meanwhile Miss Page received instructions that from 1st April all scholars were to attend full time and she made arrangements for the 303 pupils on the roll to attend school. In the event of an air raid the top class and boys of the second class would disperse to houses in George Lane, whether or not they had useable Anderson shelters. Classes III and IV used shelter No. 2 in which Infants' tables were used as seats, Classes V and VI, Infants and Class II girls used shelter No. 1 where 100 chairs were put.

The main difficulty was lack of lighting in the shelters as they just had five storm lanterns and four carriage lamps. Gradually benches and improved lighting were supplied. Although the shelters were not fully equipped, the children practised evacuating the school as quickly as possible and by 15th August managed it in one minute. The shelters were frequently used, particularly between 30 August 1940 and 31 January 1941 when there were constant air raids; these continued spasmodically until May 1941. On 24 September 1940 a large crater was made in the field by a bomb during the night and on 23rd October damage occurred to ceilings and the front door as a result of bombs falling in the neighbourhood. In November 1941, 213 pupils' gas masks were tested in the visiting gas mask van.

Miss Dorothea Page retired as headmistress at the end of November 1941 and was succeeded by Mrs Eva Butler, whose wearing of tweed suits and lacy patterned stocking is remembered by pupils. By the following September there was need for an additional class and to accommodate it the canteen was moved into the hall and a new teacher, Mrs Irene Hammond started. By August 1943 the average attendance was 304 or 78% of the nominal roll. In October the school building again suffered damage from bomb blast to ceilings, doors and some of the brickwork. Air raid wardens carried out gas mask tests and 49 had to be exchanged.

The flying bomb campaign caused considerable problems with repeated alerts. On 19 June 1944 only 47 children came to school and lunch was served in the shelters. Teachers were also affected; Mrs Shimnell, who joined the school in May 1942, had time off to deal with bomb damage to her house on 19th and 27th June. Mrs Hammond suffered damage to her property on 21st June, and the home of the groundsman, Mr Henry Timms, 16 Mounthurst Road, was very badly damaged by enemy action.[78]

The flying bomb onslaught brought about new plans for evacuation and 119 children had been taken off the roll by 28 July 1944, as they had been either evacuated officially or by private arrangement. The difficulties were reinforced when a flying bomb fell near Bolds Wood, 200 yards from the school, and caused more damage. One of the teachers, Mrs Bardgett, was chosen to accompany the Hayes schoolchildren on their journey north. The first group of about 30 pupils was taken to Leicester and the next group to Nottingham. At Bromley South they joined up with children from Bromley Parish School. The journey was relatively uneventful and she described it as 'quite fun'.[79] By the end of September the danger seemed over and the evacuees were being readmitted. A month later there were 367 on the roll with about a 75% attendance.

The roll numbers continued to increase and in January 1945, with more than the 400 pupils for which the school was built, it was decided that the top two classes under Miss Kiely and Miss Barnes should move to new classrooms that had been set up in Gadsden. It was fortunate that no pupils were involved in the V2 rocket incident that took place a few weeks later in February, although both Gadsden and the school in George Lane were damaged. The repairs and cleaning were completed over the weekend and the pupils came to school at the normal time on the Monday.

At the Golden Jubilee of the school in 1987 many former pupils recalled their wartime memories. Colin Brook recounted that during the blitz the boys and girls frequently collected shrapnel and one infant proudly brought his bag containing an incendiary bomb and placed it on his teacher's desk. A horrified Miss Mearns quickly asked all the children to leave. In the shelters the pupils were encouraged to sing to hide the noise of the guns and bombs.[80] Dorothy Dewey, a pupil at Princes Plain School, Bromley, recalled that the older children went by bus to their secondary schools and often saw raids in the distance. Lessons finished early one day when a bomb fell near the school; the girls were sent home and they walked back across the fields (the quickest way), as there were no buses. With Princes Plain School out of action for a while due to the bomb damage, the older Hayes girls returned to George Lane, shared the school shelters and were taught by two of the Princes Plain School teachers in the staff room. Many pupils considered the excursions to the shelters the most exciting part of the school day.

Sugar and, therefore, sweets were in short supply during the war. In 1943, however, the children at Hayes School received a large box of sweets from the teachers of a school in Toronto, Canada, and each child was able to have a liberal helping. Many letters of thanks were sent and it was hoped that the parcels would continue.

Changes also took place at some private schools. In March 1940 advertisements for Baston School referred to the presence of a large air raid shelter for pupils and lessons continued as normal for some months. When the situation worsened and the trips to the shelter became more frequent it was decided to evacuate. In November 1940 pupils and staff were at the Grand View Hotel, Hope Cove, Devon, but in July 1942 new premises had to be found when the hotel was requisitioned. The school moved to Barrow Court, Galhampton, Somerset owned by Colonel Boles, MP for Wells. Three happy and successful years were spent there until the end of the war and they returned to Hayes in September 1945.[81] The army took over many of the Baston School buildings. Miss Margaret Stafford Smith remained in Hayes and ran the school as a guesthouse for the wives of soldiers stationed in the area.

The fortunes of Barnhill School continued to be mixed. In November 1940 it was reported that the school had been thoroughly reorganized and had a modern ARP shelter in which teaching could continue when necessary. Colonel Sir William Waldron, at the Annual Prize Giving in December 1941, mentioned the difficulties created by the war, the evacuation of some boys and damage to the building by a bomb. He praised the headmaster, Mr P Austin, for the fact that the school had not closed its doors or suffered the loss of one day of its educational work. The reduction in pupil numbers, however, resulted in the school going into liquidation in November 1942 and as a consequence Dame Eliza Waldron became owner of the property. In June 1943 a yearly tenancy was agreed with Arthur Vincent Collier of 36 Manor Park Road, and Cecil Askey of 74 Courtfield Rise, West Wickham at £225 per annum 'to use the premises as a boys' school and for no other purpose'. The tenants had a 21-year option to purchase the freehold at £5,250 but after the war, when Arthur Collier and Cecil Askey were given a four monthly tenancy agreement, this option was withdrawn.[82] In spite of the financial upheavals the school survived into the 1960s.

One aspect of wartime schooling arrangements recalled by Miss Mercia Sansom, who lived at 37 Pickhurst Mead, was that every school in the district was involved in the Emergency Feeding Scheme and was equipped with a field kitchen. Teachers attended training courses and received certificates but thankfully their new skills were never put to the test. Mercia Sansom also joined and helped run the Girls' Training Corps, which met regularly at Hawes Down School, West Wickham. This was an organisation for girls, between the ages of 16 and 18, and the aim was to create a link between leaving school and embarking upon war work, whether in the forces, factories or as a land girl.[83]

Despite the disruptive effect of the air raids and teachers undertaking additional duties, educational standards seemed to have been maintained. Over half of the eligible children gained a county scholarship in 1944.[84]

Apart from school, children were still able to join local youth organisations, such as the Boy Scouts, Girl Guides, Cadet Force, many of which were attached to schools or churches.

## The Churches

During the war years the churches in Hayes and their affiliated organisation were affected, like other groups, by the outbreak of hostilities but continued to provide spiritual guidance and support for the inhabitants.

The Free Church, whose building plans were stopped, suffered another set back when their minister, Revd Stanley Sheppard, became a RAF chaplain in September 1941. He was replaced in April 1942 by Revd Alan Seager, who was waiting for a passage to Bechuanaland, and he left Hayes in May. A more permanent minister, Revd Harold Edwards, came in May 1943 and remained until 1950.[85]

In January 1940, Coney Hall Baptist Church appointed a new minister, Revd A J Garnier, who lived at 2 Stanhope Avenue. In June the unfortunate Revd Garnier was arrested by the police and interned in an aliens' camp on the Isle of Man because he was born in Italy. Reason eventually prevailed; Revd Garnier was released in September 1940 to return to his home and ministry.[86]

Roman Catholics, who had no permanent church, held services in a room in the New Inn but when it was bombed in September 1940 transferred to the Village Hall Annexe.[87]

Events at the Parish Church reflected matters considered in many households. In May 1941 its fire insurance was increased from £23,200 to £32,000. On 5 September 1941 the *Bromley Times* reported that the 'Parish Church clock would not go as it could not cope with double summer-time', which was introduced in 1941 and lasted to 1945. Three months later the *Parish Magazine*, a source of local news and events, was reduced to half its normal size because of the paper shortage. In April 1942, difficulty was experienced in obtaining coke for the central heating boiler. In the same month, the Rector ask for volunteers to act as Sunday School teachers as two of the current seven were being 'called-up'. When a fire practice was held at the church in June it was discovered that the ladders were too short. With the national drive to collect surplus iron from around the country, the fate of the graveyard iron railings was discussed but it was decided that there was insufficient quantity to warrant a special collection, thus the railings survive to this day. On 15 November 1942 a rare event took place when the church bells, so long silent, were rung to celebrate Britain's victory at the battle of El Alamein.[88]

Revd Edward McClintock remained at Hayes through most of the war and his entries in the Register of Services reveal the extent of enemy action and some of the demands made on him. Despite many difficulties, the numbers at services remained high. The Rector was an air raid warden as well as a minister and went immediately to follow up after any bombing incident. Frequently he recorded miraculous escapes. In one case the family had gone to the cinema. In another, when the backs of the houses at the bottom of the Rectory garden (Hayes Wood Avenue) were blown out, the woman sleeping in a back room had that very day moved her bed into another corner. If she had not done that her bed would have ended up on the ground. When numbers started to drop off at services he was told that the women could not afford to use their coupons to buy hats. His response was to place a notice on the door saying that hats did not have to be worn. The notice was torn down and the matter reached the London Evening Papers!

During 1944 Revd E McClintock was greatly concerned about the action the church should take on the return to civilian life of the Forces and POWs. 'These men and women will come back different persons and will find us also somewhat changed ... The majority will want to see things improved on 1939.' His health had suffered and very reluctantly he announced his resignation in October 1944 and left his Hayes ministry on 31 December 1944. The new Rector, Revd A Eric Smith, MA, who was from Norbiton, was inducted on 21 April 1945.[89]

*The new Rector, Revd Eric Smith, takes the first Remembrance Service after the war* [x.]

# Social Life

Social life played an important part in providing an escape from the pressure and stress of war. Home-made entertainment was the order of the day as well as a weekly outing to the Rex Cinema. From the start of the war, except in the first few weeks when places of entertainment were closed, people organised dances, socials, sports days, knitting circles and other events, which fostered the community spirit and enabled people to maintain their strength throughout the conflict. Many friendships were made, some lasting to this day.

One of the first social events to be arranged was the 1940 New Year party organised by the ARP No 3 Stretcher Party, held at Gadsden and attended by 60 people. The Hayes Chamber of Commerce also held a New Year party. The next month HVA organised a dance in the Village Hall, where it was observed that three Royal Artillery gunners attended, evidence that locals and servicemen were starting to mix.[90] As the number of troops in the area started to grow, members of ARP arranged a dance in March 1940, at which many soldiers were entertained. In April troops attended a Hayes and District Horticultural Society's party. After its formation the Home Guard often used the Village Hall for social gatherings; the first was a children's party followed by a dance, in March 1941, at which some 250 people crowded into the main hall, including senior officers from 51 Battalion. The Village Hall continued to be the main dance venue. Railway staff from Hayes Station held a dance at the hall in May 1944 and the NFS band provided the music for the evening. The dance raised £30 in aid of former Southern Railway staff who were prisoners of war.

The Village Hall stage was the platform for many concert parties and plays. In November 1943, for instance, the NFS Dramatic Society staged a grand variety concert party entitled '*Hey Presto*' and in January 1944 the NFS showed a film to more than 60 children at a party organised by the WVS and Mrs Elinor Harrold, leader of the PD3 wardens.[91] At the party Father Christmas distributed gifts, some of which American children had donated, and sweets sent by the Canadian Red Cross.

The Hayes Players performed for the Bromley Home Guard and *The Man who stayed at Home,* a topical wartime play, was taken to sixteen different camps, including RAF Biggin Hill.

The Hayes and District Horticultural Society met regularly during the war and talks were given on a wide variety of topics. In February 1940 James Grandfield, fellow of the Royal Horticultural Society, lectured on alpine plants.[92] Flower and Vegetable Shows were organised by the society or by the five District Wardens and were well supported. In September 1942 the Wardens held their second Annual Vegetable and Flower Show at the Village Hall and these events encouraged everybody to grow produce to supplement their diets.

The Civil Defence, in conjunction with Hayes and District Horticultural Society, held a major Sports and Gala Day at Gadsden in June 1944 attended by 1,600 people. Events included a 100 yards' race for women, a one mile walk for men, women's pillow fight and an ambulance duty drivers' obstacle race. The prize for winning the treasure hunt was a gold half-sovereign and the Hayes Pig Club donated two pieces of pork for the auction, the proceeds of which were presented to the Red Cross Fund.

Sport was essential for keeping up morale and fitness and was used extensively by the armed services. Most local clubs closed down temporarily or restricted their fixtures at the start of the war. In 1939 Blackheath Harriers reported in its journal:

> for the present runs will take place every Saturday throughout the winter season ...
> The only known factor to prevent this will be the destruction by enemy aircraft of
> local property, when our premises will be used as a temporary home for the
> homeless.

The Blackheath Harriers' clubhouse was used to store a 'large pile of palliasses', and by the beginning of 1941 'some 75 locals had sought shelter there for periods of up to eighteen days'. Unlike many clubs, the Harriers continued to operate and were the hosts of many a cross-country run. The Harriers' headquarters received its share of damage from enemy action with tiles dislodged, ceilings damaged and a sprinkling of incendiary bombs landing in the car park.[93]

Hayes Cricket Club had suspended most of its fixtures by the end of 1939 although one side continued to play during 1940. These were difficult times for the club but with the increase in the number of servicemen in the area they received requests in July 1941 from the RAF and the RCS to use the tennis courts and grounds. In October the RAF started to use the football pitch and by April 1942 were joined by men from the Signals Unit, who also used the cricket pitch during the summer. The Cricket Club held its annual New Year's Eve dance at the Village Hall to music provided by an RAF band. Many of the Civil Defence Units played cricket at Gadsden; one match was between the Gadsden based Light Rescue Unit and Hayes Youth Fellowship. In July 1941, HVA obtained agreement from Kent County Council, the owners of Gadsden, for ARP staff to use part of the lawn as a Bowling Green, thus providing more recreational facilities. The AFS staged a number of boxing matches and in March 1940 Firemen Presland, Boylan and Bunce, all stationed at Hayes, entered the competition.[94]

Members of the Civil Defence and Home Guard units formed brass bands. They were popular and presented many concerts, including a number given on summer evenings to large and appreciative crowds gathered on the common. Hayes Common continued to be the traditional home of the crowning of the London May Queen and, despite the war, the celebrations and pretty costumes were enjoyed by many, although the retinues had to carry gas mask boxes.

## The End in Sight

With the successful D Day landings in France in June 1944, a feeling prevailed that victory and the end of the war was near. In August the National Fire Service wound down its operations in the area and the sub-fire station at the Old Rectory was closed with the property returning to Council control on 31st October. The Rector announced during the Harvest Festival Service in October 1944 that there would be a short service of thanksgiving and dedication on the first Sunday after hostilities in Europe ceased. The following week, arrangements were made to hold a meeting in the Village Hall to consider 'post war plans' for Hayes.

In November, the slit trench shelters in the Old Rectory garden were back-filled and a start made on dismantling the tank trap roadblocks at Pickhurst Green, although the Home Guard strong points at Socket Lane and in the front garden of 210 Hayes Lane remained a little longer. These defences, so it was said, were the last of their type in the Borough of Bromley.[95] In the same month, the PCC considered 33 suggestions from parishioners about the needs of returning servicemen and women. Early in December 1944 the Home Guard held their final parade in Hyde Park, London, in front of King George VI; representatives of B Company paraded there for the last time. A week later the Invicta Association was formed by ex-Home Guard members and held its first monthly meeting in the battle-scarred New Inn.

The mood in Hayes was turning towards the future and, in March 1945, most Hayes' organisations were represented at a meeting sponsored by the Invicta Association when it was suggested that the village needed a Community Centre. The Mayor of Bromley, Councillor Arthur Collins, was present and reflected the difficulties ahead when he asked:

> speaking of the proposed centre … could anyone visualise any new buildings except houses going up for some time to come? They [the Borough Council] had a heavy programme in the housing field before them. But we must take the long view … it was all to the good that they [Hayes] should plan for a village centre.[96]

Arthur Collins was correct in his assessment.

Peace was in the air and it was proposed that HVA should resume its work as many members could spare more time, now that the Home Guard and other Civil Defence services had wound down. In April Hayes Lawn Tennis Club reopened, having disbanded in 1941.[97]

On 8 May 1945 the war in Europe ended. Despite flying bombs and rocket attacks, peace had arrived at last and local organisations and institutions, which had closed 'for the duration', once again opened their doors and pondered on the considerable task of rebuilding and repair that was necessary. In the Far East, however, the war continued until August. Many waited anxiously for their servicemen's return.

For some inhabitants there was still more bad news. Dorothy Gardiner heard that her husband, Thomas, had died in December 1944 of wounds received in Burma. Gunner Colin Clarke died in Japan in March 1945. Sergeant Albert Quinton, Trooper Walter Spencer, Driver Stanley Naylor and Lieutenant Frank Fuller were killed in Germany in the final stages of the war (Appendix 4).

For other families the ending of the war meant joyous reunions with their menfolk, some of whom had been POWs since 1940. Frank Helm returned to join his sister in 6 Redgate Drive. Peter Marchant of 38 Hayes Lane came back and was married in Hayes Church in November. The safe returns of Ronald Aldrich, Alfred Hicknott, Melfryn and Moelwyn Williams were also recorded in the local paper.

Lieutenant George Honour RNVR of 76 West Common Road was awarded the DSC in December 1944 for the part he played in 'operations' for the invasion of Normandy.[98] Wing Commander C J Hutton of Sackville Avenue was mentioned in despatches. Wing Commander D Martin Butcher received the DSO for his service in South East Asia.

I n the years when our Country

was in mortal danger

Reginald Ide STEVENS.

who served 1st March 1941 - 31st Dec 1944.

gave generously of his time and

powers to make himself ready

for her defence by force of arms

and with his life if need be.

## THE HOME GUARD

*Certificate received by members of the
Home Guard on stand down [al.]*

## BOROUGH OF BECKENHAM

### THE GREAT WAR, 1939-45.

On behalf of the Council and of the Townspeople of Beckenham, we express very cordial appreciation of the valuable services you rendered as a member of the Civil Defence Organisation of this Borough, which has suffered so much and with such fortitude during the years of War.

We convey to you our thanks and sincere good wishes.

*Mayor and Chairman of the Emergency Committee*

*Town Clerk and Hon. A.R.P. Controller.*

*August, 1945*

To Mercia Sansom,

Emergency Feeding Service

*Civil Defence certificate received by
Mercia Sansom for her work with the
Emergency Feeding Scheme [am.]*

## Counting the Cost

During 1945 Hayes, like so many communities in Great Britain, started to count the cost of the war. Over 50 houses had been destroyed and well over a thousand were damaged with shops, inns and the railway station all affected. Most of these in time would be rebuilt and repaired, leaving Hayes without too many permanent visual scars.

The loss of life of people who were born, lived, worked or were connected with the village was considerable. Twenty-nine civilians died, of whom 24 were killed in Hayes in eleven separate incidents. Five of the casualties were children under ten years of age and the oldest to die was 77. The brief biographical details of these casualties were given in *Wartime Hayes* published in 2000. Since then casualty records have become more readily accessible and recent research has uncovered many more service personnel, connected with Hayes, who died during the conflict. A complete list is in Appendix 4 with the biographical details of those who were previously omitted. Some 82 servicemen and women connected to Hayes died during the war either in action, on active service or from other causes; these deaths occurred in nearly every theatre of war. Five were buried with full military honour in Hayes churchyard; two of whom, Flight Lieutenant John Billett and Leading Aircraftsman Clement Jeans, were awarded the military medal.[99] The others were Lance Corporal Frank Balcomb, Flight Lieutenant Percy Stickland and

Corporal George Wilkinson. The names of four service men who died during the war are commemorated on family gravestones in the churchyard. Pilot Officer Gilby died when returning to base from a bombing expedition on 7 August 1942. Sergeant Ronald William Nicholson was killed on service in Malaya in September 1943 and Sergeant Pilot Kenneth Tilbury died in India in December 1943. The fourth person was Flight Sergeant Gordon Orchard whose bomber crashed over Berlin on 30 January 1945.

Of the total service casualties 36 were from the RAF, 34 from the Army, 10 from the Royal Navy, one from the Merchant Navy and one from the Home Guard. The youngest to be killed was 18 and the oldest 50. In addition, two soldiers of the RASC were killed in a road accident in May 1942 at the junction of West Common Road and Croydon Road and a bombardier died from injuries he received during a physical training exercise at the gun-site in January 1942.

The effect of the war had at times been devastating for the people of Hayes and had created all sorts of pressures for the inhabitants. Although there had been lulls in the air attacks, the inhabitants were reminded almost every month of the sacrifices being made by service people drawn from around Hayes. The coming of peace gave an opportunity to rebuild Hayes and to ensure that the community would be strengthened by the challenges that lay ahead.

# Chapter 7
# Peace comes to Hayes: 1945-1951

As soon as victory was declared on Tuesday 8 May 1945 thanksgiving services were held, led by Revd Eric Smith and the Free Church minister, Revd Harold Edwards.[1] Schools closed for two days. Numerous street parties were organised, such as those in George Lane, Bourne Vale and Hurstdene Avenue. The firewatchers of Dartmouth Road, Northbourne and Southborne provided a party for 60 children and afterwards the organisers decided to form a club, the Victory Social Club.[2] It met in the Village Hall until 1951 when a site was purchased in Kechill Gardens and eventually a clubhouse was erected that survives to this day. The largest party was probably held at the Warren when 400 children attended. The 'Quips Concert Party' gave a free show in the cinema to all local children. On 10th May the children returned to school for a service, a visit from the Mayor and a class party.

*Celebrating Victory, VE party, May 1945*

*VJ Party for the children of George Lane* [8]

When victory over Japan came in August 1945 there were more celebrations. The inhabitants of Cecil Way, Sackville and Stuart Avenues held parties at Gadsden. Families from Pickhurst Mead and Pickhurst Green had a street party for 80 children, attended by the Mayor and Mayoress of Bromley. Each boy and girl received a beaker on which was their name and 'V-1945'.[3] Bromley held official celebrations in May 1945 and June 1946, when Hayes bell ringers rang a peel of 720 changes with other local churches.[4] In July 1946 a welcome home party was held in the Village Hall for ex-servicemen and women from George Lane. Many groups did not want to lose the camaraderie that had developed in Hayes during the difficult war years. The survivors of the raid on the New Inn met for a meal each September for many years. In January 1947 the wardens on Post D4 had a reunion at Bunney's Café, Station Approach. The Invicta (Home Guard) Association decided to perform two plays each year and in November 1946 produced a highly successful performance of Blithe Spirit.[5] In June 1947 the Bromley Casualty Old Comrades Association (Hayes Branch) met at Gadsden and agreed that an oak plaque should be erected there to commemorate the work of the Light Rescue Party at Hayes.[6]

There was considerable discussion about the best way to remember those who had lost their lives during the war. In October 1945 the Rector collected the information for the Hayes Roll of Honour, which was read out at the first post-war Armistice Day parade and service held around the War Memorial. It was decided to provide an extension to the east end of the Village Hall, which had served the community so well during the war. In September 1946 the plans were approved and an estimated £5,000 was required. Fundraising events were held but national restrictions on building delayed its construction. In 1951, a second architect Ronald Pearce was consulted when funds stood at £2,227.[7] The estimated costs increased, the plans had to be altered and it was not until 1959 that the extension, the Green Room, was finally completed. The Act of Dedication took place on 13 November 1960. Miss Vera Thompson, a representative of all who were responsible for first building the Hall, unveiled a stone commemorating the fact that the Hall had been extended and improved 'in memory of all Hayes people who gave their lives in the service of their country during the World War of 1939-45'.

Meanwhile, in July 1947 it was suggested at a PCC meeting that the names of those killed from Hayes in the Second World War should be added to the base of the War Memorial. The list comprised thirteen civilians and 37 from the armed services – five from the navy and sixteen each from the army and air force.[8] In October 1950 stonemasons W Cullen & Son undertook the work.

The return of peace meant that people were eager to see the removal of the gun and searchlight sites, the tank traps, shelters and other defensive constructions that were reminders of the war and that interfered with their normal lives. One of the most visible signs was the gun and radar site on the common and the searchlight at Pickhurst. The Common Conservators, conscious of their responsibility to preserve Hayes Common, had only reluctantly agreed to the presence of the military on the common and were keen to ensure that everything was returned to normal as soon as possible.

*Gun Emplacements on Hayes Common awaiting demolition, June 1954 [m.]*

*Empty Ammunition Store on Hayes Common, June 1954 [m.]*

As early as January 1945, when peace seemed to be coming, Arthur Collins, Chairman of the Conservators, wrote to Captain Nightingale to agree an allowance to restore the site vacated by the Searchlight Unit. He also claimed from the War Department for damage caused by the construction of earthworks by the Home Guard on the common. The estimate for clearing the site opposite the Greyhound, Keston, was £60 and for the common land near Croydon Road used by the Searchlight Company £20. In September 1945 the Rangers reported that they had filled in ten slip trenches, five home guard posts, cleared the Canadian compound to the south of the Oast House, taken down the wire, cleared the bricks and levelled the ground. They had also dealt with the RCS Compound, buried the motorcycle shed that had fallen down, cleared 306 yards of barbed wire from the RCS car park, 500 yards of barbed wire from the Canadian Camp and 960 yards from the gun site.[9]

The report showed the level of activity that was required to restore Hayes Common and it could not be achieved solely by the existing Rangers. In October 1945 Fordyce Bros claimed £935, including £255 for restoration of land opposite Pickhurst Manor Hotel, refilling the anti-tank ditch, removal of five large anti-tank reinforced concrete blocks 5ft 6in deep and disposal of wire.

By the end of the year the Conservators, consisting of Mr Arthur Collins, Major Basil Binyon, Lieutenant Colonel Fulcher, Councillor Percy Jones and Mr C J Knight, had recommended payment for the clearance of:

| | |
|---|---|
| Hayes Common Gun Site (part) (Radar Mat) | £218 15s. 0d. |
| Vehicle Parking Places | £468 15s. 0d. |
| Pickhurst Green | £255 12s. 0d. |

In April 1946 Arthur Collins reported at the HVA General Meeting that five sites had been cleared but two were still occupied. The closed part of Baston Road reopened after it had been resurfaced.[10]

The Rangers continued the cleaning up operations and kept a close watch on demolition rubbish being dumped in the common's pits. In September 1946, Mr Archer, Chief Ranger, suggested that German POWs, who had not yet been repatriated, could be used to clear the searchlight site but the Military had done it by the end of October. All that was left were two brick sheds that had formed the powerhouse and transformer station and in January 1947 Fordyce's estimate for their demolition was £569 16s. 6d.

The Conservators agreed to allow Bromley Council the use of part of the hutted campsite for the provision of temporary housing accommodation. In October 1947 they were dismayed to hear that the War Office proposed to retain the gun site as a permanent position. The Town Clerk immediately raised the point that the land was 'not requisitioned under D.R.51' and that the Conservators had agreed a licence for temporary housing accommodation.

Lieutenant Colonel Fulcher represented the Conservators at a secret meeting with representatives of the War Office, Kent County Council (Town Planning Section), Bromley Borough Council and the Ministry of Town and Country Planning at the gun site in November 1947. He made it clear that the Conservators were against the camp, gun site and radar, being on Hayes Common and hoped that they would be removed as soon as practicable. It was agreed that the camp might be used for housing for ten years and that fenced enclosures would protect the radar site at the Coopers Cottages end and the gun site at the other. Lieutenant Colonel Fulcher was assured that there would be no firing at the gun site, although there might be the occasional drill. In December 1947 the Conservators sent a further letter to the Ministry of Town and Country Planning complaining about the breach of the agreement by the War Department that the site would not be used for more than twelve months after the end of war and would be restored to its natural condition.[11] It was not until 1956 that the area was finally levelled but the Conservators' earlier actions had ensured that the area was later returned to the community.

In 1947 a start was made on the removal of concrete blocks from private property and eventually they disappeared, apart from one that still remains on the railway embankment along the footpath leading from Tiepigs Lane to Hawes Lane. Some people demolished their air raid shelters, many were used as garden sheds and a few remain today. In some cases planning applications were made to convert them to another use. In November 1945 the owner of 10 Constance Crescent applied to convert his shelter into a garage and in October 1947 the shelter at Forge House, Pickhurst Lane, (now Hopton Court), was planned as a doctor's dispensary.[12] In December 1947 the Ministry of Education approved expenditure of £199 for the conversion of an air-raid shelter at Hayes School into a treatment clinic for Hayes.[13]

## Housing

The removal of the military signs of war was only one of many tasks facing the local authorities in 1945. A priority was to provide housing for those who had been bombed and had no permanent residence. The area towards the west end of Mead Way had been requisitioned in 1944 for timber storage. It was decided to build a number of prefabricated houses on the site and the first was occupied in August 1946. These 'prefabs' exceeded their design life by many years and were only removed and replaced with new town houses in around 1963.[14]

The agreement to use the army camp on Hayes Common took time to achieve but by January 1948 the Council acquired the site and in April work started on the first of the temporary housing. A schedule was drawn up showing the number of doors, sinks, WCs, stoves and cooking ranges that were required. Most of the huts were converted into two separate units and the majority were of brick construction. The first eleven units were completed and occupied by families in June. A total of 34 homes were provided although concern was expressed by inhabitants of Hayes about the effect on the common.[15]

The Council also made a compulsory purchase order for the remainder of the Hayes Place Estate, which had not been built upon and had been used as allotments during the war. It was planned to build 337 houses, 12 old people's dwellings and six shops with maisonettes. In Bourne Way tenders were also invited for the construction of 66 flats in what became Kemsing and Larkfield Closes. They were finally finished in 1950.[16] The families moved in but not all the facilities had been planned. There were no outside washing lines and consequently the tenants hung the washing out on their balconies. This was very visible to commuters and there were several objections. Eventually screens were installed on the balconies.

*Kemsing Close* [i.]

In post-war plans affecting the Greater London Area, Hayes lay astride the boundary between the 'Suburban belt' and the 'Green Belt'. The Green Belt regulations ensured the preservation of Hayes Common and the farmland east of Hayes Lane but there were still many opportunities for developers. Government restrictions and controls on new buildings, however, were very strict and priority was given to the repair and rebuilding of damaged or destroyed houses. These had the first call on the resources of wood, brick, tile, glass etc. The work needed skilled labour, which in 1945 was in great demand. In many cases individual owners could not afford repairs until their claims for war damage were approved and then they had to have a building certificate that gave the necessary permission. Many applicants experienced frustrating bureaucratic delay. Arthur Gilbey, for example, received £167 6s. 7d. for war damage but was not allowed to build a greenhouse at his nursery until April 1948. Permission was then given on the conditions that the total cost did not exceed £80, he did the work himself and did not attempt to use builders who had more important priorities.[17]

This was a normal response for those who wished to improve their properties but there were also difficulties for those people whose houses needed repair. The Poor's Land Trust properties, Brackendene, The White House and Simpson's Cottages, had all experienced damage. The repairs were carried out by William Smith & Son but it was not until 1950 that the Trustees received £269 13s. 3d. for the cost for repairs to Simpson's Cottages and the final settlement for The White House was in July 1951.[18] Although hundreds of houses and other buildings were damaged the Poor's Land Trust example is probably typical of the time taken to process war damage claims.

Agreement to pay for the damage to the roof and windows of the Parish Church was also slow but in 1950 the secretary reported to the PCC, 'that a licence had now been obtained for £1,171 and ... J & R Killick were proceeding with the work.'[19] During the repair it was found that many roof tile pegs had decayed and tiles needed to be re-laid. The War Damage Commission agreed to pay £650 for the additional work and the repair was finally completed in October 1951. Although the Old Church Schools had received very little damage from enemy action it was in an unusable state as a result of its conversion to a first aid post. In May 1945, Church groups 'needed the accommodation badly' for their activities and asked the Trustees to press Bromley Borough Council to act. Six weeks later the Council's representative inspected the building but little progress was made.

In February 1946 a repair licence was granted for one of the buildings, the Verger's house, but the work could not start until the end of 1947. It was not until October 1948 that a repair licence was finally granted for the old school buildings. The War Damage Commission's approval to start took some time but by February 1950 the Church Magazine noted that 'work was progressing on the Old Church Schools'. The first post-war function to be held there was the Annual Parochial Church Meeting on 28 March 1950. The smaller Clubroom was finished later.[20]

Of the houses built in the mid-thirties more than 45 were destroyed or damaged beyond repair. Most were rebuilt to the original design with only changes in detail but two, 22 and 24 Southbourne, were different since they were the work of Bromley architect R B Pearce. Only one, 28 Dartmouth Road, was rebuilt by the original builder, Henry Boot Garden Estates.[21] Amended plans for two houses adjacent to 42 Kechill Gardens were given a licence on 19 March 1946 and the rebuilding of 216 and 218 Hayes Lane by Howell and Brooks was approved on 17 September 1946.[22] New homes were restricted in size and in 1945 permission was only given on houses with a maximum selling price of £1,200 and subject to dimensions specified by the Ministry. Architects used clever designs to create the impression that the new houses were larger than they were in reality. That was the case for the houses built in Redgate Drive in the late 1940s, which all had wide frontages but were shallow in depth. Builders continued infilling on the Boot estate, such as 44-48 Kechill Garden in about 1947, and some bungalows were built on the Hayes Hill Estate about 1947/8. The first houses were built in Heath Rise.

Other important buildings that had suffered were not repaired until much later. The rebuilding of Hayes Station and its shops was not complete until 1957. The New Inn, extensively rebuilt with a different frontage, was not fully reopened until February 1962 although it continued to function.

Grandfield's Nursery was not rebuilt. The Roman Catholic authorities purchased the site and received planning approval to construct a prefabricated church there so that they could move from the Village Hall where they had continued to hold their Sunday services throughout the war. Father Stewart replaced Father Waller in 1947.[23] In 1951, the Hayes congregation was served from St Mark's, West Wickham and priests from the Holy Ghost Fathers, Bickley and St Mary's College, Sidcup helped out.

In November 1945 Pickhurst Lane Free Church applied to erect three huts to serve as their church. The Borough Council consented but placed a five-year time limit on the scheme. In 1948 a licence was issued for a prefabricated church until a permanent one could be built. The London Congregational Union provided the money from the proceeds of the war damage claim from Anerley Church, which it decided would not be rebuilt. The final cost was £4,025 and it was sited near the boundary to Hilldown Road, with the entrance facing Pickhurst Lane. It was opened and dedicated on 2 June 1949 and 'seemed like a cathedral' after the much smaller Pickhurst Lodge. It was used for Sunday services and other church activities, such as Brownies, during the week.[24]

*Inside Hayes Free Church prefab* [an.]

## Effects of Government Policy

The population of Hayes continued to grow rapidly and by 1950 numbered about 9,500. Various opinions were expressed about the dramatic changes resulting from the nationalisation of civil aviation, coal mining, cables and wireless, public transport, gas, electricity and iron and steel, introduced by the new Labour Government under Prime Minister Attlee. During the extremely cold winter of 1946-7 the demand for coal and electricity was so great that all fuels were severely rationed. For several weeks it was illegal to use electricity in the home between 9am and midday and between 2pm and 4pm. Factories had to close through lack of fuel and over two million people were out of work.

The introduction of the welfare state and the start of the National Health Service meant that there was no longer a need for the Hayes Nursing Association, so it was disbanded in 1948.[25] In the previous year three nurses had been supported by the Association, whose membership was about 1800. It had an income of almost £1,336. Under the new health system everyone was entitled, free of charge, to medical care from doctors, specialists and dentists. The Council paid for district nurses. The scheme was financed mainly from taxation but also from National Insurance contributions.

Rationing continued after the war. In 1946 bread was rationed to two loaves a week for adults and potato rationing was introduced in December 1947. In March 1948 the manager of Stevenson and Rush in Hayes was reported for selling sugar without cancelling the coupons and for charging more than the fixed price.[26] As the situation improved some commodities were de-rationed but in 1950 meat, bacon, butter, tea and sugar were still rationed.

Clothes rationing continued until 1949 and often caused concern. In September 1947 the Common Rangers needed leather hedging gloves to carry out their work. The appropriate forms were filled in to obtain a permit from the Kent War Agricultural Executive Committee to buy them. The request was refused because the men were not working on land cultivated primarily for essential food production. The Rangers were informed that they could only have new gloves if they provided the coupons from their own ration books. The Conservators were incensed and wrote to the local MP Sir Waldron Smithers:

> It is still difficult to believe that this country is in such a bad way that Rangers on a Public Common who are constantly dealing with cutting back growing material like gorse and heather, can only obtain protection which is absolutely essential and in the form of strong gloves, by appropriating their personal clothing coupons.

Sir Waldron Smithers raised the question in the House of Commons and the Minister of Agriculture replied that Bromley Council had the power to provide the gloves. The Rangers finally received their gloves at the end of the year.[27]

There were considerable difficulties in getting licences to open shops. At a time when most housewives shopped daily and locally for food, it was felt that the existing shops did not meet all the needs. An additional greengrocer's was required, although in October 1946 Messrs Foat, the butcher in Baston Road, and Gilbey at his nursery were granted licences to trade in such goods. In 1947 a bakery was needed. The London Divisional Food Office rejected the application for a licence but, after further pressure from HVA, one was granted in 1948. There were several applicants but they were not allowed as the regulations stated that preference should be given to an ex-serviceman. A licence was given to a serviceman for a fish shop, although the premises needed considerable alteration before he could start trading.[28]

J & R Killick opened a builders' and undertaker's establishment, at 47 Station Approach, to replace its one bombed in the war. The office survived until 2012. There were many attempts to begin small business enterprises. One of the first in April 1945 was the proposed conversion of Hawthorndene into a neurological clinic for members of the Polish armed forces. Consent was given but the clinic did not materialise.[29] An unsuccessful application was made to use the Old Church Schools for the 'fabrication of small Bakelite parts and for the purpose of furniture upholstering' until the Church Authorities were able to repair and reuse the premises. In October 1946, 1 Hillside Lane obtained approval to open as a café and tea garden. Permission was given for one of the old Hayes Place farm buildings in West Common Road, now part of Stevensons Heating, to become a workshop for the manufacture of spectacle frames and the South Eastern Optical Company was still there in 1950.[30]

*W. Foat, the butcher's shop in Baston Road, through the archway was the abattoir* [m.]

*Coal Heavers in Hayes Station Yard after the war* [m.]

A major change took place at Hayes Court that had ceased to be a school on the outbreak of war. The property was bought in November 1946 for about £19,000 by the Electrical Trades Union (ETU) to become its new headquarters. Considerable alterations had to be made before the staff moved from Ollerenshaw Hall, Whaley Bridge, Derbyshire to Hayes Court in August 1948. Permission was granted for its conversion to offices but no work was allowed for living accommodation. The Union therefore purchased Ladycroft at Keston for £6,800 and two further houses at a cost of £2,500 and £1,950 to house key staff. The building was officially opened in May 1949, the year of the Union's diamond jubilee.[31] War damages of £768 8s. 7d. were received for repairs.

*Hayes Court bought by the ETU in 1946* [m.]

In 1950 there was acrimonious correspondence with the Common Conservators who objected to the brick wall at the front of the property and the fact that in enlarging the pedestrian entrance to the mansion a considerable ditch had been dug into the common. Only the threat of legal action in October 1950 resolved the situation. Arthur Collins wrote to the Union's General Secretary suggesting that it might be good for them to meet as the Conservators were used to agreeing matters amicably and 'were not used to dealing with neighbours in a confrontational way'.[32] There is no record of whether such a meeting took place but relations seem to have been more harmonious in the future.

## Education

The increase in the number of young families living in Hayes meant that more school places were needed to cater for the demand. The 1944 Education Act raised the school leaving age to 15 and established a national system of primary schools for pupils from 5 to 11. Pupils took an examination at the age of 11 and were transferred into secondary education - grammar, technical or modern school, according to their ability. No public secondary schools were built in Hayes until the 1950s. Hayes pupils continued to be allocated to schools in neighbouring Bromley or Beckenham. The one council primary school in George Lane became increasingly crowded, despite the removal of the top forms to Gadsden at the beginning of 1945. In September 1945 there were 12 classes in Hayes County Primary School and 452 pupils. Three years later this had increased to 524 pupils in 15 classes and by January 1950 the number had risen to 561. Mrs Eva Butler remained head. Miss N Barnes and Miss D Kiely were in charge of the older age group up to 11 at Gadsden, except for the period of the fuel shortage in February 1947 when they all returned to have lessons in the main school hall.[33] Although KCC purchased the site of Longcroft to build a new primary school for infants and juniors in 1947, it was not a high priority and nothing was done until 1953, despite pressure being placed on the local Council by HVA and parents living in the Pickhurst area.[34]

The gardens at Gadsden were a magnificent stage for plays, such as a Chinese one presented by Class 1 (the oldest pupils) in July 1945 under the direction of Miss Groves. At Christmas there was a special Nativity Service in Gadsden, written to make use of the many doors opening into the central hall and the winding staircase in the turret.

The choir was very successful. Another special feature was the use of agility apparatus installed in the grounds in 1949.[35] Many visitors admired the equipment fixed between the trees and photographs of the pupils using it were featured in a Ministry of Education book on physical training called 'Moving and Growing'. Extra school holidays were still given for special occasions, such as the marriage of Princess Elizabeth and Prince Philip in 1947 or a half-day's holiday for a visit by the Princess to Bromley on 13 October 1949.[33]

*Christmas Nativity at Gadsden* [ao.]

*4th Year PE at Gadsden, 1949 [ao.]*

# Private Education

**Chatley House** continued for a few years to provide a preparatory education but ceased to exist in the 1950s.

**Baston School** re-established itself after its return to Hayes from Somerset. Many girls, who started at the school when it was in Devon and Somerset, wished to finish their education at Baston. In September 1945, therefore, it reopened in Hayes as both a day and boarding school. The 23 boarders lived in part of the main house, which was still leased and the Stafford Smiths purchased 85 Baston Road, the former home of dog lover Mrs Annesley, for their own use. In 1947 Major-General Charles Wake Norman and the newly formed Rookery Estates Company agreed to sell the sisters Baston House, the farm cottages and a further piece of land. In 1949 they bought Five Elms Cottage, which was used for staff accommodation and later became the boarding house.

The girls soon settled back into the school routine and each summer performed a play. In June 1949 the proceeds from their performance of 'The Bells of Bruges' went to the bombed churches of Bromley. [36]

*Five Elms* [s.]

**Brewood Preparatory School** was set up by the formidable Mrs Wood at her home, 9 Sackville Avenue, to drill nine-year old boys to pass the $11^+$ examination or entrance examinations to Public Schools. The one and only classroom was in the back room where 22 boys sat around a very long dark brown table. Miss C Skinner assisted. It was a hard regime and Bryan Nicholls, later deputy Permanent Secretary to the Danish Ministry of Social Affairs, remembered the experience in 2001.

For one day's homework he was supposed to:

- learn the names and titles of all the Government ministers off by heart,
- find the answers to: What is 5 times 31 pounds, 14 shillings, 5 pence and 1 farthing divided by 9? What is 13 times 6 miles, 2 furlongs, 3 chains, 7 yards, 1 foot and 2 inches?
- prepare a map of Britain marking all coal fields, rivers, mountains and cities.

The boys were told to use a pencil and not waste paper, which they did by erasing the previous day's work.[37]

**Barnhill School** continued to provide a private education for boys. It remained associated with Hayes, although from June 1947 advertisements referred to it as in West Wickham. By this time there had been a change of ownership as Eliza Waldron died in October 1946. Her husband, Sir William James Waldron, sold Barnhill to Mrs Lucy Joyce Codrington, wife of Ernest Codrington of Boxmoor, Herts for £7,000.[38] The school was popular and at the end of the summer terms invited residents to see the boys' work, such as a well displayed hobbies' exhibition in 1949.

## Social Activities

There was much discussion about the needs of the returning servicemen and women who 'had experienced to the full the advantages of mixing with others in all stations in life'. HCC set up a committee to consider whether Hayes should have a Community Centre.[39] The proposal was that the Centre should be set up separately, perhaps on the Boot's estate west of Hayes Lane or possibly at Hayes Court. Ideally, it would consist of a large and small hall with a total capacity of 100 to 150 and a number of small rooms for reading, games, handicrafts, day nursery, canteen facilities, cloakrooms, provision for billiards, table tennis, badminton and a gymnasium with cinema and wireless. Larger functions, such as dances, would still be in the Village Hall. A place was also needed for the elderly and retired.

In February 1946 Bromley Council offered HCC premises, formerly used as a gas cleansing station in the Old Rectory Gardens, for youth activities and especially for the Swift Club started in October 1945 for young people over 15. Alterations were needed and when Bromley Council discovered it would cost £900 to convert the building, the proposal was abandoned. No separate Community Centre materialised. To some extent the Village Hall fulfilled that role although 'the demand for Saturday night reservations was so great that disappointment to some organisations was inevitable'. It was used on a regular basis by no less than 29 societies and provided the opportunity for activities by both young and old. The HCC was happy to let each society organise its own programmes but supported exhibitions, handicrafts and lectures and encouraged classes for keeping fit.[40]

Some Hayes societies had continued for most of the war period including the W.I., Toc H, Royal British Legion and Hayes Social Club, although the latter's activities mainly consisted of Whist Drives. Hayes Horticultural Shows were well supported and the summer shows at Gadsden received many entries, over 400 in July 1947. The Allotments and Gardens Association, whose president was Percy Jones, had 119 members in January 1948. Hayes Players' first post war production in April 1946 was 'Fresh Fields'. The plays were normally performed in the Village Hall but in 1949 they acted 'The Ghost Train' at the Convent Hall, Plaistow Lane, Bromley, in aid of the Hayes Catholic Church Building Fund.[41]

One club that did not survive into the 1950s was the Hayes Rabbit and Poultry Club that, in spite of a record 500 entries for its show at Gadsden, appealed for members in July 1948. Other clubs, started after the war, lasted much longer and some survive to this day. The Hayes Churches Musical Society was formed in February 1945 and was open to all residents in Hayes. By September it had a membership of over 200 and in December performed Handel's Messiah under its conductor William Ballard. It also set up a string orchestra. In May 1947 the orchestra decided to form its own organisation, the Hayes Orchestral Society, which performed for the first time in December under its conductor Mr Steptoe.[42] The proceeds of £11 7s. 0d. from a concert in 1949 were given to the Hayes Free Church Building Fund. At the end of 1950 the Hayes Churches Musical Society changed its name to the Hayes Philharmonic Society that still exists today.[43]

An Over Sixty Club was founded and Major General Norman became President. By December 1947 it had sixty members.[44] The club's weekly meetings covered a variety of activities from games and music to talks and outings to Eastbourne, Folkestone or Southsea.

For teenagers there was the Swift Club with its lively programme of talks, plays and activities such as cycling that included, in 1949, trips to Brighton and Canterbury. There was rivalry with the Church Youth Fellowship, which became the 'Challengers' in January 1947, and which also had a well organised programme with many sporting events. Curate Peter Tadman, who came to Hayes in autumn 1948, was important in developing the Challengers. He was 27 years old, had been educated at Dulwich College and undertaken a number of jobs such as dock labourer, van driver and bank clerk before deciding to train for the ministry after his naval service during the war. In 1950 he left to become a chaplain with the South American Missionary Society.

Brownies, Cubs, Guides and Scouts were also popular although there were often difficulties in finding adult helpers. In March 1947 someone was urgently needed for the Brownies as there were over 30 names on the waiting list.[45] In February 1948 there were 40 Scouts, 50 Cubs and only two officers.

Another enjoyable pastime for many youngsters was the Odeon Cinema Club on a Saturday morning. It had over 500 members and in addition to watching films there were painting competitions and road safety quizzes. From June 1947 visits were made to the Beckenham Swimming Baths every Saturday morning before the film. There was even a Dog Show organised for the children in July 1947.[46]

*Odeon Cinema (formerly the Rex)* [m.]

The ceremony of the crowning of the London May Queen continued, although the 1946 ceremony was a scaled down version of the pre-war crowning. Margaret Williams was the first post war Hayes May Queen and her sister Dorothy succeeded her next year.[47]

Newcomers to Hayes had plenty of opportunity to join the sports clubs whose memberships increased with the return of peace. There were successful darts' teams at the New Inn, athletics at the Blackheath Harriers, football, table tennis, rugby, tennis and cricket. One of the most significant developments took place at the Cricket Club in Barnet Wood Road, which became incorporated in 1945 and acquired the freehold with ten acres of land. There were soon suggestions that perhaps a swimming pool could be built but the plans never materialised.[48]

*Hayes May Queen 1947* [a]

The long awaited opening of the public library in the Old Rectory took place in April 1946 and the Church Room at St Mary Cottages became available for other purposes. There was an immediate increase in the number of books taken out from 1,421 issues in March to 2,277 in May, including 410 children's books. By November there were 3,112 issues and approximately 1,000 tickets in use. Library use continued to grow and had reached 6,286 issues by January 1949.[49] For those keen on reading a Bookworm Circle started after the war, although it is not clear how long this club lasted.

What is clear is that, in spite of the many restrictions, the people of Hayes enjoyed a wide range of activities. There was a real sense of community and one that would continue in the succeeding years. The Community Council could justly conclude that whilst the spirit of comradeship survived 'Hayes would continue to be a place in which great things would be done'.

**Map 19: *Hayes in 1950***

# Chapter 8

## A changing community: 1951 to modern times

The Festival of Britain in 1951 and the accession of Queen Elizabeth II in 1952 seemed to herald a new era after the restrictions of the immediate post war years. The residents of Hayes enjoyed the festivities, which were celebrated by a pageant in the grounds of Hayes Court called 'We made History'. The play recalled memorable events that had affected Hayes, such as Cade's Rebellion, the Civil War and the time of William Pitt at Hayes Place. Queen Elizabeth II's coronation in June 1953 was another opportunity for the whole of Hayes to participate in special services, street parties, a procession through the village and entertainment on Hayes Common.[1]

The next sixty years saw remarkable changes nationally. Prosperity was increasing by the late 1950s. Harold Macmillan, MP from 1945 to 1964 for the Bromley constituency, which included Hayes, became Prime Minister in 1957 and made his memorable remark, 'You have never had it so good'. The younger generation had more money to spend and the 1960s saw the birth of a 'Pop Culture'. The death of Winston Churchill in 1965 was marked by the planting of an oak tree on the common at the top of Station Hill, near the one planted for King George V's Jubilee in 1935.[2]

In 1971, decimalisation and changes to the monetary system were introduced which many people were reluctant to accept. The following decade witnessed rapid inflation, which made life difficult for people on a fixed income but encouraged people to expect high earnings. By this time America and the USSR dominated the world and in 1973 Britain joined the European Community. The economic problems of the 1980s was followed by a recovery. In 2008, however, came a banking crisis and the last few years have seen a return to economic difficulties and great hardship for individuals.

Women became more prominent in public life. In 1979 Mrs Margaret Thatcher, whose twins, Mark and Carol, were at Baston Preparatory Department for a short time, became the first female British Prime Minister. Women started to be accepted as 'Chairmen' of various organisations in Hayes, such as Irene Ponting on the Chamber of Commerce in 1955-6 and Edith Cogswell of the HVA in 1961. More recently Beryl Grimani Harrold has played a leading role in HVA and is currently its president.

There were no more World Wars but Britain was involved in many localised conflicts, either directly or as a part of a United Nations Peacekeeping Force. Once again families in Hayes worried about relatives and friends who fought in the Malaya War from 1948, Korean War 1950-53, Suez Campaign 1956, Falklands War 1982, Northern Ireland conflicts or wars in Iraq and Afghanistan. Often, as in the First and Second World Wars, schoolchildren and other groups sent help to the soldiers. At Baston School pupils provided parcels for soldiers in the Gulf War in 1991 and wrote over 100 letters to the soldiers. Later, Captain Robert Machell spoke at an Assembly to thank the girls for their efforts and speak about what life had been like in the desert during the war.[3]

The Annual Armistice Service to remember the fallen continued to be held, led by the local branch of the Royal British Legion. By October 1989 some of the wording on the War Memorial was fading, it was refurbished and all the inscriptions were re-cut for clarity. In 2005, on the 60th anniversary of the Second World War, an additional plaque was added to commemorate those who had died in the later conflicts.[4]

Also Remembered
With Grateful Appreciation
Those who, since the Second World War
Have Given their Lives in Conflicts
And Peace-Keeping Missions
Throughout the World

There were remarkable changes in the last half of the twentieth century, particularly in technology and communications. The use of computers quickened the pace of business and government. Television brought world news into the home faster than could have been imagined fifty years before. Many people bought their first television set, with its small screen and magnifier, to watch the Queen's Coronation in 1953. Video recorders, the start of satellite television in the 1980s and the development of the internet in the 1990s, revolutionised home entertainment and communications. In 1994 cable television arrived in parts of Hayes. Very few homes were without at least one television by the end of the century. In the 21st century mobile phone technology has allowed people to use both mobile services and the internet without having to be at their offices or home. We now live in a connected world and consume information on computers, media players, mobile phones, tablets and internet enabled television, to name but a few. This thirst for information is dramatically shaping our world today. It is both difficult and exciting to imagine what advances will be made in the next fifty years.

The ownership of goods seen as luxuries in the 1950s, such as refrigerators and washing machines, increased significantly from the 1960s. In 1971 3% of households in Hayes shared or lacked a bath and 2.8% did not have their own inside lavatory. By 2001 there were only three households without sole use of a bath/shower and toilet.[5]

In 1969 man walked on the moon. It became much easier to travel around the world and the age of package holidays gave many residents the chance to visit places that their grandparents had never seen. A travel agency, J C Crane Ltd, appeared at 23 Station Approach in the early 1970s, replacing the grocers, Cave Austen & Co. The agency is no longer in Hayes but there is another at 49 Station Approach. More people came from overseas to settle in England. By the end of the century several shops in Hayes were run by people, whose families were originally from India, Pakistan or Turkey. The majority of the population, however, was born in the UK. Many residents moved from the inner cities and there was a great increase in both the ownership of houses and cars. By 1991 over 85% of homes in Hayes were owner occupied and over half the households had one or more cars.[6]

Nevertheless, there was still a great reliance on public transport. By the mid 1950s the Hayes railway line had become one of the busiest in southeast London. In 1954 the station platforms were lengthened from about 160 metres to about 210 metres to allow for the longer trains needed in rush hour. By the 1970s, however, many of the original 1930s' settlers had retired but remained in the district and fewer commuters used the station. This changed in the 1980s and the line became busier again as younger families moved into the area and more commuters used the train services. In about 2000 the platform was lengthened to 265 metres in anticipation of even longer trains. The Hayes line continues to be busy. People have been encouraged either to move to Hayes or drive in from more rural areas by the opening of the railway car park, the introduction of the London Congestion Charge, the link to the Lewisham and the Docklands Light railway and the connection to Tramlink. A recent survey found that about a quarter of the regular commuters came from outside of the area.

The 119, 138 and 146 bus routes remained and the latter became one of the first London bus routes in 1986 to be franchised to a private company as part of the Government's new policies for London's transport. Other bus routes, including Green Line express buses, came and went; route 705 to Windsor via London, and to Sevenoaks, appeared in October 1958 and ceased in April 1979. An express bus to Gatwick Airport passed through briefly about 1980, but the bus services to Hayes were in the middle of a decline, which was not reversed until 1990. Routes were added and passenger traffic grew, and Hayes became one of the best provided-for suburbs in the outer London network, with five bus routes to Bromley, three routes directly or by connection to Croydon, two to Addington and one each to Westerham, Orpington and Downe.[7]

October 1987 witnessed 'the great storm' and when dawn came on 16th October people were greeted with a scene of devastation.

***Damage caused by the hurricane in Redgate Drive, October 1987***

The sight of trees across roads and gardens, of trees leaning against houses and of trees down in such numbers on the Common as though someone had been playing ninepins, was unbelievable and heart-breaking.[8]

The community spirit was shown as everyone worked together over the next few days to clear up debris but some familiar sights disappeared. The cedar of Lebanon in the Library Gardens came down and one of the cedars in Redgate Drive also had to be felled. Over the next few months many groups, schools and individuals were involved in planting replacement trees to maintain the area's rural ambience.

By the end of the twentieth century people lived longer and leisure opportunities developed as people retired earlier and labour saving devices provided more free time. Educational opportunities expanded and a greater number of young people were able to take advantage of higher education. Employment possibilities increased and more people in the parish, almost 50% in 2001, were involved in managerial, professional and technical positions.[5] Many Hayes residents worked in London. Dorothy Dewey was one of the commuters and towards the end of her career worked for Beville Sassoon in Sloane Street, London. In 1981, when Lady Diana Spencer married Prince Charles, she was responsible for Lady Diana's going away outfit. To complete the sewing on time she often took parts back to her home in Glebe House Drive and worked on them in her front room over the weekend. On Monday she would 'smuggle' them back in, as journalists were keen to get any clues about the outfits. She also later sewed much of Princess Diana's maternity wear.[9]

The pace of change also affected the political scene. Harold Macmillan's successor as Bromley's MP in 1964 was John Hunt, who lived in Keston and was a Bromley councillor from 1953 and Mayor 1963-4. Another national politician was Peter Lilley, who was born in Hayes and went to Hayes County Primary School. He entered Parliament as MP for St Albans in 1983 and became an influential figure in the Conservative Party, joining Mrs Thatcher's Cabinet in 1990 as Secretary of State for Trade and Industry and from 1992-97 was Secretary of State for Social Security.

In 1969 the vote was extended to include all eighteen year olds and there were constituency changes in 1970 to adjust for the increasing numbers on the electoral roll. Bromley was divided into four constituencies – Ravensbourne, Beckenham, Orpington and Chislehurst. Hayes and Keston Ward was allocated to the Ravensbourne constituency and John Hunt, a very familiar figure in Hayes, remained MP for Ravensbourne until his retirement in 1997, when constituencies were again altered. Hayes became part of the newly created constituency of Bromley and Chislehurst, whose MP was Eric Forth. His death in May 2006 resulted in a by-election at which Bob Neill was elected. Further changes in 2010 placed Hayes in the Beckenham Constituency and Colonel Bob Stewart became the new MP.

Hayes was also affected by the reorganisation of the government of London and the establishment of the Greater London Council (GLC) by the London Government Act 1963. The Borough of Bromley ceased to exist and became a London Borough in 1965. The demise of the GLC in 1986, in which Dennis Barkway, a ward councillor for Hayes and leader of Bromley Council, played a part, allowed London Boroughs greater autonomy for a few years. In 2000 the Greater London Authority (GLA) was set up with an elected London Mayor and Bob Neill became the first representative on the GLA for Bexley and Bromley. The changes affected the inhabitants of Hayes in several ways, but mainly indirectly, as the elected Mayor and GLA gained more authority over what happened within the Borough and some decision-making was removed from the remit of local councillors.

Hayes continues to have three elected representatives on the London Borough of Bromley Council, although the Ward area has changed several times over the past fifty years. Many of the areas that were once part of the parish are now represented by other councillors and new areas have been added. Hayes and Keston Ward became Hayes Ward in 1974 and included land up to Bromley South Station and the railway bridge on Homesdale Road. In 2002 it became Hayes and Coney Hall Ward, losing the Bromley Town end and absorbing much of the land up to the Croydon boundary. It has the largest electorate of all the wards within the Borough.[10]

The 1950s and 60s saw the deaths of many local councillors, such as Arthur Collins and Colonel Fulcher, who had overseen and played a valuable part in the transition of Hayes from the village of the 1920s to the larger community after the Second World War. Both men's roles were recognised when they were granted the Freedom of the Borough in 1949 and 1953 respectively.[11] Others who ceased to be borough councillors, such as Percy Jones who was defeated in the 1947 election, continued to play a vital part in the life of Hayes. In 1956 he was presented with a clock 'for his invaluable work during the whole period of the existence of the Village Hall' and in 1967 celebrated his 40th anniversary as secretary of the Village Hall Management Committee. He died in December 1971, shortly after leaving Hayes to live with his daughter, and a tree was planted in Knoll Park in his memory.[12]

*Tree planted in memory of Percy Jones*
*by his son Alan Jones, 1972* [ae.]

**The Tree in 2010**

A key figure in the management of the Village Hall since that time has been Laurie Mack who became treasurer in 1970, premises manager about twenty years ago and in 2003 secretary of HCC.

Councillor John Haden, who was first elected in April 1965, became Mayor of Bromley 1968-9 and an honorary alderman. Dennis Barkway, a ward councillor from 1968, was leader of the Council for nineteen years and was granted the Freedom of the Borough in 1997. Councillor Philip Jones represented Hayes from 1971 to 1998 and was Mayor 1991-2. Since 1998 the Hayes Ward councillors have been Graham Arthur, Anne Manning and Neil Reddin. In 2004-5 Councillor Anne Manning was selected as Mayor of Bromley, joining the several inhabitants of Hayes who have become mayor since the setting up of the first Bromley Borough in 1903.[13]

Hayes Ward councillors have always tried to safeguard the integrity of the community, ensuring that the special features of the locality, preserved over many generations, are considered in decisions made by those who may not have specialist knowledge of the area. This has not always been easy. To complicate matters and to residents' consternation, following the introduction of postcodes Hayes was no longer recognised by the Post Office as a place in its own right. It was classed as part of Bromley in spite of its existence as a separate entity for over eight hundred years. Hayes, however, still retains its ecclesiastical parish, which at the southern end follows the ancient boundary but its northern limit is Mead Way.

## Housing

One issue, which greatly concerned councillors and residents, was the need to ensure that all new housing developments reflected the special character of Hayes that had been maintained, in spite of the changes that had taken place before the Second World War. The 1930s had witnessed the start of the transformation of Hayes from its small village existence. By 1950 it was unclear what would happen to the rest of the open countryside and green spaces, although most residents hoped that the village atmosphere would be retained. There were still large areas of pasture and arable land in the north and east of the parish, owned by the Norman family and farmed by the tenants of Hayesford Farm and Hayes Street Farm. The northern part of Hayes Place Estate had not yet been built upon but was scheduled for development by Bromley Council.

There was a great need for council housing and the Chilham Way estate was planned on the Hayes Place land in the late 1940s. Its construction was held up by a shortage of bricks and cement but it was built between 1950 and 1955[14] (Map 20). A number of sheltered old people's flats were built close to a small pedestrian shopping centre set up to provide essential services that included a butcher, baker, fishmonger, grocer, greengrocer and newsagent and Post Office. These flats, however, may soon be demolished to make way for a new housing development.

The 1950s' planners did not foresee the growth in car ownership and failed to provide adequate car parking facilities for their tenants. The eight shops at Chilham Way were also affected and it is one of the factors in the difficulties faced by small shopping centres in the last thirty years. In 2011 only the newsagent's shop survived alongside a tanning salon, Indian restaurant, café and Vocational Training Centre.

*Millennium Sign, showing William Pitt the Elder and Younger, Hayes Place,*
*St Mary the Virgin, Hayes Parish Church and the Kentish Horse, 2000*

*Millennium Sign and the Old Church Schools* [ba.]

*Whites Cottages, Pickhurst Green, Grade II listed building*

*Cottages that once housed Baston Farm workers but are today part of Baston House School* [bf.]

*Coopers Cottages, Croydon Road* [bf.]

*From the left, 8a Baston Road, formerly the Post Office from 1894 to 1940,*
*8 & 6 Baston Road, previously Glebe View and Elleray* [ba.]

*The Old Rectory was sold to Bromley Borough Council in 1937.*
*During the war it was used as a Damage and Casualty Centre and became Hayes*
*Library in 1946. It is a Grade II listed building [ba.]*

*Gadsden, originally built in 1875 for Henry John Norman, now part of Hayes School*

*Hayes Grove Cottage in 1987, a Grade II listed building*

*The Walnut Tree in 1987 prior to its conversion to a private house.*
*When the roof tiles were replaced, following bomb damage in World War II, a V sign*
*for Victory was created.*

*Premier Parade, Hayes Street, looking south with the Walnut Tree in the distance* [ba.]

*Hayes Street looking north, the George Inn and the Model Cottages are on the right* [ba.]

*View from Ridgeway to Station Approach.*
*The wall of the New Inn is on the right* <sup>ba.</sup>

*Station Approach, 2011* <sup>ba.</sup>

*View from Ash Lodge, Baston Road, looking south east beyond*
*Baston House School Pavilion*

*Aerial photo showing part of Hayes to the west of Hayes Primary School, 1994* [ar.]

Opposite and near the shops an open space was originally scheduled and considered for a possible community centre. However, it became The Beacon, a Public House in Farleigh Avenue. According to R W Mundy, the Council had committed itself to provide a site for the rebuilding of the Laurels, a public house in north Bromley taken over for flats and houses. By the 1950s the only sizeable piece of vacant council land was this part of the Hayes Place Estate.[15] The Beacon survived for over fifty years but has now been pulled down and replaced with housing.

*Chilham Way Shopping Precinct [i.]*

*The Beacon Public House [ap.]*

**Map 20: *Hayes in 1958***

## Mead Way

In 1956 it was proposed that the tenants of the Mead Way prefabs would be moved to Crown Lane, Bromley and the site sold for private building, but this did not occur.[48] In the 1960s plans were made to replace the prefabs in Mead Way with high quality houses. The original plan was for 72 detached and spaciously laid out houses but the government required that, owing to the housing shortage, 109 units should be built.

The plans were redrawn and town houses decided upon. One block of three-storey town houses was almost finished when a resident on the Hayesford Park Estate realised he was completely 'overshadowed' by it. With the support of a large number of residents he protested to Bromley Council who, after a great deal of public discussion, was obliged to demolish the block in Mead Way and rebuild it.

Today, many council houses are privately owned and the remainder are managed by Affinity Sutton (formerly Broomleigh Housing Association) to whom Bromley Council transferred its properties in 1992.

## Would the existing large houses survive?

Many feared that the remaining historic buildings with large gardens, such as Baston Manor, the Oast House and Hayes Grove would be sold and replaced by private housing estates. Covenants on the original land sales, made by the owner of Baston Manor in the nineteenth century, restricted further development of the land and helped to ensure that some older properties were not demolished.

### Baston Manor

Until 1952 Baston Manor remained the home of Mr and Mrs Arthur Collins, who had played a considerable part in the life of pre-war Hayes. Mrs Collins was very active in local women's groups and Arthur Collins' expertise in finance and local government continued to benefit many organisation and individuals.[16] One of his greatest contributions was as Chairman of Hayes Common Conservators where he played a significant role in ensuring the integrity of the common. He died in September 1952.

Many wondered what would happen to the house that for so long had been a significant feature in the history of Hayes. It was divided into six flats.[17] The architect was H G Payne and the builders were Messrs Barnard (Bromley) Ltd. Annie and Herbert Pettigrew moved into the first flat, No. 4, in 1953 and all six flats and Manor Cottage were occupied by 1955. The coachhouse and stable block were converted into residential premises and permission was given for the erection of eight garages.

### Hast Hill

Approval was also given for a change of use for the neighbouring property, Hast Hill, in spite of an original covenant that 'no buildings could be erected on the land nor could it be used for a hospital, convalescent home, school, public house or shop or for any purpose of a like nature other than as a private dwelling-house'. In the 1950s Howard King sold Hast Hill and permission was given for its use as offices, providing that the residential character of the house and grounds were maintained. Pattullo, Higgs & Co. Ltd, a company selling seed potatoes, feeding-stuffs and fertilisers to farmers, bought the property in January 1957. The business expanded and soon traded with most parts of the world. In 1969 Charles Wimble Sons & Co Ltd, an old established company of rice brokers, joined the group and also diversified into other basic raw materials, particularly pulses.[18] Hast Hill became the head office but by the mid 1990s it was decided to sell the property. Honeygrove Developments converted the house into six luxury apartments and refurbished the lodge and two cottages in the grounds. Therefore, by the end of the century, the house had returned to residential use - although no longer for one family.

### Oast House

Changes took place at the Oast House, after the departure in the early 1950s of Eric Hessenberg, who worked at the Midland Bank Chambers in Bromley. The Webb family purchased the property and later divided the house into two. The Oast House formed the south wing and the Pantiles the north. The architectural distinctiveness was retained and it is a Grade II listed building.[19] In 1968 the outbuildings were converted into a self-contained cottage, known as Webb's Cottage.

*Pantiles and Webb's Cottage, Croydon Road* [q.]

### Street House

Street House and its grounds were substantially altered in the post war period. Most significant was the sale of the land adjoining Hayes Wood Avenue so that the roadway could link up with George Lane. This event had been desired by residents for many years but was not practical until the garden, which had been made into allotments during the war, was returned to its owner, Major General Charles Wake Norman, in 1956. There were many plans for the use of the grounds, including an attempt by Esso to erect a garage on the land facing Hayes Street. Permission was given for two houses in neo-Georgian style, 41-43 Hayes Street and for two more in the gardens of Street House that faced George Lane.[20]

Major General Charles Wake Norman left Street House in 1949 but it remained a private dwelling until the 1970s. A successful application was made by the Rookery Estates, the group set up to manage the property of the Norman family, to turn the house into four two-bedroom flats and one one-bedroom flat. Today there are three flats. Part of the ground floor has been used as consulting rooms for over thirty years and it has been a dental surgery since 1990. It is a listed building.

***Street House showing the east end used as a dental surgery*** [ap.]

## Ivy Cottage

Ivy Cottage, Warren Road, remained a private dwelling but in its grounds approval was eventually given for the building of six distinctive properties. Mr Dennis Writer applied on several occasions between 1949 and 1953 but needed a separate access that went over common land. The Common Conservators (George Fulcher, Harold Goodway, Frederick Isard, Percy Jones and Charles Knight) finally agreed to allow two access points over the common to the proposed service road, in return for a portion of land for use as part of the common. A further agreement was drawn up when Bromley Corporation took over the powers of the Conservators in 1954. The six plots were sold separately and four architect designed bungalows and two houses were built.[21]

The properties have names not numbers and both detached houses have had only two occupiers. 'Foresters' was built to a very modern design for Mr and Mrs Hickman and later occupied by Gordon and Beryl Collis in 1966. It was featured in *House Beautiful* in March 1956 as an example of a well-constructed house that could be built for £4,000. Architects Norman Rix and his wife Margaret designed 'Southerly', the other detached house, and Margaret Rix remained there, after her husband's death, until 2005. The neighbouring bungalow, 'Pax', was built and lived in by a builder, whose wife Lily Jones was the registered owner of the plot for which she paid £850. Five years later the bungalow was sold to Edward Downer and passed to his only daughter Margaret and her husband Bernard Stenning in 1970. In the gardens of these properties a few large trees, including an oak and a lime, are reminders of the splendour of the original garden of Ivy Cottage.[22]

*Foresters, Warren Road 1968* [i]

## Hayes Court

Hayes Court remained the headquarters of the ETU, which amalgamated with other unions. In 1968 the ETU and the Plumbing Trades Union joined forces to form the Electrical, Electronic, Telecommunication and Plumbing Union (EETPU). In 1992 the AEEU was formed from the merger of the EEPTU and the Amalgamated Engineering Union (AEU) and then merged with Manufacturing, Science and Finance (MSF) to form AMICUS. On 1 May 2007 AMICUS joined forces with the Transport and General Workers Union (TGWU) and became UNITE with a membership of two million people. Over the following years activity at Hayes Court declined and there are now plans for its sale.

Since the ETU's occupancy in August 1948, Hayes Court has been the scene of momentous discussions and decisions that have affected the actions of many companies and lives of individual members throughout Britain. In the 1950s the Union had over 239,000 members and was controlled by a Communist President Frank Foulkes and General Secretary Frank Haxell. In 1959 an Anti-communist Leslie Cannon stood against the Communist General Secretary and narrowly lost. He took the matter to the High Court and the case revealed widespread ballot-rigging and intimidation. In 1961 the Trades Union Congress expelled the ETU. The Communist domination collapsed and in

1963 Leslie Cannon became the Union's President, a position he held until his death in 1970. He reformed the Union with the help of Frank Chapple, the new General Secretary, but there were still many militants in the organisation. In 1967 the General Secretary was attacked by some members who were dissatisfied with the executive's policies and in August 1968 thirty-five masked members, masked because they feared intimidation and reprisals by their executive, staged a three hours' demonstration outside Hayes Court against the 'indiscriminate expulsion' of about fifteen ETU members in the previous nine months.[23]

*Protest by ETU members outside Hayes Court 1968* [ae.]

Frank Chapple retired as General Secretary in 1984 and was made Lord Chapple of Hoxton. Eric Hammond succeeded him. In 1987 many electricians marched on Hayes Court to stage a sit-in against being sacked by Rupert Murdoch, the owner of 'News International', which printed the *Sun* and *News of the World* newspapers. Rupert Murdoch had decided to move his company from Fleet Street to new premises at Wapping and to insist that any workers transferring with him signed a 'no strike agreement'. The sacked electricians felt that they had not received appropriate support from their union.[24]

As the union's activities expanded, alterations were needed at Hayes Court. It was extended in 1961. Ten years later a fire in the canteen below the caretaker's flat, which took four fire engines an hour to extinguish, meant that the kitchen was destroyed and rebuilding was necessary. In 1984 approval was given for a three-storey extension and two years later for a first floor extension. In 2002 plans were passed for a single storey detached building.[25] Much of the original Georgian building remains in spite of the considerable additions and it is a Grade II listed building. In the grounds are part of the old brick wall of the kitchen garden and the former ice well.

*Hayes Court 1987, showing the additions to the original listed building, whose chimneys can be seen in the distance*

### Hayes Grove

Nearby is Hayes Grove, also a Grade II listed building and no longer a private house. At the end of the 1940s Lady Monroe, widow of Sir James Monroe, occupied it. Her son Hubert, who served in the Far East during the war, lived in the Mews Flat. He was 28 when called to the Bar in 1948. The following year he was selected as prospective Liberal candidate for the new Beckenham Constituency, established as a result of the 1948 Redistribution of Seats Act. He was unsuccessful in becoming an MP but became a noted specialist in tax law.[26]

He moved to Beckenham and in 1951 Hayes Grove was purchased by King Edward VII's Hospital Fund and became a home for retired hospital nurses.[27] It opened in 1953 with Miss Dorothy Stobbs as sister-in-charge. Miss Margaret Stevenson succeeded her in 1966 and the following year a group of Friends started to raise funds for the home. Lady Wilbraham, who had spent her youth at the Grove, became patron and continued to support its activities until her death in 1974.[28]

On 20 September 1979 news was received that Hayes Grove would close in March 1980 since the building was no longer considered suitable for the elderly and needed extensive repairs. Alternative accommodation was found for the residents. The announcement was a considerable shock and the Friends continued to support the former residents in their new nursing homes. The last elderly retired nurse died in 1987. The balance of the money, £1035.93, was transferred to the Hayes Mini-Ambulance Fund.[29]

The need for a Mini-Ambulance to transport elderly people to and from church and village activities had first been realised in the 1960s when a special committee was set up by HCC to raise funds and liaise with Bromley Social Services. The first ambulance was purchased in 1972 at a cost of £2,116. After a few years it was necessary to start raising money for a replacement and the one delivered in 1981 at a cost of £10,213 had done 26,000 miles by 1986. The contribution of money from the Friends of Hayes Grove was therefore very welcome. In recent years the village community spirit has again been shown with a big effort by many local organisations and individuals to raise £40,000 for a new ambulance. In 2008 the new Community Bus was finally achieved, now available for use by all clubs and organisations, not just for the frail and elderly.[30]

*Mr John Moren and Councillor Anne Manning unveiling the new Community Bus at the Hayes Fair, June 2008*

*Hayes Grove Staff, March 1980*

What happened to Hayes Grove? It was boarded up and for a while remained empty while its future was considered and plans put before Bromley Council.

*Hayes Grove closed up and awaiting a purchaser, 1980* [a.]

In January 1981 Sloane Independent Hospitals of Albermarle Road, Beckenham applied for permission to convert it, pull down outbuildings and construct a two-storey block and operating theatre. Approval was given in August 1981 for it to be changed into a hospital but in July 1982 the Grove was sold to Community Psychiatric Centres (CPC), a private American company for £300,000 and Hayes Grove Priory Hospital opened in 1983.[31] It cost CPC about £1.5 million to convert the eighteenth century mansion and to build the inpatient unit of 55 beds. The first patients were admitted on 21st November. There have been several changes of management since that time but the private hospital remains as a centre for the treatment of acute psychiatric illness. In 1990 permission was sought for an extension that was granted on appeal and in 1995 two further small applications were made, of which one was approved.[25]

**Gadsden and Baston House** remained school buildings but their interiors and grounds saw considerable changes as the schools expanded and new classrooms were built (see Chapter 9). Baston School acquired further property, including 133 Baston Road, whose land had been bought originally from the descendants of the Bath family in 1950 by Vernon Courtenay Groves. He was a builder who lived in Shirley, Surrey, and he was granted a licence to build a house in December 1951, providing that he lived in it and that its selling price was not more than £2,848. In February 1952 further permission was granted for the development of land at 'Groveland Smallholding' but in 1955 Mr Groves became bankrupt and the property was sold to Miss Margaret Stafford Smith. Mr Groves became an employee of Miss Stafford Smith and continued to live in the house that was used for the school caretaker or maintenance staff.

In 1962 Elmhurst, 87 Baston Road, was bought and converted into science laboratories until 2000 when it was leased to the Temple Academy of Performing Arts. The garages alongside the house, formerly stables, were converted into cottage accommodation for a groundsman and his family in 1990. Mr and Mrs Noel Wimble lived at 85 Baston Road from 1956 and in 1981 permission was granted for the building of a house in the grounds for their younger son Charles, who became Baston School's headmaster in 1983.[32]

### Brackendene, The White House and Simpson's Cottages

Alterations were also made to the Poor's Land Trust properties on the common, although they remained residential. The Trust experienced numerous problems as the houses became older and needed a great deal of money to maintain them.

The last tenants of The White House were Mr and Mrs James Harris, who ran the greengrocer's shop facing the Parish Church. They lived there from 1977 until 1989, by which time the rent had increased to £1,250 per annum. It was bought by Richard Taylor, who restored some of the original features of the house.[33]

*The White House, Five Elms Road* [m.]

Eric Davies moved to Brackendene after he married Peggy Frost of Glebe House in 1922 and the couple remained there for over fifty years until Eric died in 1974. They were animal lovers and in the late 1940s and early 1950s were in conflict with the Common Conservators because they allowed their goats to wander on the common, an event which Mr Davies claimed only happened for a few weeks 'after kids were born'. The Conservators rejected his claim that he had a right to graze them.

In 1964 Eric Davies sought Council approval for an animal boarding establishment for dogs. When a visit was made in 1965 there were over 30 poodles on the premises but Mr Davies maintained that they were not breeding but were simply grooming and looking after poodles. He frequently complained about the state of his property and the damp but the Trust was very reluctant to take action as it was advised that there was 'very little purpose in carrying out the work as long as the property was being occupied by the present tenants' and it should try to 'take action to stop the boarding of dogs'.

In 1974 Mr Angeolini of Hayes Hardware and Electrical, 50 Hayes Street, became the tenant and agreed to make repairs to the property. His offer to buy the property in the 1980s was rejected. Following a serious burglary in 1988 and with major repair work needed, the Trust decided to apply to the Charity Commission for permission to sell. It was hoped that a sum of £250,000 would be realised and in 1989 the Trust sold the property by tender. It was purchased by Charles Boyd, who lived there for ten years.[34]

One reason for the sale of Brackendene and The White House was to release funds for the repairs that were needed on Simpson's Cottages, which continued to provide accommodation for widows or families who were in need of help and support. Ultimately these too were put up for sale, bought and eventually, after considerable local opposition, replaced by one property in 1995.

*The four Simpson's Cottages, Five Elms Road, before they were demolished*

The new house retained the traditional Kentish style. The existing tenants left their homes with great reluctance and were housed in maisonettes in Holland Close. The residue of the Poor's Land Trust Fund was amalgamated with the Hayes (Kent) Educational Foundation in 1992 and became The Hayes (Kent) Trust. It continues to provide financial support for the needy, sick and aged in Hayes and the funds are also used for the promotion of education and 'advancement in life'.[35] A variety of people have benefited from the Trust whose funds have been used in a number of ways. Help was given to some Hayes guides to go with other guides from the Bromley North Division to Kandersteg, Switzerland, in 2007 for an international jamboree to celebrate 100 years of scouting.

*The new Simpson's Cottage, 2008*

## More large houses demolished

Some houses did not survive the pressure for development.

**Glebe House** was recommended by Bromley Education Committee in the 1950s for use as a Youth Club and Scout Centre. The proposal was not accepted. The house was pulled down and an old people's home, Isard House, named after Alderman F W Isard, a councillor for 40 years and twice Mayor of Bromley, was built on the site in 1963.[37]

Isard House had accommodation for 61 residents in 25 single, 10 double and 4 four-bedded rooms. In 1970 it housed 45 women and 16 men. Over the next thirty years, as views on the care of the elderly altered, changes were made so that rooms became single. By 2008 there were 63 individual rooms. Three years later the home was closed and the property is to be sold.

*Isard House 1974* [ap.]

**Forge House**, the home and surgery of Doctor Hopton in Pickhurst Lane, saw changes in the 1960s. Five architect designed houses were completed in its grounds by the developers Aklan Ltd in 1964 and Forge Close was formed.[38] In 1983 plans were approved for four detached houses with garages and in 1985, after much discussion, consent was received to demolish the house and construct a surgery and sheltered accommodation called Hopton Court.[39]

*Forge House, 1985* [a.]

*Forge House from back, awaiting demolition* [a.]

**Barnhill School** was sold to Noel Westbury Jones of the Cathedral School, Llandaff for £8,000 in August 1957 and he became the new headmaster. After his death in April 1961 the school closed and his wife Kathleen sold the house and lands to the builders, A J Wait & Co., in 1964. The main house was pulled down and private housing was built, although Barnhill Cottage was retained. The bungalow has been extended but survives today as 268 Pickhurst Lane.[40]

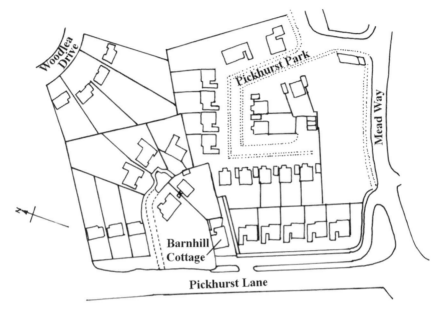

**Map 21:** *Plan of Pickhurst Park showing Barnhill Cottage*

*Barnhill Cottage*

**Fairgirth** in Baston Road was pulled down and in its place was built an attractive group of five detached houses.

**Prickley Wood**, with its 40ft long ballroom, woodland, carp pond, croquet lawn and tennis court was occupied by the Jones family until 1952.[36] It was sold, pulled down and replaced with a close of twelve houses in 1955. The coach house remained in use until the 1970s when it was demolished and two maisonettes were built facing Holland Way.

## Hawthorndene

After the war it was thought that Major Binyon might decide to sell Hawthorndene and there were numerous proposals for the house, including its use as a community centre or a school. Basil Binyon, however, stayed until 1962. In the basement he had a well-equipped workshop with a lathe and in retirement he continued his many interests. He had made a number of ingenious devices for time-lapse photography, which he used to produce accelerated motion cine films of clouds and of flowers opening. He built working model steam locomotives with which he entertained his grandchildren. In 1960 his first wife died and, after his marriage to Violet Hibbert in April 1962, he moved to Farnborough Park and sold the land for development; a fire in December 1962 destroyed the house. Hawthorndene estate was built, comprising Hawthorndene Road and Hawthorndene Close. There were eight different styles of houses and they were marketed by Sutcliffe, Son & Partners of Chipstead at prices ranging from £6,350 to £10,800.[41]

*Hawthorndene Close under construction* [i.]

*Hawthorndene Road* [i.]

## Hayesford Park

The largest private housing development in the post war period, took place on farmland to the north of Mead Way owned by the Norman family and farmed by G Hoeltschi. The land stretched from Pickhurst Lane down to Hayes Lane and was recommended for residential development in 1952. It was a continuation of the Hayesford Park estate that had been built in the 1920s and 1930s around Cameron Road and Beadon Road.

Hayesford was not scheduled for immediate development but as soon as it seemed possible that a licence to build might be granted, unsuccessful applications were made for outline permission from R B Pearce in 1952, Rookery Estates in 1953 and Messrs W E S Rumph in 1955. In 1957 a further application was made and the Borough Engineer recommended conditional permission limiting the density and restricting the site to detached and semi-detached houses. KCC refused permission but an appeal was allowed on 5 December 1958.

Donald Howard bought the farmland from C. Norman for £420,000 in 1959. On 4 May 1959 Howards of Mitcham submitted an outline application for the 71 acres.[42] Interestingly, in the light of subsequent events, the application included 336 two-storey detached houses at a height of 20ft and eight four-storey flats at a height of 45ft. It was said that Donald Howard was greatly influenced by the ideas of his grandfather Sir Ebenezer Howard, author of *First Garden Cities* and creator of Letchworth and Welwyn Garden City.[43] He was keen to provide quality housing and employed architects Messrs Grenfell, Baines and Hargreaves to plan the development. Approval was given for 403 dwellings, 12 shops, 1 café, 1 public house, 1 crèche, garages and stores to the shops.

The estate grew from the Bromley end as an 'open' layout with six detached houses to the acre until 1964 when the development south of Cheriton Avenue became intensified with maisonettes, terraced town houses and finally seven-storey flats. From 1960 there was considerable controversy. The first two stages and shopping area were built according to plan but in the third stage the builder decided to increase the density in line with government emphasis on making adequate use of land to try to meet housing demand.

Included in the revised plans were proposals for two eight-storey blocks of flats and one eleven-storey block of flats. Residents, who had bought their houses on the basis of the original brochure, showing a green area in front of their properties, were exceedingly perturbed by the rumours that started to circulate. There were petitions, letters to Harold Macmillan, to the Minister of Housing and considerable interest was shown by the local newspapers and the *Daily Mail*.[44]

Grenfell, Baines and Hargreaves had been incorporated into Building Design Partnership and said the complaints were unjustified. The house designs had won awards in national competitions and the scheme would provide an overall unity. Discussion continued over several years; the plans were amended, rejected and finally went to appeal on 26 February 1964. The appeal was dismissed but it was agreed that a residential development at a density not exceeding 88 habitable rooms could be allowed on the area scheduled for flats. In November 1965 the *Bromley & Kentish Times* reported on the latest plan for a seven-storey block of flats and three five-storey blocks. The building of the flats received favourable comment in an article in the *Sunday Times* in January 1968 that described the landscaped garden and lake created for the sole use of the flat dwellers.[45]

*Barnhill Avenue, Hayesford Park, 1968* [i.]

The estate was built for residents with one or more cars but was designed to keep other traffic out. Its closes were set off main spine roads and deliberately styled to discourage motorists from taking short cuts and to prevent the link up of Bourne Vale and Beadon Road that would have provided a fast traffic route from Hayes to Bromley.[15] Between 1961 and 1968 700 houses and 210 flats were built. The houses followed the new trend for smaller gardens and prices ranged from £5,500 to £13,000.

Included in the development was the Letchworth Drive shopping precinct with a car park and small filling station. In 1962, before the centre was opened, units had been taken by Cooper & Co Stores Ltd, R Gunner Ltd, R V Goodhew Ltd and Allied Retail Trades (London) Ltd. Only six units remained and enquiries were invited from well-established chemists, bakers, fishmongers, hardware stores, fruiterers and greengrocers.[46] By 1964 there were three vacant units, one was used as an office and a supermarket covered nos. 26-30.

*Hayesford Park Shops, Letchworth Drive* [i.]

Since then there have been many changes as the supermarket and shops suffered from competition from the nearby town centre shops in Bromley. By 2011 the supermarket had long gone. More of the units were used as offices and there were a Chinese and an Indian restaurant. The shops consisted of a newsagent's and general store, party shop and a hair and beauty products supplier. There were also a dry cleaners, launderette, care agency and gym.

Donald Howard was said to have been pleased with Hayesford Park Estate, a view supported in the 1980s by Nikolaus Pevsner and Bridget Cherry, who described the Garden City tradition of Hayesford Park with its 'small, cosily designed detached houses'.[64] An attempt to get Hayesford Park protected in the 1990s failed but some residents would still like that to happen.

The difficulties Donald Howard encountered in the estate's construction contributed to his company's liquidation in 1972. The development also had an impact on Hayesford Farm. The loss of much of the farmland meant that it was no longer a viable separate entity – a factor that opponents of the scheme had pointed out when the original building plans were approved. The leaseholder, G Hoeltschi senior, moved to Hayes Street Farm where his son still lives, although it is no longer a dairy farm. Instead of cows there are fruit and vegetables, horse livery & riding, a trout lake and regular boot fairs that started in 1990 – a result of the need in the late twentieth century for farmers to diversify if they were to survive.

## George Lane

The Rookery Estates, which owns Hayes Street Farm, built four estate houses, 34-40 George Lane, for its farm workers in the 1950s. They were sold in 1990. Two years later there was a successful application for a detached house in the ground behind the properties in Hayes Wood Avenue.

George Lane is perhaps one of the most altered roads in Hayes. Georgian Close was built in the early 1960s. A new house was constructed at 29 George Lane and the old cottages at 13-15 George Lane were pulled down and replaced by detached houses in the 1970s. When Miss Vanderplank died, the adjacent cottages, 9-11 George Lane, which had been in her family since 1928, were left to Hayes Church, sold in 1997 and made into one property.

Five of the 1920s utility bungalows were pulled down and replaced by sixteen terraced houses, five built by Jones and Rogers of Wallington in 1966 and the others about 1971. Permission for the demolition of the last utility bungalow and the building of a pair of semi-detached houses and a detached house was given in 2011.

After several years of discussion, permission was given on appeal in 2003 for two detached houses on the site of 'Fort George', the former headquarters of the Army Cadets.[47] More recently, the bungalow at 87 George Lane has been demolished and replaced with two semi-detached houses.

## Kechill Gardens

Most housing developments took place in the gardens or land belonging to the original large houses. In 1977 there was considerable disquiet when the Victory Social Club decided to sell off part of its ground in Kechill Gardens.[49] It had originally been reserved on the Hayes Place plan for 'an estate club and recreational use' and many residents felt that it should remain as an open space. The majority of the members, however, agreed to accept an offer of around £40,000 for some of the land's development and Ferndale built eight houses on the site.

## West Common Road

There were also changes in West Common Road. In the late 1970s, Neo-Georgian houses, Nos.7-11, replaced the buildings destroyed by the V2 attack. Permission was given for a house and two bungalows in the garden of 108 West Common Road and in 1988 approval was finally given, on appeal, for its replacement by three new houses.

*Demolition of 108 West Common Road*

Such infilling has been seen at other places in Hayes and continues on a relatively small scale. For example, in 1979 a house in Pickhurst Mead was demolished to provide access to a new housing development, Sedgewood Close.[50] When Mr E A Cooke died, his house at 55 Pickhurst Lane was modernised and in 2004 planning permission was granted for a detached house in its grounds.

## Bourne Way Flats

Three private developments of flats were allowed in Bourne Way. Thirty maisonettes were built at Meycroft in 1969/70. Woodgrange, 54 Bourne Way, was pulled down and a block of twelve flats, named Woodgrange Court, was built in its place.

On the other side of the road there was considerable opposition to proposals to develop a block of flats. However, in 1978 the development company won its battle for new homes at 51-55 Bourne Way and the nine Oakdene flats were constructed in the 1980s.

*Woodgrange Court, Bourne Way* [i.]

## Opposition to development

During the last sixty years there have been many occasions when planning applications have been considered to be against the interest of the community. Residents, with the support of the HVA and sometimes the Chamber of Commerce, have mobilised to try to prevent what they regarded as inappropriate development.

In the 1960s some of the building yards and other depots in Hayes closed. Various schemes were proposed to make the best use of the available land. The Express Dairy depot in Station Approach originally had stables with a flat for the groom. The depot was adapted for electric milk floats about 1950 and the horses were retired. When it closed in 1965 the building was swept away to make room for Bromley Council's car park. Global House was built on the former Ray's Yard for Global Homes Southern Ltd in 1988. It became the finance and human resources centre for the Bromley Health Authority and later Bromley Hospitals Trust.[51]

The goods yard of Hayes Station shut in 1965. It was used by a number of companies including a builders' merchant until 1988/89 when the site was cleared for the construction of the Barratt's development, Saville Row and Farnborough Crescent. Known as The Mews, it consists of 50 one and two bedroom houses arranged in two crescents. A commuter car park was also built accessed by Old Station Yard. This was the culmination of a very long campaign in which there had been many proposals for the yard, including plans for a supermarket, offices and car parking that was turned down in 1979 but granted on appeal. The option was not taken up.

*Hayes Station in the 1950s before the station yard (on the right) was closed*

*Disused station yard, 1968 [i.]*

*The former station yard in the 1970s [ap.]*

In 1971, there was great agitation when Bromley and Sheppard's College, a home for clergy widows situated in London Road, Bromley, wanted a new site. Application was made at seven different places in Hayes for 30 two-storey homes, a chapel, chaplain's house, nurse and porters' accommodation and car parking space. The proposed sites were on Norman land which General Norman, President of Bromley College, had offered at its agricultural value. The trustees favoured five acres of land behind Burwood Avenue. The application was turned down and there was general relief when the appeal was quashed, since the land was in Metropolitan Green Belt. Then, as now, it was felt vital to maintain one of the distinctive features of Hayes – its farmland and green spaces.[52]

Croudace in 1972 and Global Homes in the 1980s made several unsuccessful attempts to build houses on the allotments at Wickham Sports Club in Pickhurst Rise and to the rear of Crest Road.[53]

Another area of land of concern to the residents of Hayes had stood unoccupied for many years at the junction of Tiepigs Lane and Bourne Way. This site, originally a gravel pit, had been used for the dumping of waste and the Council decided in 1984 that it would be an ideal place for a council lorry depot. A vigorous campaign against the proposal was launched, spearheaded by the HVA.[54] Finally, the site was approved for private housing and Bovis started to develop it. Heydon Court, Deer Park Way, was designed as single retirement apartments by Blenbury Retirement Homes. The prices in 1987 ranged from £42,000 for a first floor studio apartment to £47,000 for one with a balcony.[55]

In 1984 plans for three detached houses on the former Killick's site off Hillside Lane were rejected as 'backland development'.[56] From 1987 various applications were made, including a proposal to build 24 sheltered units. Eventually, in 1993 and 1994 Wentworth Close was built, consisting of four detached houses priced from £199,950 and developed by Howard Homes.

*Knoll Park* [m.]

By the end of the century the majority of land available in Hayes for development had been utilised but fortunately sufficient green land remained as common, farmland or public parks to provide a link with its early history. Knoll Park and Husseywell Park are reminders of the earlier gardens of Hayes Place; Pickhurst Park was formerly part of the grounds of Longcroft. In 1949, the Council accepted the gift of several open spaces on the Hayes Place Estate and these survive.[57] The Library Gardens were once the grounds of the Old Rectory. The Friends of Hayes Parks was formed in 2003 to ensure that the parks remain for the enjoyment of future generations.

*Pickhurst Park, 1953* [m.]

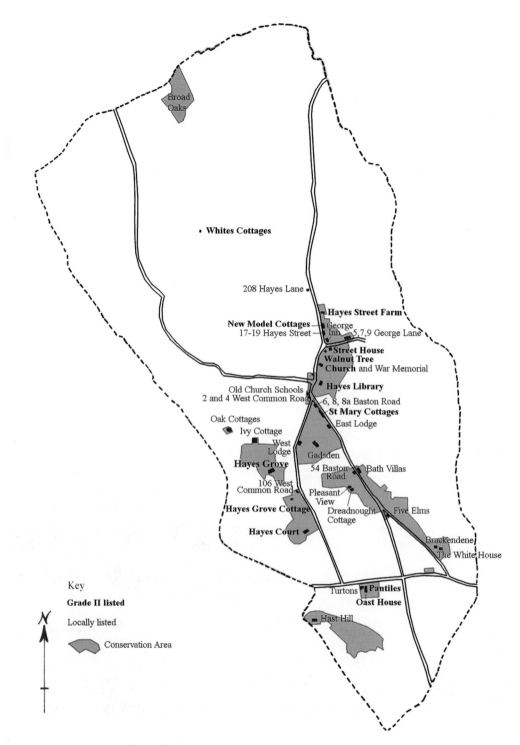

Broad
Oaks

• **Whites Cottages**

208 Hayes Lane •

•**Hayes Street Farm**
**New Model Cottages**— •George
17-19 Hayes Street — Inn •5,7,9 George Lane
•**Street House**
**Walnut Tree**
**Church** and War Memorial
Old Church Schools •**Hayes Library**
2 and 4 West Common Road •6, 8, 8a Baston Road
**St Mary Cottages**
Oak Cottages •East Lodge
• Ivy Cottage
West
Lodge •Gadsden
**Hayes Grove** 54 Baston• •Bath Villas
106 West Road
Common Road Pleasant
View
**Hayes Grove Cottage** •Dreadnought• •Five Elms
Cottage
**Hayes Court** Brackendene•
The White House

Turtons •**Pantiles**
**Oast House**

Key

**Grade II listed**

Locally listed

Conservation Area

Hast Hill

**Map 22: *Conservation Areas and Listed Buildings 2011***

As well as some of the grounds of the former mansions, many of the older cottages and houses also survive and can be found alongside the post 1920s' developments that now form the majority of the households. Over a quarter of the houses that existed at the time of the 1841 tithe map and 128 of the 197 properties recorded at the end of Queen Victoria's reign remain today. Most are nationally or locally listed or are in Conservation Areas, of which there are several. One covers Hayes Village, a second affects the houses within Bromley Common, Hayes and Keston Commons and another is in the north of the old parish - Broad Oaks Way (Map 22). The increase in the number of houses from around 300 in 1929 to about 4,000 in 2001 resulted in many more people settling in Hayes. The population was about 9,000 in 1950 and fifty years later had increased to around 12,000. Exact comparative statistics are difficult to determine since the present ward boundary of Hayes is very different from the former parish boundary.

The population now appears to be relatively stable, although there will continue to be changes as many of the inhabitants who came to Hayes in the immediate post war period require smaller accommodation and new families arrive, often influenced by the quality of the local schools. One constant feature is the way in which most residents wish to remain and are unwilling to leave or move elsewhere, unless work or other factors require them to seek housing in other areas. Hayes is still regarded as an attractive place to live in spite of the many changes from its rural origins.

## Shops

The rise in population was accompanied by an increase in the number of shops. It was usual in the 1950s, when ownership of refrigerators and freezers was uncommon, for housewives to shop daily for their food provisions. The original Premier Parade shopping area at Hayes Street, known by locals as 'Old Hayes', continued for many years to provide grocers, greengrocers, a butcher's, post office and hairdresser's.

*Premier Parade, Hayes Street, about 1952* [bb.]

*Hayes Street June 1969, showing the additional shops
built in Premier Parade in the 1950s [m.]*

Mr F Tidbury, whose shop in West Common Road was bombed, moved into Premier Parade after his request to rebuild on the site of his original shop was rejected in 1949. New shops were built about 1955/56 to complete the Parade and sold tools, garden supplies, toys and clothes. Ron Holland moved to Oaklands, a garden shop, at 48 Hayes Street in 1956/7. It became R.B. Holland Ltd in 1974 and was sold in 1985. Today it is a Dry Cleaners.

*View from Ridgeway about 1956. Some of the re-built shops near the station can be
seen in Bourne Way in the distance [m.]*

In 1952 the Council refused permission for three-storey shops on the bombed area of Hayes Station but four years later the wartime damage to the station concourse and shops was repaired. Most shops in Station Approach were occupied and the area began to be known as 'New Hayes'. There was a great variety of stores which, by 1953, included MacFisheries, F W Woolworth, Home & Colonial, Boots the Chemist, David Greig, W H Smith, South Suburban Co-operative Society, Stevenson & Rush and Hall & Company. The latter supplied coal and coke for heating and cooking. The South Eastern Electricity Board also had a showroom.[58] There were four cafés, one in Bourne Way, two in Station Approach and one in Baston Road.

*Station Approach, 1950s* [m.]

The northern end of Station Approach witnessed great change with the closure of the Odeon (Rex) Cinema on 27 October 1956. High entertainment tax was given as the reason for its closure but the Chamber of Commerce thought it was inferior films. By 1956 the cinema was earning £22,000 but had a deficit of £4,500. For a few months after its closure it was used by Rank-Cintel in the development of projection television.[59]

There were many suggestions for the future use of the building. A swimming pool conversion was proposed but the purchase price was £35,000 and the Council decided against it. The cinema was eventually demolished and was replaced with two small shop outlets and a Fine Fare supermarket that opened in 1962.

The growth of larger supermarkets in places such as Locksbottom and West Wickham and the greater ownership of cars affected the viability of local shops. As a result several of the well-known High Street multiple stores left, including the department store F W Woolworth which ceased trading in Hayes in the late 1970s. Fine Fare, the one remaining supermarket, altered its form of retailing to accommodate the changing demand for goods in the locality and transferred about 1977 to its subsidiary, Shopper's Paradise, an early experiment in 'no frills' shopping.

*Northern end of Station Approach*

Boots the Chemist closed in 1981 although returned to Station Approach in 2008, following the merger two years earlier of Alliance Unichem with Boots. Another chemist, Rumseys, celebrated its fiftieth year in 1982. Its mahogany shop-fittings and bow fronted windows are remembered by many residents. Mr Rumsey died in the 1950s but his partner Horace Crowhurst, a founder member of the Chamber of Commerce and its chairman in 1951, continued and retained the original 1930s fittings. He retired in the summer of 1981 and handed over to a younger pharmacist. By this time another chemist, Ivor Shipley, whose original premises were at 16 Station Approach, had moved across the road to No. 15, the former site of the Home & Colonial Store. The Hayes Co-operative Society closed in 1984, following the merger between the South Suburban Co-operative Society and the CWS.[60] In 1987 there were reports that Shoppers Paradise was to be sold to the highest bidder. Today the site is occupied by Iceland.

The Hayes Chamber of Commerce, formed in 1936, became very concerned from the 1970s over the future for small shops. In 1981 Station Approach was described as essentially a local convenience centre selling mainly foodstuffs and other day-to-day purchases. Nearly half the shops sold non-food goods and food goods were concentrated in grocery stores. Vacant premises frequently occurred in the shopping frontage and there was a tendency for these to be filled in time by non-retail use e.g. offices, building societies, restaurants etc. In the winter of 1984 the editor of the Hayes Review made a plea for residents to support their local shops:

> Supermarkets have killed off the grocers, freezers in supermarkets have killed off the fishmongers and large chain stores have proved a difficult competition for the dress, electrical and hardware shops.

The effects of new technology, new marketing and design techniques conspired to change the character and purpose of the old-style shopping centre. Superstores continued to take custom away from Hayes.

The greater use of the motor car, free public transport for the over 60s and the development of internet shopping, have resulted in local shops often being unable to compete on price. Nevertheless, these shops still provide a valuable service for many residents, particularly the elderly, although it has not been possible to halt some of the changes, such as the closures of the Post Offices in Chilham Way and Hayes Street.[61]

There has been a revival of some specialist shops, a considerable increase in Charity Shops that did not exist in the 1950s, and in 'ethnic' restaurants and takeaways, a trend found in many areas of the country. The site of the former Woolworth store became a Socold Freezer Centre. In 1980 there was controversy over plans to make it a nightclub. A petition against it had 1,300 signatures and was a factor in the decision not to proceed. It later became a 'Handy Store'. In 1997 it was a health shop and fitness gym run by TV Gladiator 'Wolf' but this closed in 1999.[62] A few months later in 2000 a Sainsbury's 'local' store opened.

By the end of the 20th century, the number of food shops in Hayes had declined by almost two thirds from those in existence in 1950, although the non food shops with their specialist services remained at about the same number. Some of the former food provision shops are now used as offices by estate agents and there is still a betting shop.

Only one of the original businesses in Station Approach, Barclays Bank, survives in 2012. It was only in 2007 that the family business, Bromley & Co, wallpaper and decorating suppliers, closed in Hayes Street after more than fifty years.

*Bromley & Co, Hayes Street [m.]*

Another regretted closure in Hayes Street in 2003 was the Walnut Tree, known as Nicholls at the end of the nineteenth century. For most of the twentieth century it was a newsagent's/confectioner's shop. Peter and Ethel Sheath, who managed the shop from 1937, bought it from the Rookery Estates in 1953. Fifty years later, the Grade II listed building was granted permission for conversion to a house. The barns were made into accommodation.

*The Walnut Tree after its conversion to a house* [ba.]

The Chamber of Commerce represented the interest of traders in 'Old' and 'New' Hayes, Hayesford Park and Chilham Way and the committee worked hard to safeguard the interests of its members. Matters that concerned the Chamber included rates, rents, parking, hypermarkets, the appearance of Station Approach, pedestrian crossings, the retention of units as retail stores, Christmas lights and Christmas window decorations.[63] In 1982 there was some dissatisfaction with the role of the National Chamber of Commerce and the local group was unable to finance the affiliation fee. A few years later the Chamber ceased to exist as a formal body but a small group of Hayes traders continued to work together when critical matters arose. Without the active support of the traders, in cooperation with HVA, many of the events that have taken place in the past sixty years, including special fairs and the Christmas Lights could not have taken place. A key figure in the organisation of these events in the past thirty years has been Alan Williams, chairman of the Hayes Fair and the Lights Committees.

## The Inns

The only new inn to appear in the post war period was the Beacon Inn that, as we saw earlier, was set up to cater for the population of the council houses that were built in the 1950s. In recent years it closed, reopened and then closed again. The Inn has now been pulled down for the building of semi-detached houses. Its history reflects the general difficulty that has faced public house owners in Hayes and nationally as they respond to changes in people's eating and drinking preferences, the effect of drink/drive legislation and more recently the smoking ban. The George Inn and New Inn have survived and also The Pickhurst, which although technically in the Parish of West Wickham is still regarded by many as part of Hayes.

The George Inn remained in the hands of the same family until 1971. Stanley Poole was the landlord from 1939 until his death in 1959 and his widow remained in charge until 1962. Her son-in-law Toley Cooper and daughter Pat took over the licence, which they held until 1971. During the next forty years there were many changes in ownership and different attempts to attract customers. Watney Mann Ltd submitted plans to turn the George Inn into a Schooner Inn and approval to convert it to a restaurant was given in October 1972. Watney Mann merged with Grand Metropolitan Estates. The George was converted into a Berni Inn but by the late 1990s British tastes had changed through foreign travel and the chain started losing money heavily. In 1991 there was another major refurbishment when it became part of Whitbread and four years later it was a steak-oriented Beefeater Restaurant. Mitchells and Butlers became the owner in 2006 and converted it to an Ember Inn. Four years later the restaurant was again redesigned as a 'country inn'.

*146A Bus outside the George Inn*[m.]

Mitchells and Butler also, until recently, owned the New Inn, which after the Second World War was run by the brewers Courage and extensively refurbished in 1962. Since 1984, when it was developed as a Harvester Steak House, there have been a number of owners including Imperial Inns Taverns Ltd in 1986, Pier House Inns and Bass Taverns in 1996. It has now moved into private ownership. In 2010 it was greatly altered and the gardens are once again in use.

*The George Inn, 2011*

*The New Inn and Station Approach, 2011* [ba.]

These alterations reflect the changes in Hayes that have taken place in the last sixty years. Most of the land that became available through the sale of the large Hayes mansions from the 1920s has been built upon, and the increase in residential accommodation has been significant. Shops and inns have adapted to meet demand and in recent years there have been many changes, created in part by the greater use of the motorcar. In spite of all the developments, the basic structure of the old village, centred on the Parish Church and the George Inn, survives.

# Chapter 9

# A vibrant community: 1951 to modern times

The additional population created by the new housing in Hayes, particularly in the 1950s and 1960s, meant that the traditional infrastructure was stretched. There was increasing demand for better educational and leisure facilities and these demands reflected the changes that were taking place in the wider society.

## Education

### Nursery Schools

There was considerable pressure on local schools. As more mothers went to work there was a greater need for nursery and childminding facilities. Mrs Margaret Grist started a nursery school in her own home in 1949 and two years later moved to the Hayes Free Church Lodge with 28 pupils where she remained in charge for over twenty years. The Pickhurst Lodge Pre-School Group still exists today as does St Mary's Nursery School that started in the hall of the Old Church Schools on 25 April 1963 under Mrs Moores. By the time she moved to Manchester in 1970 there was a movement towards taking children at a younger age and for fewer days. A number of playgroups were set up. One started in the Roman Catholic Church Hall and was run by Mrs Jean Murdoch until 1979 when the Roman Catholic Church authorities wanted the hall for church activities. Other playgroups were set up using the facilities at the Sports Clubs in Barnet Wood Road.

*St Mary's Nursery School, 1993* [ax.]

In 1965 a Play Centre for Handicapped Children was started in the Old Church Schools' Club Room with help from surplus money from St Mary's Nursery School. It was run by Mrs R Glover SRN, Mrs C Still, a deacon of the Free Church, and by voluntary helpers, who worked in close liaison with Bromley Health Department. It was open until the end of the summer term 1972, when an Act of Parliament transferred the responsibility for the education of handicapped children from the Ministry of Health to the Ministry of Education. It was considered that as far as possible the pupils should join children in a normal situation and they were transferred to special opportunity classes at certain primary schools.[1] The Club Room was then used by St Mary's Nursery School for the youngest pupils.

### Primary Schools

In the early 1950s there was only one primary school in Hayes. At the age of five, children went to the Infant Department of the County Primary School in George Lane. The older juniors transferred to the Gadsden site until they were eleven years of age when they moved to secondary schools that were in the borough but not in Hayes. Many former pupils recall with fondness their time at Gadsden and the influence that Miss Nellie Barnes and Miss Doris Kiely had on their school days.

*Gadsden Staff 1951 [ao.]*

The numbers of pupils continued to grow and there was great demand for a primary school in the Pickhurst area of Hayes. The land at Longcroft was available but there were delays. By 1953 there were seven senior classes at Gadsden, including one using the squash court. At George Lane the former canteen kitchen, dining room, school hall and medical inspection room were in use as classrooms. It was calculated that a maximum of

745 pupils could be catered for at George Lane and Gadsden. On 22 May 1953 there were 780! By this time Mrs Eva Butler had retired and for four months from September to December 1952 Miss Nellie Barnes acted as head until Miss Pat Furse started in January 1953.[2]

*Recorder Group at Gadsden, 1952 [ao.]*

Eventually work started on the construction of Pickhurst County Primary School that finally opened in 1953 with 105 infants in four classes under Miss K Gay.

*Pickhurst County Primary School under construction, 1953 [m.]*

*Pickhurst County Primary School 1953 [m.]*

*Miss K Gay, first head of Pickhurst Infant School*
*and Mr F Harmer, head of Pickhurst Junior School, 1957 [aq.]*

The original four classes were moved to the newly completed lower Infants wing and the upper Infants wing was used by the Juniors. By September 1954 the pupil roll totalled 415 but the school still had only nine classrooms. The dining hall was divided with a curtain to provide two additional areas.

With pupil numbers growing Miss Gay remembered that:

> by April 1955 the school role was 463 and consequently the Medical Room was brought into use. It held just 18 children and an agile master who could climb over the desks.

The situation improved when the first block of the Junior School was ready for occupation in April 1956 and the remainder of the building was finished in May.[3] With the appointment of Mr F Harmer as headmaster, the Junior School formally opened its doors in September 1956. Sir William Nottidge JP, Chairman of Kent County Council officially inaugurated the two schools, Pickhurst Infant and Pickhurst Junior, on Saturday 13 July 1957.

Expansion continued and today there are about 270 pupils in the Infant School under Mrs Leonie Osborne and around 500 in the Junior School, whose current head is Mark Rampton. In 2010/11 the buildings of Pickhurst School were again being enlarged.

*Aerial Photo of Pickhurst School, late 1990s [aq.]*

The phased opening of Pickhurst County Primary School produced a gradual reduction in numbers at Hayes County Primary School and in July 1956 it became practical for the junior classes at Gadsden to return to George Lane. By 1960 there were 310 pupils in 10 classes and this had increased to 390 in 13 classes by the time Tony Hayes became head in 1996. Ambitious plans were made to extend the school to a three form entry. Twelve new classrooms and a large new hall were built and opened in 2001. Today at Hayes Primary School, under the head Mrs J Brinkley, there are around 630 pupils and the annual intake is about 90.

*Hayes Primary School pupils, 1993* [ar.]

*Aerial Photo of Hayes Primary School showing the 2001 extension* [ar.]

In 1965 Bromley Education Authority took over responsibility for the running of the schools from KEC. With the boundary changes, Pickhurst Junior and Infant School today have a West Wickham address, although most people still think of them as part of Hayes.

Both Hayes Primary School and Pickhurst Junior and Infant Schools have seen considerable additions to their buildings and to their resources in the past fifty years and have recently become Academy Schools. One of the most noticeable differences for pupils who attended in the 1950s and 1960s would be the introduction and use of computers and its associated technology, particularly in the last decade. The main aim remains as it has been over the past century to provide the most effective education for the local schoolchildren.

## Secondary Education

### Hayes School

The departure of the older juniors from Gadsden in 1956 provided the opportunity to open Hayes County Secondary School for Boys with 77 pupils. The first headmaster was R W Bigg. Three years later girls were admitted. Gadsden was used for teaching and administration and in a new building there were fourteen classrooms, two art & craft rooms, a metalwork shop, woodwork shop, two science laboratories, two domestic science rooms, needlework room, large hall, gymnasium and two changing rooms. When R W Bigg retired in 1967 a copper beech was planted in the grounds in his memory. By this time views on secondary education were changing. There was a movement away from entry to schools as a result of a pupil's result in the 11+ examination to the development of mixed ability schools.

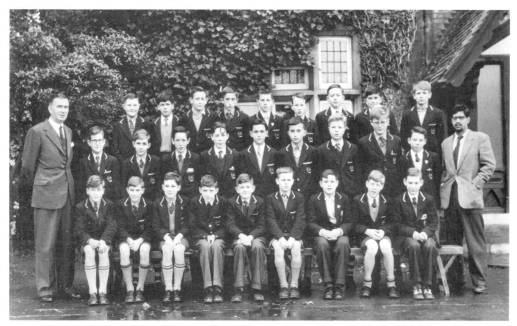

*Some of the first pupils at Hayes Secondary School, 1956* [as.]

Under the next head, Dr J S Leeming, Hayes School developed into a, six form, 180 pupil entry, comprehensive school. By 1973 there were 1,200 pupils. The dramatic increase in numbers resulted in the creation of a sixth form centre, library, sports centre, language laboratories, nine science laboratories and an art workshop complex.

*Hayes Secondary School 1971 ae.*

John Catmull became head in 1990 and lead the way to the school becoming grant maintained. More facilities were built with a greater emphasis on technology and media studies. The school expanded to an eight form entry. In 2002 Hayes School, by this time a Foundation School, was awarded Media Arts Status. Mr Kieran Osborne became head in 2004 and a master plan for phased extensions and alterations has been proposed. To date a new classroom block has been built that includes a special unit for pupils with speech, language and learning difficulties. The school, where there is now a very large sixth form, has become an Academy.

*Bike marking by Police Community Support Officers at Hayes School, 2010 ay.*

By the end of the twentieth century some pupils came from a wider area than Hayes but the majority were from the immediate environs. No other secondary school was built in Hayes, although in 1974 a planning application was made for an eight-form entry Roman Catholic Comprehensive School in Hayes Lane to replace one in Orpington.

## Baston School

The only independent school in Hayes to survive to the end of the twentieth century was Baston School for Girls that saw great growth in the immediate post war period. In 1951 Mrs Joy Wimble, who had been with the school since 1937, became headmistress. Miss Marian Stafford Smith remained as Principal until her death in 1953 when there were many tributes to her remarkable headship. Her sister Margaret Stafford Smith, who received the Freedom of the Borough in 1953, died in 1955 and the following year Mrs Joy Wimble and her husband Noel bought the school from the executors. In 1956 it provided both primary and secondary education and had over 300 pupils.

*Mr Charles Wimble, Head of Baston School and the Principal, Mrs Joy Wimble, 1983*[s.]

Five Elms, at the junction of Baston Road and Five Elms Road, became the boarding house and 83 Baston Road the preparatory department. In 1983, the year of the School's Golden Jubilee, Charles Wimble became head and his mother Principal, a position she held until her retirement in 2005.[4] Many additions were made to the school buildings, including a swimming pool, sports pavilion and science block. The return of Hong-Kong to the Chinese in 1997 halted the flow of overseas students and the boarding house was closed in 2001. Five Elms was put up for sale and permission granted to make it into flats. Its use by the new owners as a cannabis factory was foiled by a police raid in 2008.

By the time Mr Wimble became Principal in 2005 Baston School provided education for girls up to the age of 16.[5] It was affected by the recession and closed in 2009. Hillcrest Autism Services purchased it in 2010 and opened a school for autistic children, known as Baston House School.

## Organisations and Leisure Activities

A vital part of the life of Hayes is created by its many organisations and clubs, which provide the opportunity for those with similar interests to share their experiences. There are so many societies that it is only possible to indicate some developments since the Second World War that reflect both national changes and the local impact and importance of specific individuals.

One of the most important local organisations, Hayes Village Association, celebrated its 75th year in 2008. Its aim remains:

- To protect and watch over the interests of all residents in matters of local government and public services.
- To promote efficient and economic administration of the affairs of the district.
- To preserve local amenities.

Membership remains voluntary. The HVA represents over 2,500 households and offers an important focal point for those who wish to maintain the heritage of Hayes and to ensure it remains an enjoyable place to live. Its elected committee considers a vast range of matters. When Alice Coward wrote *Hayes Village on the Heath* in 1973 she referred to the Association's success in keeping an eye on building development, the efficiency of street lighting, improvement of local transport services by bus and rail, car parking, the layout of the parks. Similar matters have occupied HVA since that time including lorry routes, conservation areas, the appearance of the environs, policing and vandalism. Close relations are maintained with the police, local traders and other bodies.

Frank Ruler, who died in July 1970, was president of the HVA for a number of years and treasurer of HCC for about twenty years. He was also president of the county ratepayers' association and the Hayes delegate to the Ravensbourne Federation of Ratepayers' Associations. He studied traffic developments extensively and represented the residents' interests at transport tribunals considering fare rises. Like many officers of the HVA, he worked tirelessly for the community where he had lived since his marriage in 1933. He was also a trustee of the Hayes Educational Trust and a treasurer of the Keston branch of the Council for the Preservation of Rural England.

The HVA arranged an exhibition called 'Meet the Clubs' at the Village Hall in 1993. It covered 65 local organisations, most of whom met in the Village Hall or Old Church Schools.[6] Many societies, such as the Hayes Philharmonic Choir, had existed for almost fifty years but some were more recent, such as the Hayes (Kent) Flower Club established in 1970.[7] Inevitably, some of the clubs founded in the 1930s and 1940s did not survive changing times and other organisations moved to different venues. The Hayes, West Wickham and District Scottish Society, set up in 1952, moved to West Wickham in the 1970s. The Hayes Orchestral Society, now the Hayes Symphony Orchestra, met in West Wickham from 1960. Edward Lee was the leader from the early 1950s and only gave up playing at the age of 77 in 1979.

In 1967 the Hayes WVS office was closed after 27 years and the work of the organisation continued from the Borough Office in Bromley. At the time there were 70 active members who helped with Meals on Wheels, Trolley Shops, Mother and Baby Clubs, and collecting and distributing clothing.[8] Muriel Adamson, who later lived in Hawthorndene Road, was the District Organiser from February 1954.

The Hayes Council Tenants' Association ceased to use the Village Hall for its Bingo nights by 1970, as did the National Cactus and Succulent Society for its monthly meetings, although this society continued to hold its annual show in Hayes until about 2000.[9] In June 1998 the *Hayes Review* reported on the successes of the Chess Club, which had met in the Green Room of the Village Hall for almost fifty years. 'The club has produced more than 20 Junior British/English champions, two or three grandmasters … and even Nigel Short [British chess champion and Grandmaster] has visited.' In spite of its successes, the club had stopped meeting by the end of the decade. St Mary's Young Wives group finished in the 1980s when more mothers went out to work and younger mothers did not come forward as leaders, although some of the members from the 1970s and 1980s still live in Hayes and meet together monthly. Wyn Pellow ran St Mary's Women's Fellowship until she was almost 90 years old but, when she gave up in 2002, the society folded although the Women's Fellowship at the Free Church continues.

The meetings of many early organisations for women were in the afternoon, since most wives were at home, but changing employment patterns resulted in more evening societies. Today, however, as over 30% of the population are over the age of 60 and retired there is a return to more daytime activities such as Tea Dances and Keep Fit. The Hayes Over 60s Club continues to be active and the Hayes Men's Fellowship has a membership of over 100 men who enjoy its outings, walks and guest speakers.

For many years Hayes Players continued to rehearse or build their sets in the cellar under 'Vanda's', later 'Marjorie's', at 48 Station Approach. In the late 1960s a large outhouse became available for rent behind Street House in George Lane and the Players spent several years there until it was redeveloped. Fortunately this coincided in 1972 with a plot of land becoming available in George Lane on Hayes Street Farm, which was duly rented from Rookery Estates.

*Hayes Players celebrate the purchase of the Studio in 1994* [at.]

The Players built their own rehearsal room/workshop and storage facility. The base was laid and the building erected under the direction of Reg Purnell and Derek Moore. The new building was appropriately named 'The Merrill Studio' after the group's founder Joe Merill. In 1994 the Players bought the land for its permanent home. They produce four plays each year, mainly in the Village Hall where, in October 1992, a sound and lighting control loft was installed. They were the first amateur society in England to stage 'The Accrington Pals', which won the Kent Festival in 1983.

***The Accrington Pals performed by Hayes Players*** [al.]

The Hayes Players have had a long involvement in drama festivals and have been finalists 17 times in the Kent Full Length Play Drama Festival and 6 times winners. In the Bromley Theatre Guild Full Length Play Festival they have won on no fewer than 15 occasions. Julian Agnew, who was a leading member of the Hayes Players in the 1980s and 1990s, has since become a professional actor.[10]

Some Hayes residents have a great interest in gardening and those who have limited garden space use allotments. During the war many parts of Hayes had been made into allotments that were due to be returned to the owners by the end of October 1954, later extended to 1955. The Old Rectory and Gadsden allotments were handed over and those in the grounds of Street House were returned on 31 March 1956. Agreement was reached with the Norman family to extend the time on the 47 plots at the Old Bromley Sports Ground, apart from the ones that fronted Hayes Lane that were sold for building in 1955. The rest of the allotments were used until 1962 when KEC leased the land for additional playing fields for the then Bromley Grammar School for Boys. The Bourne Vale allotments (80 plots) and those behind the old Longcroft site at Pickhurst (40 plots) remain and the Hayes (Kent) Allotments Association founded in 1940 continues to manage and allocate them.

Many of those using the allotments participate in the five annual shows held by the Hayes (Kent) and District Horticultural Society, who have their own allotments in Constance Crescent. The Society remains flourishing and has provided the judges for the best front garden competition run each year by the HVA since 1994.[11]

## Sport

Cricket continued to be played until the 1990s on the Sports Ground in West Common Road purchased by Courage in 1949.

*Cricket in the 1950s, Courage's Sports Ground, West Common Road* [m.]

Just after the war Hayes Cricket and Sports Club Ltd bought their ground in Barnet Wood Road with a loan from the club president Arthur Collins and the rent from Catford Bridge Rugby Football Club's use of the ground during the winter months. After Arthur Collins' death in 1952, the executors required the repayment of the loan. Bill Warman, President of the Rugby Club and Vice President of the Cricket Club, paid it and provided for the building in 1955 of a new pavilion, designed by Bruce-George. The Warman Sports Trust was set up to administer the ground on behalf of the Cricket, Rugby and Tennis Clubs, all of which remain active. The ground has changed little over the years and one can still look across open country and see relatively few buildings in the distance.

> The most obvious sound that the cricketer or spectator often hears complementing the sound of bat on ball is that of the skylark rising from the adjoining field, whilst on a Sunday evening the sound of the church bells still rings across the meadows from the village church as it has done for centuries.[12]

Hayes is one of the leading cricket clubs in the Metropolitan area of Kent. A significant change took place in 1995 when women were allowed to play. Called the Hayes Hurricanes in 2001, it is now one of the top women's clubs in the south east of England. Lydia Greenway and Lynsey Askew both play for England and were in the successful side that beat New Zealand in 2008.

Catford Bridge RFC was renamed Bromley Rugby Football Club in the 1964/1965 season and continues to prosper with around 600 members. In recent years Jim Staples, a former junior went on to captain Ireland. Paul Collins (Ireland and London Irish) played, on occasions, for the 1st XV until his retirement. Mike Friday, formerly of London Wasps and ex-captain and coach of England's 7s team, was also a member.[13]

Barnet Wood Road is also the site of Park House Rugby Football Club. On 24 March 1962 disaster struck when its pavilion was completely destroyed by fire shortly after a new agreement had been made to lease the land for ten years. A temporary structure was quickly erected and a more permanent clubhouse was started in 1971. It finally opened on 7 October 1973. In 1978 the club's landlords sold them the freehold of thirteen acres of playing field.[14]

A badminton club was started in the new Warman Pavilion in the late 1950s and badminton continues to be played there today. Several of the badminton clubs that originally met in the Village Hall, such as the Glanville Club and the Ladies Afternoon Group, ceased to exist. Other groups flourish as do a number of tennis clubs including Hayes Tennis Club, Glebe Tennis Club formed in 1976 that plays in Hayes Library Gardens, and the Old Wilsonian Lawn Tennis Club at Hayes Hill.

*Tennis in the 1950s, Barnet Wood Road* [m.]

Hayes Bowling Club started in 1951 and used the bowling green of Courage's Sports Ground in West Common Road. Its original name was Courage's (Associate Members) Bowls Club but it became Hayes (Kent) Bowls Club and affiliated to the English Bowling Association, the Kent County Bowling Association and the Bromley and District Bowling Association.

By 1985 Courage no longer needed the Sports Ground and Clubhouse for its own use and it was bought by Mr F Woods in 1990.[15] The clubhouse was converted into a Country Club and the Bowls Club changed its name to Hayes Country Bowls Club. At the beginning of the twenty first century the clubhouse and land was sold to Direct Build Services. After an appeal, the company was given permission to pull down the pavilion and replace it with a three-storey block of flats, Burton Pynsent House, so changing the nature of land that had been used for sports for ninety years. The Bowls Club survived and in 2006 became Hayes Common Bowling Club.

*New Pavilion for Hayes Common Bowls Club, West Common Road
and Burton Pynsent House under construction, 2008*

*Blackheath Harriers' Sunday morning run, starting from the Clubhouse in
Bourne Way, 1969* [az.]

In athletics, the Blackheath Harriers continued to operate from its clubhouse in Bourne Way and in 1969 was included in Division 1 of the newly formed national league. Though relegated in the seventies Blackheath Harriers returned to the national league in 1979 and to Division 1 in 1984. Since then it has hovered between Divisions 1 and 2. In 1992 the club allowed women to join. In 1994 and 1995 the club was winner of the National Cross Country Championship, the National 6-Stage Relay in 1994 and the 12-Stage relay in 1995. In 1997 the National Young Athletes Boys Final was won for the ninth time and in 1998 Julian Golding became the Commonwealth 200m champion in Kuala Lumpur. In March 2000 the Club changed its name to Blackheath Harriers Bromley and in 2003 merged with Bromley AC to become Blackheath and Bromley Harriers AC. The club manages the track at Norman Park.

At the end of 2007 the Junior Athletes and Young Athletes were National Champions and the latter also headed the Southern Premier League for the fourth consecutive year. The male and female veteran teams were the Kent Division and Southern Counties Area champions.[16]

For those who preferred to cycle, an informal club was organised by Bigfoot Bikes of Hayes Street in 2004. The club is now relatively large and on many occasions groups of cyclists may be seen assembling in Hayes Street for their day's outing.

## Youth Organisations

There have been many changes in youth organisations over the last half-century as people's aspirations and interests altered. In the 1950s the activities of both the Challengers, led by Claude Pierce until 1963, and the Swift Youth Club were very varied and ranged from lectures and socials to excursions, walking and cycling expeditions. As its members became older a senior section was set up for Challengers aged 18 to 25.

*Performance of 'Cinderella' by the Challengers, 1952*

*Challengers at Church Service, late 1950s*

*Victory Social Youth Club presented with the Challenge Cup*
*by the Mayor of Bromley John Hunt, 1963* [au.]

A youth club was started by the Victory Social Club for ages 12 to 25 and met in Hayes Primary School one evening a week. The three clubs were members of the Bromley Council of Youth that consisted of about a dozen local youth groups. These organisations competed against each other in a number of activities that culminated in Bromley Youth Week that was held in the summer. This began with a procession through Bromley High Street with floats and ended the following Saturday with an athletics meeting, where all clubs took part. In the evening a dance was held at which the cups were presented. Swimming competitions were held at Downham Baths, cycle racing at Biggin Hill airfield, and athletics at Bromley Grammar School for Boys. These activities led to lifelong friendships. Many Challengers still keep in touch with each other and meet up regularly. At a Millennium Reunion Weekend in Eastbourne, 100 former members, some travelling from Australia, Canada and Singapore, met and exchanged memories.[17]

After the retirement of Claude Pierce the Challengers Youth Club continued for a few years but, like other youth groups in the 1960s, was no longer so popular. The needs of teenagers seemed to change. It was the time of the 'mods and rockers' and youth clubs generally went out of vogue. In 1974 HVA set up a young people's section but on many occasions damage was caused to the Village Hall and its fittings, often by outsiders denied admission. Initially, HVA tried to cover the cost of the damage and hoped that it could continue to provide a youth club. It proved impossible and, by the 1980s, the general feeling was that what was needed was a purpose-built youth centre. It was considered that it might be possible to build such a centre in the Rectory Garden but this was not practicable.

In the 1980s the Hayes Free Church also had a popular youth club which ran for many years on a Friday evening. By the end of the century there were small youth groups attached to the various churches in Hayes. Most youngsters, however, were involved in specific activities run through their schools, such as the Duke of Edinburgh Scheme, or by the Borough, such as the Youth Orchestra, rather than in any general club catering for a wide range of activities and taste.

During the war a Kent Cadet Gunner unit was formed at Gates Green Road, Coney Hall and had soon grown to such proportions that approval was given to raising its status to a regiment. Lieutenant Colonel Short assumed command. The regiment also met at its hut known as 'Fort George' in George Lane, Hayes, as well as Wickham Common School, Cyphers Cricket Club, Beckenham and the Drill Hall at Penge and had over 200 cadets. In 1950 it amalgamated with the 1st ACF Battalion RWKR. Hayes Cadets were in 'G' troop and continued to use Fort George as their headquarters until 2001.

In the 1950s an active Parents and Friends Association was started to support the cadets of 'G' troop. Colonel Chamberlain of Glebe House, West Wickham, agreed to be its President in 1955 and attended the Annual General Meetings until at least 1961. Army Cadets were aged from 14-18 but in 1956 the cadet roll dwindled as the emphasis changed to citizenship rather than military training. In 1958 there were 40 boys when Captain D S Garrett retired and was succeeded by Captain P C Lewis and then Lieutenant Foster.[18]

During the 1960s Lieutenant Colonel Philip Jones TD was appointed Officer Commanding of the Battalion. On 3 April 1968 it became 10 (Kent) Cadet Regiment Royal Artillery and Hayes became detachment 104. David Hart, a cadet in the late seventies, recalls the tough discipline and training exercises held in nearby woods. In 1984 the MoD negotiated a 21 years lease on the George Lane site, the old buildings were demolished and two new huts erected. Company Sergeant Major David Hart became Officer Commanding 104 in 1990. A year later, Hayes was badged to the Irish Guards. At the beginning of the twenty first century there was a period of change and uncertainty. David Hart left to pursue a staff job at headquarters and handed over command to 2nd Lieutenant Mark Ryan. The first female cadets were recruited and in 2007 Sarah Golding became the first female Officer Commanding 104.

*Lieutenant Stan Cox and Tom Exton, 22 January 1956, outside Fort George* [g.]

The Rookery Estates, from whom the land was leased, applied in 2001 for planning permission to build two detached houses on the site of Fort George. It was allowed on appeal and as a consequence the Cadets were forced to look elsewhere for a new home when their lease expired. The Rookery Estates tried to find them an alternative site; one on farmland at the end of George Lane was rejected and in 2004 an application was made to demolish some of the farm buildings at Hayes Street Farm and erect a single storey building in its place. The appeal was dismissed on the grounds that its use was likely to create an unacceptable amount of noise.[19] The unit moved to Ravensbourne School and met twice a week under Paul Stevens. It is now based in the new Kingswood Cadet Centre in Hayes Lane.

In September 1981 an Air Training Corps (ATC), 768 Squadron, moved to Hayes School under Flight Lieutenant Godfrey Smith MBE MIMgt. It soon had 85 members and in 1983 girls were allowed to join. The ATC hut was erected by the tennis courts and officially opened by Group Captain G J Oxlee OBE, an ex-768 Squadron cadet in 1984. In April 1985 two cadets took part in the NATO exercise 'Handy Forge' attached to 33 Wing, RAF Regiment in West Germany. During the nineties several new activities appeared, including parachute courses at RAF Weston-on-the-Green, full bore rifle shooting and sub-aqua diving courses. In 1996 the Bulldog aircraft replaced the Chipmunk for air experience flying. In the same year the Squadron Banner was dedicated at a special service in Hayes Church in the presence of Group Captain the Earl of Ilchester. In May 2002 Flight Lieutenant Smith retired and was succeeded by Flight Lieutenant Steve Penny, a former RAF Wing Commander, who had seen active service during the Falklands War. At about the same time, although due for replacement, the army cadet hut was moved because it was in the way of a proposed turning area for coaches. The new site, still in the school grounds, was by the Lodge. A much larger headquarters' building was planned but there were considerable difficulties with the proposal and the project was eventually abandoned.

*ATC, 768 Squadron, Remembrance Sunday 2005 [av.]*

Flight Lieutenant Penny resigned as CO in January 2004 and was replaced on 1st April 2005 by Flight Lieutenant James Dyer, a former 768 cadet from Hayes. His knowledge and experience in the field of adventure training greatly benefited the cadets. Pressure was directed at the Squadron to become an 'Open Unit' rather than school based. This, compounded with the difficulties of accommodation, resulted in the Ministry of Defence suspending the squadron. It was closed on 31 March 2006 and the remaining cadets moved with Flight Lieutenant James Dyer to 228 Bromley Squadron.[20]

## Scouts and Cubs

In 1950 there was one Scout Group, 1st Hayes Scouts (12th Bromley), which met in the tin hut in the Library Gardens. A second group, 2nd Hayes Scouts (20th Bromley) attached to St Mary's Church, was formed in 1951 under scoutmaster Gordon Smith and met in the Old Church Schools and a third group, 3rd Hayes (22nd Bromley) Free Church Scouts, started at Hayes Free Church under Harold Gentry in 1955. As their numbers grew the new groups decided that they needed larger headquarters and both the 2nd and 3rd groups built their own.

The Parish Church leased land behind the Old Church Schools to the 2nd Hayes Scouts who selected a Butler Block Building by Stephenson Developments. In 1958 work started under scoutmaster Rennie Hoyland, assisted by parents, friends and scouts.

*Parents and 2nd Hayes Scouts preparing the base for the Scout Hut [ac.]*

*The completed Scout Hut [ac.]*

They removed three large trees, cleared years of growth and rubble, laid foundations and raised funds for the new building. The roof was still being erected on 18 June 1960 when the Scout Hut was formally opened by the Prime Minister, Harold Macmillan, an event commemorated by a plaque, carved by two of the scouts, on the outside of the building. The building was finally dedicated and used from June 1961 until the early 1990s. In 1965 a prefabricated concrete garage was erected behind the headquarters and proved very useful when the scouts built several canoes later in the decade.[21]

***Prime Minister Harold Macmillan arrives to open the Scout Hut, 18 June 1960*** [ac.]

In 1956 Fred Wyatt took over as leader of the 3rd Hayes Scouts, a post he held for 25 years. At his suggestion a piece of land off Mounthurst Road was purchased and Burroughs Wellcome Research Laboratories donated a large wooden hut. Volunteers dismantled derelict greenhouses, cleaned and levelled the ground and under Sid Daws' supervision laid a concrete and brick foundation, on which to erect the hut. The Mayor of Bromley, Alderman John Hunt, formally opened it on 5 October 1963.[22] The hut is still used today although the group under Mrs Brenda Petts, who became Acting Group Scout Leader in 2004, are raising funds to build a new one.

In 1979 the lease on the tin hut used by 1st Hayes Group ran out and it was demolished. Ray Hollister, who became Group Scoutmaster in 1982, was instrumental in establishing a temporary building, made out of old motorway site buildings, on a parcel of land in George Lane leased from Rookery Estates. In the 1990s this also become the home of the 2nd Hayes Scouts, who were unable to renew the lease on their site because there were plans to redevelop the Old Church Schools. The two scout groups – 1st Hayes (12th Bromley) under Ray Hollister and 2nd Hayes (20th Bromley) under Frank Rhodes – were amalgamated and became 32nd Bromley.[23] In 1991 great efforts were made to raise funds to renovate the

George Lane Hut which the scouts eventually bought. Planning consent was given for it to become permanent but it was only to be used for scouting purposes.

Without the dedication and enthusiasm of these volunteers the history of scouting in Hayes would have been very different.

In 1967 Senior Scouts started with seven boys from 3rd Hayes troop and Fred Wyatt ran their meetings, some in the garage of Gordon Scott's father where they built a canoe. Senior Scouts became known as Venture Scouts, and many later became Scout leaders. In 1992 they won the Judd Trophy for the best Venture Unit in the District and Gavin Martin was leader from 1994 until 2002. In that year all Venture Units were closed and a new section, the Explorer Unit for 15–18 year olds opened in September 2002.

For younger boys there were cubs. 1st Hayes Group had one pack until 1974 when two were formed, the Rikki pack under Mrs D Pretty and the Kaa pack under Mr B Hubbard. Similarly the 2nd Hayes Group soon had a large waiting list and in 1961 Kim Pack was formed to exist alongside Baloo.

*Baloo Cub Pack 1976* [ae.]

At the Free Church the Mowgli Cub Pack was started in 1953 but due to lack of leaders closed in 1985/1986. By this time a second Free Church pack, Baloo, had been started in the 1960s and continues to be successful, winning the District Cub Challenge Cup in 1991, 2005 and 2007.

For boys aged six to eight the first Beaver Unit in Bromley, the Woodchippers Colony, was started in 1985/6 by Mrs Sylvia Humphrey and was part of the 2nd Hayes (20th Bromley) Group. This colony had ceased by the end of the 1990s but a second colony, formed under Marion Graham, continued. At the Free Church a Beaver Colony was opened in 1994.[24]

*Woodchippers Colony 1992* [ax.]

## Guides and Brownies

The number of Brownie packs for girls over the age of seven has varied over the fifty years and in the mid 1970s there were seven groups. In 2009 three groups met in the Old Church Schools and one at the Free Church. The 1st Hayes Brownies started in 1932, the 2nd Hayes Brownies began in 1947, closed in 1964 but restarted in 1972 under Mrs Rosemary Humphrey who retired in 1992. The 5th was formed in 1957 and Marie Green, former District Commissioner, led it from 1991 until her retirement in 2010. At one stage there were three groups attached to the Free Church but a shortage of leaders has resulted in the survival of only the 3rd Hayes Brownies that was formed in 1946, met originally in Pickhurst Manor Lodge and was run by Doris Bellringer for 21 years. Like the cubs the brownies participate in numerous activities and have raised funds for several charities, such as the Wishing Well Appeal for Great Ormond Street Children's Hospital in 1988 and the Blue Peter 'Bring and Buy for Romania' in 1991.[25]

The demand by younger girls to participate in similar activities led to the setting up of Rainbows for the under 7s in 1994. The difficulty of finding helpers resulted in its closure in 1999 but it has reopened in recent years.

By 1948 the original brownies at the Free Church were ready for guides and the 4th Hayes Guides were started under the captaincy of Mrs Plater. The 1st Hayes Guides formed in 1919 was still active and a 2nd and 3rd troop linked to the Parish Church had also been set up and met in the Old Church Schools. In the early 1950s the 1st and 3rd Hayes Guides shared joint camp holidays. One year while they were away there was a storm, which ripped the tents and they had to sleep in an Oast House until the farmer said that they had to go home as 'the animals would not eat the hay after the guides had slept in it'!

*Brownies supporting the Great Blue Peter Bring & Buy Sale, 14 May 1981*

*5th Hayes Brownies, 1993 [ax.]*

Unfortunately the 2nd Hayes Guides ceased in 1981 and the 4th Hayes Guides more recently, but the remaining guide groups were able to enjoy the many activities held both locally and nationally to mark the Guides' centenary year in 2010. It started with *Party in the Park* at Crystal Palace and later in the year in October there was a District event at Hayes Free Church. A County Church Parade took place in Sidcup in November and the County Flag was carried by Zoe Kingsmell, leader of the 1st Hayes Guides, escorted by two assistant guiders, Vickie Jones and Helen Barclay, also from 1st Hayes Guides.

*1st Hayes Guides 1956*

*1st Hayes Guides, 1993* [ax.]

## May Queen

Many Hayes girls have been involved in the festival of the Crowning of the London May Queen that takes place on Hayes Common each year and is a good reminder of the rural origins of Hayes. There are now three local groups; the original Hayes May Queen, with its realm colour of madonna blue and lily of the valley flowers, the Hayes Common May Queen with its colour of eau-de-nil and primrose flowers and a Hayes Village group with the colour of magenta and forget-me-not flowers.[26]

*Hayes Common May Queen 1985,*
*Elizabeth Wilson May Queen and Janice Randall Prince [ae.]*

## Hayes Common

The 79 hectares of Hayes Common remain one of the delightful features of Hayes and provide enjoyment for all ages. Bromley Council took over its management in 1954 after the passing of the Bromley Corporation Act 1953.[27] The scheme of management was modernised and the ancient rights of tenants of the Manor to cut heather and bracken or dig up the turf were repealed. Since then there has been an increase in the growth of woodland and birch, there is less heather and broom and in places dense patches of holly threaten to dominate. The Friends of Hayes Common was formed in 2000, under its chairman Dr Keith Royston, and regular working parties tackle the worst areas. Keith Royston reported in 2010 that great improvements had been made to many areas of the common.'Our clearances of dense holly are benefiting both people and the wildlife by getting sunlight and warmth back down to ground level again, after years of deep gloom.'

The main heathland area is on the four corners of the Baston and Croydon Roads' crossroads and an area of 2.4 hectares is designated as a site of Special Scientific Interest.[28] The pond off Baston Road has a good amphibian population and the pond near Prestons Road/Warren Road is good for bats. In recent years deer have become bolder and have been seen in some of the gardens bordering the common, particularly enjoying the roses. Dog walking is a favourite pastime. In summer, many clubs organise walks over the common either to see the flora and fauna or to explore the evidence for the earlier history of Hayes. In 2010, the area was made part of the Hayes Common and Keston Local Nature Reserve.

## The Churches

In the immediate post-war years there were significant changes to the churches in Hayes as the various denominations tried to meet the needs of the increasing population. Both the Roman Catholic Church and the Congregational Church (Hayes Free Church) built new places of worship in Hayes in the 1950s.

### Roman Catholic Church

Although the Roman Catholics bought the bombed site of Grandfield's Nursery soon after the ending of the war, they continued to meet in Hayes Village Hall. In December 1952, an architect was commissioned to draw up plans for a building, which was completed by 1954. The original suggestion to call the building 'Our Lady's Hall' was not agreed by the Bishop of Southwark but Rosary Hall was accepted. At first, to meet the cost of its building, the Rosary Hall was used for badminton and dances but in the early 1960s it was decided to use the building only as a church. The original intention had been to build a hall and church but with limited resources the hall site was converted into the church that exists today.

*Rosary Hall* [ap.]

In 1965 the priest's house was built in the grounds and the present church, Our Lady of the Rosary, was completed in 1966 with Father Donald Dorsett officiating. By 1968 a Philips Philicorda Electronic Organ replaced the harmonium and early in 1971 limed oak benches replaced the metal chairs. In 1972 the church interior was painted white ready for a new altar of Botticino marble. A Millennium Window was installed in 2000. Father Dorsett remained in Hayes until his death in 1978 and was succeeded by Father Stuart and then by Monsignor Peter Strand in 1986. The end of the century saw a succession of

Roman Catholic priests, Father John Hennessey in 1997, Father Serafin in 1998, Father William Keogh in 1999 and Father David Hutton in 2003.[29]

## Hayes Free Church

In 1951 Revd Henry Jacquet replaced Revd Harold Edwards as Minister of the Free Church and during his ministry the aims of the congregation for a permanent church were achieved. The membership grew to over 300 and at various times the large afternoon Sunday School had to seek additional rooms for one or more of its departments. Space was used in the Pavilion of the Goldfields Consolidated Company in Hayes Hill (now the Old Wilsonians Sports Club), two classrooms at Barnhill School and in the home of Mr and Mrs Steadman, teachers in the Sunday School. Mrs Eva Butler started a morning Junior Church.

Mr J Colvin, architect at the Bromley office of Messrs Gordon Jackson & Partners, drew up plans for a permanent hall and church. Pickhurst Lodge was demolished to make way for the first stage of the building programme. J Rider Smith, chairman of the planning committee of the London Congregational Union, laid the foundation stone for the new hall on 16 April 1955 and the building was opened on 19 November 1955. With the removal of building restrictions, plans were soon made for the building of the church, whose foundation stone was laid on 5 May 1956 by Revd Hugh Wallace, the minister at Anerley from 1905 until his church was bombed. The builders were R Mansell Ltd and it was equipped to seat 400 people.

*Opening Hayes Free Church Hall, 19 November 1955* [an.]

Mrs Dorrett gave an oak table and chair, in memory of her husband Herbert who had been a highly respected member and local councillor. A portable oak christening font was donated in memory of Flying Officer K G Richards, Miss Muriel Cooke presented an oak reading desk and Miss E Manning's executor gave an oak lectern. Mr Douglas Davidson of Kingsgate Davidson, Organ Builders, was a member of the church and choir in 1956 and on his recommendation an organ was installed and officially commissioned on 15 April 1957. For many years Ralph Arnold maintained it. The new building was dedicated on 13 April 1957 and, with the money left over, a brick wall was put round the site and a gallery made inside. The work was completed just in time for the televising of the morning service by ITV on Sunday 22 February 1959.[30]

Revd Allan Butler, son of the former head of Hayes Primary School, took over in 1962 and it was during his ministry that Congregationalists and Presbyterians came together to form the United Reform Church. It was also the start of greater ecumenical activity between the churches in Hayes and on 23 January 1968 a joint service for Anglicans, Catholics and members of the Free Church was held at St Mary's with all three clergy taking part. Joint services continue, including an Open Air Service each summer. The next Free Church minister, John Robinson, led several inter-church group trips to the Holy Land. Norman Healey became Minister in 1992 and a joint service started to be held on Good Friday when a procession of witness made its way from the Parish Church, St Mary The Virgin, to the Free Church for a family service.

During the ministry of Robert Bushby, who was appointed in 1996, an experiment was held of a Christmas Tree Festival in which Hayes' organisations could sponsor and decorate a tree in the Free Church. A series of concerts and other events were organised and the money went to charity. At the first Festival in 2001 there were about 20 trees and £2,080 was collected. The experiment was so successful that it has continued as an annual event. In 2007 there were 31 trees and £7,020 was raised for Demelza Hospice Care for Children.[31]

Revd Sue Powell became the first woman to lead the Free Church in 2006, although she was not the first female minister in Hayes. Revd Cilla Matthews, who became the curate at the Parish Church, was licensed by the Bishop of Tonbridge on 4 March 1990. She retired in 2002.

## Hayesford Park Baptist Church

In 1992 the Baptists decided they needed a place for a second congregation because of the rapid increase in people attending Coney Hall Baptist Church. Hayes and Hayesford Park were chosen but it proved difficult to find a suitable venue and Revd Peter Thomas, Rector of Hayes Parish Church, suggested the congregation met in the Village Hall until a suitable place was found. They started in September 1993. In 1996 the Community Centre in Letchworth Drive on the Hayesford Park Estate was identified as a possible venue, and on Palm Sunday 2000 the congregation moved from the Village Hall to the new location. The Community Centre was used for some time but in 2004 the Baptists returned to the centre of Old Hayes and used the Village Hall on a Sunday morning for worship. Their pastor is Revd Simon Grey.[32]

*Knoll Park, part of the original grounds of Hayes Place* [ba.]

*Husseywell Park, part of the original grounds of Hayes Place* [ba.]

*The open space of Hayes Common at the top of Station Hill, site each year of the Crowning of the London May Queen* [bc.]

*Friends of Hayes Common having a tea break during one of their working parties*

*Hayes Village Association Float, Hayes Fair, 1977* [be.]

*Hayes Horticultural Society Float, Hayes Fair, 2000*

*Young Wives as Mister Men, Hayes Fair in the late 1970s*

*May Queen procession in Station Approach on the way to the common in the 1980s* [bd.]

*A group from 'Churches Together in Hayes', Hayes Millennium Fair [ax.]*

*Hayes Millennium Fair on Hayes Common, 2000 [ax.]*

*Fun day in the Rectory gardens, 1997* [ax.]

*Hayes Fair held at Baston School, 2008* [bc.]

*Miss Beatrice Russell, a pupil at Hayes Church School 1908 - 1916, opens an exhibition to celebrate the Old Church School's two hundredth anniversary in 1991*

*Interest shown in the 'Wartime Hayes' Exhibition in the Village Hall, 1989*

*The cast and crew of 'Edge of Darkness' performed by Hayes Players, 2004* [at.]

*Gathering in Village Hall on the retirement of Canon Peter Thomas, 27 May 2001* [ax.]

## The Church of God

In 1950 the Assembly Hall of the Church of God in George Lane was extended to create more space for youth work and again in 1961 to house 'The Needed Truth Publishing Office' which later became the Hayes Press. The Hayes Press has since moved but the church is still active with Sunday and Thursday services and has recently restarted a youth group on a Friday.[33]

## The Parish Church

*St Mary the Virgin, 2011* [ba.]

The Parish Church remains at the centre of the old village, a symbol of past centuries and a landmark in the community. Like many old buildings it constantly has needed repairs. The first post-war task was to deal with war damage and reshingle the tower. Then woodworm was discovered in the floor of the pews on the north side of the church and in 1958 it was replaced with concrete and covered with cork tiles. Two years later an infestation of deathwatch beetle resulted in the removal of the Victorian matchboarding from the roof and the remarkable ancient wooden roofing timbers were revealed. Some of these were replaced in the 1980s because of dry rot. The 1970s saw the overhaul of the bells by the Whitechapel Foundry, the rebuilding of the organ by Mander, the renewal of the tower and installation of a weathercock. In 1993 the roof was completely renovated and a new finial installed on the Lady Chapel.

There were many proposals to enlarge the church including one in 1962 to remove the east wall and extend the chancel. A plan to build a porch at the southwest corner, close up the north door and provide new clergy and choir vestries was approved in 1963. The builders were S E Wright and Son Ltd and a generous donation to the cost of the porch was made by the widow of Sir Charles Jocelyn Hambro, who was buried in the family grave in August 1963. The font was moved to a new position behind the pews on the south side of the nave. The total cost of the porch and new vestries was over £9,000.

***Revd Frank Mitchell and Mr Clare on the church roof
replacing the stolen lead, 1974*** [ae.]

No further enlargement was needed during the ministry of Revd Frank Mitchell 1966-1977 but in the 1980s discussions started on ways to provide a church hall within or close to the existing church. The Sunday Schools used the Old Church Schools for their meetings and it was considered difficult for the children to feel part of the church. A highly controversial plan was made with Burton & Deakin, a BMW garage situated on the corner of Pickhurst Lane and West Common Road, to take over the Old Church School site. As part of the arrangement, a hall would be built in the Rectory Gardens. In spite of considerable opposition and planning appeals the scheme was finally approved but, by the time this occurred, Burton & Deakin had changed its plans. Instead, the church decided to modernise the Old Church Schools and create another hall incorporating the old Scout Hut and this was finally achieved in 2000.[34]

***Burton & Deakin Garage, 1968*** [i.]

***The car showroom on the former Burton and Deakin site, 2011*** [ba.]

There have been four rectors in the post-war period. Revd Eric Smith was the first and during his ministry many new groups were set up and flourished. He went to Knockholt in 1966. Revd Frank Mitchell succeeded him. He and his wife played an active role in the community. The Drama Group flourished and a Children's Choir grew. Another new development was the setting up of a popular Pram Service in 1976. His successor, in

1977, was Revd Peter Thomas who remained for 24 years and was known to most people in the parish. He and his wife Sheena had an 'open house' at the Rectory, where coffee mornings, fetes, barbecues, dog shows, bonfire nights and picnics all took place. He was chairman of many local organisations, a Governor of Hayes School and had a great involvement with the young, holding a weekly session at Baston School and frequently visiting the local primary schools. Like his predecessors he was made an Honorary Canon of Rochester Cathedral shortly before his retirement in 2001.

*Father Peter Strand on his retirement 27 July 1996, with Revd Peter Thomas* [ax.]

During the ministry of the most recent Rector, Revd David Graham, who retired in April 2012, the plans for an extension to replace the 1965 vestry addition and provide a meeting room, office, priest and choir vestries were finally realised. The planning process took a long time. Although first proposed in 1996, the extension was not built until 2005 and was opened on 1st May by the Bishop of Rochester, Dr Michael Nazir-Ali.

The new Church Meeting Room provided another place where inhabitants of Hayes could meet to share in fellowship and enjoy a wide range of activities. On special occasions the whole community has come together, such as for the 1977 Queen's Silver Jubilee and for the Millennium when a carnival parade and entertainment was organised on Hayes Common. Historical exhibitions, such as the ones for the 'Centenary of Hayes Railway' in 1982, 'Wartime Hayes' in 1989, the 'Bicentenary of the Old Church Schools' in 1991, and the 'Millennium Exhibition' in 2000, have engendered a great deal of enthusiasm for the past and offer a chance for newcomers to learn about Hayes and its interesting history. In 2009 a special service was held in the Parish Church, after the unveiling of a blue plaque, to mark the birthplace of Pitt the Younger in Hayes in 1759.

*New Parish Church Meeting Room 2010*

Hayes today is very different from the Hayes of sixty years ago but the signs are there of a past that gives Hayes its uniqueness. It is the reason why so many people are reluctant to leave a place where they have spent most of their life. That special nature has been achieved through the efforts of many people to ensure that the vestiges of that past are not swept away in a rush for modernization and financial gain. As John Payne, chairman of Hayes Chamber of Commerce 1979-80, said:

> It is like living in a village community with a large town on our doorstep. We believe we have the best of both worlds – a big town [Bromley] and we are on the edge of the countryside, with lots of lovely fresh air.

Change will continue to alter the appearance of the former village but there is still sufficient green land to evoke its farming origins. The area of green belt remains an important feature to the east and south of the former parish. Almost any walk whether on the common, in the fields or in the streets will show the signs of the development of Hayes revealed in the previous chapters. The importance of the people and their determination to maintain the spirit of the community cannot be underestimated. Hayes is what it is today because of the actions of individuals in the past. It may have become part of the London Borough of Bromley but it retains a separate identity. The words of Canon Thompson in his *History of Hayes* seem apt: 'there still remains in Hayes some pride in ancestry….something gracious in the memories of former days.' It will require future generations to ensure that this legacy is maintained.

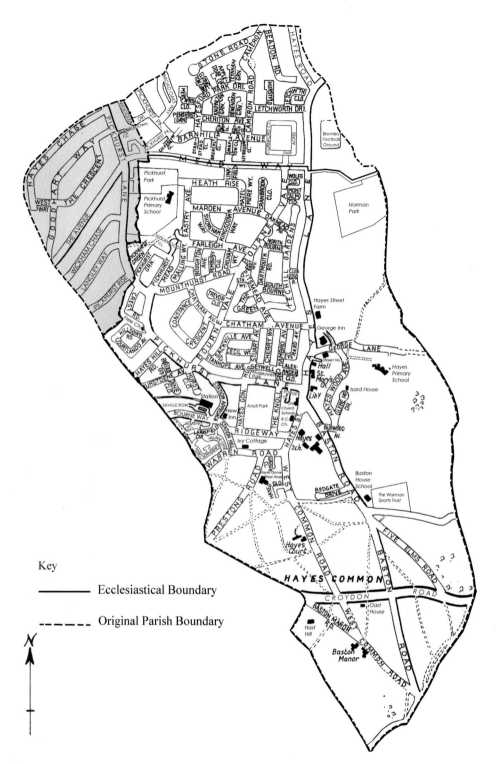

**Map 23:** *Modern Hayes, the area within the original Parish Boundary of 1895 and the present boundary of the Ecclesiastical Parish*

# Appendix 1: First World War Recruits from Hayes

| Surname | Forename | Home | Hayes Family | House | Report Date | Service | Bible Entry | Hayes Roll of Honour | On Hayes War Memorial | Date Died CWGC | Age at death |
|---|---|---|---|---|---|---|---|---|---|---|---|
| Alexander | Frederick | Hayes | Y | Pickhurst Manor | | | Y | | | | |
| Andrews | Cyril E | Hayes | Y | Hazelcot, Croydon Road | 06-Nov 1914 | Army | Y | | | | |
| Andrews | Eric | | | | | | Y | | | | |
| Andrews | Raymond | Hayes | | Hazelcot, Croydon Road | | | Y | | | | |
| Arnold | Alfred H | Hayes | Y | St Mary Cottages | 06-Nov 1914 | Army | Y | | | | |
| Arnold | Percy F | Hayes | Y | St Mary Cottages | | Army | | Y | Y | 15 Sep 1916 | 30 |
| Arnold | Walter | Hayes | Y | St Mary Cottages | | | Y | | | | |
| Attenborough | Stanley | Hayes | Y | Longcroft | 22-Jan 1915 | Army | Y | | | | |
| Barnes | Edgar | Hayes | Y | Hayes Court Lodge | | | Y | | | | |
| Barnes | Egbert C | Hayes | Y | Elmhurst Villa | | | Y | | | | |
| Batten | Albert E | Hayes | Y | Hayes Place Gardens | 11-Sep 1914 | Army | Y | | | | |
| Batten | Ernest | Hayes | Y | Hayes Street Farm Cottages | 14-Dec 1914 | Army | Y | | | | |
| Batten | Walter H | Hayes | Y | Hayes Street Farm Cottages | 06-Nov 1914 | Army | | Y | Y | 09 Apr 1917 | 21 |
| Beagley | John | | | | 14-Aug 1914 | | | | | | |
| Beavis | Albert W | Hayes | Y | Flint Cottages, Croydon Road | | | Y | | | | |
| Beavis | Edward | Hayes | Y | Flint Cottages, Croydon Road | | Army | | | | | |
| Beavis | George | Hayes | Y | Flint Cottages, Croydon Road | 06-Nov 1914 | Navy | Y | | | | |
| Beavis | Henry C | Hayes | | Pickhurst Mead | 10-Mar 1916 | | | | | | |
| Beeston | Harold L | Hayes | Y | Hayes Road | Aug 1914 | Army | | Y | Y | 24 Oct 1918 | 29 |

| Surname | Forename | Home | Hayes Family | House | Report Date | Service | Bible Entry | Hayes Roll of Honour | On Hayes War Memorial | Date Died CWGC | Age at death |
|---|---|---|---|---|---|---|---|---|---|---|---|
| Bennett | David | Hayes | | Gadsden Gardens | 04-Sep 1914 | Army | | | | | |
| Bensted-Smith | Francis | Hayes | Y | Solway Bank | 1915 | Army | | | | | |
| Bignall | Albert E | Hayes | Y | Baston Farm Cottages | 06-Nov 1914 | Army | | | | | |
| Bingham | Thomas | Hayes | | | | | Y | | | | |
| Bingham | William B | WW | Y | Warren House Lodge | 24-Dec 1915 | RFC | | Y | Y | 05 Jul 1916 | 32 |
| Bingley | Edwin | Hayes | | | | | Y | | | | |
| Boakes | George | Hayes | | Spilman's Grove | 03-Dec 1915 | Army | Y | | | | |
| Boniface | Harry | Hayes | | Tythe Cottage | 10-Dec 1915 | | | | | | |
| Borer | Walter H | WW | | | 21-Aug 1914 | Army | Y | | | | |
| Bower | Cyril | Hayes | Y | | 14-Aug 1914 | Army | Y | | | | |
| Bowles | Arthur | Hayes | Y | Hayes Bottom | | | Y | | | | |
| Bowles | Harry | Hayes | Y | Hayes Bottom | 06-Nov 1914 | Navy | Y | | | | |
| Brown | Henry | Hayes | Y | Baston Cottages | 1918 | Army | | | | | |
| Bryant | Frederick | Hayes | Y | Baston Cottages | 11-Sep 1914 | Army | Y | | | | |
| Campbell | Lyon | Hayes | | | 14-Aug 1914 | Army | | | | | |
| Carter | Arthur W E | Hayes | | Hayes Village | 26-Nov 1915 | | Y | | | | |
| Cassam | Arthur E | Hayes | Y | Baston Road | April 1916 | Army | | Y | Y | 11 Sep 1916 | 25 |
| Chapman | Henry | Hayes | Y | No.3 Station Rd | 11-Sep 1914 | Army | | | | | |
| Churcher | Horace F | Hayes | Y | Stationmaster's House | 06-Nov 1914 | Army | | | | | |
| Clark | Charles D | Bromley | | | | Army | Y | Y | Y | 22 Jan 1920 | 37 |
| Clark | Robert | Hayes | | Waites Cottage | | | Y | | | | |
| Clark | Thomas W | Hayes | | Waites Cottage | | | Y | | | | |
| Clibbon | William G | Hayes | | Hayes Place Gardens | 21-May 1915 | Army | | | | 22 Jul 1916 | 24 |
| Cogger | George | Hayes | Y | Hayes Lane | 26-Nov 1915 | Army | | Y | Y | 08 Jun 1917 | 29 |
| Cole | William J | Hayes | | Hayes Common | 11-Sep 1914 | Army | Y | | | | |
| Cook | Cecil B | Hayes | Y | Hayes Road | | RNAS | | Y | Y | 20 Aug 1917 | 18 |

| Surname | Forename | Home | Hayes Family | House | Report Date | Service | Bible Entry | Hayes Roll of Honour | On Hayes War Memorial | Date Died CWGC | Age at death |
|---|---|---|---|---|---|---|---|---|---|---|---|
| Cope | Sydney | | | | 14-Aug 1914 | | | | | | |
| Cowan | James | Hayes | | Meadow Way | | Army | Y | | | | |
| Dance | James | Hayes | Y | Baston Farm Cottages | | | Y | | | | |
| Davis | Claud | Hayes | | Pickhurst Mead | 28-May 1915 | | | | | | |
| Devas | Geoffrey C | WW | Y | Hartfield | 1915 | Army | | | | | |
| Devenish | Lennox N | Hayes | | Pickhurst Manor | 17-Dec 1915 | | | | | | |
| Dodd | Charles | Hayes | | The Village | | | Y | | | | |
| Dodd | Victor | Hayes | | The Village | 06-Nov 1914 | Army | Y | | | | |
| Farnham | Edward J | Hayes | Y | Brewery Cottages | 04-Sep 1914 | Army | | | | | |
| Field | Arthur | Keston | Y | Woodside | 11-Sep 1914 | | | | | | |
| Fossey | Leonard A | Hayes | | Clematis House | 30-Apr 1915 | | Y | | | | |
| Friend | Mark | Hayes | Y | Wood Cottages | | | Y | | | | |
| Frost | Arthur C | Hayes | Y | Glebe House | 1914 | Army | | Y | Y | 25 Sep 1915 | 18 |
| Frost | James J | Hayes | Y | Glebe House | 08-Jan 1915 | Army | | Y | Y | 07 Jul 1916 | 21 |
| Gamble | William | Hayes | | | 14-Aug 1914 | | | | | | |
| Garrard | Percy | Hayes | | Alpha, George Lane | Regular | Army | | Y | Y | 18 Sep 1918 | 38 |
| George | Arthur | Hayes | | Pickhurst Farm | | | | | | | |
| Gilbert | Charles | Hayes | Y | Thatched Cottages | | | Y | | | | |
| Gilbert | Edward H | Hayes | Y | Thatched Cottages | 14-Apr 1916 | | Y | | | | |
| Gilbert | George | Hayes | Y | Thatched Cottages | | | Y | | | | |
| Gilbert | Leonard | Hayes | Y | Thatched Cottages | | | Y | | | | |
| Gilbert | P Ronald | Hayes | Y | Thatched Cottages | | | Y | | | | |
| Gilbert | Walter | Hayes | Y | Thatched Cottages | | | Y | | | | |
| Goldsmith | Charles | Hayes | Y | Warren Cottages | 06-Nov 1914 | RM | | Y | Y | 30 Apr 1915 | 24 |
| Goldsmith | Edward | Hayes | Y | Warren Cottages | 13-Aug 1915 | Army | Y | | | | |
| Goldsmith | Leonard S | Hayes | Y | Warren Cottages | 04-Sep 1914 | Army | Y | | | | |

| Surname | Forename | Home | Hayes Family | House | Report Date | Service | Bible Entry | Hayes Roll of Honour | On Hayes War Memorial | Date Died CWGC | Age at death |
|---|---|---|---|---|---|---|---|---|---|---|---|
| Goldsmith | Robert | Hayes | Y | Warren Cottages | | | Y | | | | |
| Goode | John | Hayes | | | | | Y | | | | |
| Grandfield | James | Hayes | Y | Hayes Place | | RFC | Y | | | | |
| Hambro | Charles | Hayes | Y | Pickhurst Mead | | | Y | | | | |
| Hambro | Harold | Hayes | Y | Hayes Place | | | Y | | | | |
| Hambro | Ronald Olaf | Hayes | Y | Hayes Place | | | Y | | | | |
| Hardy | Charles | WW | | Park Farm | 06-Nov 1914 | Army | | Y | Y | 13 Oct 1915 | |
| Hardy | Percy | WW | | Park Farm | | Army | | Y | Y | 23 Aug 1918 | |
| Harris | Norman | Hayes | Y | White House | | Navy | | Y | Y | 26 Nov 1914 | 16 |
| Harris | William G | Hayes | Y | Hayes Court Stables | 27-Nov 1915 | Army | | | | 07 Oct 1916 | 25 |
| Harrod | Charles E | Hayes | Y | Spilman's Grove | 19-Nov 1915 | Army | Y | | | | |
| Hawkings | Claude | Hayes | Y | Greenways | 14-Aug 1914 | | | | | | |
| Hawkings | Wilfred | Hayes | Y | Greenways | 06-Nov 1914 | Army | Y | | | | |
| Hawkins | George | Hayes | | 3 Station Road | 27-Oct 1915 | | | | | | |
| Hill | George M | Hayes | Y | | 21-Aug 1914 | Army | | | | | |
| Holroyde | John S | Hayes | Y | Hayes Road | | RFC | | Y | Y | 10 May 1917 | |
| Hold | Frank | Hayes | | Hayes Lane | 26-Jun 1916 | | | | | | |
| Huxley | Ernest | Hayes | Y | Woodland Cottage | | | Y | | | | |
| Huxley | Sidney | Hayes | Y | Woodland Cottage | | | Y | | | | |
| Jackson | Francis | Hayes | | | | | Y | | | | |
| Jagger | Frank | Hayes | | | | | Y | | | | |
| James | Edwin A | Hayes | Y | Tithe Cottage | | Army | | | | 23 Oct 1918 | 28 |
| James | Wallace A | Hayes | Y | | 17-Mar 1916 | | | | | | |
| Janes | Herbert | Hayes | Y | St Mary Cottages | | | Y | | | | |
| Jones | Leslie | Hayes | | Hayes Road | | | | | | 05 May 1916 | 24 |
| Keech | Edward | Hayes | Y | Spilman's Grove | | | Y | | | | |

| Surname | Forename | Home | Hayes Family | House | Report Date | Service | Bible Entry | Hayes Roll of Honour | On Hayes War Memorial | Date Died CWGC | Age at death |
|---|---|---|---|---|---|---|---|---|---|---|---|
| Keech | Frank | Hayes | Y | Spilman's Grove | | | Y | | | | |
| Keech | Simon H | Hayes | Y | Spilman's Grove | 06-Nov 1914 | Army | Y | | | | |
| Knights | Thomas H | Hayes | Y | Pleasant View | | | Y | | | | |
| Knights | Reginald | Hayes | | Glencot | | | Y | | | | |
| Lander | William H | Hayes | Y | Brewery Cottages | 04-Jun 1915 | Army | | | | 18 Nov 1916 | 35 |
| Lane | Reginald D | Hayes | Y | Greenways Cottage | 21-Feb 1917 | Army | | Y | Y | 30 Nov 1917 | 19 |
| Lane | Thomas | Hayes | Y | Thatched Cottages | | Army | Y | | | | |
| Lane | William | Hayes | Y | Thatched Cottages | | Army | Y | | | | |
| Langridge | Frederick | Hayes | Y | Hayes Place Lodge | | | Y | | | | |
| Langstone | Sidney E | Hayes | Y | Pickhurst Mead Lodge | 06-Nov 1914 | Army | | | | | |
| Lee-Warner | Harry G | Hayes | Y | Hawthorndene | Regular | Army | | | | | |
| Legge | Walter H | Hayes | Y | The Nest | | RFC | | Y | Y | 11 Feb 1917 | 33 |
| Mahon | Brian M | | | | 28-Aug 1914 | Navy | Y | | | | |
| Maidment | Robert | Hayes | Y | Hayes Place Farm | 17-Mar 1916 | | Y | | | | |
| Mann | T B D | Hayes | Y | Hayes Grove Cottage | Regular | Army | | | | | |
| Marchant | Francis GW | Keston | Y | Woodside | 1915 | RFC | | Y | Y | 22 Oct 1916 | 19 |
| Marden | James | WW | Y | Coney Hall Farm | 05-Jan 1917 | | Y | | | | |
| Marriage | John | Hayes | Y | Glebe House Stables | | | Y | | | | |
| Masham | Arthur | Hayes | | | | | Y | | | | |
| Masham | Howard E | Hayes | | Alpha, George Lane | 19-Nov 1915 | | | | | | |
| Meade | Edward C | Hayes | | Spilman's Grove | 18-Dec 1914 | Army | | | | | |
| Mills | Ernest | | Y | | 06-Nov 1914 | Army | | | | | |
| Mills | James | | Y | | 06-Nov 1914 | Army | | | | | |
| Mills | John | | Y | | 06-Nov 1914 | Navy | | | | | |
| Mills | Robert | Hayes | Y | Gadsden Gardens | 06-Nov 1914 | Army | | | | | |
| Mitchell | Alfred G | Hayes | Y | Rose Cottage | 18-Dec 1914 | Army | Y | | | | |

| Surname | Forename | Home | Hayes Family | House | Report Date | Service | Bible Entry | Hayes Roll of Honour | On Hayes War Memorial | Date Died CWGC | Age at death |
|---|---|---|---|---|---|---|---|---|---|---|---|
| Mitchell | Herbert | Hayes | Y | | | | Y | | | | |
| Mitchell | Peter | Hayes | Y | | | | Y | | | | |
| Mitchell | Richard | Hayes | Y | Rose Cottage | 18-Dec 1914 | Army | | | | | |
| Mitchell | William | Hayes | Y | Rose Cottage | 18-Dec 1914 | Army | Y | | | | |
| Moore | Arthur | Hayes | | Myrtle Cottage | | | Y | | | | |
| Moore | Harold | Hayes | Y | | | | Y | | | | |
| Morris | Norman H | Hayes | Y | Five Elms | 06-Nov 1914 | Army | | | | | |
| Nash | Alec | Hayes | | | 14-Aug 1914 | Navy | | | | | |
| Ord | Robert | Hayes | | | 14-Aug 1914 | | | | | | |
| Oswick | Cecil | Hayes | Y | Greenways Lodge | 24-Dec 1915 | | | | | | |
| Parkinson | William H | Hayes | | Hayes Court Stables | 24-Dec 1915 | | | | | | |
| Pascoe | Richard | Hayes | Y | Baston Manor Lodge | 06-Nov 1914 | Army | Y | | | | |
| Pascoe | William | Hayes | Y | Baston Manor Lodge | May 1915 | Navy | Y | | | | |
| Pattenden | Albert T | Hayes | Y | Baston Manor | 22-Jan 1915 | | Y | | | | |
| Pattenden | Edward J | Hayes | Y | Redgate Cottage | 24-Dec 1915 | Army | Y | | | | |
| Pattenden | Harry | Hayes | Y | Bath Cottage | | | Y | | | | |
| Payne | John O | | | | | Army | | Y | Y | 25 Apr 1915 | |
| Peagram | George | | | | 21-Aug 1914 | Army | | | | | |
| Pearce | Alfred | Hayes | Y | Glebe View | | | Y | | | | |
| Pearce | Robert | Hayes | Y | Glebe View | | | Y | | | | |
| Pennington | William | Hayes | | | 14-Aug 1914 | | | | | | |
| Plant | Frederic G | Hayes | Y | School House | 06-Nov 1914 | Army | | Y | Y | 25 Sep 1915 | 22 |
| Plant | Ronald G | Hayes | Y | School House | 06-Nov 1914 | Army | Y | | | | |
| Plant | Harold W | Hayes | Y | School House | | Army | Y | | | | |
| Porter | Harold | Hayes | | | | | Y | | | | |
| Potter | Benjamin | Hayes | Y | Brewery Cottages | | Army | | Y | Y | 03 May 1917 | 23 |

| Surname | Forename | Home | Hayes Family | House | Report Date | Service | Bible Entry | Hayes Roll of Honour | On Hayes War Memorial | Date Died CWGC | Age at death |
|---|---|---|---|---|---|---|---|---|---|---|---|
| Potter | John | Hayes | | Brewery Cottages | | | Y | | | | |
| Price | James A | WW | | Warren Wood | 28-Aug 1914 | Army | | | | | |
| Price | William F | Hayes | Y | Hillside Cottages | | | Y | | | | |
| Robbins | Frederick J | Hayes | Y | Tithe Cottage | 15-Nov 1915 | Army | | Y | Y | 15 Sep 1916 | 20 |
| Robbins | George | Hayes | Y | Alders Cottage | | | Y | | | | |
| Robjant | John A | Hayes | Y | Nest Cottage | 26-Nov 1915 | Navy | | | | | |
| Robson | Arthur J | Hayes | Y | Simpson's Cottages | 06-Nov 1914 | Army | Y | | | | |
| Rust | Edward W | Hayes | Y | Elleray | 28-Aug 1914 | Army | Y | Y | Y | 23 Jul 1915 | 21 |
| Rust | John W | Hayes | Y | Elleray | | | Y | | | | |
| Rust | Robert F | Hayes | Y | Elleray | 11-Sep 1914 | | Y | | | | |
| Rust | Roland E | Hayes | Y | Elleray | 11-Sep 1914 | Army | | | | | |
| Sands | Percy | Hayes | Y | St Mary's Cottages | | Army | Y | Y | Y | 11 Apr 1917 | 32 |
| Saunders | Benjamin T | Hayes | | Elmhurst | 04-Jun 1915 | | Y | | | | |
| Skinner | Douglas H | Hayes | Y | Ash Lodge | 06-Nov 1914 | Army | | Y | Y | 16 Jul 1916 | 24 |
| Skinner | Duncan | Hayes | | Ash Lodge | | | Y | | | | |
| Smith | Arthur W | WW | | Warren Wood | 28-Aug 1914 | Army | | | | | |
| Smith | James | Hayes | Y | 2 Simpson's Cottages | 17-Dec 1915 | | Y | Y | | | |
| Smith | Julian M | WW | Y | The Warren | 04-Aug 1914 | Army | | Y | Y | 7 Sep 1914 | 27 |
| Snow | Geoffrey | WW | Y | Prickley Wood | | | Y | | | | |
| Staplehurst | John H | Hayes | | | 21-Mar 1916 | | | | | | |
| Stiles | Thomas P | Hayes | | | | | Y | | | | |
| Taylor | Arthur V | Hayes | Y | Hayes Cottage | 27-Nov 1914 | Army | | | | | |
| Taylor | John C | Hayes | | Hayes Place | 06-Nov 1914 | Army | | | | | |
| Thomson | John A | Hayes | | Woodgrange | 10-Dec 1915 | | | | | | |
| Tidbury | Edward | WW | | Coney Hill Lodge | | | Y | | | | |
| Tidbury | Frederick | Hayes | | Hayes Place | | | Y | | | | |

| Surname | Forename | Home | Hayes Family | House | Report Date | Service | Bible Entry | Hayes Roll of Honour | On Hayes War Memorial | Date Died CWGC | Age at death |
|---|---|---|---|---|---|---|---|---|---|---|---|
| Timms | Henry Arthur | Hayes | Y | 2 Hillside Cottages | 16-Jul 1915 | | Y | | | | |
| Tombs | H T | WW | | Warren Gardens | 04-Sep 1914 | Army | | | Y | | |
| Torrens | Attwood A | Hayes | Y | Baston Manor | 01-Feb 1915 | Army | | Y | Y | 08 Dec 1916 | 42 |
| Tulett | William A | Keston | Y | | | Army | | Y | Y | 17 Sep 1915 | 19 |
| Tuson | Arthur W | Surrey | | | | Army | | Y | Y | 01 Dec 1917 | 32 |
| White | Edward | Hayes | Y | Whites Cottages | | | Y | | | | |
| Whitehead | Philip J | Hayes | Y | Spilman's Grove | 17-Dec 1915 | | Y | | | | |
| Wilding | Joseph | Hayes | | | | | Y | | | | |
| Williams | Charles J | Hayes | Y | Flint Cottage | 14-Jan 1916 | | Y | | | | |
| Williams | Harold D | Hayes | Y | Spilman's Grove | 20-Nov 1914 | Army | | | | 20 Dec 1920 | 26 |
| Williams | Harold L | Hayes | Y | Hawthorndene | | Army | Y | | | | |
| Williams | Henry V | Hayes | Y | Glencot | | RNAS | | Y | Y | 26 Nov 1917 | 35 |
| Williams | Herbert W | Hayes | Y | Mayes Cottage | | Navy | | Y | Y | 09 Jul 1917 | 29 |
| Wood | Albert | Hayes | | Tithe Cottage, Pickhurst | 03-Dec 1915 | | Y | | | | |
| Wood | Charles F | Hayes | Y | | | | Y | | | | |
| Wood | Charles H | Hayes | Y | Glebe House | 06-Nov 1914 | Army | | Y | Y | 25 Aug 1916 | 21 |
| Wood | John F | Hayes | Y | Tithe Cottage, Pickhurst | | Army | | Y | Y | 17 Nov 1916 | 36 |
| Wright | Amos | WW | | Warren Wood Stables | 22-Jan 1915 | | | | | | |
| Wynn | Edward W | Hayes | Y | Simpson's Cottages | | | Y | | | | |

# Additional information from CWGC for casualties not recorded in *Hayes in World War 1* by Jean Wilson

**Calder,** Private, Frederick G/19974, 11 Bn Royal Sussex Regt transferred to (424679) 125 Coy Labour Corps 10 December 1917. Age 28. Son of Mr and Mrs William Calder of Springfield Woodlea Road, Worthing. Born at Hayes, Kent. Buried Bucquoy Road Cemetery, Ficheux, Pas de Calais, France.

**Croft,** Gunner A, 163409, 'B' Bty 291 Bde Royal Field Artillery, 8 August 1918. Age 35. Son of Frederick and Louise Croft of Hayes, Kent; husband of Blanche A E Croft of "Bassingbourne", Church Path, North Finchley, Middx. Buried Montigny Communal Cemetery Extension, Somme, France.

**Devas,** Lieutenant, Bertrand Ward, 2nd Bn Suffolk Regiment. 13 November 1916. Age 34. Son of Charles Stanton Devas; husband of Elizabeth Helen Devas of Hayes Grove Cottage, Hayes Common, Kent. Barrister-at-Law (Inner Temple). Buried Luke Copse British Cemetery, Puisieux, Pas de Calais France.

**Frost,** Private Montague Clarence G/1360 8 Bn Queen's Own (Royal West Surrey Regiment) 26 September 1915. Age 18. Son of H J and Eleanor Frost of Ringwood, Station Road, Hayes, Kent. Named on Loos Memorial, France.

**Jones,** Lance Corporal, Leslie Oscar, 1659, 21 Bn London Regiment (First Surrey Rifles) 5 May 1916. Age 24. Buried Cabaret-Rouge British Cemetery, Souchez, Pas de Calais, France.

**Linning,** Major (Quartermaster) John, I Bn Black Watch (Royal Highlanders) 16 September 1914. Age 50. Son of John and Janet Linning; husband of Lillian Ann Linning of Glencarn, Pickhurst Lane, Hayes, Kent. Buried Perth (Wellshill) Cemetery, Perthshire, United Kingdom.

**Manchip,** Private, Thomas Alexander 62843, 20 Bn Royal Fusiliers. 25 April 1917. Son of Thomas Alexander and Elizabeth Manchip of Deddington, Oxon; husband of Grace Lilian Manchip of 89 Hayes Road, Bromley. Arras Memorial Pas de Calais, France.

**McDonald,** Captain (Adjt.) Albert William MC, mentioned in Despatches, 3rd Regiment South African Infantry. Died of wounds, received at the battle of Menin Road 21 September 1917. Age 42. Son of Donald and Elizabeth McDonald; husband of Mary Goodger McDonald of Colne Cottage, Iver, Bucks. Born Hayes, Kent. Buried Nine Elms British Cemetery, Popeeringe, West-Vlaanderen, Belgium.

# Appendix 2: New Shops and Businesses in Hayes in the 1930s

## Station Approach - West Side

| Number | Name | Business | Approx date |
|---|---|---|---|
| 12 | National Provincial Bank Ltd. | Banking | 1934 |
| 14 | Charles H Wheeler | Tobacconist | 1934 |
| 16 | T J Treves Brown | Chemist | 1934 |
| 18 | J H Dewhurst Ltd. | Butcher | 1935 |
| 20 | South Suburban Co-op Society | Grocer | 1935 |
| 22 | South Suburban Co-op Society | Butcher | 1935 |
| 24 | West Kent Electric Co. Ltd. | Electrical Engineers | 1935 |
| 26 | Florence Louise | Milliner | 1934 |
| 28 | Jackson's (Croydon) Ltd. | Boot Repairer | 1934 |
| 30 | George Lavington | Radio Dealer | 1934 |
| 32 | M A Ray & Sons | Builders' Merchant | 1933 |
| 34 | Leslie Cuckney | Draper | 1933 |
| 36 | Mac Fisheries Ltd | Fishmonger | 1934 |
| 38 | William Arthur Pitt | Baker | 1933 |
| 40 | Belson & Co. Ltd. | House Furnisher | 1933 |
| 42 | Express Dairy Co. Ltd. | Dairy | 1933 |
| 44 | Stevenson & Rush Ltd. | Provision Merchant | 1933 |
| 46 | Hylda & John | Café | 1933 |
| 48 | Killick & Knight | Auctioneer | 1933 |
| 50 | E.W. Jones | Boot Repairer | 1933 |
| 52 | Irene Ponting | Draper | 1933 |
| 54 | J E Francis | Hairdresser | 1933 |
| 56 | The Flower Shop | Florist | 1933 |
| 58 | Ferdinand Straub | Hairdresser | 1934 |

## Railway Station Shops

| Number | Name | Business | Approx date |
|---|---|---|---|
| 60 | Arthur Ray & Co | Estate Agent | 1935 |
| 62 | Hy J Rough. | Tobacconist | 1933 |
| | W H Smith & Sons | Newsagent | 1935 |
| | Sage Shoe Repairing Service | Shoe Repairer | 1936 |
| 64 | Rickett Smith & Co. Ltd. | Coal Merchant | 1935 |
| 66 | Nathaniel Pegg & Co Ltd. | Coal Merchant | 1933 |
| 68 | F C Smith | Fruiterer & Dining Rooms | 1933 |
| 70 | F C Smith | Café | 1933 |
| 72 | J & R Killick Ltd. | Builder | 1935 |

## Bourne Way

| Number | Name | Business | Approx date |
|---|---|---|---|
| 2 | A Moore & H Chetham | Grocer & General Store | 1935 |
| 4 | Thomas Howson | Radio Engineer | 1934 |
| 6 | Arthur T Staples | Hosier | 1934 |
| 8 | Hayes Cleaners | Dyers & Cleaners | 1935 |

| Number | Name | Business | Approx date |
|---|---|---|---|
| 10 | E Wilder (Miss) | Baker & Cooked Meats | 1935 |
| 12 | F T Speakman | Hardware Merchant | 1934 |

## Station Approach – East Side

| Number | Name | Business | Approx date |
|---|---|---|---|
| 1-3 | R Surridge's | Garage & Service Station | 1932 |
| 5 | T Latham & Co. Ltd. | Confectioner | 1938 |
| 7-9 | F W Woolworth & Co. Ltd. | General Store | 1938 |
| 11 | J Sears & Co. | Boot & Shoe Dealer | 1938 |
| 13 | | | |
| 15 | Home & Colonial Stores Ltd. | Grocer | 1935 |
| 17 | Eastman & Sons | Dyers & Cleaners | 1937 |
| 19 | Norgates Ltd. | Gents Outfitter | 1936 |
| 21 | T Walton (London) Ltd. | Fruiterer | 1935 |
| 23 | Sanders Brothers (Stores) Ltd. | Grocer | 1935 |
| 25 | Bata Shoe Co. Ltd. | Boot Retailer | 1935 |
| 27 | Jubilee Cleaners Ltd. | Dyers & Cleaners | 1935 |
| 29 | William G Seager | Hardware Store | 1932 |
| 31 | Leonard A Pullen | Wool Store | 1933 |
| 33 | Walter Terry | Ladies' Hairdresser | 1933 |
| 35 | R J Smith & Sons | Builders' Merchant | 1933 |
| 37 | H B Hicking | Cycle Dealer | 1932 |
| 39 | Walters (Purveyors) Ltd. | Butcher | 1932 |
| 41 | Barclays Bank Ltd. | Banking | 1933 |
| 43 | Ernest W Griffiths | Café | 1935 |
| 45 | David Greig Ltd. | Provisions Merchant | 1933 |
| 47 | White's Fruit Stores | Fruiterer | 1934 |
| 49 | J Rumsey & Son. | Chemist | 1932 |
| 51 | H C Enright | Confectioner & Post Office | 1933 |
| 53 | United Dairies London Ltd. | Dairy | 1932 |
| 55 | Westminster Bank Ltd. | Banking | 1933 |
| 57 | Hugh F Thoburn Ltd. | Estate Agent | 1933 |

## Premier Parade, Hayes Street

| Number | Name | Business | Approx date |
|---|---|---|---|
| 18 | W H Cullen Ltd | Grocer | 1933 |
| 20 | James R Bane | Confectioner | 1935 |
| 22 | H A Doerr | Decorators | 1938 |
| 24 | Henry Boot & Sons Ltd. | Estate Office | 1934 |
| 26 | Minnie Nicholl (Mrs) | Home Made Cakes | 1937 |
| 28 | Edgar Matthews | Butcher | 1935 |
| 30 | Stanley Hider | Fruiterer | 1934 |
| 32 | Jennifer | Ladies' Hairdresser | 1937 |
| 34 | Smith & Boylan | Boot Repairer | 1934 |
| 36 | D M Hunt (Mrs) | Domestic Stores | 1935 |
| 38 | C A Smallbone Ltd. | Wines & Spirits | 1933 |
| 40 | Edith May Moore (Mrs) | Ladies' Hairdresser | 1934 |

# Appendix 3: Origin of Hayes Road Names

| Road Name | Date Approved Or in use | Estate/ Builder | Origin |
|---|---|---|---|
| Alexander Close | 11/1932 | Boot | After Sir Everard Alexander Hambro |
| Appledore Close | 1960s | Howard | After a Kentish Town |
| Barnet Wood Road | 2/1924 | | Leading to Barnet Wood |
| Barnhill Avenue | c.1964 | Howard | Named after house called Barnhill |
| Baston Manor Road | | | Leading to Baston Manor |
| Baston Road | 1/1931 | Various | Was called Keston Road, then Common Road |
| Beadon Road | 2/1927 | Norman | After Charlotte Beadon, who married George Norman in 1792 |
| Beckenham Lane | | | Name given to the road from parish boundary with Beckenham and junction with Hayes Street |
| Benenden Green | 1960s | Howard | After a Kentish Town |
| Bidborough Close | 1960s | Howard | After a Kentish Town |
| Boughton Avenue | 4/1950 | BBC | After a Kentish village |
| Bourne Vale | 6/1932 | Boot | Proposed as Valley Road, developers had suggested Boethar Avenue (early English for Boot). Refers to the occasional stream or Bourne that flows through the area |
| Bourne Way | 11/1931 | Various | Had been Station Road from 1882 and changed to prevent confusion with Station Road, West Wickham and elsewhere |
| Brenchley Close | 1960s | Howard | After a Kentish Town |
| Briar Gardens | 8/1933 | Spencer | Unknown |
| Broad Oaks Way | 1/1936 | | Originally approved as Broad Oaks Avenue in 9/1936 from line of oak trees |
| Burwood Avenue | C1937/38 | | Unknown |
| Cameron Road | <3/1933 | | From Archibald Cameron Norman |
| Cecil Way | 11/1932 | Boot | After Lord Sackville Cecil |
| Chatham Avenue | 11/1931 | Boot | After William Pitt, the Earl of Chatham |
| Cheriton Avenue | 1960s | Howard | After a Kentish Town |
| Cherry Walk | 11/1932 | Boot | Thought to be named after a walk in the garden of Hayes Place |
| Chilham Way | 4/1950 | BBC | After a Kentish village |
| Church Road | | | At one time the name for the north section of Baston Road from St Mary's Cottages to Pickhurst Lane |
| Club Gardens | 11/1931 | Boot | Name for the road leading from Hayes Lane to the area set aside for a club, now Victory Social Club |
| Common Road | | | See Baston Road |
| Constance Crescent | 3/1936 | | Possibly named after the daughter of builder Mr Harris |
| Courtlands Avenue | 9/1935 | Spencer | Was to be called Manor Road in July 1935 but changed to Courtlands Avenue and Hilldown Road |
| Cornford Close | 1960s | Howard | |
| Cranbrook Close | 4/1950 | BBC | After a Kentish village |
| Crest Road | 4/1934 | | Thoburn originally wanted 'The Crest' indicating the top of the hill |
| Croydon Road | 1/1931 | Various | The name of the road between Farnborough, West Wickham and Croydon; previously referred to as 'Croydon to Farnborough Road'. |
| Culverstone Close | 1960s | Howard | After a Kentish Town |
| Dartmouth Road | 11/1931 | Boot | Approved as Dartmouth Gardens, named after the 3rd Earl of Dartmouth (Viscount Lewisham) who owned and lived at Hayes Place. |

| Road Name | Date Approved Or in use | Estate/ Builder | Origin |
|---|---|---|---|
| Dene Close | <3/1933 | Spencer | Related to an early field name |
| Eastry Avenue | 4/1950 | BBC | After a Kentish Village |
| East Way | 11/1931 | Boot | One of the four proposed 'compass named' roads in the central area of Bourne Vale |
| Elvington Green | 1960s | Howard | After a Kentish Town |
| Everard Avenue | 11/1932 | Boot | After Sir Everard Alexander Hambro |
| Farleigh Avenue | 4/1950 | BBC | After a Kentish village |
| Five Elms Road | | | After Elm Cottage which changed its name to Five Elms Cottage between 1861 and 1871. The road name was in use 11/1934. |
| Forge Close | 1964 | | Named after Forge House that was built on land adjacent to the old Forge |
| Furze Lane | | | Hayes Hill Road was called Furze Lane when the Tiepigs Lane extension was created in 1831. The name was still in use in 1927-28. |
| George Lane | c.1927 | HPC | Name taken from the George Inn, first part of the Lane was Spilman's Grove but when extended for Hookfield Cottages the new name was applied to complete lane. |
| Georgian Close | Early 1960s | | Extension of George Lane |
| Glebe House Drive | 3/1933 | Morells | Commemorating the Glebe House estate |
| Goodhart Way | 7/1930 | Langley | After the Goodhart family who owned the Langley Park estate |
| Grove Close | 5/1931 | | Part of the grounds of Hayes Grove in Prestons Road |
| Hambro Avenue | 11/1932 | Boot | After Sir Everard Alexander Hambro |
| Hawthorndene Close | 1962 | | In grounds of former house called Hawthorndene |
| Hawthorndene Road | 1962 | | As above |
| Hayes Chase | 9/1931 | Langley | |
| Hayes Close | 10/1932 | | |
| Hayesford Park Drive | 1960 | Howard | The principal road in Hayesford Park estate, preserves the name of ford which existed and gave name to the area in Victorian times. |
| Hayes Garden | 9/1931 | | Name of existing nursery |
| Hayes Hill | 8/1928 | Thoburn | After the area, name predates the development |
| Hayes Hill Road | By 1931 | Spencer | The road leading to Hayes Hill |
| Hayes Lane, | <1500 | Various | Principal ancient road |
| Hayes Mead Road | 1930 | | Was called 'The Mead' and 'Hayes Mead' in 1929 and Hayes Mead Road by 1930; name confirmed by Beckenham Council in 1938. |
| Hayes Road | c.1895 | | |
| Hayes Street | | | Known as the Street in Victorian times; from 1938 applied to road from Chatham Avenue to cottage south of the Old Church Schools. |
| Hayes Wood Avenue | 3/1933 | Morells | Unknown |
| Hazelmere Way | 9/1939 | HP Cook | After a house called 'Hazelmere |
| Heath Rise | 5/1939 | HP Cook | Unknown |
| | | | |
| Hilldown Road | 9/1935 | Spencer | Unknown |
| Hillside Lane | | | From the hill leading to and from the common |
| Holland Close | | Warren Wood | After Holland Way |

| Road Name | Date Approved Or in use | Estate/ Builder | Origin |
|---|---|---|---|
| Holland Way | 3/1936 | Warren Wood | Originally proposed 'Newland Avenue' and approved by Bromley BC in 11/1935. Renamed 'Holland Way' at the request of the builders. It is suggested that the builder was part of the Dutch Vanden Bergh family. |
| Hurst Close | 7/1933 | Spencer | Unknown |
| Hurstdene Avenue | 4/1933 | Spencer | Unknown |
| Husseywell Crescent | 11/1932 | Boot | After 'Hussey Well' in Pickhurst Lane |
| Kechill Gardens | 11/1931 | Boot | After the Kechill family who were land owners in Hayes during the 15th Century |
| Kemsing Close | 4/1950 | BBC | After a Kentish village |
| Kingsdown Way | 4/1950 | BBC | After a Kentish village |
| Knowlton Green | 1960s | Howard | After a Kentish town |
| Langley Way | 7/1928 | Langley | Commemorating Langley Park estate |
| Larkfield Close | 4/1950 | BBC | After a Kentish village |
| Letchworth Drive | By 1962 | Howard | Named by builder Donald Howard after his grandfather Ebenezer Howard, creator of Letchworth and Welwyn Garden cities |
| Leybourne Close | 1960s | Howard | After a Kentish town |
| Linkfield | 5/1939 | HP Cook | Probably named as the road that linked the Cook development with Meadway |
| Malling Way | 4/1950 | BBC | After a Kentish village |
| Mapleton Close | 1960s | Howard | After a place in Kent |
| Marden Avenue | 4/1950 | BBC | After a Kentish village |
| Matfield Close | 1960s | Howard | After a place in Kent |
| Mead Way | 11/1931 | Boot | Probably so called because constructed through open meadows |
| Mereworth Close | 1960s | Howard | After a place in Kent |
| Montcalm Close | 11/1931 | Boot | Tenuous connection with Hayes and the Pitts; named from the French General at the battle of Quebec. |
| Mounthurst Road | 3/1936 | | A road that rises towards the top of Pickhurst |
| New Farm Avenue | 5/1935 | | Commemorating New Farm |
| New Road | C1760 | | Name given to the road that William Pitt diverted away from Hayes Place. Name covered the road from junction with Hayes Street and roughly where Bourne Vale enters Pickhurst Lane. Name changed to Pickhurst Lane in the early 1930s. |
| Northbourne | 12/1931 | Boot | Close to the Bourne stream |
| Oakmead Avenue | 11/1931 | Boot | Unknown |
| Pembury Close | 4/1950 | BBC | After a Kentish village |
| Penshurst Green | 1960s | Howard | After a place in Kent |
| Pickhurst Green | 4/1936 | | Road borders the southern edge of Pickhurst Green |
| Pickhurst Green Road | | | Thought to be the old name used to describe the track / road from Tiepigs Lane to Pickhurst Green and beyond |
| Pickhurst Lane | 4/1932 | Various | Comprises New Road, Pickhurst Green Road and Beckenham Lane; consolidated and in use by 1932 |
| Pickhurst Mead | 3/1936 | | After the house 'Pickhurst Mead |
| Pickhurst Park | c.1938 | | From the estate name |
| Pickhurst Rise | 4/1926 | Langley | From the area 'Pickhurst' |
| Pittsmead Avenue | 11/1931 | Boot | After William Pitt |
| Pondfield Road | 2/1928 | | Pond in the estate |
| Prestons Road | | | After the Preston family who lived at Hayes Court from 1894 to 1917 |

| Road Name | Date Approved Or in use | Estate/ Builder | Origin |
|---|---|---|---|
| Prickley Wood | c.1953 | | After the house 'Prickley Wood' |
| Redgate Drive | 3/1938 | | After the house called 'Redgates' |
| Ridgeway | 6/1931 | | Unknown, may be geographical |
| Sackville Avenue | 11/1932 | Boots | After Lord Sackville Cecil who lived at the Oast House |
| Sandiland Crescent | 2/1936 | Warren Wood | Suggested as an area in the Netherlands. |
| Sedgewood Close | c.1979 | | Unknown |
| Shoreham Way | 4/1950 | BBC | After a Kentish village |
| School Road | | | Early name for the section of road by the Old Church Schools; became part of Hayes Street and West Common Road. |
| Socket Lane | | | Derivation unknown; old farm track name in excess of 200 years old. |
| Southbourne | 11/1931 | Boot | Close to the Bourne stream |
| South Way | 11/1931 | Boot | One of the four proposed 'compass named' roads in the central area of Bourne Vale |
| Speldhurst Close | 1960s | Howard | After a place in Kent |
| Spilman's Grove | 15th Century | | Early name for the first part of George Lane; went into disuse in the late 1930s. |
| Stanhope Avenue | 11/1932 | Boot | After Charles, Lord Viscount Mahon, later 3rd Earl Stanhope who married Hester Pitt |
| Stanstead Close | 1960s | Howard | |
| Station Approach | 7/1931 | Various | Was part of Station Road but renamed in 1931 to prevent confusion with West Wickham road of the same name |
| Station Hill | | | Road built about 1884 for access to the common from the Railway Station |
| Station Road | c.1882 | Taylor | Original name for Bourne Way and Station Approach |
| Stone Road | 6/1933 | | Possibly after Sibella or Emma Stone, who married into the Norman family |
| Stuart Avenue | 11/1932 | Boot | After the Stuart sisters who lived in Hayes and were connected to the Hambro family |
| The Avenue | 11/1928 | Langley | Unknown |
| The Green | 11/1932 | Boot | Planned open space on the estate |
| The Knoll | 9/1931 | | Unknown origin |
| Tiepigs Lane | | | Unknown origin – ancient |
| Trevor Close | 3/1936 | | After Charlotte Trevor who lived at Warren Wood or after the son of the builder Mr Harris |
| Warren Road | 1/1931 | | After The Warren and Warren Wood houses |
| West Common Road | 1/1931 | Various | |
| Westland Drive | 10/1936 | Warren Wood | Originally Dale Rise in 1935 but changed to Westland Drive; Dutch influence |
| West Way | 11/1931 | Boot | See East Way |
| Wickham Chase | | Langley | |
| Wolfe Close | 11/1931 | | General Wolfe defeated Montcalm at battle of Quebec. |
| Woodlea Drive | Late 1930s | | |
| Workhouse Lane | | | Lane to Parish Workhouse, later West Common Road |

BBC = Bromley Borough Council

Grateful thanks to Laurie Mack for permission to use his research on the origin of the roads, which forms the basis of this appendix.

# Appendix 4: Casualties in World War II

## Civilian Casualties

| Name | | Age | Date died | Where died | Lived at | Hayes Roll of Honour |
|---|---|---|---|---|---|---|
| Olga | Bowman | 29 | 24-Oct-1940 | 6 Cherry Walk, Hayes | 6 Cherry Walk | No |
| Ronald | Bowman | 29 | 24-Oct-1940 | 6 Cherry Walk, Hayes | 6 Cherry Walk | No |
| Stanley | Bowman | 32 | 24-Oct-1940 | 6 Cherry Walk, Hayes | 6 Cherry Walk | No |
| Michael John | Brooker | 10 | 17-Sep-1940 | At Sea | 189 Bourne Vale | Yes |
| Harry | Bruck | 7 | 26-Oct-1940 | 216 Hayes Lane | 216 Hayes Lane | Yes |
| Harry John | Carden | 29 | 20-Apr-1941 | Old Palace School, Poplar, London | 7 Mounthurst Road | No |
| Robert Morton | Crawford | 34 | 11-Jan-1941 | Bow Streeet, London | 20 Hurstdene Avenue | Yes |
| Patricia Anne Custins | Crowhurst | 6 | 25-Mar-1944 | Station Approach | 49a Station Approach | Yes |
| John Sheridan | Foster | 8 | 16-Oct-1940 | 103 Hayes Lane | 103 Hayes Lane | No |
| Albert Leslie | Goodenough | 39 | 24-Sep-1940 | 24 Southbourne | 24 Southbourne | No |
| Albert Theophilus | Goody | 77 | 26-Oct-1940 | 216 Hayes Lane | 6 Morley Road, Lewisham | No |
| Florence Edith | Grandfield | 62 | 9-Feb-1945 | 14 West Common Road | 14 West Common Road | Yes |
| James | Grandfield | 62 | 9-Feb-1945 | 14 West Common Road | 14 West Common Road | Yes |
| Stanley Jack | Grandfield | 34 | 9-Feb-1945 | 14 West Common Road | 32 West Common Road | Yes |
| Charles W | Hammond | 47 | 16-Sep-1940 | The New Inn | 142 Kingsway, West Wickham | No |
| Sidney | Harper | 53 | 24-Sep-1940 | 24 Southbourne | 24 Southbourne | No |
| Elsie Amy | Hawtin | 30 | 23-Mar-1943 | Southend Road, Beckenham | 33 Dartmouth Road | No |
| Reginald Francis William | Knight | 21 | 14-Nov-1940 | Invicta Road, Greenwich | 196 Croydon Road | Yes |
| Nora Patricia | Marfleet | 40 | 6-Sep-1940 | 101 Bourne Way | 101 Bourne Way | No |
| Vera May | Marfleet | 36 | 6-Sep-1940 | 101 Bourne Way | 101 Bourne Way | No |
| Pamela Anne | Mote | 4 | 25-Mar-1940 | Station Approach | 41 Station Approach | Yes |
| Charles John | Pinhorn | 75 | 9-Feb-1945 | 24 The Knoll | 24 The Knoll | Yes |

| Name | | Age | Date died | Where died | Lived at | Hayes Roll of Honour |
|---|---|---|---|---|---|---|
| Dorothy Emma | Robbins | 51 | 3-Jan-1944 | 6 Tiepigs Lane | 6 Tiepigs Lane | No |
| Frederick John | Scates | 33 | 16-Sep-1940 | The New Inn | 184 Wickham Chase | No |
| James | Stevens | 18 | 17-Apr-1941 | 154 Pickhurst Lane | 50 Greenway, Bromley | No |
| Mary Louisa | Stoner | 8 | 26-Oct-1940 | 216 Hayes Lane | 216 Hayes Lane | Yes |
| Eric Harold | Strouts | 32 | 16-Apr-1941 | Hayes Common | 6 Redgate Drive | Yes |
| Josephine | Sullivan | 28 | 6-Sep-1940 | 101 Bourne Way | 74 Nutfield Road, Thornton Heath | No |
| Winifred | Taylor | 33 | 11-Jul-1944 | 2 Marion Road, Croydon | 3 Kechill Gardens | Yes |

## Service Casualties

| Name | | Service | Rank | Number | Age | Date died | Where died | Lived at |
|---|---|---|---|---|---|---|---|---|
| Walter James | Abbott | RAFVR | Corporal | 1308868 | 33 | 29-Nov-1943 | Singapore | |
| Joan Margaret | Ashburner | WRNS | Leading Wren | 45374 | 20 | 9-Jun-1944 | Fife | 4 Cecil Way |
| Sidney Walter George | Avent | RAF | Sergeant Pilot | 1283173 | 21 | 28-Apr-1942 | At Sea | 96 Pickhurst Lane |
| Frank William | Balcomb | Army | Lance Corporal | 486300 | 28 | 29-Jun-1942 | United Kingdom | 40 Pickhurst Lane |
| John Victor | Billett | RAF | Flt Lieutenant | 135865 | 27 | 20-Feb-1945 | United Kingdom | 3 Burwood Avenue |
| Derek John William | Billinghurst | RAF | Sgt Navigator | 1628300 | 20 | 12-Jul-1945 | Italy | 2 Hurst Close |
| Roger Basil | Binyon | Army | Captain | 219665 | 30 | 24-Sep-1944 | Netherlands | Hawthorndene, Warren Road |
| Albert Henry | Breck | Army | Private | 7391326 | 26 | 21-Aug-1943 | Japan | |
| Kenneth Roy | Bryant | RAF | Sgt Observer | 755318 | 21 | 2-Aug-1940 | Netherlands | 105 Chatham Avenue |
| Arthur William | Bunn | Army | Lance Corporal | 6105081 | | 25-Oct-1942 | Egypt | 14 Hurst Close |
| George Leonard | Burden | Royal Navy - FAA | Leading Air Mech. | C/FX 81324 | 25 | 9-Apr-1942 | At Sea | 33 George Lane |
| Ernest Stanley | Butcher | Army | Captain | 72734 | 50 | 2-Sep-1945 | United Kingdom | |
| Bernard | Chipperton | Army | Trooper | 1456247 | 18 | 6-Sep-1943 | United Kingdom | |
| Colin Arthur | Clarke | Army | Gunner | 985724 | 24 | 17-Mar-1945 | Japan | |
| John Peter Dixon | Clarke | RAF | Pilot Officer | 121537 | 21 | 9-May-1942 | Germany | 62 Bourne Way |
| Brian Robert | Clover | RAF | Flying Officer | 50694 | 31 | 16-Dec-1943 | United Kingdom | 18 Hayes Gardens |
| Clifford Charles | Collins | Royal Navy | Ord. Seaman | C/JX 316031 | 18 | 18-Nov-1942 | At Sea | 34 Pittsmead Avenue |

| Name | Service | Rank | Number | Age | Date died | Where died | Lived at |
|---|---|---|---|---|---|---|---|
| Ernest Ronald Peter Shackle Cooper | RAF | Pilot Officer | 87050 | 26 | 26-Jul-1941 | Germany | |
| Stanley Wilson Charles Culmer | RAF | Sergeant Pilot | 1283606 | 26 | 14-Apr-1942 | United Kingdom | 12 Abbotsbury Road |
| Charles Sidney Darwood | RAF | Flight Lieutenant | 37085 | 26 | 18-May-1940 | France | |
| Arthur James Davis | Royal Navy | Petty Officer Stoker | P/KX 79741 | 29 | 17-Oct-1939 | At Sea | |
| Leslie Robert Davy | Army | Sergeant | 6090099 | 23 | 11-Oct-1944 | Netherlands | |
| Robert Stanley Deason | RAFVR | Sgt Observer | 1390632 | 20 | 9-Aug-1943 | United Kingdom | 15 Hayes Gardens |
| Gordon Elmy | RAFVR | Flying Officer | 159691 | 22 | 31-Mar-1944 | Germany | 78 Kechill Gardens |
| Kenneth Arthur Fairclough | RAFVR | Flt Sergeant | 1339199 | 23 | 13-Jul-1944 | Italy | 32 Sackville Avenue |
| Shadrach Morton Frost | RAFVR | Sergeant | 1379682 | 30 | 14-Jun-1943 | Unknown | 78 Kechill Gardens ? |
| Frank William Fuller | Army | Lieutenant | 243186 | 34 | 5-Apr-1945 | Germany | 131 Pickhurst Lane |
| Gerald Alan Gale | RAFVR | Sergeant | 1375303 | 19 | 14-Apr-1942 | Unknown | 178 Hayes Lane |
| Thomas William Gardiner | Army | Lieutenant | 314935 | 30 | 16-Dec-1944 | Burma | 32 Kechill Gardens |
| Alfred Robert Goodall | Merchant Navy | Chief Steward | | 39 | 2-Dec-1940 | At Sea | 8 The Green |
| Jack Goodenough | Army | Lance Bombardier | 952288 | 23 | 24-Sep-1940 | United Kingdom | 24 Southborne |
| Clifford Roy Grandfield | RAFVR | Sergeant | 1253914 | 20 | 8-Dec-1942 | Malta | 14 West Common Road |
| Arthur Ellis Harris | Army | Lance Sergeant | 6096488 | 29 | 9-Sep-1943 | Italy | 7 Montcalm Close |
| Raymond Keith Hoer | Army | Rifleman | 14419119 | 19 | 14-Jun-1944 | France | 67 Keswick Road, WW |
| Ronald Henry Imeson | RAFVR | Flying Officer | 68179 | 21 | 15-May-1942 | United Kingdom | 21 Constance Crescent |
| Bernard Weymouth Isles | Army | Signalman | 6474343 | 29 | 15-Feb-1943 | Sri Lanka | |
| Clement Jeans | RAuxAF | Leading Aircraftsman | 842271 | 46 | 12-Feb-1945 | United Kingdom | 126 Goodhart Way, WW |
| Edmund John Charles Joyce | RAFVR | Leading Aircraftsman | 1873279 | 39 | 22-Dec-1945 | Iraq | |
| Cyril Caister Langley | RAFVR | Sergeant | 1804334 | 21 | 24-Nov-1943 | Unknown | 17 Hayes Hill Road? |
| Frank Mark Le Bosse | RAFVR | Leading Aircraftsman | 1290760 | 37 | 15-Feb-1945 | Italy | 106 Hayes Lane |
| Geoffrey Bevington Legge | RNVR | Lt Commander | | 37 | 21-Nov-1940 | United Kingdom | Nash Farm, Keston |
| John Desmond Lenahan | RAF | Pilot Officer | 41302 | 20 | 9-Sept-1940 | | |
| Norman S D Mack | RAF | Flt Sergeant | | | | | 21 Bourne Vale? |
| Leslie James Mallows | RAFVR | Sergeant Pilot | 1377970 | 21 | 6-Jul-1942 | Uganda | 37 Chatham Avenue |
| Derek Graham Mayley | RAFVR | Sergeant | 1800825 | 22 | 7-Jul-1944 | Austria | 178 Pickhurst Lane |
| Robert Mays | Home Guard | Private | | 18 | 21-May-1944 | United Kingdom | 148 Bourne Vale |

| Name | | Service | Rank | Number | Age | Date died | Where died | Lived at |
|---|---|---|---|---|---|---|---|---|
| Thomas Jeffrey | Morley | Army | 2nd Lieutenant | 259434 | | 30-Oct-1942 | Egypt | 14 St Mary Cottages |
| William John | Mortlock | Royal Navy | Able Seaman | P/JX 380181 | 19 | 23-Oct-1943 | At Sea | 16 Pickhurst Mead? |
| Stanley Owen | Naylor | Army | Driver | 6352135 | 21 | 24-Mar-1945 | Germany | 98 Chatham Avenue |
| John Brittenden | Neal | Army | Lance Sergeant | 867002 | 26 | 10-Dec-1942 | Italy | 15 Cecil Way |
| Robert Gunn | Nicoll | Royal Canadian Army | Gunner | M/4154 | 23 | 25-Jul-1943 | Italy | |
| Leslie Thomas | Nicholls | Army | Gunner | 1119288 | 32 | 9-Apr-1943 | Egypt | 23 Pickhurst Mead |
| Peter Derek | Norman | RNVR | Acting Sub Lieut. | | 19 | 21-Nov-1944 | At Sea | 11 The Knoll |
| Alan Charles | Parker | RAFVR | Sergeant Navigator | 912468 | 32 | 20-Jan-1944 | United Kingdom | 182 Pickhurst Lane |
| Vincent James | Pattison | RAF | Pilot Officer | 33442 | 21 | 6-Jul-1940 | At Sea | 28 Ridgeway |
| John | Payne | Royal Navy | Leading Stoker | C/KX 88568 | 26 | 8-Nov-1942 | At Sea | |
| Alfred William | Peyton | Army | Lieutenant | 201786 | | 15-Apr-1943 | Burma | Pondfield Road |
| Henry Arthur | Pocock | RAFVR | Sergeant WO/AG | 1310474 | 23 | 5-Oct-1942 | United Kingdom | Hayes Lane |
| Albert Reginald | Quinton | RAFVR | Sergeant Air Bomber | 914247 | 25 | 17-Mar-1945 | Germany | 17 Glebe House Drive? |
| Barty Reddie | Reid | Royal Navy | Able Seaman | C/JX 153441 | 20 | 17-Dec-1942 | At Sea | 143 Pickhurst Lane |
| Robert Alexander | Renno | Army | Private | 6096197 | 27 | 19-Jul-1943 | Italy | |
| Donald Alfred | Robson | Army | Lieutenant | 293927 | 20 | 16-Dec-1944 | Belgium | |
| Peter Guy | Rogers | Army | Private | 5572484 | 24 | 29-Jun-1944 | France | 15 Everard Avenue |
| Frederick | Sansom | Army | Bombardier | 1573338 | 31 | 13-Apr-1942 | At Sea | 37 Pickhurst Mead |
| Philip Donn | Scarr | Army | Corporal | 2084786 | 24 | 27-Sep-1944 | Netherlands | |
| Arthur P T | Shelley | Army | Lieutenant | 113825 | 43 | 7-Apr-1941 | United Kingdom | 6 Husseywell Crescent |
| Ronald | Smith | Army | Gunner | 1827637 | 34 | 4-Jun-1944 | Egypt | 10 Crest Road |
| Walter Frederick | Spencer | Army | Trooper | 7954409 | 37 | 23-Mar-1945 | Germany | 30 Constance Crescent |
| Percy Jack | Stickland | RAFVR | Flight Lieutenant | 101033 | 27 | 21-Jul-1945 | United Kingdom | 14 Bourne Vale? |
| Leonard Walter | Stiles | Army | Rifleman | 6852316 | 23 | 24-Nov-1943 | Italy | |
| Charles Oliver | Taylor | Army | Sergeant | 1833908 | 35 | 11-Jul-1944 | United Kingdom | 3 Kechill Gardens |
| Henry John Anthony | Thicknesse | Army | Brigadier | 6851 | 44 | 23-Oct-1944 | Netherlands | 107 Harvest Bank Road, WW |
| Leonard William | Thompson | RAFVR | Sergeant WO/AG | 1129556 | 31 | 24-Aug-1943 | Germany | |
| Frederick Albert | Timms | Army | Sergeant | 880834 | 20 | 7-Jun-1940 | At Sea | 16 Mounthurst Road |

| Name | | Service | Rank | Number | Age | Date died | Where died | Lived at |
|---|---|---|---|---|---|---|---|---|
| Robert Douglas | Walker | RAF | Sergeant | 568505 | 23 | 5-Apr-1942 | Singapore | 120 Hayes Lane |
| Jack Ronald | Wallis | RAFVR | Sergeant Flt Engineer | 1803333 | 21 | 22-Jun-1944 | Germany | 107 Chatham Avenue |
| John Gordon | Walshe | RAFVR | Sergeant Navigator | 1317945 | 20 | 5-Aug-1944 | Cyprus | 29 Hambro Avenue |
| Cecil Horace | Walters | Royal Navy | Leading Cook | LT/MX 87033 | 42 | 12-Jul-1944 | At Sea | 13 Hurstdene Avenue |
| Alexander George | Whitehead | Army | Lance Corporal | 2885491 | 29 | 12-Aug-1943 | Italy | |
| George Millar | Wilkinson | RAuxAF | Corporal | 841738 | 34 | 29-Nov-1940 | United Kingdom | |
| Harold Oliver | Wilson | Army | Corporal | 7934291 | 24 | 21-Aug-1944 | France | 138 Pickhurst Lane |
| Raymond Howard | Wilton | RAFVR | Flying Officer | 143921 | 21 | 13-Jun-1944 | Germany | 31 Hayes Wood Avenue |

## Additional information – CWGC entries not recorded in *Hayes at War* by Trevor Woodman

**ABBOTT**, Corporal, WALTER JAMES, 1308868, 242 Sqdn Royal Air Force Volunteer Reserve. 29 November 1943. Age 33. Son of Percy Ernest and Miriam Maud Abbott, of Hayes, Bromley, Kent. Column 426, Singapore Memorial

**BRECK**, Private ALBERT HENRY, 7391326, Royal Army Medical Corps. 21 August 1943. Age 26. Son of Albert and Dorothy Breck; husband of Helen Breck, of Hayes, Kent. Grave Ref. Brit.Sec. J.D. 15 Yokohama War Cemetery, Japan

**BUTCHER**, Captain, ERNEST STANLEY, 72734, Royal Corps of Signals. 2 September 1945. Age 50. Son of Edward Ernest and Elizabeth Mary Butcher; husband of Elizabeth Frances Butcher, of Hayes, Kent. Grave Ref. Block I, Grave 158. Bromley Hill Cemetery [Hayes Directory 1950 – 69 Hayes Wood Avenue, Hayes]

**CHIPPERTON**, Trooper, BERNARD, 14526247, Royal Armoured Corps. 6 September 1943. Age 18. Son of Frank and Rosa Chipperton, of Hayes, Bromley, Kent. Grave Ref. Panel 2, Newcastle-upon Tyne (West Road) Crematorium

**CLARKE**, Gunner, COLIN ARTHUR, 985724, 5 Field Regt, Royal Artillery. 17 March 1945. Age 24. Son of Arthur W.M. and Maud Elizabeth Clarke, of Hayes, Kent. Grave Ref. Brit. Sec. F. A. 14, Yokohama War Cemetery, Japan

**COOPER**, Pilot Officer (Pilot) ERNEST RONALD PETER SHACKLE, 87050, 35 Sqdn, Royal Air Force. 26 July 1941. Age 26. Son of Frederick Arthur Marrison and Doris Cooper; husband of Monica Cooper, of Hayes, Bromley, Kent. Grave Ref. Coll. grave 8. Z. 4-7 Berlin 1939-45 War Cemetery

**DARWOOD**, Flight Lieutenant (Pilot) CHARLES SIDNEY, 37085, 111 Sqdn, Royal Air Force. 18 May 1940. Age 26. Son of Arthur John and Nita Darwood; husband of Elizabeth Darwood, of Hayes, Kent. Grave Ref. Plot 8. Row B. Grave 31. Longuenesse (St Omer) Souvenir Cemetery, France

**DAVIS**, Petty Officer Stoker, ARTHUR JAMES, P/KX 79741, H.M.S. Iron Duke, Royal Navy. 17 October 1939. Age 29. Son of Arthur John and Eliza Davis; husband of Elizabeth Mary Davis, of Hayes, Kent. Panel 35, Column 1, Portsmouth Naval Memorial

**FAIRCLOUGH**, Flight Sergeant (Pilot) KENNETH ARTHUR, 1339199, 142 Sqdn, Royal Air Force Volunteer Reserve. 13 July 1944. Age 23. Son of Arthur Henry and Maud Lilian Fairclough, of Hayes, Bromley, Kent. Grave Ref. Coll. grave V. D. 1-5. Milan War Cemetery, Italy. [Hayes Directory 1950 – 32 Sackville Avenue, Hayes]

**FROST**, Sergeant, SHADRACH MORTON, 1379682, 220 Sqdn, Royal Air Force Volunteer Reserve. 14 June 1943. Age 30. Son of Morton Bennett and Eva Frost, of Hayes, Kent. Panel 150.Runneymede Memorial

**GOODENOUGH**, Lance Bombardier, JACK, 952288. Royal Artillery Attd to HQ X Corps. 23 September 1940. Age 23. Son of Alfred and Annie Goodenough of Addington, Berkshire. Buried at Bromley (St Lukes) Cemetery. He was the third person to be killed at 24 Southbourne, Hayes

**IMESON**, Flying Officer (Pilot Instr.) RONALD HENRY, 68179, Royal Air Force Volunteer Reserve. 15 May 1942. Age 21. Son of Frank and Annie Elizabeth Imeson, of Hayes, Kent. Grave Ref. Plot South. Row E. Grave 8. Little Rissington Churchyard, Glos[Hayes Directory 1950 – 21 Constance Crescent, Hayes]

**ISLES**, Signalman, BERNARD WEYMOUTH, 6474343, Royal Corps of Signals. 15 February 1943. Age 29. Son of Alfred William and Mary Ann Isles, of Hayes, Kent. Grave Ref. Plot 6C. Row F. Grave 11. Colombo (Kanatte) General Cemetery, Sri Lanka

**JOYCE**, Leading Aircraftman, EDMUND JOHN CHARLES, 1873279, Royal Air Force Volunteer Reserve. 22 December 1945. Age 39. Son of John Charles and Mary Florence Joyce; husband of Eileen Joyce, of Hayes, Bromley, Kent. Grave Ref. 6. C. 7.Habbaniya War Cemetery, Iraq

**LENAHAN**, Pilot Officer (Pilot) JOHN DESMOND, 41302, 607 Sqdn., Royal Air Force. 9 September 1940. Age 20. Son of John Martin and Sarah Edith Lenahan, of Hayes. Grave Ref. Sec. O, Grave 58 Cranbrook Cemetery, Kent

**MACK**, No record can be found confirming the death of Flt Sgt Mack

**NICHOLLS**, Gunner, LESLIE THOMAS, 1119288, 65 Field Regt, Royal Artillery. 9 April 1943. Age 31. Son of Thomas Joseph and Alice Eliza Nicholls; husband of Karoline Nicholls, of Hayes, Kent. Grave Ref. 4. J. 6. Alexandria (Hadria) War Memorial Cemetery. Egypt

**NICOLI**, Gunner, ROBERT GUNN, M/4154, 3 Field Regt, Royal Canadian Artillery. 25 July 1943. Age 23. Son of William and Annie Nicoll; husband of Nellie May Nicoll, of Hayes, Kent, England. Grave Ref. A, C, 44 Agira Canadian War Cemetery, Sicily. Had married Nellie Hancock of 20 Station Approach 24 September 1941

**PAYNE**, Leading Stoker, JOHN, C/KX 88568, H.M.S. Cowdray, Royal Navy. 8 November 1942. Age 26. Son of James and Beatrice Payne, of Hayes, Kent. Panel 61, 2. Chatham Naval Memorial

**QUINTON**, Sergeant (Air Bomber) ALBERT REGINALD, 914247, 153 Sqdn Royal Air Force Volunteer Reserve. 17 March 1945. Age 25. Son of Walter Alfred and Violet Marie Quinton (nee St. John), of Hayes, Kent. Grave Ref. Coll. grave 8. G. 26-29. Durnbach War Cemetery, Germany [Hayes Directory 1950 – 17 Glebe House Drive?]

**RENNO**, Private, ROBERT ALEXANDER, 6096197, 2nd Bn, Devonshire Regiment. 19 July 1943. Age 27. Son of George Robert and Nellie Renno; husband of Doris Eileen Renno, of Hayes, Bromley, Kent. Panel 5.Cassino Memorial, Italy

**ROBSON**, Lieutenant, DONALD ALFRED, 293927, 191 (The Hertfordshire and Essex Yeo.) Field Regt,  Royal Artillery. 16 December 1944. Age 20. Son of Robert and Florence Amelia Robson, of Hayes, Bromley, Kent. Grave Ref. V. D. 109. Schoonselhof Cemetery, Antwerp

**SCARR**, Corporal, PHILIP DONN, 2084786, 89 Parachute Security Sec.,  Intelligence Corps. 27 September 1944. Age 24. Son of William Donn and Margaret Alice Scarr, of Hayes, Kent. Grave Ref. 10. E. 8. Jonkerbos War Cemetery, Netherlands

**SHELLEY**, Lieutenant, ARTHUR P. T., 113825, Royal Army Service Corps. 7 April 1941. Age 43. Son of Philip Samuel and Clara Louisa Shelley; husband of Gladys Annie Shelley, of Hayes, Bromley, Kent. Grave Ref. Ward 4. Sec. A. Grave 2. Carlisle (Stanwix) Cemetery[Hayes Directory 1950 – 6 Husseywell Crescent Hayes]

**SMITH**,  Gunner RONALD, 1827637, 86 Lt A.A. Regt,  Royal Artillery.  4 June 1944. Age 34. Son of Walter and Rosalie Smith;  husband of Ethel Smith, of Hayes, Kent. Grave Ref. 4. D. 16 Moascar War Cemetery, Egypt

**STILES**, Rifleman, LEONARD WALTER, 6852316,  2nd Bn King's Royal Rifle Corps. 24 November 1943. Age 23. Son of Arthur and Caroline Stiles,  of Hayes, Bromley, Kent. Grave Ref. XIV. E. 1. Sangro River War Cemetery, Italy

**THOMPSON**, Sergeant (WO/AG) LEONARD WILLIAM, 1129556, 156 Sqdn Royal Air Force  Volunteer Reserve.  24 August 1943. Age 31. Son of Henry John and Martha Thompson; husband of Jacqueline Yvonne Monica Thompson, of Hayes, Bromley, Kent. Grave Ref. Coll. grave 14. B. 7-8. Berlin War Cemetery

**WALLIS**, Sergeant (Flt Engr) JACK RONALD, 1803333, 619 Sqdn., Royal Air Force Volunteer Reserve. 22 June 1944. Age 21. Son of Frederick William John and Lily Ellen Wallis, of Hayes, Bromley, Kent. Grave Ref. Coll. grave 8. F. 13-14. Hanover War Cemetery [Hayes Directory 1950 –107 Chatham Avenue]

# Acknowledgement of illustrations

We are fortunate that in the 1930s and 1940s Horace Crowhurst took a number of photographs of Hayes that his daughter Maureen has kindly agreed that we may publish. We are grateful to Howard King's son Tony for donating his father's photographs, mainly taken in the 1950s, to the Hayes Archives and for agreeing to their publication. In the late 1960s Professor Martin Lee produced a geographical survey of Hayes that has provided many interesting photographs and in 1974 Gordon Wright took a complete photographic record of Hayes that is in Bromley Library. Our thanks go to all who have given permission to use their photographs.

a.  Mr R Manning
b.  Miss M Fuller
c.  Miss D Timms
d.  Mrs W Weaver
e.  Mrs G Willis
f.  Mrs N Chamberlin
g.  Miss B Jarvis
h.  Mr L Smith
i.  Mr M Lee
j.  Miss M Crowhurst
k.  With the kind permission of the Ordnance Survey
l.  Bromley Library, Local Studies Collection
m. Mr H King
n.  Mr D Rowedder
o.  Mrs V Blinks
p.  Mrs L Frost, MBE, widow of Mr D R (Dick) Frost of Bencewell Orchard
q.  Sales Brochure
r.  Mr C Legge
s.  Mr C Wimble - Baston School Archives
t.  Mr W Sparrowe
u.  Mr G W Tookey QC
v.  Mr P Rose
w. Mrs E Belsey
x.  Mrs M Nelson
y.  Mrs R Witcombe
z.  Mrs C Timms
aa. Mr J Ruler -Hayes & District Horticultural Society Records
ab. Mr W Dance
ac. Mr B Neville - Scout Records
ad. Bromley Mercury
ae. Kentish Times Group
af. Mrs R Knopp
ag. Mr A Parkin
ah. Mrs S Pettitt
ai. Mr A Pettitt
aj. Bromley Library Archives
ak. Mr P Gilbey

al. Mr R Stevens
am. Miss M Sansom
an. Hayes Free Church Archives
ao. Miss N Barnes
ap. Mr G Wright
aq. Pickhurst School Records
ar. Hayes Primary School Records
as. Hayes School Records
at. Mrs M Whytock, Hayes Players Archives
au. Mr P Groves - Victory Social Club Records
av. Mr S Swainsbury
aw. Mrs A Manning
ax. St Mary the Virgin, Hayes - Church Archives
ay. PCSO M Jacobs
az. Mr B Saxton - Blackheath and Bromley Harriers AC Archives
ba. Mr M Howe
bb. Mr P Leigh
bc. Mr S Howe
bd. Mr O Pereira
be. Mr P Harrold
bf. Mr D Wilson

# Bibliography

## Primary Sources

**Australian War Memorial, Canberra**
Roll of Honour cards 1914-18: AWM 131;145
**Bromley Public Library: London Borough of Bromley Archives and Local Studies**
Appraisal Area Report, Hayes, 1980
Bromley Rural District Council Records: C/BRORDC minutes; planning etc
Bromley Borough papers: C/BROB compulsory purchase orders; council minutes
Bromley Borough Planning files
General: 396; 811; 891; 933; 1003; 1082; 1116; 1215; 1233; 1315; 1506; 1532; 1605; 1626; 1630
Hayes Common Records: 298
*Hayes Directories*
Hayes Library Issues 1939-1950
Hayes Nursing Association: 140
Hayes Parish Council Records
Hayes Parish Records: P180 various; 687/2 Parish Rates
Sales Catalogues: 1200 various
**Centre for Kentish Studies**
WKR/B1: Records of Royal West Kent Regiment
**Commonwealth War Graves Commission**
*Debt of Honour Register*
**Hayes Church Archives**
PCC information
Baptism, Death and Marriage Registers
Great Lectern Bible listing the men who safely returned in 1918/1919
Hayes Roll of Honour
**House of Lords Record Office**
FCP/2/311
**Library and Archives Canada**
Canadian Convalescent Hospital, Bromley, Kent: RG9.III; Anti-Aircraft Units: RG24
**London Metropolitan Archive**
London Congregational Records 1936-9, 1952
**The National Archives**
Census information: RG11 - 17
Home Office: HO198
Inland Revenue Assessment 1910-13: IR/58
Metropolitan Police: MEPO 2; 4; 5
Military records and home casualties: WO166; 199
National Farm Survey 1941: MAF 32; 73

## Primary Material held by individuals or the authors

12th Bromley (1st Hayes) Scout Records - Mr Bob Neville
Baston School Archives – Mr Charles Wimble
Chamber of Commerce Records - Mr Ron Holland
Frost Family Papers include correspondence, photograph albums, Glebe House Furniture Sale Catalogue, 15.12.30
Gilbey, Arthur R, Personal Diaries
Hayes Allotment Holders Register – Mr John Ruler
Hayes Community Council Records
Hayes Primary School: Log Book 1937 - ; 70th Anniversary Records
Hayes Village Association Records
Hayes Village and District Association Records
Hayes Women's Fellowship Minutes
Hayes Women's Institute: Branch Records;  History Notes
Pattulo Higgs Brochure
Pickhurst Primary School: Records;  Miss K Gay's memories
Plant Family Scrapbook
Poor's Land Trust Records
Robson Family Papers
Sales Brochures and Catalogues: various, including *Coneyhall Estate, Forge Close, Hast Hill, Hawthorndene, Hayesford Park, Hayes Grove Estate, Hayes Mead, Hayes Park Estate, Hayes Place Estate and Heydon Court*
Sidcot School Archives
Victory Social Club Archives - Mr Peter Groves

# Secondary Sources

Architect and Building News, *Hayes Place, Kent,* 1937
Bellringer, Doris, *In the beginning were the Girls, 1910-1930*
Bellringer Doris & Graham Linda, *The 3rd Hayes Brownies 1946-1996*
Blake L, *Bromley in the Front-line*, 2nd edition, Bromley 1980
Collier B, The *Defence of the United Kingdom*, London, 1957
Cooksley, Peter G, *Aviation Enthusiasts' Guide to London and the South-East.,* Cambridge 1982
Coward, Alice, *Hayes – Village on the Heath,* Hayes, 1973
Cresswick Paul, Pond G Stanley, Ashton P H, *Kent's Care for the Wounded*
Golding K, *The Story of Hayes Philharmonic Society*
Goyder, Roma, *Hayeseed to Harvest,* 1984
Green G D, *The Story of Hayes Free Church, 1937 – 1997,* 1997
Harrold, Elinor, *Hayes Remembered,* Hayes 1982
Hayes Philharmonic Society, *Golden Jubilee 1945-1995*
Heinecke P, *St Mary Cray Paper Mills,* Industry and Enterprise, BBLHS No 9
Hook J, *The Air Raids on London during the 1914 – 1918 War, Book II,* London 1989
Imperial War Graves Commission, *Civilian War Dead of the United Kingdom, Volume II,* London 1954
Knowlden P, *The Long Alert,* Bromley 1988
LDV, *The Bromley Home Guard, A History of the 51st Kent Battalion,* 1945
Lee M E, *A Geographical Account of the development of a Kentish Parish*, transcript 1968
Mack L, *Bus to Coney Hall: The first few years*
Mack L, *Hayes Place Estate,* typescript, 2000
Mack L, *Hayes (Kent) Village Association Golden Jubilee Souvenir Guide*, 1983.
Mack L, *Notes on the Spencer Estate*, 2000 unpublished typescript
Mack L, *The Building of the Hayes Estates,* c1982
Mack L, *The Village Hall,* unpublished notes, May 2005
Mercer, Derrik ed, *Chronicle of the 20th Century,* Longman 1988
Moody G T, *Southern Electric,* 4th edition, Ian Allen,1968
Mullin M, *Design by Motley,* University of Delaware Press, 1996
Mundy R W, *An outer London suburb: Hayes, Kent: a case study of the growth processes of a 20th century Suburb,* typescript,1967
Pile, General Sir Frederick, *Ack-Ack,* G Harrap & Co, London 1949
Player, John, *The Story of our Club House – The Warren,* 2nd edition
Ramsey W G, editor, *The Blitz, Then and Now,* Volume 1, 1987, Volume 2, 1988
Rason, Denise, Hospital Memorial Boards and Plaques Rescued, *Bromleag*, June 2003.
Rason, Paul, *Bromley's War Memorials, Volume 5,* LBB, 1999
Rawlinson A, *The Defence of London, 1915 – 1918,* London 1923
Roth-Nicholls K & Nicholls B, *My dearest Lini*, privately printed 2006
Saunders D K and Weeks-Pearson A J, *The Centenary History of the Blackheath Harriers,* 1971, 2nd edition 1989.
Smith, Flt Lt Godfrey, *No 768 Squadron ATC 1941-2006 Requiescat in pace*, typescript
Tapsell, Martin, *The Big Screen in the Big Borough*
Thompson P. A, *The History of Hayes (Kent) Cricket Club, 1828-1978,* Hayes 1978.
Taylor, Richard, *The White House,* typescript
Timms, Christiana B, *Historical Happenings in Hayes,* typescript 1994
Trimming R J, *Proposal for Hayes Area of Special Residential Character,* typescript 1993
Wagstaff J S, (ed.), *Bus Crew,* Sheaf Publishing Ltd, 1979
Walker, Joyce, *West Wickham and the Great War,* West Wickham1988
Walker, Joyce, *West Wickham in the Second World War,* West Wickham,1990.
Wilson J M, *Hayes in World War 1,* Hayes, 1989
Wilson J M, *The History of Baston,* Hayes, 1983
Wilson J M, Mabel Winifred Knowles 1875-1949, The Angel of Customs House, *Bromleage* August 1993
Wilson J M, *The Village School, Hayes 1791-1987*, Hayes 1987
Wilson J M & Woodman T C, *Hayes Church School 1791-1991,* Hayes 1991
Woodman T C, *Wartime Hayes,* Hayes, 2000
Woodman T C, Hayes in the Spring of 1941, *Bromleage,* May 1991

**Newspapers & Magazines**

| | | |
|---|---|---|
| *Beckenham Advertiser* | *Daily Mail* | *News Shopper* |
| *Bromley Borough News* | *Hayes Parochial Magazine, later Hayes Herald* | *Sunday Express* |
| *Bromley & District Times* | *Hayes and West Kent Gazette* | *Sunday Times* |
| *Bromley and Kentish Times* | *The Guardian* | *The Sheffield Daily Independent* |
| *Bromley Mercury* | *The London Gazette* | *The Times* |
| *Bromley Property News* | *Morning Post* | *West Kent Mercury* |
| *Daily Herald* | | |

# References

BDT     *Bromley and District Times*

BKT     *Bromley and Kentish Times*

BLA     Bromley Archives, Bromley Public Library

BM     *Bromley Mercury*

BPL     Bromley Libraries, Local Studies Collection

BT     *Bromley Times*

CWGC     Commonwealth War Graves Commission

DNB     *Oxford Dictionary of National Biography*

HCC     Hayes Community Council

HPC     Hayes Parish Council

HPM     *Hayes Parish Church Magazine*

HVA     Hayes Village Association

HVDA     Hayes Village & District Association

IWGC     Imperial War Graves Commission

NMR     National Monuments Record

PCC     Parochial Church Council

TNA     The National Archives

## 1   Village life and sacrifice: 1914-1921

1   *Bromley & District Times*

2   BLA: HPC Minute, 14.3.14

3   BLA: BRDC Minute, Vol. VII, 24.4.14; *BDT*, 27.2.14

4   Longman *Chronicle of the 20th Century*

5   The figure has been extrapolated from various editions of *BDT*, Hayes Roll of Honour Book and the names in the Parish Church Lectern Bible

6   *BDT*, 14.8.14, 6.11.14

7   *BDT*, 13.10.16

8   J M Wilson, *Hayes in World War 1*, Hayes, 1989

9   Personal Communication from Joyce Walker

10   M. Mullin, *Design by Motley* 1996

11   Paul Cresswick, G Stanley Pond, P H Ashton, *Kent's Care for the Wounded*, 1915; information from Joyce Walker

12   *BDT*, 28.8.14

13   *BDT*, 7.5.15

14   National Archives of Canada:Canadian Army Convalescent Hospital, Bromley, 1916 War Diary RG 9.III, Vol. 3750

15   National Archives of Canada:Canadian Army Convalescent Hospital, Bromley, Sept 1915 to Dec 1916. RG 9.III Vol. 5039

16   *BDT*, 26.11.15; Op cit. 8

17   The official death date of Edward Rust is Friday, 23 July 1915. The War Diaries of 6 Bn RWKR show 22 July 1915

18   Plant Family Scrapbook, obituary from unnamed London daily newspaper, 6.11.15

19   CWGC: *Debt of Honour Register*; Frost family papers

20   Joyce Walker, *West Wickham and the Great War*, 1988

21   BLA: P180/25/11; op.cit. 8

22   *BDT*, 17.3.16, 31.3.16, 30.6.16

23   Arthur Robson's papers have been given to the Imperial War Museum

24   The memorial in the Parish Church gives death date

of 23 August and age 20, which is a variance to the CWGC records. His name is on the Hayes Cricket Club Memorial.

25   CWGC: *Debt of Honour Register*; RWKR records WKR/B1/A2

26   Op cit.8 . There is a memorial stone to him in the churchyard of St John's Church West Wickham.

27   *BDT*, 24.8.17; BLA: P180/1/8; William Harris is not listed in the *Hayes Roll of Honour Book* nor on the War Memorial.

28   CWGC: *Debt of Honour Register; BDT,* 30.11.17

29   Op cit.8; *BDT,* 22/29.12.16

30   BLA: P180/1/30

31   Op cit.8; correspondence with Colin Legge

32   Information from his sister Mrs. Frances Jane Capon of Downe; Australian War Memorial, Canberra

33   Op cit.8; CWGC *Debt of Honour Register*

34   Op cit.8 and information provided by the family

35   *BDT,* 28.6.18; Op cit.8

36   A Rawlinson, *The Defence of London, 1915 – 1918;* Peter G Cooksley *Aviation Enthusiasts' Guide to London and the South-East.* There was a searchlight sited at Downe, Kent, known as an 'advanced light' to give early warning of approaching enemy aircraft and *Zeppelin* airships.

37   Hook J, *The Air Raids on London during the 1914 – 1918 War*

38   BLA: P180/25/11

39   Op cit.8; *BDT,* 16.12.17

40   Paul Rason, *Bromley's War Memorials, Volume 5*

41   *BKT,* 24.1.19

42   *BKT,* 1.2.18, 15.10.15, 2.3.17

43   *BKT,* 25.7.19, 30.1.20; Rachel Orr's memories

44   CWGC: *Debt of Honour Register*; BLA: P180/1/5, P180/1/8, P180/1/30

45   *BM,* 14.5.20

46   Personal communication from his daughter Mrs Christiana Timms

47   BLA: Hayes Rate Book 1917; *BM,*10.2.22

48   Hayes Census Summaries for 1911 and 1921; BLA: P180/1/8, P180/1/22, P180/1/30

49   *BKT,* 29.11.18; BLA:1138

50   *BM,* 30.5.19

51   *Brass Memorial Plaque,* Hayes Parish Church

52   Plant Newscuttings; *BKT,* 25.7.19

53   Personal communication by Mr. Leonard Smith, grandson of the founder.

54   BLA: HPC Minute, 5.8.16

55   BLA: BRDC Minute, 4.6.18, 19.11.18, 8.4.19

56   BLA: HPC Minutes, 27.5.20

57   *BM,* 29.8.19

58   BLA: HPC Minutes, 15.11.19, 13.12.19, 17.4.19, 30.4.21

59   *BKT,* 31.1.19; *BM,* 2.6.33

60   *BKT,* 22.8.19; P.A. Thompson, *Hayes (Kent) Cricket Club, 1828-1978,* Hayes, 1978

61   BLA: P180/25/19

62   *BDT,* 20.6.19

63   *BKT,* 24 .10.19

64   see Appendix 1

65   *BKT,* 7.1.21

66   *HPM,* January 1923

67   *HPM,* May 1924

68   CWGC: *Debt of Honour Register*

69  *BDT, 30.5.15*

## 2  A new beginning 1921-1939

1   *BM*, 1.12.25
2   Elinor Harrold *Hayes Remembered* ;  *Hayes Directories*, 1927 to 1940 editions; Lewis family papers.
3   *BM, various.*
4   *HPM,* November 1927
5   Elinor Harrold, *Hayes Remembered; BKT*, 29.1.37
6   BLA: P180/1/27
7   *BM, 25.11.27*
8   *BKT, 7.1.38*
9   *BM, 26.11.37, 10.12.37*
10  Mrs Perrett – Conveyance Documents 145 Hayes Lane
11  Laurie Mack, *The Building of the Hayes Estates,* c1982
12  HPC Minute, 27.4.30; *BM*, 24.4.30, 2.5.30, 4.7.30
13  *BM*, 12.10.34, 7.12.34, 19/26.7.35, 4.10.35; *Hayes Directori*es, 1935 to 1938 editions
14  HPC Minutes, 21.11.21, 29.10.25, 8.1.28
15  *BM*, 5.8.21; *HPM*, July 1923
16  *BM,* 22.6.23, 4.7.24, 10.10.24; *HPM,* September / December 1924
17  *HPM*, February 1926; *BM,* 18.12.25
18  HPC Minute, 12.2.26
19  HCC Minute, 3.2.26, 10.3.27
20  *HPM,* August 1926
21  HCC Minute, 25.3.27
22  Conveyance 1.1.1928
23  HCC Minute, 11.7.27;  HPC Minute, 21.7.27;  notes on the Village Hall by Laurie Mack, May 2005; Personal communication by Mr William Smith to Mr. Laurie Mack
24  *BM*, 29.7.27
25  HCC Minutes, 20.10.27, 5.11.27
26  HCC Minutes, 9.11.27, 20.4.28; HPC Minute 27.10.27; *BM*, 20.1.28
27  HPC Minutes 24.11.27, 12.1.28
28  HCC Minutes 20.4.28, various minutes 1930, 13.3.31, 7.5.31
29  HCC Minutes 25.10.29, 30.3.36
30  HCC Minutes, various 1932 to 1935
31  HCC Minute 17.4.35
32  *BM*, 15/ 22/ 29.5.36, 5.6.36; Plant Scrapbook, June 1936
33  HCC Minutes 29.4.36, 23.4.37; Laurie Mack, unpublished notes May 2005; *BT*, 12.2.37
34  HCC Minute 29.4.37; HVA: Minutes 4.1.37, 15.3.37, Plant Scrapbook
35  *BT*, 12.2.26
36  *BM,* 25.10.29
37  Laurie Mack, *Hayes (Kent) Village Association Golden Jubilee Souvenir Guide*, 1983. In 1983 the HVA celebrated their Golden Jubilee with an exhibition on the development of Hayes. Much of the original research into the building of new housing estates was undertaken for the exhibition by Mr Mack and the authors are indebted to him and the HVA for permission to use this material.
38  *BM*, 6 March 1936
39  NMR: RAF air photograph, LA33/3009, 14.8.44
40  Abstract of Title of Pickhurst Manor; *The Morning Post*, 28.10.35; *Hayes and West Kent Gazette,* 17.1.36

41  Killick & Knight, *Hayes Mead Estate Brochur*e, undated; Baxter, Payne & Lepper, *The Hayes Hill Estate Brochure*, undated
42  *DNB*
43  Interview with Mrs Jean Partridge (nee Ballentyne) in 1991
44  BPL: L55.8
45  TNA: IR 58/14205/8021
46  Certificate of Redemption of Tithe Rent Charge, 20 July 1930
47  *BM*, 18.2.27, 9.12.27
48  Martin Hood & Larkin (The Estate Gazette Ltd.)
49  *BKT,* 23.8.29
50  *BM*, 19.11.30
51  Henry Boot Garden Estate Brochure, plan dated 24.2.1930; separate plan May 1932
52  *BT*, 20.12.29; HPC Minute, 29.12.29
53  *BKT*, 1.5.31; *BM*, 8.1.32
54  Hayes Place Estate Sales Catalogue, 29.5.31; *Di*stinctive Houses by Henry Boot & Sons Ltd, Messrs. Summersell & Wadsworth
55  *BM,* 5.6.31
56  *BKT*, 26.4.35
57  William Agg-Large 2nd Schedule; *BM,* 22.5.23
58  *BM*, 23.5.30
59  *BM,* 8.1.32; *BT*, 8.1.32
60  HPC Minutes, 27.2.30, 26.6.30; *BM,* 7.2.30, 25.4.30, 27.6.30; *BKT,* 8.1.32
61  *BKT*, 3.3.33
62  *The Sheffield Daily Independent*, 20.4.32
63  *Hayes Directories*, 1924 to 1928;William Edward Agg-Large papers
64  *DNB; BKT*, 3.4.31; *BM*, 17.4.31
65  Interview with Mr. Richard (Dick) Frost, son of James Frost. The house had a large dining room, drawing room, lounge, library and 12 bedrooms.
66  *BKT,* 11.7.26
67  The Glebe House Antique and Modern Furniture Sale Catalogue, 15 December 1930; *BM,* 28.11.30
68  *BT,* 12.6.31; *BM*, 23.10.33
69  *BM*, 9.10.31
70  Interview with Mr Bill Dance
71  *BM,* 24.5.35; J M Wilson, *The History of Baston,* 1983.
72  BLA:298, minutes 2.1.36, 26.11.36, May 1937
73  *BM,* 16.4.37, 4.6.37
74  BLA:298/3, 22 April 1938
75  *BKT*, 6.5.38, 16.9.38, 13.10.39
76  NMR:RAF Air Photograph, LA33-3008, 14 August 1944
77  BLA:298, 19 June 1934; *BKT*, 20.9.35
78  P Heinecke, *Industry and Enterprise, Bromley Local History No.9; BM*, 16.5.30
79  *BKT*, 19.1.36;  *Hayes Park Estate* brochure, undated
80  BLA: Hayes Common Conservators, Minute 8.2.20; *BM,* 20.10.22
81  *BKT*, 28.9.23;  *BM*, 26.2.37
82  *BKT*, 24.2.24
83  *BM*, 9.1.31, 27.2.31,16.2.34
84  *BM*, 19.9.30, 14.11.30;  *Hayes Directories,* 1933 to 1940
85  *BM*, 15.8.35, 18.10.35, 2.2.40
86  *BT*, 22.2.24; J M Wilson, 'The Angel of Customs House', *Bromleage*, August 1993

87  *BT*, 21.3.24, 12.12.24
88  *BM*, 26.10.28
89  *BM*, 13.9.20
90  TNA:RG11/0736/76
91  *BM*, 7.2.30; *BT*, 23.9.21; Interview with Bill Dance
92  J M Wilson, *The History of Baston*, 1983
93  BLA: Hayes Parish Rating book. Tenants include Thomas Scott 1920-22, George Simmons to 1924
94  BLA:806, Sales Catalogue, 1927
95  HVA General Meeting, 10.10.35
96  T C Woodman, *Wartime Hayes*, 2000. In Munich, in September-October 1938, Neville Chamberlain tried to resolve Hitler's claims in the Sudetenland.
97  Roma Goyder, *Hayeseed to Harvest*, 1984
98  *BM*, 31.8.31
99  *Hayes Directories*, 1916 onwards; *BT*, 8.1.26; *HPM*, November 1928; *BM*, 20.11.36
100 *BM*, 5 June 1935
101 *Hayes Directories*; John Player, *The Story of our Club House – The Warren*, 2nd edition
102 *BKT*, 16.3.34, 31.5.34
103 TNA:MEPO 5/550 part1, 1936
104 BLA:298, minute 22 June 1936
105 *BM*, 10.11.39
106 *BM*, 19.8.21, 16.3.23
107 *BM*, various editions
108 *BKT*, 14.5.26; *HPM* June 1926
109 *BM*, 18.3.38
110 *BM*, 8.1.31, 29.6.34, 3.2.39
111 *BM*, 16.1.31, 31.3.33. The Young Conservatives were again a thriving group in the late '50s and early '60s
112 *BM*, 20.4.36
113 HPC Minutes, 31.1.29, 8.3.29
114 HPC Minutes, 23.5.29, 19.9.29, 30.9.29
115 HPC Minutes, 27.3.30, 8.5.30, 27.1.32
116 HPC Minute, 20.3.34; *District Times* 23.3.34; *BM*, 13.4.34
117 BLA:1531A
118 *The London Gazette*, 13.3.38, 23.12.38
119 *BKT*, 23.2.34
120 Recalled by Mr. Hughes on his resignation from the HVA Committee in 1935. Minute, 25 April 1935
121 HVA: *Hayes – Village on the Heath*, 1973; HVDA: Minutes 9.11.33, 7.12.33
122 HVDA:Minutes 25.1.34, 4.4.34
123 HVA:Minutes 31.1.34, 26.2.34, 15.3.34, 22.4.35
124 HVA:Minute 21.2.35; Alice Coward *Hayes – Village on the Heath*, 1973

## 3  The end of the village?

1  *BM*, 5.8.27. The fire mark referred to was above the front door of the Walnut Tree and remained there until the late 1960s.
2  *BT*, 29.2.28; *BM*, 24.4.31
3  G T Moody, *Southern Electric*, 1968, 4th edition
4  J S Wagstaff, (Ed.) *Bus Crew*, 1979; *BM*, 25.3.27
5  *The Times*, 2.9.21
6  *BM*, 18.8.22
7  *BM*, 25.5.24; BRDC Minute 9.12.24
8  *BM*, 7.8.25
9  *BM*, 15.1.26, 24.9.26, 19.8.27; *HPM*, September 1927
10  *BM*, 5.8.27; HPC, Minutes 11.4.29, 24.6.31
11  *BM*, 14.3.30, 21.8.31
12  *BM*, 7.6.35; Council Order 5 June 1935
13  *BM*, 25.10.35
14  House of Lords Record Office:FCP/2/311
15  *BM*, 22.11.34, 7.12.34, 5.4.35;  Bromley Borough Council: Public Works Facilities Act 1930, Compulsory Purchase Order No.3 – 3 April 1935
16  BLA:396/1 & 2
17  *BKT*, 6.3.36
18  *BM*, 12.6.31
19  L Mack, *Hayes Place Estate*, typescript, 2000
20  *BKT*, 28.8.31, 4.9.31
21  *Hayes Directories* 1932 to 1939 editions
22  *BM*, 8.10.37;  *Distinctive Houses by Henry Boot & Sons Ltd*, Messrs. Summersell & Wadsworth
23  *Daily Herald*, 17.2.34
24  Henry Boot Garden Estates Ltd brochure, undated but after 24 February 1936
25  *Hayes Directories*, 1934 to 1940 editions
26  Henry Boot (Garden Estates) Ltd, drawing 340, 24.2.36
27  *BM*, 12.9.24; HPC Minute, 27.6.29; *BT*, 28.6.29, 16.8.29; BRDC Minutes
28  R H Goodsall, *A Third Kentish Patchwork*, 1970
29  Henry Boot & Sons Ltd, drawing dated May 1932; *BM*, 13.4.33
30  *BM*, 23.10.36; L Mack, *Hayes (Kent) Village Association Golden Jubilee Souvenir Guide*, 1983
31  The houses later built were 1-11 and 2 Hazelmere Way, 11-19 and 2-16 Heath Rise
32  F Hugh Thoburn brochures, undated; *Hayes Directories*, 1932 to 1939 editions
33  L Mack, *Hayes (Kent) Village Association Golden Jubilee Souvenir Guide*, 1983
34  HPC Minutes, 27.9.33, 31.5.33; Interview Dorothy Dewey 2006
35  *BM*, 31.8.34, 9.4.37
36  *BM*, 28.9.34; *BT*, 18.1.35
37  *BM*, 1.5.31, 27.10.33; *BT*, 16.2.34; HVA: Minute 15.11.37; Op.cit. 33
38  *Morrell's Coneyhall Estate, Hayes, Kent* brochure, undated but pre 1934
39  L Mack, *Bus to Coney Hall: The first few years*. Typescript.  Morrell's Leyland Cub bus had the registration index AUC 144
40  Killick & Knight brochure, undated
41  *Hayes Directories*, 1933 to 1940. Houses in Hurstdene Avenue were occupied 1933-35, Hurst Close 1934-35, Dene Close 1935, Hayes Hill Road, Courtland Avenue, 1935-38 and Hilldown Road 1936-37
42  L Mack, *Notes on the Spencer Estate*, 2000, unpublished typescript. The first to receive Council approval were Nos.31 to 53 Pickhurst Lane on 9.6.32. Nos.35 and 37 are different from the others and were built to revised plans approved 3.4.33.
43  *BM*, 8/29.8.30, 19.9.30
44  *BM*, 23.5.30, 3.10.30, 9.1.31, 24.4.31; *Hayes Grove Estate* brochure, published before December 1930
45  Conveyance documents held by Roger Rowe
46  Hugh F Thoburn Ltd, Crest Road and Pickhurst Lane, Pickhurst Mead and Pickhurst Lane House brochures, undated
47  Hugh F Thoburn Ltd, Pickhurst Green House brochure, undated
48  *BM*, 12.11.37, 17.12.37
49  *BT*, 20.9.35

50  R J Trimming, *Proposal for Hayes Area of Special Residential Character,* typescript 10.6.93; Hugh F Thoburn Ltd, Warren Wood (Extension) brochure, undated
51  Hugh F Thoburn Ltd, Bourne Way house brochure
52  L Mack, *The Building of the Hayes Estates,* c1982
53  *BT*, 12.2.26
54  Hugh F Thoburn Ltd, Auction Catalogue, about March 1935
55  *BM*, 4.2.36, 5.6.36, 11.9.36; Compulsory Purchase Order 5 February 1936.
56  *BM*, 12.6.36
57  *BT*, 5.5.33
58  *BKT*, 7.7.33, 2.11.34, 29.11.34; Correspondence with Mr. Martin Tapsell.
59  *BM*, 31.3.35*;* BLA:C/BROB/F/684
60  Mericia Cinema Society, Gallery 2003 article
61  *BM*, 9.4.36, 26.6.36; HVA:Minutes 13.5.36, 15.7.36, 16.9.36, 16.11.36, 14.1.37
62  *Hayes Directories*; *BM*, 4.9.31
63  *BT*, 7.9.34, 6.12.35; Bromley Borough Planning file
64  *BKT*, 24.7.31; *HPM*, June 1931
65  *BKT*, 10.7.31, 11.8.33, 16.3.34, 22.3.35; *BM*, 23.3.34
66  Hayes Place Estate Sales Catalogue, 29 May 1931; Plant Scrapbook, 30.11.31
67  *BKT*, 9.12.32, 27.1.34, 14.9.34; *BM*, 20.1.33, 10.2.33
68  *BKT*, 6.7.34, 30.11.34, 21.12.34
69  *Morning Post,* 23.11.35, Column by S P B Mais *A Countryman looks at the Suburbs*
70  *BT,* 14.9.23; *Hayes Directories*,1922 -1927; *BM,* 11.11.39
71  *BM*, 14.2.36
72  *BM,* 23.10.36, 26.2.37, 5.3.37, 2.9.38
73  *BT*, 23/30.9.21; *BM*, 2.12.21
74  *Hayes Directories*, 1925 and 1929; interview with Mr. Peter Rose in March 2002; *BM*, 27.6.24, 11.7.24
75  *HPM,* December 1929
76  *BM*, 16.9.27, 7.10.27, 17.1.36; *Hayes Directories;* TNA: IR58/14205/8037-8039
77  *Bromley Directories*, editions 1915 to 1925; *BM*, 20.2.24, 1.8.30
78  *BM*, 29.3.34, 7.12.28, 24.12.31, 3.9.37, 9.9.38
79  *BM*, 10.12.20; *Hayes Directory,*1926 edition
80  Arthur R Gilbey's personal diaries.

## 4  Response to change: 1921-1939

1  BLA: 140/2; *BM,* 12.6.31
2  *BM,* 3.2.33, 12.5.33
3  *BM,* 21.12.34
4  *BM,* 14.9.34, 17.5.35, 6.3.36, 1.10.37
5  *BM,* 7.5.37, 27.5.38, 5/12.5.39
6  J M Wilson, *The Village School, Hayes 1791-1987*
7  BLA: P180/25/7
8  BLA: P180/25/6
9  Conversation with Dorothy Dewey 2006
10  Hayes Parish Church Chest
11  BLA: P180/25/18
12  *BKT,* 11.6.37; *West Kent Mercury,* 29.10.37
13  J.M. Wilson & T C Woodman, *Hayes Church School 1791-1991,* Hayes 1991
14  Rona Goyder, *Hayeseed to Harvest*, 1985
15  The chair suffered from the English climate and no longer exists but the brass plaque survives.
16  See entries in *DNB*
17  *The Guardian,* 30.10.2006
18  Information from L G Smith, W Dance
19  *Hayes Directories*; *BM,* 20.12.35
20  HPC Minute, 4.1.32
21  *BM,* 16.7.37, 19.11.37
22  *BM,* 8.7.38, 7.7.40; Barnhill Cottage Conveyance documents
23  J M Wilson, *The History of Baston* 1983
24  Baston School Archives. Mary (Robin) Place became a well known archaeologist and author
25  *HPM,* May 1924
26  *BM,* 3.4.25, 5.2.37; *HPM,* October 1930
27  *BT,* 7.2.19; *BM,* 21.8.31
28  *HPM*, September 1924; J M Wilson, Mabel Winifred Knowles 1875-1949*, Bromleage* August 1993
29  *BT*, 7.1.21, 6.1.28; BLA: P180/25/13
30  *Hayes Church Magazine*, July 1930
31  Calvary Church Archivist: In the early 1950s the stones were moved to St Paul's Cathedral, Boston.
32  *BM*, 4.10.29
33  *HPM*, June 1930, November 1929
34  *BM*, 8.7.38, 7.8.31, 20.10.36, 16.6.39
35  *HPM*, October 1928, November 1930, January 1932
36  *BM*, 3.6.33
37  *BM*, 25.8.33; Information from Mrs Rhoda Witcombe, 2001
38  Papers held in Hayes Parish Church Chest; *BM*, 3.6.36, 24.7.36
39  *BM*, 28.7.39
40  BLA: P180/3/10. Buchman's process revolved around conversion in small groups in which members would confess all their sins to each other.
41  *BM*, 8.6.34; BLA: P180/3/10
42  *BM*, 18.2.38, 1.3.35, 25.10.35
43  *BM*, 4.6.37, 30.7.37
44  *BM*, 24.6.38, 7.10.38
45  Sidcot School Archives: Old Scholars Annual Report 1992
46  *BM*, 13.1.39, 10.3.39, 15.12.39
47  BLA: 622/C/3/1
48  G D Green, *The Story of Hayes Free Church, 1937 – 1997*, 1997
49  *BM*, 7.1.38, 20.1.39, 12.5.39; BPL: L14.9
50  *BM*, 13.5.37
51  *BM*, 3.11.39
52  *BM*, 12.1.34, 6.7.34; HPC Minute, 31.1.34
53  Interview with Mr Bill Dance
54  *BM*, 20.9.29
55  *HPM*, April 1925
56  *BM*, 16.7.26, 3.9.26
57  *BM*, 14.2.36
58  *BM*, 3.1.36, 22.1.37, 14.5.37
59  *BM*, 17.3.39
60  *BM*, 11.9.31
61  *BM*, 26.1.34; reminiscences of Mrs Muriel Adamson
62  *BM*, 3.4.36, 17.2.39, 28.4.39
63  Mrs M Adamson's reminiscences
64  *BM*, 17.9.37, 13.4.38, 4.11.38
65  *BM*, 22.9.22, 6.9.29; *HPM*, January 1923
66  *BM*, 14.4.39, 12.8.38, 12.11.37
67  *BM*, 4.11.36, 21.4.39
68  D K Saunders and A J Weeks-Pearson, *The Centenary History of the Blackheath Harriers,* 1971, 2nd edition 1989
69  *BM*, 19.3.26, 7.2.30, 3.3.39

70  *BM*, 17.9.37; *BKT*, 10.2.39
71  *BM*, 17.7.36, 21.4.39
72  *HPM*, November 1929; *BT*, 27.2.31
73  *BT*, 6.10.33, 29.10.37
74  *BM*, 18.10.35
75  *BM*, 20.7.23, 30.7.26, 18.3.27, 20.6.28
76  *BM*, 4.12.31, 10.11.33
77  HVA: Minutes, 18.4.34, 16.5.34, 20.6.34, 18.7.34, 12.9.34
78  HVA: Minutes 3.10.34, 16.1.35
79  HVA: Minute 19.9.35; *BM*, 16.7.36, 18.9.38
80  HVA: Minutes 15.3.34, 16.5.34, 12.9.34
81  *BM*, 21.9.34, 28.4.39
82  *BM*, 11.3.27, 13.7.28; *HPM*, July and August 1928
83  *BM*, 22.11.29
84  HVA: *Review*, April 2006; *BM*, 28.7.22, 11.7.24
85  *HPM*, January 1931; *BM* 14.6.35; HVA: *Review*, July 2006
86  *BM*, 1.6.34, 27.7.34, 14.12.34
87  *BM*, 21.7.39
88  *HPM*, March 1924, January 1927, May 1930; *BM*, 4.8.33
89  *BM*, 17.1.36
90  *BM*, 4.6.37
91  *BM*, 7.8.36, 6.11.37
92  *BKT*, 4.2.38, 7.7.36
93  British Pathe News: 234.08-1921, 340.06-1924, 392.16-1925, 680.40-1927
94  *BM*, 9.5.19
95  *BM*, 12.5.33, 24.1.36, 19.3.37; British Pathe News: 762.03 1928
96  *BM*, 12.5.39
97  *BM*, 10.5.35, 17.3.39
98  Doris Bellringer, *In the beginning were the Girls, 1910-1930*
99  *HPM*, July & September 1923
100 *BM*, 26.7.35, 26.5.39, 8.10.37
101 *HPM*, September 1925, December 1926, August 1927; *BM*, 3.2.39
102 BLA:298/7, 9.6.20, 6.5.21; *BM*, 9.9.21
103 *BM*, 12.6.31; BLA:298/7, 28 May 1934
104 BLA:298/1/4; HPC Minute 11.5.34
105 *BM*, 20.10.22; HPC Minute 31.1.29; BRDC Minute 11.11.29
106 HPC Minutes, 17.4.23, 19.9.29; BLA:298/1/4
107 BLA:298/7, 20.6.34, 7/ 8.8.34, 30.10.35
108 TNA: IR58/14206/8189
109 BLA:298/1/4, 26.5.20, 9.6.20
110 BLA:298/1/5, 28.1.28, 24.3.28, 3.4.28, 5.5.28, 27.6.28
111 BLA:298/2/9, 28.2.36; 298/2/10, 15.1.37
112 BLA:C/BROB/F/48/E
113 *BM*, 6.5.38; HVA: Minute 16.5.34
114 HVA: Minutes 20.6.34, 18.7.34, 3/26.10.34, 16.1.35, 21.2.35
115 BLA:298/7, 19.9.34, 298/10, 19.3.37
116 BLA:298/2 file 9; 298/3, 3.3.38
117 BLA:298/3, 30.3.38, 21.6.38, 5.4.38, 5.9.38
118 BLA:298/7, 8.8.34, 5.1.23
119 BLA:298, 28.8.37, 7.10.38. The SAAD unit was on the common from 27 September to 4 October 1938
120 *BM*, 6.5.38, BLA:BROB/F/48/E/2

## 5   Towards war

1  HVA:Minutes 26.7.37, 22.9.37

2  HVA:Minute 15.4.37. Later Lt Col Heilbron was appointed chairman of the London Region Committee of the KCC Civil Defence Emergency Committee. The HVA sub-committee included Messrs Drawmer, Nash, Pinfield and Wallis; *BM*, 27.4.38
3  HVA:Minute 5.10.38; T C Woodman, *Wartime Hayes*, 2000; *BKT*, 13.12.38
4  Hayes and the other three centres were subordinate, and reported to the main borough ARP centre located under Bromley Town Hall. Later this centre moved to the basement of F Medhursts Ltd now the Primark store.
5  The others were at Keston Mark, Hook Farm, Bromley Common, Widmore Green, Langley Park, Assembly Rooms at Coney Hall and Quernmore School, which later became the National Fire Service (NFS) headquarters for No.37 Area.
6  *BM* 5.4.39
7  HVA:Minute 19.4.39
8  Interview with Mrs Peggy Jackson in 1998
9  Interview with Mr & Mrs Alan Pettitt in 1988
10 BKT, 23.6.39
11 BLA:298/2, 28.8.37
12 BLA:Hayes Civil Records, 8.6.39, 29.6.39; BLA:298, 25.5.39, 29.6.39, 8.10.39
13 Borough of Bromley, Minutes of the General Purposes Committee, 2 September 1939
14 *BKT*, 8.9.39; Hayes Parish Chest: Marriage Register 1939-1946
15 *BKT*, 24.1.41, 26.7.40, 4.10.40, 7.3.41
16 Sidcot School: *Old Scholars' Annual Report 1992*
17 BKT 6.9.40, *BM* 27.9.40
18 *BKT* 18.2.44
19 *BKT*, 2.9.39; BLA:Borough Map 10.10.39; 1506; conversation Dorothy Dewey 2007. Full list of wardens in T C Woodman *Wartime Hayes*, 2000
20 BLA:1605
21 BLA:1506 Log 1
22 Miss Dorothy Timms' memories, 1989
23 *BKT*, 13.10.39, 24.11.39
24 *BKT*, 17.11.39; NMR:RAF Air Photograph, 3G/TUD/UQQK/12/29 Part III, 15 January 1946
25 *BKT*, 8.9.39; BLA: P180/8/4
26 HCC Minutes, 8.5.40, 23.4.43; HVA:Minute 11.1.40; *BKT*, 20.10.39; HVA:General Meeting Chairman's Report, 18 April 1940
27 Bromley Council Minutes, 21.11.39, 30.7.40, October 1940; BLA:1506/1. The Station Approach shelters were built to accommodate 45 persons at No. 42, 37 persons at No.44 and 73 persons at No.48.
28 Interview Mr & Mrs Alan Pettitt, February 1989; *BKT*, 22.11.40; communication Canon W B Norman
29 Interview Mrs Vera Bardgett, 16.3.89; BLA:Hayes Common Conservators, Minute 14.4.40
30 BLA:Hayes Common Conservators, Minute 8.10.39
31 BLA:Hayes Common Conservators, Minutes 30.3.41, 19.1.41, 8.10.40; BLA:298, Maps MR.1.411651, MR.854839
32 BLA:Hayes Common Conservators, Minute 25.7.40
33 BLA:Hayes Common Conservators, Minute 19.1.41

34 TNA: WO166/2389, WO166/2579, WO166/2543, List of the units occupying ZS10:-

| Regiment Number | Battery Number | Date From | Date To |
|---|---|---|---|
| 99 | 303 | 30/10/39 | 07/12/39 |
| 99 | 302 | 07/12/39 | 18/04/40 |
| 99 | 303 | 18/04/40 | 04/06/40 |
| 84 | 263 | 04/06/40 | 15/06/40 |
| 84 | 261 | 15/06/40 | 28/06/40 |
| 101 | 317 | 28/06/40 | 10/07/40 |
| 162 | 158 | 10/07/40 | |
| 54 | 162 | 12/09/40 | 27/03/41 |
| 97 | 319 | 14/05/41 | 28/07/41 |
| 54 | 312 | 28/07/41 | 10/11/41 |
| 109 | 343 | 10/11/41 | 21/04/42 |
| 141 | 493 | 21/04/42 | |
| | 394 | 30/08/42 | |
| 155 | 525 | | 30/08/42 |
| 163 | 565 | 15/09/42 | 20/10/42 |
| 155 | 537 | 20/10/42 | 29/12/42 |
| 129 | 444 | 29/12/42 | |
| 155 | 537 | 31/12/42 | 15/03/43 |
| 141 | 490 | 15/03/43 | 11/05/43 |
| 170 | 568 | 11/05/43 | 24/05/43 |
| 141 | 490 | 24/05/43 | 25/11/43 |
| 160 | 556 | 25/11/43 | 27/07/44 |
| 130 | 443 | --/03/45 | 20/04/45 |
| 160 | 458 | - -/09/45 | --/12/45 |

35 B Collier *Defence of the United Kingdom*, London, 1957
36 TNA:WO166/927
37 TNA:WO166/1159, WO166/12434 and others; Correspondence Mr Peter Nowers, 10.2.99
38 BLA:Hayes Common Conservators, Minute 18/ 25.7.40, 19.1.41
39 TNA: WO166, WO199/ 1202
40 TNA: WO166/927 and /1159; BLA:1506, 12.7.40
41 BLA:891/1 J H Boswell, E G Brice, T A Davey, S E Dowley, W T Elwood, H R Gooch, A G Hancock, A A Hodgkin, W Ironside, J Merrill, V T Rand, S H G Rose, F T Spearman. Not stated to have war experience W A S Ballard and F A Tottem.
42 BLA:891/1
43 Conversation with Mr Gordon Johnson in 1989
44 BLA:1506, September 1943; Hayes Village Hall Management Committee 26.6.41
45 BLA:811 Known ammunition and explosive dumps used by the Home Guard: The Pickhurst Hotel garden; B/1 Bombing Post Hayes Street Farm; Crest Road Post; Isolated lock-up shed on Baston Farm along Barnet Wood Road; Stables (outhouses) Hayes Street (probably behind The Walnut Tree shop). The inflammable stores were kept in a ditch on Hayes Street Farm, 12 Pickhurst Green in the back garden of Mr F A Tottem and in a field next to Barnet Wood.
46 BLA:811
47 51 Battalion, Kent Home Guard Operational Instructions, 16 April 1942
48 LDV, *The Bromley Home Guard*
49 BLA: Hayes Common Conservators, Minutes 8.10.39, 25.7.40, 31.8.41, 30.3.41, 28.5.40

## 6  Hayes at war: 1940-1945

1 BLA:1233; *BKT*, 17/ 24.5.40
2 *BM*, 7.6.40; *BKT*, 30.1.42; *Sunday Express* 17.7.60; Conversation Dorothy & Winifred Timms 1989
3 BLA:P180/1/15
4 TNA:WO166/2541,/2291,/2449,/2111,/2291,/2453
5 T C Woodman, *Wartime Hayes*, 2000
6 Robson Family Papers
7 IWGC, *Civilian War Dead of the United Kingdom, Volume II,* London 1954
8 *BKT*, 20.9.40. BLA:1116, the survivors included Mr Frank Clarke, the licensee, his wife Jean, Mr, Mrs & Miss Grimble, Mr & Mrs R E Stevens, Mr & Mrs W Oates, Mr & Mrs W Cole, Mrs Maud Hammond, Miss Maud Scales, Mrs P O'Neill, Mr E O Hall, Mr W Kemp, Mrs Ann Owens, Miss Audrey Clarke, Miss Joan Clarke
9 TNA:WO166/2453; National Archives, Maryland, USA: Ref 6x10438(S6), 18.8.40; IWGC, *Civilian War Dead of the United Kingdom, Volume II,* London 1954 and *Debt of Honour Register*
10 TNA:WO166/2435
11 W G Ramsey, editor, *The Blitz, Now and Then,* Vol 2, 1988
12 *BKT*, 17.5.47
13 BLA:P180/1/15
14 *BKT*, 23.10.40; J M Wilson, *The Village School Hayes, 1791 – 1987*, Hayes 1987
15 Originals with Mrs U Tollman
16 *Bromley Borough News*, 3.5.90; the medal, owned by LBB, is in the care of the Borough's Museum, The Priory, Orpington; IWGC, *Civilian War Dead of the United Kingdom, Volume II,* London 1954
17 *Hayes Review,* January 1990. His widow lived in Vienna until her death in the early 1990s and was occasionally visited by David Stoner and his brother
18 Poor's Land Trust Records
19 BLA:811/27; TNA:WO166/3901
20 BLA:Hayes Common Conservators, Minute 19.1.41
21 *BKT*, 10.1.41
22 BLA:1506 Log 3
23 TNA:WO166/2453; HO198/48; J M Wilson, *The Village School Hayes, 1791 – 1987*, Hayes 1987
24 TNA:HO198/48; W G Ramsey, editor, *The Blitz, Then and Now, Volume I,* 1987
25 TNA:HO198/48; IWGC, *Civilian War Dead of the United Kingdom, Volume II,* London 1954
26 IWGC, *Civilian War Dead of the United Kingdom, Volume II,* London 1954; Joyce Walker, *West Wickham in the Second World War,* West Wickham,1990
27 TNA:WO166/2589
28 *BKT*, 12.9.41
29 TNA:WO166/7477, /7508
30 TNA:WO166/7530,/2105, /7313; BLA:298
31 BBC Archive: WW2 The People's War
32 BLA: Hayes Common Conservators, Minute 19.1.41
33 National Archives of Canada: RG 24, volume 15582,

volume 15548

34 National Archives of Canada: RG 24, volume 15548, entries for 1, 3, 7 and 10  September 1942

35 'Local marriages involving overseas servicemen' compiled from St Mary the Virgin's Marriage Register.
- 20 September 1941 Edmund Welsh, Royal Canadian Artillery, to Hazel Ewing of No.88 Pickhurst Lane.
- 24 September 1941 Thomas Nelson, Royal Canadian Artillery, to Margaret Tidbury of No.50 George Lane.
- 24 September 1941 Robert Nicoll, Royal Canadian Artillery, to Nellie Hancock of No.20 Station Approach.
- 4 July 1942 Hugh Maynard, a mariner from Canada, to Muriel Maynard of No.49 Hurstdene Avenue.
- 15 January 1944 Leonard Warren, an Australian soldier, to Gladys Brewster of No.61 George Lane.
- 16 January 1944 William Gammon, a Canadian soldier, to Denise Ramsey of No.92 Pickhurst Lane.
- 4 May 1945 Clifford Sorenson, Royal Canadian Air Force, to Elsie Kemp of No.1 Hambro Avenue.
- 24 May 1945 Robert Down, a Canadian soldier, to Edna Jordan of No.35 Dartmouth Road.
- 23 June 1945 Albert Stacey, an Australian soldier, to Jean Davey of No.8 Glebe House Drive.
- 3 July 1945  Addison Cameron, a Canadian soldier, to Joan Birch of No.297 Pickhurst Rise.
- 23 September 1945 Charles Joudrey, a Canadian soldier, to Doris Arthur of No.41 Baston Road.
- 29 November 1945 Melvin Clark, a Canadian soldier, to Frances McAllister of No.20 Stanhope Avenue.
- 17 January 1946 Jack Kellam, a United States soldier, to Brenda Marchant of No.38 Hayes Lane.
Of the brides, two were in the ATS, two serving with the WAAF, one in the Land Army and one was listed on the marriage certificate as a lathe worker.  The remainder are recorded as holding teaching and clerical posts.

36 Instruction 'Withdrawal and immobilisation of Locomotives Ashford to the Hayes Branch' 29 June 1942

37 National Fire Service papers dated January and March 1943

38 The Baedeker raids, so named after the famous travel guides, were against major English cathedral cities such as Exeter, Canterbury, Bristol, etc.

39 BLA:Hayes Common Conservators, Minutes 10.3.42, 17.8.42, 25.11.42

40 TNA:WO166/11641

41 TNA:WO166/11622

42 TNA:WO166/11491; the aircraft included Junkers 88s, Dornier 217s, Heinkel 111s and Focke Wulf 190s

43 TNA:WO166/11622; HO198/19

44 Mr Arthur Gilbey Diaries via Mr. Peter Gilbey

45 Sergeant Pilot Sidney Avent (Kiel), Pilot Officer John Clarke (Rostock), Sergeant Pilot Stanley Culmer (returning from Dortmund), Flying Officer Elmy (Nuremberg), Sergeant Gerald Gale (Hamburg), Sergeant Cyril Langley (Berlin), Sergeant WO/AG Henry Pocock (en route to Aaachen). BKT, 18.12.43

46 BKT, 22.10.43, 5.11.43, 19.3.43

47 op.cit 11; the aircraft were Focke-Wulf, Fw 190 and twin-engine Messerschmitt, Me 410. TNA:HO198/19 and HO198/425

48 TNA:WO166 and HO198 series; HO198/23

49 Interview Maureen Crowhurst 2008; BKT, 31.3.44

50 Denise Rason, Hospital Memorial Boards and Plaques Rescued, Bromleag, June 2003

51 BKT, 31.3.44; TNA:HO198/23

52 TNA:WO166/14816

53 General Sir Frederick Pile, Ack-Ack, G Harrap & Co, London 1949

54 The times and duration of air raid warnings on Saturday 17 June 1944

| 00.45 to 02.30 | 16.50 to 16.57 | 20.32 to 21.10 |
| 02.35 to 06.30 | 17.12 to 17.56 | 21.30 to 21.55 |
| 14.05 to 14.30 | 18.05 to 18.38 | 23.10 to 06.27 |
| 15.50 to 16.20 | 19.35 to 20.13 | |

55 TNA:HO198/80, HO198/81

56 TNA:WO166/14864; HO198/84, HO198/86, HO198/91

57 TNA:HO198/107;  BKT, 16.2.45

58 TNA:MEPO 4/310; Princess Royal University Hospital: Bromley Hospital Archives

59 BKT, 22.11.40, 30.5.41, 28.4.44;  HVA:Minute 12.4.45

60 BKT, 29.9.44

61 HVA:Minute 12.4.45

62 HCC Minute, 17.4.44

63 WI Hayes Branch, Annual Reports 1939 – 45

64 Bromley's presentation Supermarine Spitfire Mk.1, serial R7262, was built at Eastleigh, Hampshire and flew for the first time on 22.3.41. It was allocated to 122 and 313 Squadrons

65 Conversation Mr Edward Searle; BKT, 28.7.44, 11.12.44

66 BKT, 14.1.44; Hayes Women's Fellowship Minute 24.6.41

67 William Foot, Maps for Family History, TNA Readers Guide No.9

68 TNA:MAF 32/82/16 and MAF 73/20/15, /16

69 Interview with Mr Peter Rose, 26.3.2002; TNA:MAF 32/82/12 and 73/20/15, /16;  BKT, 20.7.56

70 TNA:MAF 32/82/52, MAF 73/20/15

71 Discussion with Miss Winifred Timms 1989; BKT, 22.9.44, 6.7.45

72 Memories of Mr David Moxon

73 BKT, 5.4.40; The Allotment Holders Register, via Mr John Ruler; Hayes Directory 1953; NMR:RAF Air Photograph, 106 GLA30,3091, 7 August 1944, LA33, 3008/9, 14 August 1944

74 HCC Minute, 24.4.41

75 BKT, 1.11.40; Interview with Mr & Mrs Alan Pettitt, Feb 1989

76 BKT, 9.10.42, 26.7.40, 27.9.40; Conversation with Mrs Jean Hadley, 1989

77 Correspondence with Mr. Edward Searle, 1987; discussion Miss Dorothy Dewey 2007

78 Hayes School logbook from 1937

79 TNA:HO 198/91; Conversation Mrs Bardgett 1989

80 Correspondence Mr Colin Brook; J M Wilson The

*Village School, Hayes 1791- 1987*

81 J M Wilson, *The History of Baston*, Hayes 1983; *BKT*, 22.3.40

82 *BM* 24.12.41; Barnhill Conveyance Documents, 28.8.45

83 Interviews with Miss Mercia Sansom, 1998.

84 *BKT*, 29.9.44

85 *BKT*, 1.8.41; Gwen Green, *The Story of Hayes Free Church*, 1937-1997

86 *BKT*, 16.8.40

87 *BKT*, 25.10.40

88 *BKT*, 5.9.41, 20.11.42; BLA: P180/8/3 13.2.43, 29.9.43

89 BLA: P180/8/3; Parish Chest:Church Council Minute Book 1934-1947; Conversation Mrs Rhoda Witcomb (née McClintock) 2001; *BKT*, 20.10.44, 22.12.44, 20.4.45

90 *BKT*, 5.1.40, 16.2.40

91 *BKT*, 3.11.43

92 *BKT*, 16.2.40

93 D K Saunders & A J Weeks-Pearson, *The Centenary of the Blackheath Harriers*, London, 2nd Edition 1989

94 P A Thompson, *History of Hayes (Kent) Cricket Club, 1828-1978* Hayes 1978; *BKT*, 18.7.41,15.3.40

95 *BKT*, 6/13.10.44, 10.11.44

96 *BKT*, 30.3.45

97 *BKT*, 27.4.45

98 *BM*, 19.1.45, 18.5.45, 25.5.45, 1.6.45; *BKT*, 8.12.44

99 *BKT*, 20.4.45 MM to L/Cp Colin Frederick Jeans – 'on 10 Sept 1944 ordered into Nijmegen and to seize bridge across the river. He was the gunner in the troop leader's tank of the leading troop. By his accurate shooting and great coolness in the face of intense enemy anti-tank gun fire, the Lance-Corporal made an enormous contribution to the clearing of the roundabout.'

## 7 Peace comes to Hayes: 1945-1951

1 *HPM*, June 1945

2 Victory Social Club Archives

3 *BM*, 7.9.45, 31.8.45

4 Bromley Borough Council official programme: *Victory celebrations in Bromley, June 8-10* 1946

5 *BT*, 3.5.46; *BM*, 17.9.48, 17.1.47, 1.11.46, Arsenic and Old Lace 23.4.48

6 *BT*, 20.6.47

7 *BM*, 25.4.47; HCC Minute, 17.11.51

8 BLA:P180/8/4

9 BLA:298, 10.1.45, 23.9.45

10 HVA: Minutes April 1946

11 BLA:298, 22.1.47, 20.10.47, 6.11.47

12 T. Woodman, *Wartime Hayes,* Hayes 1999

13 *BM*, 24.12.47

14 M Lee, *Hayes A geographical account of the development of a Kentish Parish*, 1968 thesis

15 BLA:298, 13.11.47; *BKT*, 3.10.47

16 *BM*, 9.1.48, 15.10.48; *BKT*, 25.8.50

17 BLA:1215/4, 1215/8

18 Poor's Land Trust Records: Minute 4.10.50

19 BLA:P180/8/4

20 J Wilson & T Woodman *Hayes Church School 1791-1991*

21 Borough of Bromley: General Purposes Committee Minutes 1944-50

22 Information from Laurie Mack

23 *BM,* 16.12.48

24 Gwen D Green, *The Story of Hayes Free Church 1937-1997*

25 BLA:140

26 *BM*, 25.3.48

27 BLA:298, September 1947

28 HVA Records: Committee Minutes

29 *BM,* 13.4.45

30 HVA Records: General Meeting and Committee Minutes 1946-48

31 *BM,* 6.5.49; ETU Records seen at Hayes Court 1987

32 BLA:298

33 Hayes Primary School: Log Book 1937 -

34 HVA Records: Special Meeting 22.11.45; *BM,* 14.12.45, 30.4.48, 29.4.49

35 J Wilson, *The Village School Hayes* 1791-1987

36 J Wilson, *The History of Baston*

37 K Roth-Nicholls & B Nicholls, *My dearest Lini*

38 Barnhill Conveyance documents

39 HCC Minute, 16.4.45

40 HCC Minute, 20.2.46; General Purposes Committee 11.9.45

41 *BM*, 25.7.47, 30.1.48, 4.2.49

42 *BM*, 23.7.48, 6.2.45, 20.2.48, 12.3.48, 5.12.47

43 K Golding, *The Story of Hayes Philharmonic Society*

44 *BM*, 24.12.47

45 *BM*, 14.10.49, 15.10.48; *HPM*, March 1947

46 *BM*, 1.11.46, 27.6.47, 11.7.47

47 *BM*, 10.5.46, 25.4.47

48 *BM*, 19.10.45

49 *HPM*, June 1946; Hayes Library: *Hayes Library Issues 1939-1950*

## 8 A changing community: 1951 to modern times

1 BLA: Programme *We Made History;* HCC Minute, 21.9.53

2 HVA:*Quarterly Review,* Autumn 1965

3 Baston School Archives

4 *Hayes Herald,* November 2005

5 Ward Profile 2001

6 Ward Profile 1991

7 Survey of Railway Use provided by Anne Manning. Transport information provided by Laurie Mack, 1981-2005 Transport Users Consultative Committee for London, London Regional Passengers' Committee and London Transport Users Committee

8 HVA:*Quarterly Review,* January 1988

9 Conversation Miss D Dewey, 2007

10 Information from Councillor Anne Manning

11 Bromley Borough Records: 1949 & 1953

12 *BKT*, 17.9.71

13 Mayors include:
  • Thomas Dewey 1903, lived Beadon Road
  • Bertram Pearce 1922-23, moved to Hayes 1929
  • F W Isard 1926-27 & 1947-9
  • Margaret Stafford Smith 1938-40
  • Arthur Collins 1944-45
  • John Hunt 1963-4
  • H W John Haden 1968-9
  • James Frederick David 1979-80
  • Philip G Jones 1991-2
  • Anne Manning 2004-5

14 HVA:*Review,* October 1950

15 R W Mundy, *An outer London suburb: Hayes, Kent: a case study of the growth processes of a 20th century Suburb,* 1967
16 *The Times* 28.7.52
17 BLA:Hayes Common Conservators, letter 25.4.53
18 Conditions of Sale, Hast Hill 1913; Pattulo Higgs Brochure, undated
19 Land Registry Title No K35799 for Pantiles in Shefford Sales Catalogue, undated
20 HVA:General Meeting Autumn 1955, *Newsletter* Spring 1959; *BKT,* 3.12.71
21 BLA:298, Correspondence Box 4
22 Information from Mrs Margaret Stenning and Mr Gordon Collis
23 *The Times* 29.6.61, 16.10.67, 13.8.68
24 *BKT,* 12.3.87
25 Bromley Borough Council: Planning Records
26 *BM,* 10.6.49; *The Times* 9.6.82
27 Land Registry Title Number P84935; KCC permission to develop land WK/3/51/160
28 BLA:1003
29 St Mary's *Pew Sheet,* November 1988
30 HVA: *Review,* January 2009
31 *BKT,* 6.8.81, 29.7.82, 25.8.83
32 J M Wilson, *The History of Baston,*1983
33 Richard Taylor, *The White House*
34 BLA:C/BROB/F/48/E/2; Poor's Land Trust Records
35 HVA: Records, letter 1.5.99. The Rector, Revd David Graham, remains the chairman
36 *Beckenham Advertiser* 21.1.54; correspondence with Philip Geoffrey Jones and Jennifer Lee Jones
37 HVA: *Review* Winter 1962/63
38 Aklan Ltd, Developers' House Plans - ready for occupation Summer 1964
39 *Bromley Advertiser,* 23.6.83, *Bromley Property News,* 21.6.84, 21.2.85
40 Barnhill Conveyance documents
41 *DNB:* Basil Binyon; Hawthorndene 'Exclusive New Development Plans' brochure
42 BLA:BROB/F/1090/3/25 & 1713/A
43 *BKT,* 8.11.84
44 *Daily Mail,* 16.9.63
45 *Sunday Times,* 11.1.68
46 BLA: BROB/F/1090/3/25
47 Bromley Borough: Planning Application 04/02997
48 HVA: *Newsletter,* Winter 1955/56
49 Victory Social Club Records
50 *Beckenham & Penge Advertiser* 18.12.80
51 Bromley Borough: Planning Application 88/01829, untenanted 2011
52 *BKT,* 1.10.71
53 *BKT,* 5.1.73, 1.10.81, 17.2.83, 31.3.83; *Bromley Advertiser,* 9.6.83
54 *News Shopper,* 8.11.84
55 *BKT,* 2.1.88; Blenbury Sales Information; *News Shopper,*15.3.89
56 *BKT,* 1.3.84
57 HVA:General Meeting 26.10.49.
58 *Kelly's Directory* 1953
59 Tapsell Martin, *The Big Screen in the Big Borough;* information from Roger Rowe
60 *BKT,* 18.6.81, 17.12.81, 20.9.84
61 *BKT,* 28.4.88, 16.2.84; HVA: *Review,* October 1985
62 *BKT,* 14.2.80, 10.7.80, *Bromley Borough News,*

27.11.97
63 Chamber of Commerce Records via Ron Holland
64 Bridget Cherry & Nikolaus Pevsner, *The Buildings of England - London 2: South,* 1983

# 9    A vibrant community: 1951 to modern times

1 Jean Wilson and Trevor Woodman, *Hayes Church School 1791-1991*
2 Hayes Primary School: Log Book 1937 - , 70th Anniversary Records ; J M Wilson, *The Village School Hayes, 1791 – 1987,* Hayes 1987
3 Pickhurst Primary School: Records & Miss K Gay's memories
4 Jean Wilson, *History of Baston* 1983; Baston School Archives
5 HVA: *Review,* October 2005
6 HVA: Meet the Clubs Programme, Hayes Village Hall 3 April 1993
7 Hayes Philharmonic Society : *Golden Jubilee 1945-1995*; Kathleen Golding, *The Story of Hayes Philharmonic Society;* Information from Miss Christine Rees
8 HVA: *Review,* Autumn 1968
9 Information supplied by Laurie Mack
10 HVA: *Review* January 1998; Mrs Mary Whytock
11 BLA:C/BROB/F/923; HVA: *Review,* July 1994
12 HVA: *Review,* Summer 1972; P Thompson, *History of Hayes Kent Cricket Club* 1828-1978
13 Bromley RFC website, Neil Harris Membership Secretary
14 Park House Rugby Football Club website
15 HVA:General Minute 19.6.85, *Review,*Spring 1976
16 *The Centenary History of the Blackheath Harriers;* www.bandbhac.org.uk
17 Challengers information from Mrs Elizabeth Woodman, Mr Richard Marshall and *HPM*
18 BLA:811 Box 22
19 Bromley Borough planning application 04/02997; information David Hart
20 Flt Lt Godfrey Smith, *No 768 Squadron ATC 1941-2006 Requiescat in pace*
21 12th Bromley Scouts: Records held by Bob Neville
22 Gwen D Green, *The Story of Hayes Free Church* 1937-1997; information on Scouts and Cubs provided by Mrs Brenda Petts
23 *Hayes Herald* August 1991
24 Information from Mrs S Humphrey
25 Doris Bellringer  & Linda Graham, *The 3rd Hayes Brownies 1946-1996;* Information on Guides & Brownies from Mrs Joyce Hales and Mrs E Barclay
26 Mrs L Vistuer
27 BLA:Bromley Corporation Act, 1953
28 Information from Keith Royston, Chairman, Friends of Hayes Common; Friends of Hayes Common Circular 37
29 Mrs Alice Coward, *Hayes, Village on the Heath;* Information from Miss Maureen Crowhurst
30 Gwen D Green, *The Story of Hayes Free Church* 1937-1997
31 Information from Mr Tony Russell 2007
32 Information from Hayes Baptist Church
33 Assembly of God Information leaflet
34 Hayes Parish Chest: PCC Minutes

# Index